Let's spend the night together

Manchester University Press

Let's spend the night together

Sex, pop music and British youth culture, 1950s–80s

The Subcultures Network

MANCHESTER UNIVERSITY PRESS

Copyright © Manchester University Press 2023

While copyright in the volume as a whole is vested in Manchester University Press, copyright in individual chapters belongs to their respective authors, and no chapter may be reproduced wholly or in part without the express permission in writing of both author and publisher.

Published by Manchester University Press
Oxford Road, Manchester M13 9PL
www.manchesteruniversitypress.co.uk

British Library Cataloguing-in-Publication Data
A catalogue record for this book is available from the British Library

ISBN   978 1 52615998 4   hardback

First published 2023

The publisher has no responsibility for the persistence or accuracy of URLs for any external or third-party internet websites referred to in this book, and does not guarantee that any content on such websites is, or will remain, accurate or appropriate.

Typeset
by New Best-set Typesetters Ltd

Contents

List of figures and tables *page* vii
List of contributors viii
Acknowledgements xiii

Introduction: Let's spend the night together: sex, pop music
and British youth culture, 1950s–80s 1
*Matthew Worley, Keith Gildart, Anna Gough-Yates, Sian Lincoln,
Bill Osgerby, Lucy Robinson, John Street, Pete Webb*

1 Where were you? UK chart pop and the commodification
of the teenage libido, 1952–63 16
Tom Hennessy

2 The Jerry Lee Lewis scandal, the popular press and the
moral standing of rock 'n' roll in late 1950s Britain 38
Gillian A.M. Mitchell

3 'I'm different; I'm tough; I fuck': attitudes towards young
men, sex and masculinity in Nik Cohn's *Awopbopaloobop
Alopbamboom: Pop from the Beginning* (1969) 58
Patrick Glen

4 'We are no longer certain, any of us, what is "right" and
what is "wrong"': *Honey*, *Petticoat*, and the construction
of young women's sexuality in 1960s Britain 75
Sarah Kenny

5 Lovers' lanes and haystacks: rural spaces and girls' experiences
of courtship and sexual intimacy in post-war England 94
Sian Edwards

6 Queering modernism: social, sartorial and spatial intersections
between mod and gay (sub)culture, 1957–67 113
Shaun Cole and Paul Sweetman

7 'You just let your hair down': lesbian parties and clubs in
   the 1960s and early 1970s   132
   Alison Oram
8 Singing Elton's song: queer sexualities and youth cultures in
   England and Wales, 1967–85   152
   Daryl Leeworthy
9 'Nothing like a little disaster for sorting things out': *Blowup*
   (1966) and the free hedonism(s) of Swinging London   170
   Marlie Centawer
10 'Everything gets boring after a time': *Deep End* and
   swinging sex   185
   David Wilkinson
11 Run the track, but no bother chat slack: overstanding
   the relationship between slackness and culture within
   the reggae dancehall, 1960s–80s   205
   William 'Lez' Henry
12 'This could be a night to remember': authenticity,
   historicising and the silencing of sexual experience in
   the northern soul scene   220
   Sarah Raine and Caitlin Shentall
13 'Mummy … what is a Sex Pistol?': SEX, sex and British
   punk in the 1970s   238
   Matthew Worley
14 The 'style terrorism' of Siouxsie Sioux: femininity, early
   goth aesthetics and BDSM fashion   258
   Claire Nally
15 Coming of age Asian and Muslim in post-punk West
   Yorkshire   275
   Nabeel Zuberi
16 'I'm your man': heartthrobs and banter in *Smash Hits*   293
   Hannah Charnock

Index   310

Figures and tables

Figures

1.1	Stylistic distribution in the UK Top 100 pop charts – 1953	18
1.2	Stylistic distribution in the UK Top 100 pop charts – 1956	19
1.3	Stylistic distribution in the UK Top 100 pop charts – 1960	20
1.4	Stylistic distribution in the UK Top 100 pop charts – 1963	21

Tables

1	Singles containing references to dreams in their titles, 1954–63	31

Contributors

Marlie Centawer is a lecturer with the Centre for Studies in Arts and Culture at Brock University, and PhD candidate at Liverpool John Moores School of Art and Design under the supervision of Professor Colin Fallows. She is also assistant and archivist to the British Pop artist, art collector and Indica Gallery co-founder John Dunbar. Her research interests include popular music and youth culture, sixties counterculture, photography, cinema, visual culture, psychogeography and rock and roll.

Hannah Charnock is a lecturer in Modern British History at the University of Bristol. Hannah specialises in the history of relationships and has published work on female friendship, teenage sexuality, and marriage in twentieth-century Britain. She is currently writing her first book, a history of English teenagers' experiences of heterosexuality in post-war Britain.

Shaun Cole is a writer, lecturer and curator. He is associate professor in Fashion at Winchester School of Art, University of Southampton, and Co-Director of the 'Intersectionalities: Politics – Identities – Cultures' research group. He has written on the subject of menswear and gay fashion and his publications include *'Don We Now Our Gay Apparel': Gay Men's Dress in the Twentieth Century* (2000), *The Story of Men's Underwear* (2010) and *Dandy Style: 250 years of British Men's Fashion* (2021).

Sian Edwards is a senior lecturer in Modern British History at the University of Winchester. Her first monograph, *Youth Movements, Citizenship and the English Countryside*, was published in 2018 and explores the place of the countryside in the citizenship training of mid-century youth organisations. Her most recent research focuses on experiences of the rural teenager in post-war Britain and aims to conceptualise and understand post-war rural youth cultures.

Keith Gildart is Professor of Labour and Social History at the University of Wolverhampton, UK. He has published widely in the field of youth culture and popular music. He most recent books include *Images of England through Popular Music: Class, Youth and Rock 'n' Roll 1955–1976* (2013) and *Keeping the Faith: A History of Northern Soul* (2020).

Patrick Glen is a social and cultural historian, journalist and musician based in the School of Performance and Cultural Industries at the University of Leeds. Patrick is the author of *Youth and Permissive Social Change in British Music Papers, 1967–1983* (2018).

Anna Gough-Yates is Deputy Provost of the Academic Department at the University of Roehampton. She has published widely on women's magazines and with regard femininity, feminism and representation in television.

Tom Hennessy is an independent scholar and academic quality professional working in Swansea University. His work focuses on dance records, dancefloors and authenticity in urban Britain.

William 'Lez' Henry was born in the London borough of Lewisham, of Jamaican Parentage and is the British Reggae Deejay Lezlee Lyrix. He is a professor of Criminology and Sociology in the School of Human and Social Sciences, University of West London, where he is the Equality, Diversity & Inclusivity Lead and Course Leader for the MA: 'Global Black Studies, Decolonisation and Social Justice'. Professor Lez is a writer, poet and community activist who is a renowned public speaker, both nationally and internationally, featuring in numerous documentaries, current affairs television and radio programmes. He lectures in the areas of criminology, sociology, anthropology, race, education, ethnicity, black history, youth crime and cultural studies. As a passionate educator, he delivers educational, interventionist, programmes such as his 'Goal Models: Pathway to Personal Success Programme' in various school settings. Professor Lez has a passion for martial arts and holds a Shodan Black Belt in IKK Kyokushinkai Karate, and is a 3rd Degree Black Belt, senior instructor with Hung Kuen Southeast, Five Animals, Shaolin Kung Fu.

Sarah Kenny is Assistant Professor of Modern British Studies at the University of Birmingham with particular interests in youth culture, lifestyle, and leisure spaces in the post-war period. She has published on a range of topics including urban regeneration, the night-time economy, and cultural identity. Her first monograph, *Growing Up and Going Out: Youth Culture, Commerce, and Leisure Space in Post-war Britain* is forthcoming with Manchester University Press.

Daryl Leeworthy is the Rhys Davies Trust Research Fellow at Swansea University. His several books include *Labour Country* (2018), *A Little Gay History of Wales* (2019), *Causes in Common: Welsh Women and the Struggle for Social Democracy* (2022), and, most recently, *Fury of Past Time: A Life of Gwyn Thomas* (2022).

Sian Lincoln is an independent scholar who has published widely in journals and anthologies on aspects of youth culture. Her monograph *Youth Culture and Private Space* was published in 2012 and her book co-written with Brady Robards, *Growing up on Facebook*, was published in 2020. She is co-editor of two book series: Cinema and Youth Cultures (Routledge) and Palgrave Studies in the History of Subcultures & Popular Music.

Gillian A.M. Mitchell is a senior lecturer in History at the University of St Andrews. She specialises in the socio-cultural history of popular music in Britain and North America from the 1950s to the 1970s. Her most recent books are *Adult Responses to Popular Music and Intergenerational Relations in Britain, c.1955–1975* (2019) and *The British National Daily Press and Popular Music, c.1956–1975* (2019).

Claire Nally is a professor in Modern and Contemporary Literature at Northumbria University. Claire has written and edited several books, but her most recent work now focuses on Neo-Victorianism. She has published articles on burlesque, as well as gender and sexuality in goth magazines, and her latest monograph was *Steampunk: Gender, Subculture and the Neo-Victorian* (2019). She is the co-editor (with Angela Smith) of the Bloomsbury International Library of Gender and Popular Culture.

Alison Oram is a senior research fellow at the Institute of Historical Research, School of Advanced Study, University of London and Professor Emerita at Leeds Beckett University. She has published widely on lesbian and queer history in twentieth century Britain, as well as on queer heritage. Her books include *'Her Husband was a Woman!' Women's Gender-Crossing and Modern British Popular Culture* (2007) and, with Matt Cook, *Queer Beyond London* (Manchester University Press 2022). She led 'Pride of Place: England's LGBTQ Heritage' for Historic England in 2015–16, https://historicengland.org.uk/research/inclusive-heritage/lgbtq-heritage-project/

Bill Osgerby is Emeritus Professor of Media, Culture and Communication at London Metropolitan University. He has published widely on British and American cultural history. His books include *Youth in Britain Since 1945* (1998); *Playboys in Paradise: Youth, Masculinity and Leisure-Style in Modern America* (2001); *Youth Media* (2004); *Biker: Style and Subculture on Hell's Highway* (2005); *Youth Culture and the Media: Global Perspectives* (2016); and *American Pie: The Anatomy of Vulgar Teen Comedy* (2021). He has also co-edited numerous anthologies, including *Action TV: Tough Guys, Smooth Operators and Foxy Chicks* (2013); *Subcultures, Popular Music and Social Change* (2014); and *Fight Back: Punk, Politics and Resistance* (2017).

Sarah Raine is a lecturer in Cultural Industries at the University of Leeds (UK). Sarah's published research considers issues of gender and generation, authenticity and identity, and the construction of the past and present in the popular music scene and industry. In addition to a range of articles and book chapters, she is the author of *Authenticity and Belonging in the Northern Soul Scene* (2020) and the co-editor of *Towards Gender Equality in the Music Industry* (with Catherine Strong, 2019) and *The Northern Soul Scene* (with Tim Wall and Nicola Watchman Smith, 2019). Sarah is the co-Managing Editor of *Riffs* and acts as a book series editor for Equinox Publishing (Music Industry Studies / Icons of Pop Music) an editor for *Jazz Research Journal*.

Lucy Robinson is part of the Subcultures Network team and Professor of Collaborative History at the University of Sussex. She is currently finishing a book for Manchester University Press on popular culture and politics in the 1980s.

Caitlin Shentall is an independent researcher based in Sheffield with an interest in youth culture in post-war Britain. Caitlin is currently a copywriter in Student Recruitment at the University of Sheffield. Her co-authored chapter draws upon and further develops the work she undertook for her MA thesis entitled *Do all Roads Really Lead to Wigan? A Reassessment of the History of the Northern Soul Scene in the 'Crisis Decade' of the 1970s* (University of Sheffield, 2017). As a freelance writer, Caitlin has been involved in projects documenting Sheffield's music and DIY scenes and has contributed to local publications, including *Exposed Magazine*, *Now Then* and The Foodhall Project's *Open Journal*.

John Street is an emeritus professor of politics at the University of East Anglia. Among his publications are: *Music and Politics* (2012), *From Entertainment to Citizenship: Politics and Popular Culture* (2013) (with Sanna Inthorn and Martin Scott), and *Media, Politics and Democracy* (2021).

Paul Sweetman is a senior lecturer in Culture Media & Creative Industries at King's College London. He was previously based at the universities of Durham and Southampton. He has written and published on the sociology of the body, fashion, subcultures, visual methods of research and social and cultural theory. He is currently working on issues of subculture and place (both separately and together), partly through the lens of Actor Network Theory (ANT).

Pete Webb is a writer, lecturer and musician who specialises in research into popular and contemporary music, subcultures, politics, social theory and his concept of 'milieu cultures'. He is a senior lecturer in sociology at the University of the West of England, Bristol. He previously worked in the music industry (1990–2002) as an artist and tour manager, He is the owner and creative director of PC-Press, publishing books on Test Dept., Killing

Joke, Massive Attack and the fanzine *Vague*. His current music project is New Brand.

David Wilkinson is senior lecturer in English at Manchester Metropolitan University. As a member of the Subcultures Network, he is the author of *Post-Punk, Politics and Pleasure in Britain* (2016) and is currently working on a British Academy/Leverhulme funded research project investigating the contested legacy of the British counterculture.

Matthew Worley is Professor of Modern History at the University of Reading and a co-founder of the Subcultures Network. He has written widely on British politics and culture, focusing initially on the interwar period and more recently on the 1970s and 1980s. His research on British punk-related cultures has been published across a range of journals, including *History Workshop*, *Popular Music* and *Twentieth Century British History*. A monograph, *No Future: Punk, Politics and British Youth Culture, 1976–84*, was published in 2017. He is currently researching towards a book-length study of fanzines (*Zerox Machine*) and has recently published an article on punk and the Marquis de Sade for *Contemporary British History*.

Nabeel Zuberi is associate professor in Media and Screen Studies at the University of Auckland. His publications include *Sounds English: Transnational Popular Music* (2001), *Media Studies in Aotearoa/New Zealand 1 & 2* (2004 and 2010, co-edited with Luke Goode), and *Black Popular Music in Britain since 1945* (2014, co-edited with Jon Stratton). He is currently working on a book about music, race and media after 9/11, to be published by Bloomsbury.

Acknowledgements

The Subcultures Network would like to acknowledge all those who follow us and contribute to our Facebook page. Thanks also to the anonymous readers of the proposal and manuscript for their advice and encouragement.

This book is dedicated to Jordan.

Introduction: Let's spend the night together: sex, pop music and British youth culture, 1950s–80s

Matthew Worley, Keith Gildart, Anna Gough-Yates, Sian Lincoln, Bill Osgerby, Lucy Robinson, John Street, Pete Webb

When the Rolling Stones released 'Let's Spend the Night Together' as a double A-sided single in January 1967, it was quite obvious that Mick Jagger had more on his mind than a long evening's chat about Sartrean existentialism or number crunching figures left over from his accounting degree. In his lyric, Jagger became tongue-tied as he got high, offering no apology for the feelings he could not disguise. Mutual satisfaction was promised and guidance offered as his voice jittered and twitched, pushing and persuading the 'baby' of his lustful attention for some fun 'groovin' around'. By the end of the song, Jagger was literally begging for 'it'. 'Now I need you more than ever', he pleaded. 'Oh my', he gasped as the song pounded towards a climax, 'oh my-my-my-my-my'.[1]

Whatever the gendered mores revealed by Jagger's lyric,[2] post-war pop music and sex were evidently joined at the hip. Our version of *Let's Spend the Night Together* is therefore intended to explore how this relationship between sex and popular music informed post-war British youth culture through to the 1980s. From the moment rock 'n' roll crossed the Atlantic in the mid-1950s, its jerking rhythms and lyrical tics transmitted missives of desire that soon moved from the ribaldry nonsense of songs such as, say, Jerry Lee Lewis's 'Whole Lot of Shakin' Going On' to the blunter appeals of the Rolling Stones's aforementioned single. In Britain as in the USA, pop stars rivalled and sometimes overtook movie stars as objects of libidinal obsession, expressions of which were captured forever in films of screaming fandom and collated – voyeuristically, revealingly – by Fred and Judy Vermorel in their *Starlust* (1985) collection of pop-fan fantasies.[3] For those in a band or on a stage, self-transformation became possible: from suburban nobody to media-projected *somebody*; from one desiring to being desired. In lives lived after dark (or in the head), the promise of sexual experience and sexual sensation found opportunity in pop, sometimes reaffirming but also challenging socio-cultural norms. In turn, music infused and helped define wider cultures that generated media-framed simulacrums and permeated spaces both private (the bedroom) and public (the club, bar, street and discotheque). Within those spaces, sex and sexuality were felt, dreamt, pursued, discovered, stylised, spurned and abused to soundtracks that stoked the imagination and moved the body. Not for nothing do 'jazz', 'rock 'n' roll', 'funk' and 'punk' have sexualised etymologies.[4]

Ann Powers, in her excellent *Good Booty: Love and Sex, Black and White, Body and Soul in American Music* (2017), traces this relationship between sex and music from a US perspective. Named after the expurgated lyrics to Little Richard's 'Tutti Frutti', the book acknowledges pre-Second World War antecedents before drawing a line that connects rock 'n' roll's initially all-but inarticulate expression of stifled teenage urges to the choreographed hyper-sexuality of twenty-first-century pop. In between, the 'erotic pull' of music's communal, physical and sensual charge is revealed across various genres, positioning pop as a driver of socio-cultural change that brokered race relations and posited – albeit sometimes problematically – sexual freedom.[5]

Let's Spend the Night Together is not intended as an Anglicised companion to Powers's study, even if the pop-cultural dialogue between Britain and the USA means her narrative broadly applies to the UK. From the 1950s, as pop music helped distinguish the increasingly media-saturated (Western) world of commodified spectacle, the relationship between music and sex became ever more explicit. In both countries, pop music and sexuality were codified and channelled through the mechanisms of cultural consumption. To be sure, a British narrative would warrant more attention to class and style than Powers's US account. Jamaican and wider Caribbean influences would also need to be incorporated, given ska-then-reggae's contribution to British music and youth culture.[6] But a journey from rock 'n' roll to the 1980s would necessarily take in the studied innocence of late 1950s/early 1960s pop before detouring through beat groups and The Beatles en route to girl groups, soul, rock, glam, disco, punk, post-punk, hip hop and the technologically advanced chart and dancefloor sounds that pushed towards the millennium.[7]

As such, *Let's Spend the Night Together* is compiled with a broader remit in mind. For the Subcultures Network, established to explore how youth cultures and popular music relate to processes of social change, the *youth culture* aspect is important. Not only was music integral to the formation of youth cultures over the later twentieth century, but the sounds, spaces, styles and places they encompassed also bore significance. As portents of the future, young people served (and serve) as conduits for a combustible mixture of hope, fear and anxiety.[8] What teenagers did, what they wore, where they went, what they said and thought all gave indication of the state of the world and where the world was heading. A 'generation gap' was determined and exacted over the 1950s–60s, through which emerged new modes of thinking and being.[9] An important part of this was sexual, be it in terms of personal identity or personal practice.[10] The sexual liberation of the late twentieth century, however disputed and awkward and incomplete, was bound to a cultural 'youthquake' that tested how far the freedoms promised by capitalism, consumerism and democracy could go.[11]

Given all this, our objective is not to assess how music correlates to gender and/or sexuality. Sheila Whiteley and others have already produced a range of insightful studies on such a relationship.[12] Nor does it dwell on what youth cultural forms and styles *suggest* about sex and gender. Again, important work from Nik Cohn and Angela McRobbie onwards feeds into many of the chapters included here.[13] Instead, our aim is to home in on experiences and representations of sex in the physical and media spaces opened up through music-based cultures. Our attention is focused on what was said and done, examining how and where sex was engaged with and imagined through pop music and youth cultural style. It means capturing the longings and lustings – the frustrations and fumblings – of being young. It concerns how sex, beyond the drugs and rock 'n' roll, was mediated and understood in (and as) practice.

Historical and logistical reasons inform our timeframe. *Let's Spend the Night Together* begins from the post-war period underpinned by the Labour governments of 1945–51 and concludes as the tenets of Thatcherism begin to take effect. During the 1980s, the advent of AIDS and the reweaponising of gender politics necessitated a repositioning of sexual relations and sexual representation. These, given their complexities, warrant a book of their own. Put simply, *Let's Spend the Night Together* examines how youth culture and pop music informed young people's sexual experience and understanding in a period of apparent liberalisation. That this was messy should not be in doubt. As always, however, youthful libidos made sure to find a way.

Time Is On My Side:[14] background and context

The period covered by *Let's Spend the Night Together* saw youth culture and popular music emerge as defining motifs of British post-war history. Both 'youth' and 'pop' helped signal a new world built on the rubble of the Second World War. They embraced and relied upon the technological advances that drove towards a suitably modernised consumer society. Their evolution and performance gave expression to, or at least hinted at, the faultlines generated by ongoing processes of socio-economic and socio-cultural change: the post-war baby boom, deindustrialisation, (im)migration, liberalisation.

In such a way, the cut of youth cultural style and the sounds of pop music from a particular time now define popular memories of the late twentieth century. No documentary is complete without a pop-sourced soundtrack or a pop-star studded montage to locate the viewer.

That said, British history between the 1950s and 1980s was multifaceted and multi-layered.[15] In geopolitical terms, the Cold War and Britain's own processes of decolonisation provoked existential questions as to the UK's position in the world.[16] 'Bomb Culture', Jeff Nuttall called it: here was a generation born into a world primed for destruction but filling with purchasable playthings and commodified leisure time.[17] In other words, knowledge of the Holocaust – and the possibility of a nuclear war made real by the US bombing of Hiroshima/Nagasaki – cast a shadow over the post-war period that never quite disappeared, despite the ideals for living promised by the advertisers.

Politically and economically, the governments of 1945–51 provided for a post-war 'settlement' built on a mixed economy of public and private ownership and committed to a welfare state and full employment.[18] This buckled during the 1970s and was largely dismantled by the Conservative administrations presided over by Margaret Thatcher from 1979.[19] In between, however, the rationing and austerity that ushered in the 1950s gave way to steadily rising living standards into the 1970s.[20] This, as always, should not be overstated. But the 'teenage consumer' was constructed and recognised as a product of the 'affluent society' developing through the 1950s–1960s, their frequenting of coffee bars and embrace of new styles and sounds noted and dissected.[21]

Quite clearly, Britain's economic basis was shifting during the post-war period, transitioning from primary industry and manufacturing towards an ever-expanding service sector.[22] Partly as a result of this, women entered the workforce in greater numbers. The sons of blue-collar workers found jobs in offices, with new industries and extended educational opportunities providing a semblance of social mobility. Immigration, too, began to transform Britain's demographic. New towns and new homes were built as slums were cleared and motorways constructed. In the process, communities were reconfigured and high streets reimagined.[23]

Given such circumstances, old certainties around class and gender began to weaken. By the 1960s, even the British establishment was losing its veneer, succumbing to scandals that demystified the pre-eminence of power and privilege. That these were often sexual in nature should be noted. The 1962–63 Profumo affair was exposed, in part, through tabloids gaining a taste for the salacious.[24] Thereafter, the Labour governments of 1964–70 became known for seeking to embrace the 'white heat of technology' and enacting liberalising reforms that better reflected the changing times.[25] Among them were the decriminalisation of homosexuality, the widening availability of the contraceptive pill, the reforming of divorce law and broader access to abortion. Censorship, too, was relaxed as modernism and media challenged the boundaries of what was permitted; of what could be said, imagined, shown and seen.[26]

Political and socio-economic change was bound to socio-cultural change. Disposable income and extended leisure time enabled new patterns of life, as did the products and appliances that defined an age of consumption.[27] In a media-driven society of the spectacle, new possibilities revealed themselves via celluloid portals into visual worlds soundtracked by purchasable music and codified in images collated by magazines and, increasingly, broadcast on television. Researched brilliantly by Claire Langhamer, an 'emotional revolution' rolled over the 'short' twentieth century, altering how people understood socio-sexual relations. The centrality of sexual satisfaction to love and matrimony served as a destabilising factor, Langhamer argues, not only affecting how people approached marriage but also the pursuit and expectations of romance.[28] Youth cultures were in the vanguard of all this, precipitating media-driven 'panics' about delinquency and paving the way for concerns about 'permissiveness' corroding the morality of British society.[29]

Young people undoubtedly became more visible over the 1950s–70s, not just as a proportion of the population but in terms of their presence and purchasing power. If the teds, beats, mods, rockers, hippies, rude boys and skinheads delineated recognisable – or 'spectacular' – youth subcultures, then a far wider tableau of sounds, spaces, behaviours and consumables catered for young people more generally. Youth culture, for our purposes, is not thereby confined to style- or music-based 'subcultures', which were always amorphous and open to differing interpretation. Rather, youth cultures are here understood to comprise particular ways of life expressing certain meanings and values through common behaviour across a range of contexts.[30] As well as looking to young punks and reggae sound systems, the book ventures into gay clubs, out to the countryside, and back towards the charts and high-street magazine racks – tracing youth cultural and pop interactions with sex across both marginal spaces and the commercially popular. The counterculture, incubated in part on further and higher education campuses over the 1960s–70s, also brought attention to a growing number of students, many of whom embraced radical politics and helped cultivate much of what transformed into pop.[31]

Of course, the embrace and experience of youth culture could be relative and neither evenly distributed nor equally felt. Part of the romance of youth culture and pop music was their juxtaposition with the British landscape and the day-to-day experience of life itself: Teddy boy drape-coats worn beside still-to-be-cleared bombsites; the temporary escape of the dance hall;

the glitter glistening and heels clopping along wet terrace streets; the glimpse of hidden or forbidden behaviours stirring feelings and temptations; glamorous dreams born in drab suburban enclaves. But these moments were often fleeting, their realisation forever challenged, denied or decried. More significantly, and as many of the chapters that follow demonstrate, the dynamics of class, race, gender, age and sexuality still generated struggles and reactions that played out across the late twentieth century. As Emily Robinson, Camilla Schofield, Florence Sutcliff-Braithwaite and Natalie Thomlinson have argued, an age of 'popular individualism' was dawning.[32] That is, the post-war period was defined, in part, by a growing desire for autonomy and control over the definition and expression of individual rights, identities and perspectives. For youth, such popular individualism found an outlet in terms of aspiration, style and cultural choices. Politically, too, such impulses might seek a route through campaigns for social equality or a genuine antipathy to the socio-economic structures and hierarchies that hindered self-determination. If not quite a 'magical solution' to the class, gender and racial inequities thrown up in such a period of change, then the sounds, styles and spaces of youth culture arguably provided the means to navigate – or temporarily deflect – their impact.[33]

The relationship between youth culture and sexual behaviour was fuelled by other factors. Like young people, sex became more visible from the 1950s, as if the 'discursive explosion' recognised by Michel Foucault over the previous periods now found full display in the expansion of a media that often aligned youthful freedom with increasingly explicit depictions of sex and sexuality.[34] Tabloids sold sex as scandal; advertisers used sex to sell products pertaining to be more than simply functional.[35] Clothes, lipsticks and cigarettes held a sexual cachet, presented and directed towards youthful consumers. In magazines, bodies meshed with material satisfaction across images ever glossier and more colourful.[36] Most explicitly, in London's Soho, a seedy underground moved overground as sex shops flourished and bent policemen succumbed to vice.[37] As this suggests, pornography found commercial outlets and – though still bound by censorship laws – permeated the mediascape.[38] Just as the top shelf of the newsagents began to fill with an array of titles, so the bottom shelf saw *The Sun* use its page 3 to showcase topless models from late 1970, their teenage years often presented as part of the appeal.[39]

In the arts, the 1960 publication of D.H. Lawrence's *Lady Chatterley's Lover* is typically seen as a turning point, the court ruling in Penguin's favour paving the way for sex and nudity to proliferate through other books, in film and on stage.[40] Here, again, a cultural dialogue between the UK, USA and Europe was evident, even if Britain's particular relationship with sex revealed itself in distinct ways. Where European art house cinema and writers such as William Burroughs began to explore subconscious sexual impulses and the multiplicity of sexual desire, bawdy English humour found expression in the *Carry On* films and, later, the tawdry titillation of 1970s sexploitation. Space opened for low cultures as well as high cultures to test at the limits of sexual expression.[41] And while Britain's kitchen sink dramas often told tales of unwanted pregnancies and wayward bohemians that tapped into concerns close to youth culture, the 'new Hollywood' auteurs of the 1960s–70s (Polanski, Scorsese et al.) depicted sex and violence in ways more graphic than hitherto. By the end of the decade, sex and nudity were commonplace on film and television: even buying peanuts in a pub might lead to the sight of a naked woman pictured beneath the strategically placed packets.

That representations of sex and sexuality were overwhelmingly informed by heteronormativity and the male gaze need hardly be said. By the 1970s, however, this was being confronted and critiqued by advancing feminist and gay liberation movements.[42] Popular culture (like the personal) became a site of political struggle, both in terms of contesting existent social structures and imagining new ways of living and being. Indeed, the counterculture that flowered in the 1960s was important here, demonstrating how the propagation of 'free love' could at once challenge convention whilst also revealing sexual and gendered fissures coexisting behind the utopian rhetoric. In practice, the 'sexual revolution' tended to afford greater sexual licence to heterosexual men than it did to women, gay men and lesbians; nevertheless, debates ensued and openings emerged. More to the point, the counterculture marked the moment when youth culture and the possibilities of sexual liberation conflated, overtly politicising the behaviour of young people and confirming the fears of those who felt 'permissiveness' embodied the 'moral collapse which characterised the sixties and seventies'.[43] To now read the *International Times* and *OZ*, both of which emerged at the forefront of the underground press and both of which were subject to police raids and prosecution for obscenity, is to see sexual politics pushed to the forefront of the youth-led 'revolution'.

Beyond these media projections, the sexual lives of young people received more sober attention, with sexological studies slowly filtering into the social consciousness to inform the language and expectations of sexual experience.[44] By the end of the 1950s, a growing acceptance of sex before marriage was registered in relation to heterosexual couples 'going steady'.[45] According to Callum Brown, 38 per cent of 'first intercourse' took place within marriage between 1950 and 1965, falling to 15 per cent during 1965–75.[46] Even so, 'moral panics' still ensued in relation to teenage pregnancies and delinquency, feeding into concerns about the well-being of young women attracted to the spaces opening up around youth culture or the degenerating effects of the 'teenage revolution' on traditional gender roles.[47] In school, sexual awareness found only a circumscribed conduit through sex education, while families often remained sites of embarrassed convention.[48] As a result, hearsay and gossip continued to provide more typical ways to sexual (mis)information, enabling another space to be filled by media-generated advice columns or images as prurient as they were 'instructive'.[49]

For this reason, Michael Schofield's 1965 survey into *The Sexual Behaviour of Young People* offers us a dry but insightful snapshot of Britain on the cusp of the so-called 'Swinging Sixties'. The survey was prompted by a growing belief that teenagers were having sex earlier and more often. A 'teenage mythology' was developing, Schofield argued, integral to which was teenage consumption and recognisable youth cultures.[50] Through a combination of 'uncommitted income' and expanding leisure options, young people began to 'challenge [the] outworn ideas of the older generation'. Girls and boys were deemed to be maturing earlier, with their dancing, dress and style all setting them aside. According to Schofield, female 'emancipation' and secularisation further informed ideas that monogamy and marriage were under threat.[51]

As it was, the 15- to 19-year-olds surveyed suggested only relatively minor shifts in sexual behaviour. Marriage and monogamy remained the 'norm', even if variations in experience were registered between the genders, ages and classes of those interviewed. The 'double standard' with regard to the sexual activity of young males and females remained clearly set. Nevertheless, accounts of the disappointment experienced by young people having sex for the first time and the layers of 'petting' negotiated en route to consummation raised as many questions as answers. Likewise, and despite the survey's heteronormative expectations, the reporting of same-sex encounters among both boys and girls was revealing. Where 21 per cent of boys claimed to know of homosexual activity in their school (with 5 per cent 'admitting' to taking part themselves), 12 per cent of girls said the same (with 2 per cent taking part).[52] All in all, the survey concluded that if young people were having more sex than previously believed, then their experience remained within quite traditional codes and conducts.

Schofield's study reminds us not to exaggerate the depth and breadth of social change ongoing over the 1950s–70s.[53] Gaps existed between media representation and lived experience, gaps that pop music and youth culture arguably aestheticised or filled in vicarious fashion. Then again, the cultural and sexual landscape was evidently transforming by the onset of the 1980s. What Peter Bailey calls the 'parasexual' had widened, meaning the remit of what was deemed sexual but licit.[54] Questions of sex and sexuality were far more openly discussed than thirty years previously, with the advances of feminism and gay liberation disputed but apparent. At the same time, sex was commodified in ways that caused concern, while sexual politics moved to the forefront of debates about personal identity and moral rectitude. Both Mary Whitehouse (who founded the National Viewers and Listeners' Association in 1965) and Margaret Thatcher signalled a reaction to the liberal reforms of the 1960s, even if their attempts to stem the tide of 'permissiveness' eventually submerged beneath the radical economic policies celebrated by the latter and the cultural spaces forced open by those committed to social change. In such a context, antipathy towards sexual minorities remained all too common and later found official sanction in the infamous Clause 28 of the 1988 Local Government Act that prohibited the 'promotion of homosexuality' by local authorities.

The relationship between sex, popular music and youth culture was complex and contested. In the midst of it, as scholars of female adolescence have demonstrated especially, were real people living real lives, finding themselves as they traversed their way through the shifting cultural contours of the late twentieth century.[55] If pop music served only to provide a soundtrack to such experience, then it offered a valuable purpose. More often than not, the sounds and spaces of youth culture formed a backdrop to formative moments that were never forgotten (even if they were not always cherished).

Undercover of the Night: content and non-content

Reflecting on sex in connection with pop music and youth culture might appear contentious in the wake of the criminal abuse enacted by people such as Jimmy Savile, Paul Gadd (Gary Glitter) and Jonathan King. That the industries disseminating pop music and servicing youth culture proved exploitative was hardly a revelation in itself. Feminists had long critiqued both the patriarchal structures of the music industry and the misogyny bound up in much popular music.[56] Related scandals – from Jerry Lee Lewis's marrying his 13-year-old cousin (once removed) to the Rolling Stones', Bill Wyman's relationship with Mandy Smith of the same age – recurred from the 1950s onwards. As noted already, pop's sexual connotations and the formation of youth cultural spaces immediately generated fears of immorality. Nevertheless, the concentrated detail of sexual abuse – exacerbated by similar stories relating to young people in other sections of society (from care homes to football cubs and the church) – combined to reaffirm the sleazy reputation of the 1960s and 1970s in particular. Heard post-Savile, Mick Jagger's predatory tale of a 15-year-old girl scratching his back on 'Stray Cat Blues' does indeed appear to imply a 'capital crime'.[57]

None of the chapters included here focus specifically on paedophilia or sexual abuse, though such themes arise. From a historical point of view, it remains important to recognise the ongoing tensions that infuse social attitudes towards youthful – and especially teenage – sexuality. Throughout the period under review, debate ensued as to how the behaviours expressed through youth culture and pop music related to wider processes of social change. At the same time, 'permissive populism' – defined by Leon Hunt as 'the popular appropriation of elitist "liberationist" sexual discourses' – ensured that youthful sexuality became a totem of the 1960s–70s.[58] A veritable Pandora's box appeared to open, unleashing an array of hopes, anxieties and possibilities. These, in turn, were pored over and exaggerated by a media rehearsed in moral outrage and, simultaneously, obsessed by all things prurient.[59]

As it is, *Let's Spend the Night Together* locates youth culture and pop music as a space and a means by which these processes played out. One the one hand, music and youth culture enabled young people to explore and experience their developing sexualities. On the other, they provided sites for prevailing attitudes to reproduce and exploitation to occur. By reading *Let's Spend the Night Together*, residues may be found of teenage pleasures and adolescent pains, thereby explaining, perhaps, why the 1950s–70s can appear both revelatory and repulsive.

The structure of the book is broadly chronological, moving from the 1950s to the early 1980s. The chapters consider how the relationships between sex, pop music and youth culture were shaped by the media; how spaces relating to youth culture and popular music served to inform sexual experience; how youth cultural sounds and styles gave expression to sexual practice; how subcultures and marginal spaces informed popular culture and vice versa; how cultural mediums engaged with and represented youthful sexuality. In many cases, youthful agency is seemingly refracted through pressures and structures either commercial or conservative. As a result, questions of class, gender, race and sexual identity are considered in relation to the evolving political and socio-cultural context. By the book's end, the 1980s have arrived. In January 1984, the Rolling Stones issued the final single from their latest *Undercover* album before taking a brief hiatus. Titled 'She Was Hot', the cover depicted a naked young woman kneeling down to embrace a large red candle. In the song, Jagger is pinned to the ground as he 'rid[es] the pleasure trails', taking passion where he finds it on a cold night with a 'honey […] young and fresh'. Oh my. Oh my-my-my-my-my.

Notes

Our thanks to Natalie Thomlinson for reading and commenting on the draft of this introduction. Her help and insights were invaluable.

1 Rolling Stones, 'Let's Spend the Night Together' b/w 'Ruby Tuesday' (Decca, 1967).
2 Sheila Whiteley, 'Little Red Rooster v. The Honky Tonk Woman', in Sheila Whitely (ed.), *Sexing the Groove: Popular Music and Gender* (London: Routledge, 1997), pp. 67–99; Marcus Collins, 'Sucking in the Seventies? The Rolling Stones and the Aftermath of the Permissive Society', *Popular Music History*, 7:1 (2012), 5–23; Andrew August, 'Gender and 1960s Youth Culture: The Rolling Stones and the New Woman', *Contemporary British History*, 23:1 (2009), 79–100.
3 Fred [and Judy] Vermorel, *Starlust: The Secret Fantasies of Fans* (London: Faber & Faber, 2011). See also Carol Dyhouse, *Heartthrobs: A History of Women and Desire* (Oxford: Oxford University Press, 2017); Norma Coates, 'Teenyboppers, Groupies, and Other Grotesques: Girls and Women and Rock Culture in the 1960s and early 1970s', *Journal of Popular Music Studies*, 15:1 (2003), 65–94.
4 Nik Cohn, *Awopbopaloobop Alopbamboom* (London: Paladin, 1970); Jon Savage, *England's Dreaming: Sex Pistols and Punk Rock* (London: Faber & Faber, 1991); LaMonda Horton Stallings, *Funk the Erotic: Transaesthetics and Black Sexual Cultures* (University of Illinois Press, 2015); Will Sawyer, 'The Etymology of Jazz: One More Time', *ANQ: A Quarterly Journal of Short Articles, Notes and Reviews*, 34:4 (2021), 267–70.
5 Ann Powers, *Good Booty: Love and Sex, Black and White, Body and Soul in American Music* (New York: Dey St, 2017).
6 William 'Lez' Henry and Matthew Worley, *The System is Sound: Narratives from Beyond the UK Reggae Bassline* (Basingstoke: Palgrave Macmillan, 2020).
7 For a comprehensive overview, see Bob Stanley, *Yeah Yeah Yeah: The Story of Modern Pop* (London: Faber & Faber, 2004).
8 Bill Osgerby, *Youth in Britain since 1945* (London: Routledge, 1998).
9 Arthur Marwick, *British Society since 1945* (London: Penguin, 1996 edn); Axel Schildt and Detlef Siegfried (eds), *Between Marx and Coca-Cola: Youth Cultures in Changing European Societies, 1960–1980* (New York: Berghahn Books, 2006).
10 Pete Doggett, *Growing Up: Sex in the Sixties* (London: Bodley Head, 2021)
11 Kenneth Leech, *Youthquake: The Growth of a Counter-Culture Through Two Decades* (London: Sheldon Press, 1973).
12 For a 'way in' to a wide-ranging literature, see Simon Frith and Angela McRobbie, 'Rock and Sexuality', *Screen Education*, 29 (1978), 3–19; Jenny Taylor and Dave Laing, 'Disco-Pleasure-Discourse: On "Rock and Sexuality"', *Screen Education*, 31 (1979), 43–8; Simon Reynolds and Joy Press, *The Sex Revolts: Gender, Rebellion and Rock 'n' Roll* (London: Serpent's Tail, 1995); Sheila Whiteley (ed.), *Sexing the Groove: Popular Music and Gender* (London: Routledge, 1997); Freya Jarman-Ivens (ed.), *Oh Boy! Masculinities and Popular Music* (London: Routledge, 2007); Jodie Taylor, *Playing it Queer: Popular Music, Identity and Queer World-Making* (New York: Peter Lang, 2012); Stan Hawkins (ed.), *The Routledge Research Companion to Popular Music and Gender* (London: Routledge, 2020). See also, Lucy O'Brien, *She-Bop: The Definitive History of Women in Popular Music* (London: Penguin, 1995); Sheila Whiteley, *Women and Popular Music: Sexuality, Identity and Subjectivity* (London: Routledge,

2000); Sam de Boise, *Men, Music, Masculinity and Emotions* (Basingstoke: Palgrave Macmillan, 2015); Rhian E. Jones and Eli Davies (eds), *Under My Thumb: Songs That Hate Women and the Women Who Love Them* (London: Repeater, 2017); Stan Hawkins, *Queerness in Pop Music: Aesthetics, Gender Norms and Temporality* (London: Routledge, 2020).
13 Nik Cohn, *Today There are No Gentlemen: The Changes in Englishmen's Clothes since the War* (London: Weidenfeld & Nicolson, 1971); Angela McRobbie, *Feminism and Youth Culture* (Basingstoke: Palgrave Macmillan, 2000 edn); Mike Brake, *The Sociology of Youth Culture and Youth Subcultures: Sex and Drugs and Rock 'n' Roll?* (London: Routledge, 1980). For contemporary youth cultures, see Victoria Cann, *Girls Like This, Boys Like That: The Reproduction of Gender in Contemporary Youth Cultures* (London: Bloomsbury 2019). Studies relating to particular youth cultures (mod, punk, goth etc) are also numerous.
14 Recorded by the Rolling Stones in 1964, 'Time Is On My Side' was originally released by Kai Winding in 1963 and Irma Thomas in 1964.
15 Paul Addison, *No Turning Back: The Peacetime Revolutions of Post-War Britain* (Oxford: Oxford University Press, 2010).
16 Brian Harrison, *Seeking A Role: The United Kingdom, 1951–1970* (Oxford: Oxford University Press, 2009); Brian Harrison, *Finding A Role? The United Kingdom, 1970–1990* (Oxford: Oxford University Press, 2010). See also, Paul Gilroy, *After Empire: Melancholia or Convivial Culture?* (Abingdon: Routledge, 2004).
17 Jeff Nuttall, *Bomb Culture* (London: MacGibbon & Gee, 1968).
18 Kenneth Morgan, *Labour in Power, 1945–51* (Oxford: Oxford University Press, 1985).
19 Richard Vinen, *Thatcher's Britain: The Politics and Social Upheaval of the 1980s* (London: Simon & Schuster, 2009).
20 Albert Helsey, *British Social Trends since 1900* (Basingstoke: Macmillan, 1988).
21 Mark Abrams, *The Teenage Consumer* (London Press Exchange, 1959); Richard Hoggart, *The Uses of Literacy: Aspects of Working Class Life* (London: Chatto & Windus, 1957); Keith Gildart, *Images of England Through Popular Music: Class, Youth and Rock 'n' Roll, 1955–1976* (Basingstoke: Palgrave Macmillan, 2013); Bill Osgerby, 'Well, It's Saturday Night an' I Just Got Paid: Youth, Consumerism and Hegemony in Post-War Britain', *Contemporary Record*, 6:2 (1992), 287–305; Penny Tinkler, 'A Material Girl? Adolescent Girls and Consumer Culture, 1920–1958', in Penny Tinkler and Maggie Andrews (ed.), *All the World and Her Husband: Women in 20th Century Consumer Culture* (London: Cassell & Co., 2000); Selina Todd and Hilary Young, 'Babyboomers to Beanstalkers: Making the Modern Teenager in Post-war Britain', *Cultural and Social History*, 9:3 (2013), 451–67.
22 Jim Tomlinson, 'De-industrialization Not Decline: A New Meta-Narrative for Post-War British History', *Twentieth Century British History*, 27:1 (2016), 76–99.
23 Pat Thane, *Divided Kingdom: A History of Britain, 1900 to the Present* (Cambridge: Cambridge University Press, 2018).

24 Adrian Bingham, *Family Newspapers? Sex, Private Life, and the British Popular Press 1918–1978* (Oxford: Oxford University Press, 2009).
25 Mark Donnelly, *Sixties Britain: Culture, Society and Politics* (London: Routledge, 2005).
26 Robert Hewison, *Too Much Too Soon: Art and Society in the Sixties, 1960–1975* (London: Methuen, 1986).
27 Vernon Bogador and Robert Skidelsky (eds), *The Age of Affluence, 1951–64* (London: Macmillan, 1970); Lawrence Black and Hugh Pemberton (eds), *An Affluent Society? Britain's Post-War 'Golden Age' Revisited* (London: Routledge, 2017).
28 Claire Langhamer, *The English in Love: The Intimate Story of an Emotional Revolution* (Oxford: Oxford University Press, 2013).
29 Stanley Cohen, *Folk Devils and Moral Panics* (London: MacGibbon & Kee, 1972); Marcus Collins (ed.), *The Permissive Society and its Enemies: Sixties British Culture* (London: Rivers Oram, 2007).
30 Raymond Williams, *Keywords: A Vocabulary of Culture and Society* (London: Harper Collins, 1976), pp. 87–93.
31 Simon Frith and Howard Horne, *Art into Pop* (London: Methuen, 1987); Mike Roberts, *How Art Made Pop and Pop Became Art* (London: Tate, 2018); Lisa Tickner, *London's New Scene: Art and Culture in the 1960s* (New Haven: Yale University Press, 2020); Arthur Marwick, *The Sixties: Cultural Revolution in Britain France Italy and the United States, c.1958–c.1974* (Oxford: Oxford University Press, 1998).
32 Emily Robinson, Camilla Schofield, Florence Sutcliffe-Braithwaite and Natalie Thomlinson, 'Telling Stories about Post-war Britain: Popular Individualism and the "Crisis" of the 1970s', *Twentieth Century British History*, 28:2 (2017): 268–34.
33 Stuart Hall and Tony Jefferson (eds), *Resistance Through Rituals: Youth Subcultures in Post-War Britain* (London: Hutchinson, 1975).
34 Michel Foucault, *The History of Sexuality, Volume 1: The Will to Knowledge* (London: Penguin, 2020).
35 Clarissa Smith and Feona Attwood with Brian McNair (eds), *The Routledge Companion to Sex, Sexualities and the Media* (London: Routledge, 2017).
36 Jon Stratton, *The Desirable Body: Cultural Fetishism and the Erotics of Consumption* (Champaign: University of Illinois Press, 1996).
37 Frank Mort, *Capital Affairs: London and the Making of the Permissive Society* (New Haven: Yale University Press, 2010); Martin Tomkinson, *The Pornbrokers: The Rise of the Soho Sex Barons* (London: Virgin, 1982).
38 Gillian Freeman, *The Undergrowth of Literature* (London: Panther, 1969).
39 Marcus Collins, 'The Pornography of Permissiveness: Men's Sexuality and Women's Emancipation in Mid Twentieth-Century Britain', *History Workshop Journal*, 47 (1999), 99–120; Bingham, *Family Newspapers*, pp. 201–28.
40 John Sutherland, *Offensive Literature: Decensorship in Britain, 1960–1982* (London: John Sutherland, 1982); Alan Travis, *Bound & Gagged: A Secret History of Obscenity in Britain* (London: Profile Books, 2000); Nick Thomas,

'"Tonight's Big Talking Point is Still That Book": Popular Responses to the Lady Chatterley Trial', *Culture & Society*, 10:4 (2013), 619–34.
41 Leon Hunt, *British Low Culture: From Safari Suits to Sexploitation* (London: Routledge, 1998).
42 Jeffrey Weeks, *The World We Have Won: The Remaking of Erotic and Intimate Life* (London: Routledge, 2007); John Walker, *Left Shift: Radical Art in 1970s Britain* (London: I.B. Tauris, 2001); Margareta Jolly, *Sisterhood and After: An Oral History of the UK Women's Liberation Movement, 1968 to the Present* (Oxford: Oxford University Press, 2019); Lucy Robinson, *Gay Men and the Left in Post-War Britain: How the Personal Got Political* (Manchester: Manchester University Press, 2011); Stephen Brooke, *Sexual Politics: Sexuality, Family Planning and the British Left from the 1880s to the Present Day* (Oxford: Oxford University Press, 2011).
43 Mary Whitehouse, *Whatever Happened to Sex?* (London: Hodder & Stoughton, 1977), p. 15.
44 Hera Cook, *The Long Sexual Revolution: English Women, Sex and Contraception, 1800–1975* (Oxford: Oxford University Press, 2004); Marcus Collins, *Modern Love: An Intimate History of Men and Women in Twentieth-Century Britain* (London: Atlantic Books, 2003); Harry Cocks, 'Saucy Stories: Pornography, Sexology and the Marketing of Sexual Knowledge in Britain, c.1918–70'. *Social History*, 29:4 (2004), 465–84.
45 Lesley A. Hall, *Sex, Gender and Social Change in Britain since 1880* (Basingstoke: Palgrave Macmillan, 2013); Simon Szreter and Kate Fisher, *Sex before the Sexual Revolution: Intimate Life in England, 1918–1963* (Cambridge: Cambridge University Press, 2010).
46 Callum Brown, 'Sex, Religion and the Single Woman *c*.1950–75: The Importance of a "Short" Sexual revolution to the English Religious Crisis of the Sixties', *Twentieth Century British History*, 22:2 (2011), 189–215.
47 Penny Tinkler, 'Going Out or Out of Place? Representations of Mobile Girls and Young Women in late-1950s and 1960s' Britain', *Twentieth Century British History*, 32:2 (2021), 212–37; Janet Fink and Penny Tinkler, 'Teetering on the Edge: Portraits of Innocence, Risk and Young Female Sexualities in 1950s; and 1960s' Britain', *Women's History Review*, 26:1 (2017), 9–25; Carol Dyhouse, *Girl Trouble: Panic and Progress in the History of Young Women* (London, Zed Books, 2013); Louise A. Jackson, 'The Coffee Club Menace: Policing Youth, Leisure and Sexuality in Post-War Manchester', *Cultural and Social History*, 5:3 (2008), 289–308. See Peter Laurie, *Teenage Revolution* (London: Anthony Blond, 1965) and Christopher Booker, *The Neophiliacs* (London: Fontana, 1969) for concern over gender roles.
48 Lesley Hall, 'Birds, Bees and General Embarrassment: Sex Education in Britain, from Social Purity to Section 28', in Richard Aldrich, *Public Or Private Education? Lessons from History* (London, Woburn Press, 2004), 93–112; Amy Gower, 'Schoolgirls, Identity and Agency in England, 1970–2004', University of Reading PhD thesis (2022).
49 Penny Tinkler, '"Are You Really Living?" If Not, "Get With It!" The Teenage Self and Lifestyle in Young Women's Magazines, Britain 1957–70', *Cultural*

and Social History, 11:4 (2014), 597–619; Mary Jane Kehily, 'More Sugar? Teenage Magazines, Gender Displays and Sexual Learning', *European Journal of Cultural Studies*, 2:1 (1999), 65–89.
50 Michael Schofield, *The Sexual Behaviour of Young People* (London: Pelican, 1968), p. 26.
51 Ibid., pp. 23–8.
52 Ibid., pp. 60–2. Schofield thought these were probably underestimations.
53 See Melanie Tebbutt, *Making Youth: A History of Youth in Modern Britain* (Basingstoke: Palgrave Macmillan, 2016), chapter four.
54 Peter Bailey, 'The Victorian Barmaid as Cultural Prototype', in Peter Bailey (ed.), *Popular Culture and Performance in the Victorian City* (Cambridge: Cambridge University Press, 1998).
55 For examples relevant to this collection, see Hannah Charnock, 'Teenage Girls, Female Friendship and the Making of the Sexual Revolution in England, 1950-1980', *The Historical Journal*, 63:4 (2020), 1032–53; Ros Watkins, '"(Today I Met) The Boy I'm Gonna Marry: Romantic Expectations of Teenage Girls', in Subcultures Network (eds), *Youth Culture and Social Change: Making a Difference By Making a Noise* (Basingstoke: Palgrave Macmillan, 2017), 119–46; Helena Mills, 'Using the Personal to Critique the Popular: Women's Memories of 1960s Youth', *Contemporary British History*, 30:4 (2016), 463–83.
56 See, for example, the feminist punk fanzine *Brass Lip* (1979).
57 Rolling Stones, 'Stray Cat Blues' on *Beggars Banquet* (Decca, 1968).
58 Hunt, *British Low Culture*, p. 2.
59 Adrian Bingham, '"It Would Be Better for the Newspapers to Call a Spade a Spade": The British Press and Child Sex Abuse, *c*.1918–90', *History Workshop*, 88 (2019), 89–110.

1

Where were you? UK chart pop and the commodification of the teenage libido, 1952–63

Tom Hennessy

In the post-war period pop music became a distinctive and powerful cultural force in the United Kingdom, rising on the same tide as that which brought the teenager into the public imagination. In the 1950s a particular alchemy took place, combining economic, social, entrepreneurial and musical factors, engendering the previously staid, backwards-looking popular music industry with greater urgency and modernity. By 1963, British pop was on the cusp of changing music forever, as Beatlemania emerged to permanently redefine the meaning and potentialities of pop and pop fandom. To become what it became, pop music needed teenagers just as much as teenagers needed pop music. They were, in effect, two manifestations of the same arousal: deeply sublimated, emergent desires of both a sexual and consumerist nature, imbued with distinctively American qualities. While the rock 'n' roll boom of 1956–58 is widely recognised as a major moment of libidinal release,[1] a close analysis of the pop charts across this period – the first decade of their existence in the United Kingdom – shows that sex and romance were materialising in pop music in a multitude of complex and surprising ways. This chapter is concerned with mapping the post-war teenage libido through chart pop. It is an attempt to describe the inner lives and drives of young people through their musical taste and consumer habits, but also an analysis of how the commodification of teenage sexuality implicated producers, performers, consumers and the uninvested parent culture in the formation of new subjectivities and new cultural formations in which sex and sexuality were dramatically repositioned.

There are two broad perspectives on this subject I wish to acknowledge as informing my approach. The first, stemming from Lacanian psychoanalysis and Foucauldian poststructuralism considers the intersection of capital and sex/sexuality to be a matter of fetishism – sexually charged economic drives experienced by the human psyche. Jon Stratton has demonstrated how from the nineteenth century onwards, advertising, spectacle and the development of mass markets were closely bound to a rise in interest in sex – its categorisation, standardisation and commodification.[2] This perspective, concerned with power relations and the oppressive technologies of state and capital, understands (implicitly at times) human desire to be coerced and manipulated in the service of prevailing systems of control. The second approach considers how people experience and creatively navigate – even reconstitute – such structures. Social histories may encompass this approach, granting individuals and groups a more central role in the characterisation of structural forces, often couched in terms of 'negotiation' and 'conformity' and 'transgression'. I draw on work by Judith Walkowitz, Lesley Hall and Claire Langhamer who have each influenced my thinking on the history of the post-war period and/or sex and sexuality.

An early example of this approach is Anthony Giddens's text *The Transformation of Intimacy* (1994), in which he reflected on the popularity of romance novels amongst women:

> Avid consumption of romantic novels and stories was in one sense a testimony to passivity. The individual sought in fantasy what was denied in the ordinary world. The unreality of romantic stories from this angle was an expression of weakness, an inability to come to terms with frustrated identity in actual social life. Yet romantic literature was also (and is today) a literature of hope, a sort of refusal … romantic love may end in tragedy, and feed on transgression, but it also produces triumph, a conquest of mundane prescriptions and compromises.[3]

My research of the pop charts and the individual records contained within indicates that pop provided the same sense of 'unreal' transcendence within life experiences marked by control and perplexity. Indeed, close study of these texts reveals the fundamental interdependencies between the personal and the structural in the cultural sphere, producing texts capable of simultaneously articulating dominant power relations and implying their subversion. Establishing the role of emergent forms of commerce, such as chart pop, in summoning and sustaining these cultural modes is a central preoccupation of this chapter.

Additionally, it remains an important and ongoing project to ensure that a range of lived experiences – in this instance the role of queer men and adolescent girls – are situated in historical discussions about popular music. On a purely narrative level there is a great deal more to be said about the music of this era, and it is in the service of this ongoing discourse that this chapter is dedicated.

The charts

The British pop charts, or 'Record Hit Parade', began life as an analogue of the USA's hugely popular Billboard charts. The *New Musical Express*

(*NME*) posted their first top 12 on 14 November 1952, initially compiling their data by simply phoning around a select number of record shops to find out what was selling.[4] The charts grew in popularity through the mid-1950s and became (somewhat) more rigorous in their construction, using till receipts and then wholesale figures. Their appeal came from the weekly competition they provided. Bob Stanley has described 'excitement in league table form, pop music as sport'.[5] As the industry saw the value in pushing records towards chart success the hit parade took on a life of its own, becoming an important means through which the industry interpolated its product into the everyday life of its consumers. As Figures 1.1–1.4 illustrate, chart pop changed significantly in its first decade, moving from a singular 'traditional' style derived from older forms of musical production – principally variety theatre and sheet music – towards a more diverse and unstable tapestry of musical style that we might be more familiar with today. By

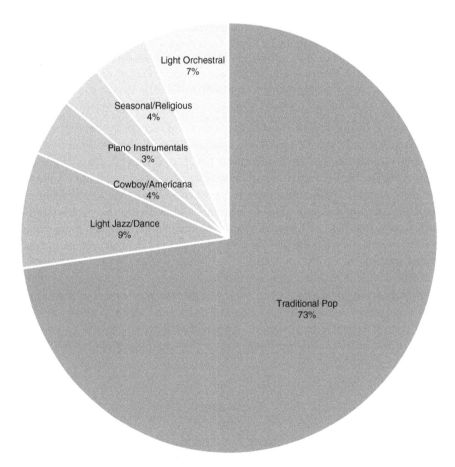

Figure 1.1 Stylistic distribution of the UK Top 100 pop charts – 1953

1963 the charts were stylistically freewheeling. They had also become the be-all-and-end-all of pop success: a year later the BBC first aired *Top of the Pops*, a television show that adopted the Top 40 as its own and became the 'circus maximus' of British pop.

It is significant that the charts were first published in the *NME*. Under the proprietorship of Maurice Irving Kinn, one of several high-profile Jewish promoters in the pop industry at this time, the paper focused on glamour and the *popular* at a time when the market was dominated by the more sober *Melody Maker* (*MM*). An institution in the music world since the 1920s, *MM* was the unofficial mouthpiece of the professional musical establishment, at this time dominated by high-profile bandleaders, the Musicians' Union, the BBC and two record companies: Electric Musical Industries (EMI) and Decca. These institutions, while not always in complete harmony, acted mutually to ensure that British musicians and composers

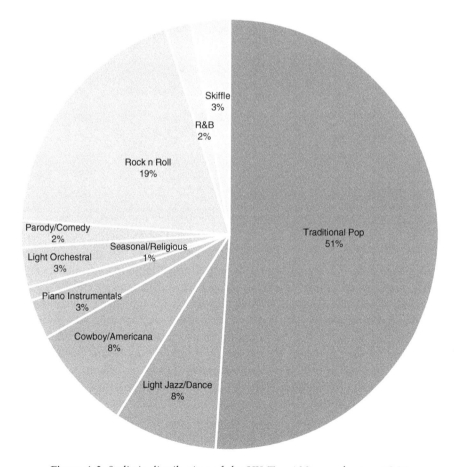

Figure 1.2 Stylistic distribution of the UK Top 100 pop charts – 1956

20 *Let's spend the night together*

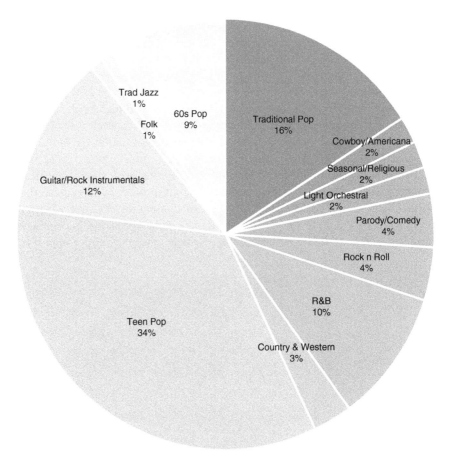

Figure 1.3 Stylistic distribution of the UK Top 100 pop charts – 1960

were promoted, and that at least only respectable, 'high quality' music was made available to the public. From an ideological perspective the BBC set the tone – in some respects it was created to resist the ever-expanding commercial music sector when it was formed in 1922. During this period, it was staunchly wedded to the principles of its founder John Reith, whereby the public service mandate to 'educate, inform and entertain' led to the systematic exclusion of a large proportion of 'low brow' forms of music. As Director General William Haley put it, 'the aim of the BBC must be to conserve and strengthen serious listening ... while satisfying the legitimate public demand for recreation and entertainment the BBC must never lose sight of its cultural mission'.[6] Inevitably a prominent feature of this mission was the suppression of any forms of entertainment deemed salacious or

Where were you?

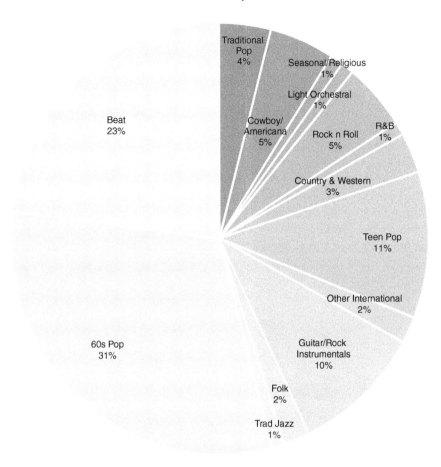

Figure 1.4 Stylistic distribution of the UK Top 100 pop charts – 1963

offensive to the buttoned-up sensibilities of the time, guaranteeing that the bulk of music heard in the UK during this period was middle-brow classical, dance music or light jazz, played by tame British bands. As Matthew Horn explains, the BBC tried to avoid playing American records, preferring instead to commission its own bands to cover the most popular songs, undoubtedly with the approval of the Musicians' Union.[7] The exception to this rule were the weekly request programmes, such as *Two Way Family Favourites* and *Pick of the Pops*, which were among the few permitted to play pop records.

In the context of BBC, *MM* and the Musicians' Union efforts to restrain popular taste, traditional pop was the compromise provided to listeners. This style of music featured unimpeachably respectable singers, clad in dinner suits and ballgowns, delivering Tin Pan Alley material – the British equivalent of the famous New York music-mill based in Denmark Street in Soho – or stage and screen. Traditional pop was coy about sex, often deploying deeply encoded allusions and assimilated sounds from marginal musical genres, such as country, R&B (Black American pop) and jazz to add a sense of *frisson*. Most of the biggest stars were, even at this point, American – Al Martino, Johnnie Ray, Doris Day and Nat King Cole being foremost among them – providing glamour and prestige far in excess of their British counterparts.

Nat King Cole's 'Somewhere Along The Way' (Capitol Records, 1952), the seventh best-selling record in the UK chart's first year, is one such example. Written by Broadway stalwart Jimmy Van Heusen under a pseudonym, the song is pitch-perfect traditional pop, with swooning strings and a placid sentimentality. In Cole's hands the song has a hint of swing, and the by-the-numbers lyric gains a deeper melancholy. Escalating his pitch through the middle line of each verse, the gentle slide back towards the blues that follows communicates plain lovesickness in a direct and uncontrived way.

> I used to walk with you
> Along the avenue
> Our hearts were carefree and gay
> How could I know I'd lose you
> Somewhere along the way.

The song is typical of traditional pop, rendering romance in highly literal terms. Emotions and events within the rituals of courtship were enacted as brief vignettes and made ideal – that is, liberated from the anxieties, uncertainties or complications that generally afflict this process in the real world. Elsewhere, song titles such as 'Walking My Baby Back Home' (Columbia, 1952), 'Hold Me Thrill Me Kiss Me' (Coral, 1952), 'Got You On My Mind' (Columbia, 1953) and 'Hold My Hand' (Coral, 1953) illustrate this. Rejection and disappointment were handled in a similar fashion, often abstracted into polite imagery, such as 'Outside Of Heaven' (RCA Victor, 1952) and 'Downhearted' (RCA Victor, 1953), 'Someone Else's Roses' (London, 1954). The vocabulary about romantic engagement privileged restrained, heterosexual relations that could be issued publicly without risking censure. The singer (generally male; by 1954 75% of hit records were by male singers)[8] was invariably positioned as the protagonist of the situation, granted the right to ask questions, state their desires and expectations of the song's subject, 'you', as referred in the second person. Within the text of the song, the singer was the subject (male), while the ideal listener was the object (female).

As the male perspective was privileged, male listeners were invited to 'stand in' for the song's subject. This position grants the listener the pleasures of articulacy and control over romantic scenarios, offering fantasies of perfected agency. The female listener gets to 'want' the singer, while the male listener gets to 'be' the singer. This is the structure that underpinned the pop vocabulary of the post-war period: a form of language that functioned to assert, justify and reproduce the norms signified in the structure.[9]

Other ways of being, while not entirely absent from traditional pop, remained deeply encoded. Johnnie Ray prefigured rock 'n' roll by a few years with his highly emotive style, a product of his struggle with his sexuality. Martin Aston has shown that even turgid mid-1950s song-writing could break through into imaginations poorly served by a relentlessly heteronormative society: 'lyrics that evoked feelings of hope, romance and validation became even more crucial now that there were so many boy/girl love songs on the radio ... when you're gay you take any clue you can get'.[10]

In concert with other mass entertainments like cinema, and other sociocultural institutions, pop music provided the public with an orderly and modest emotional repertoire featuring literal depictions of courtship. Because of the way sex and desire was positioned in the culture at large – as a predominantly private and adult subject – it was necessary to compose and produce records in this way to ensure that they could be broadcast and sold. There was little incentive to push moral boundaries in an industry dominated by conservative establishment institutions, such as the BBC. Importantly, at this stage, there was no obvious youthful subject position available in traditional pop. Romance – and especially sex – were adult matters, expressed with minimal angst, force or uncertainty.

It might be concluded that it was the arrival of the charts themselves that accelerated the decline of traditional pop and its rigid framing of sex and romance. With its roots in the sheet music era and on the variety and musical theatre stage, it was perhaps inevitable that traditional pop would be swamped by records custom built for chart success in an increasingly commercialised music culture. Changes in chart pop were a result of a symbiosis between exciting transatlantic music industry trends, cheaper playback equipment, a younger audience and the growing sophistication of the packaging, recording and marketing of pop music by Jewish promoters such as Kinn.[11] Adjacently, as Judith Walkowitz has shown, the Jewish tradesperson in the interwar Soho garment trade was perceived as 'an ethnic trickster, who negotiated the social boundaries of Jew and non-Jew by deploying both old and new resources; he or she was symbolic of the pressures of the back regions and the new commercial pleasures of mass media and fashion'.[12] A decade later Jewish pop managers like Kinn, Lew Levinsohn, Bernard Delfont and Brian Epstein can still be seen leading significant innovations, such as the 'clean' presentation of Black, Jewish and Hispanic performers Winifred Attwell, Frankie Vaughan, Cleo Laine, Lita Roza and Shirley Bassey. Another influential outsider was Larry Parnes, a relatively 'out' homosexual for the time, who pioneered the British teen pop boyfriend persona in the late 1950s.

Gradually, under the guidance of a group of entrepreneurs from the social margins, the record industry was becoming better attuned to the habits and desires of young people. Social outsiders were important entrepreneurial wild cards within the industry's institutions, often exhibiting a far greater degree of enterprise and imagination than their paymasters in seeking out and developing new markets for their products. The charts were therefore a highly significant innovation, emerging from outside of the establishment and reconstituting pop music as a modern, youth-oriented consumer product, divorced from the dusty sheet music, dance band and BBC request show era. The techniques used were almost entirely copied from the USA, and it was in the wake of one of their most significant cultural exports that sexual and consumerist desires could be truly and profitably aroused.

The rock 'n' roll moment

British commentators had long wrestled with the anxiety that American produce such as popular music, cinema and fashion had begun to colonise domestic culture. Objections to this ranged from a snobbish disdain for the American accent and deportment, to a perception of moral laxness and anxiety about the USA's muscular presence on the world stage. On the left, anti-capitalist and anti-nuclear sentiment combined with the protectionist tendencies of the labour movement to form another strand opposed to Americanisation.[13] J.B. Priestley, writing just before the Second World War, noted that British popular culture:

> Lacks something of its old genuine gaiety, its amusements are becoming too mechanised and Americanised ... the entertainments are more calculating, their shows more standardised, and the audiences more passive. It has developed a pitiful sophistication – machine made and not really English – that is worse than the hearty old vulgarity.[14]

The presence of hundreds of thousands of American and Canadian servicemen in Britain during the Second World War brought these concerns into dance halls and nightclubs around the country, cementing a decades-long association between America (especially Afro-America) and sexualised, aspirational music cultures.[15] Throughout the 1950s and 1960s young people were drawn in waves to the energy and musical quality of American pop, absorbing a wide range of mannerisms, body language, hairstyles, fashion, accent, jargon, dances and consumer habits. This unsubtle assimilation was often viewed unfavourably. In the context of the BBC's ideological agenda, it was a conventional position to view Americanisation, particularly the forms most favoured by the young, as malignant. A propensity towards 'declinism' also weighed heavily on British attitudes, a tendency that the Suez crisis in 1956 brought spectacularly to the surface.[16]

It was no coincidence that the autumn of that year presented a broader series of crises, including the unravelling of the Communist Party of Great Britain in the wake of the Hungarian uprising, a major factor in the emergence of the youthful, activist–academic New Left movement. In popular culture the release of the film *Rock Around The Clock* – not much more than a sequence of performances by rock-adjacent acts such as Bill Haley and The Platters – was met with disruptive behaviour from some boys in cinemas around the country, including damage to seats and confrontations with ushers and police. The press hysteria that followed spoke of some profound anxieties about Americanisation on the one hand, and about class, youth and social change, now becoming apparent after a decade of welfarism, on the other. Changes in the pop charts were, therefore, directly implicated in contemporary perceptions of social change, and New Left-influenced thinkers were quick to articulate these themes in terms of theory and action. Nearby, in France and the USA, psychoanalytical thinkers were also beginning to draw together the same threads, building a soon-to-be influential body of work concerned with the interplay of sex, commerce and desire.[17] In this sense the teenager emerged in Britain as a physical manifestation of Americanisation; an impulsive and sexually active consumer highly responsive to modern, transatlantic trends, and expressive of certain urges habitually suppressed by the parent culture.

Rock 'n' roll records brought about a major change in pop vocabulary; however, it was a gradual process. The first wave of UK rock hits did not evidence a significant lyrical shift as far as courtship goes. Records such as 'Rock Around The Clock' (Decca, 1954) and 'Blue Suede Shoes' (RCA Victor, 1956) were as much about a shift in attitude towards fun-loving assertiveness than about an evolving sexuality. Others, such as 'Ain't That A Shame' (Imperial, 1955) and 'Heartbreak Hotel' (RCA Victor, 1956) were simple tales of heartbreak, lyrically very similar to the traditional material that they shared the charts with. This began to change when the boom reached its peak in 1957 and the music's more sordid material came to the surface. Records like 'Be Bop A Lula' (Capitol, 1956), 'All Shook Up' (RCA Victor, 1957), 'Long Tall Sally' (Speciality, 1956) and 'Whole Lotta Shakin' Goin' On' (Sun, 1957) began to introduce some very suggestive language.

The idea of sex as something to repress and control was beginning to loosen; however, sex education in schools was still rare, and public discourse about sex was uneasy. This new 'bad boy' masculine subject, in concert with other images circulated by a new generation of films and magazines, directly assaulted this cultural reticence to talk about sex openly. Claire Langhamer has argued that in the post-war period 'the promise of romantic meetings was central to the attraction of particular leisure activities; the expansion of commercial, youth-orientated leisure provided more scope for romantic encounters'.[18] It is likely this was one of the reasons why the bad boy rocker was so attractive to young people: he offered a physical and musical language with which to say what was normally unsayable. Rock 'n' roll specifically formulated a new, confident, inappropriate and unquestionably *youthful* masculinity.

Rock 'n' roll was inherently subterranean in origin, with deep roots in Black and queer American music cultures. Little Richard, whose career began as a drag queen, crossed over into mainstream stardom in the mid-1950s, establishing a gay vocal and sartorial presence at the heart of rock 'n' roll that would be echoed for decades. In records such as 'Good Golly Miss Molly' (Speciality, 1958), Little Richard lyrically tethered bawdy drag banter to commercially successful pop music. Listeners of every persuasion were invited to a high energy party, presided over by a tiny man with a powerful falsetto and very obvious make-up, encouraging all sexes and ethnicities to 'ball' and intermingle. Even the less (to modern eyes) obviously camp rock performers exuded queer signifiers. 'Before Elvis, you'd only seen that kind of sugar lacquer on the hair and the eye shade on geisha girls', claims British fashion designer Antony Price. 'He had the campest image ever by that point.'[19] As writers such as Martin Aston have made clear, rock 'n' roll was a part of a long lineage of gay dance hall culture, and while the signs and symbols it projected were not widely understood at the time, pop records were beginning to provide a language that helped people realise more about themselves and their sexual/romantic interests.

Because of this unsettling effect, rock 'n' roll was rapidly brought to heel by the transatlantic music industry. A heavily blanched and manufactured style best described as 'teen pop' evolved, assimilating the surfaces of rock 'n' roll while dampening its sound and diminishing the wild individualism and sexual energy of its performers. Much like traditional pop, teen pop was mass produced for a relatively affluent, white record-buying demographic, who might be alarmed by the invitation to 'ball'. Pat Boone was perhaps the emblematic performer of this style, building a hugely successful career with a repertoire of squeaky-clean covers of Black pop records. However, the association of pop music with sexual/romantic adventure had now been set, and those outsider entrepreneurs in the industry increased their influence by infusing American style into specifically British configurations. At the forefront were gay songwriters and industry promoters such as Larry Parnes, Joe Meek and Brian Epstein who transformed the puerile sexuality of rock 'n' roll into a new, commercially savvy and carefully targeted pop process.[20]

Girls were now specifically catered for and had pop star 'boyfriends' built for them from scratch, as it were. Parnes's boys, plucked from the skiffle cellars and coffee bars of Soho, had their image – their name even

– carefully selected from the outset. They sang rock covers, along with some original material, with lyrics centred around simple romantic scenarios or melancholic narratives about love gone wrong. Adam Faith's 'Poor Me' (EMI, 1960) for example expresses the sorrows of being rejected, while Billy Fury's 'Last Night Was Made for Love' (Decca, 1962) is about being stood up on a date, or possibly just pining for an impossible romance. A certain moody introspection infused the image of the most successful performers. The complaints and doubts in their records were backed up by the steady stream of interviews and photo shoots circulated by the pop press, in which they talked about what kind of girls they liked, what their favourite colours were and so on, building up an unthreatening persona onto which their young fans could project their fantasies. The emotional investments made into these texts correlates with what Langhamer has perceived as 'a hardening of attitudes towards the "arranged marriage" [which] demonstrates the extent to which "true love" was increasingly believed to be the basis for everyday happiness'.[21] This was a component of a more general promotion of domesticity and matrimony across the mass media, reflected in a sharp spike in marriage rates.[22] In this sense the aim of teen pop was to provide listeners with a boyfriend: handsome, kind, vulnerable, brooding and talented, whose demands were limited to those of 'love'. All that was required to complete the picture was the female object. As Fury's refrain goes: *Last night was made for love, but where were you?*

Born too late?

In the early 1960s teen pop was rivalled by a new style I have termed '60s pop'. The term deliberately refers to the decade, as it was a clear move away from the orthodoxies of the 1950s – traditional pop, rock 'n' roll and teen pop. Again, 60s pop was a fusion of the styles that preceded it, but with an ever-increasing degree of musical hybridity. Rhythms and instrumentation were borrowed, often ham-fistedly, from musical traditions such as mambo, calypso, folk or R&B, representing the changing tastes of an increasingly diverse, curious and ageing (the first generation of chart pop consumers would now be in their mid-late 20s) record-buying public. Pop in the 1960s represents attempts within the industry – from both its creative and marketing wings – to synthesise this diversity and meet the changing tastes of their audience. It was also notable for featuring a greater range of female performers. All female (and Black) vocal groups such as The Shirelles, The Ronettes and The Crystals found success blending R&B vocal style back into rock 'n' roll, while solo performers such as Dusty Springfield, Connie Francis and Helen Shapiro brought a breezy, modern gloss to high quality song writing.[23]

A succession of dance crazes in the early 1960s, such as the twist, indicate a further intersection of Black American and white British musical style. Hits by Chubby Checker, such as 'The Twist' (Parkway, 1960) and 'Let's Twist Again' (Parkway, 1961), Sam Cooke 'Twisting the Night Away' (RCA Victor, 1962) and English singer Petula Clark 'Ya Ya Twist' (Pye, 1962) extended into the repertoires of many early Beat bands. In addition, the twist – a solitary dance step – conformed to a general change in music culture away from the dancehall and towards the nightclub and discotheque, driven by older teenagers and young adults. Aston has identified the twist as a significant moment:

> The twist not only allowed people to express themselves from the hips and with a lower centre of gravity, it gave adults permission to dance to teenage music for the first time; boys didn't have to lead and girls didn't need to follow. Gay men and women got the chance to dance together, since they weren't touching and so not breaking the law[24]

The transition into 60s pop accordingly expanded upon pop's relationship vocabulary. It provided a female counterpart voice to teen pop's strictly male subjectivity and acknowledged new forms of dancing less encumbered by adult inhibitions; however, the opening up of sex and romance to wider consumption came at a cost. Unlike the (occasionally) more demanding, grown-up female performers of the pre-rock phase, female singers of the 60s pop phase were invariably compliant and child-like. The Poni-Tails' song 'Born Too Late' (Paramount, 1958) is an early example of this:

> Born too late for you to notice me
> To you, I'm just a kid that you won't date
> Why was I born too late?

The narrative here is not only about a young girl being infatuated by an older man. It implies, through its bright and perky delivery by a group of young female singers, that this scenario might (should?) be a pleasurable fantasy for its ideal female audience. By 1962 this had reached an extreme with Louise Cordet's barely credible 'I'm Just A Baby' (Decca, 1962). While in each case the singers were female, the songwriters and promoters of this material were male. Male singers dealing with these scenarios were also common, including Mark Wynter's 'Go Away Little Girl' (Pye, 1962) and 'Heart of A Teenage Girl' by Craig Douglas (Top Rank, 1960), while the age of consent also took on an almost mythic status in records like 'Only Sixteen' by Craig Douglas (Top Rank, 1959), 'You're Sixteen' by Johnny Burnette (London, 1960), 'Happy Birthday Sweet Sixteen' by Neil Sedaka (RCA, 1961) and (although not a top 100 record) 'Sweet Little Sixteen' by Chuck Berry (London, 1958). This formula – older men commodifying sexualised teenage femininity in pop records, for whom the same teenagers were the primary market – was consistently successful, although we might question the effect it had on its young audience.

It has been noted in several texts that attitudes towards sex were changing with increasing rapidity as the 1960s began[25] – what Jeffrey Weeks has described as 'the eruption of highly sexualised popular music and culture'.[26] For boys this involved a progressive opening-up of heterosexual urges, projected into tabloids, such as the *News of the World*, and new mainstream pornographic publications, such as *King* and *Penthouse*. While there was something vaguely progressive about moving sex and desire from out of the shadows, as Hall has noted 'this was more about liberating men from sexual guilt than emancipating women'.[27] Girls, on the other hand, were still expected to manage and control physical intimacy in their romantic lives. Virtue was theirs to lose, and many articles in magazines such as *Jackie* were devoted to warning girls of the dangers of 'going too far'.[28] Pop was a significant and emerging zone in which these double standards were enforced. Indeed, knowing today what we do about the sexual habits of some of this era's most prominent pop figures – Jimmy Savile, Rolf Harris and so on – this turn should cast a deep shadow over this era of pop.

There were signs, however, that female pop fans were finding ways of pushing back against such compromised representations. 'Beatlemania' in Britain peaked around 1963–64 with an outbreak of hyper-fandom among girls aged roughly 10–15 that was far in excess of anything that had been seen before. The Beatles generated an all-encompassing sense of excitement and a devotional following among this group. It created some extraordinary scenes, such as the moment when The Beatles, while being driven through the gates of Buckingham Palace, caused a violent surge of young fans through police lines. It was shocking to many, and caused a great deal of concern and confusion in the press.[29] These were only the sporadic public manifestations of an obsession that was conducted largely in private or in small groups, fed by a steady stream of photo spreads and interviews in the music press, and in new teen-specific publications like *Jackie*. It has since been proposed that this seemingly unaccountable phenomenon was actually closely linked to the pressures of girlhood in the post-war period. For the feminist writers Ehrenreich *et al.*,

> It was rebellious (especially for the very young fans) to lay claim to sexual feelings. It was even more rebellious to lay claim to the active, desiring side of a sexual attraction: The Beatles were the objects; the girls were their pursuers. The Beatles were sexy; the girls were the ones who perceived them as sexy and acknowledged the force of an ungovernable, if somewhat disembodied, lust.[30]

This perspective pitches Beatlemania against the orderly, compliant representations of fandom and femininity promoted by teen and 60s pop. Ehrenreich draws this explosive phenomenon towards what is now known as second-wave feminism, suggesting that it was perhaps a vanguard for the growing intellectual and activist reaction to patriarchy over the previous decades. In the early 1960s the effects of new feminist movements were by no means clear, and the majority of women (and men) did not consider their gender as a point of oppression or resistance. Beatlemania is interesting, however, because it was the globally dominant mode of fandom for the most high-profile band of the 1960s. Rock-centred histories struggle with this fact, and often gloss over it as an immature aberration before the band found their true voice and started making valuable music.[31] The feminist reading of hyper-fandom problematises this by suggesting a radical potentiality in female desire enabled by pop.

Brian Epstein has been widely credited with masterminding The Beatles early career. A closeted gay man, and a prominent Jewish impresario, he might be thought of as perfecting commodification of teenage sexual impulses in pop form. As Sasha Geffen puts it: 'Beatlemania slotted the Beatles into a feminine position, the object of ravenous desire, and so enabled their female fans to assume a place of relative masculinity. By curating the band's aesthetic, Epstein primed teenage girls to see the Beatles the way a gay man might see them.'[32] This leads us to consider whether it is not enough to consider a gay influence, or presence, in pop music. Might pop be, at a fundamental level, a *consequence* of the queer gaze – an elemental drive present in all pop that aligns the psychosocial and aesthetic meaningfully within the text? A case can certainly be made for this during the late 1950s and early 1960s when the template of modern pop music was effectively set.

Dreams

While girls were obliged to struggle with narratives of romance that implicated them in fully formed relationships with pop stars on the one hand and placed them as objects of adult sexual desire on the other, boys were presented with greater opportunities. Led by a small group of male American performers who had obtained some control over their creative direction, a strand of pop emerged which deployed 'dreams' as its primary euphemism for explorations of youthful desire. This development is illustrated in Table 1 below, which shows the dispersal of records which contain reference to dreams and dreaming in their title.

What is notable about this list is the high profile of the performers and the 'classic' status of many of the records. Nat King Cole, the Crew Cuts, the Everly Brothers, Pat Boone, Bobby Darin, Johnny Burnette, Little Richard and Roy Orbison were major figures in pop's rock 'n' roll era, without ever really being considered *rockers* in the way that Elvis Presley, Buddy

Table 1 Singles containing references to dreams in their titles, 1954–63

Year	Charting position	Performer	Record title
1954	48	The Crew Cuts	Sh-Boom (Life Could be A Dream)
1955	80	Johnnie Ray	Song Of The Dreamer
1956	70	Nat 'King' Cole	Dreams Can Tell A Lie
1958	1	The Everly Brothers	All I Have To Do Is Dream
1958	88	Pat Boone	If Dreams Came True
1959	4	Bobby Darin	Dream Lover
1960	42	Johnny Burnette	Dreamin'
1961	27	Cliff Richard	Theme For A Dream
1962	21	Roy Orbison	Dream Baby
1962	64	Billy Fury	Once Upon A Dream
1963	17	Roy Orbison	In Dreams
1963	20	The Springfields	Island Of Dreams

Holly or Gene Vincent were. These performers had long careers producing high quality, middle-of-the-road pop and often had significant input over their creative direction, if not actual song-writing credits. This is, in short, a roll call of some of post-war pop's most gifted blanchers, harmonisers and arousers.

The use of the theme of dreams in these records represents a turn towards introspection in chart pop. Johnnie Ray's plea is a simple one, using the dream in the common way to describe a deeply felt but unrequited emotional desire: 'To the heavens above, I'm praying that you, Give me that which I love, Let this dream come true' (Columbia, 1955).

In a fashion common for the 1950s, Ray invokes religious terminology as well. This lyrical tactic communicated intensity but also virtue, thus ensuring that any sexual passion was at least partially restrained. Nat King Cole's dream on the other hand accesses a deeper plain of desire:

> For where there's smoke, you'll find a fire
> And in my dreams I saw the gleam of your desire
> Tonight we'll meet along the street
> And all my fears will fly
> Your loving arms will hold me
> And as they enfold me
> Your kiss will soon have told me
> That dreams can tell a lie.
> (Capitol, 1956)

Here, the glorious pronouncement of love – so familiar to Cole's fans from his traditional material – is called into question. The sensation, the desire of love, is not trustworthy. Indeed, it only creates more doubt and a greater need to dream even more to dispel it. This is not a simple pronouncement of love from a man to a woman; this is a man battling with feelings that have no hope of immediate satiation. These are songs of inhibition under a veneer of gentlemanly integrity. This is in keeping with traditional measures of masculinity, but also shows signs of strain and doubt that prefigure the more open disruptions about to emerge.

Rock 'n' roll of the boom period did not go in for dreams very much. It was more about the here and now. That there are no such charting records in 1957 at the boom's peak suggests this. Dreams return just as teen pop on both sides of the Atlantic had consolidated economically and stylistically and successfully purged the charts of rock's aggressive streak. The Everly Brothers' 'All I Have To Do Is Dream' (London, 1958) was a monumental hit. The high point of country-tinged teen pop, it epitomises the safe, proxy-boyfriend persona that had been perfected at this point. The brothers' dream takes the form of a solitary adolescent fantasy; a dream brought to mind so perfectly that it appears to the dreamer as if it were real. 'I can make you mine, taste your lips of wine, any time, night or day. Only trouble is, gee wiz, I'm dreamin' my life away'.

Unlike earlier representations of courtship, the protagonist of the narrative is distant, thwarted even, yet he seems quite content to be a lonely dreamer. The spike in records dealing with dreams over the following years indicates that the dream metaphor was an effective one in creating a space that listeners could occupy comfortably. Perhaps many young people found dreams and fantasies easier to identify with than the smouldering romances or the wild party-chasing being presented elsewhere. It is certainly a notable shift in the representation of teenage romance and desire, now described as personal, solitary fantasies of alienation from social/romantic normality.

Roy Orbison was a particularly prominent exponent of this 'lonely dreamer' figure. His first hit 'Only The Lonely' (London, 1960) and post-1963 classic 'Pretty Woman' (London, 1964) are typical of his tales of isolation and withdrawal. Combined with his dark glasses, rigid appearance and bluesy style, these records celebrate shyness and the private pleasures of the voyeur. Perhaps because he lacked the jaw dropping charisma of his fellow Sun Records alumni – Elvis Presley, Johnny Cash, Jerry Lee Lewis – he nurtured this persona and lyrical formula as an alternative, which, it would seem, hit home with a section of the record-buying public. 'Dream Baby' (London, 1962) is a well-constructed pop record which doesn't develop the idea of dreams much beyond that expressed by Johnnie Ray seven years earlier. However, through sheer repetition ('dream' is mentioned in every single line of the song at least once) the song actually creates a strange overlap of the literal, metaphorical and euphemistic uses of the term that preceded it. The singer is simultaneously dreaming of a dream woman while hoping to be snapped out of this dream and have it become a reality – a complex proposition, but one made very much in rock 'n' roll's absurdist lyrical traditions.

'In Dreams' (London, 1963) arrived a year later and took dreaming to its musical and poetic high point in post-war chart pop. Musically complex, with Latin rhythms and an ambitious progression through several melodic themes, this record should be considered a major landmark in the evolution of post-war pop. Its lyric pursues the Everly Brothers's onanistic dreaming further, combining it with the grand confession of traditional pop to produce a representation of the truest love, yet one that is completely alienated from its object: not immature teenage fantasy but a full suite of adult desires. A gentle idyll of the coming of sleep marks the gateway to a dreamscape in which full physical and emotional contact with the listener-object is confirmed. Yet the dream must end, and the second half of the song speaks of the tragedy of the dreamer, a sad, solitary figure whose imagination is nonetheless noble, heroic:

> But just before the dawn
> I awake and find you gone
> I can't help it, I can't help it if I cry
> I remember that you said goodbye
> Too bad it only seems
> It only happens in my dreams
> Only in dreams
> In beautiful dreams.

In 1963 it was a major departure for a pop record to meditate in such a fashion. The lyric holds on to the uncomplicated sentiment and rhyme-structures familiar to all pop listeners over the previous decade, yet in combination with the symphonic style of the record the components build an edifice of emotion both monumental and absurd; overblown yet somehow truthful to how desire might actually feel when one lies in bed alone. The record upholds one of pop's primary functions – an immediate, undemanding 'relationship' between subject and object – while teasing out degrees of emotional sincerity and relevance appropriate to a new audience and a new pop terrain at the turn of the 1960s.

Conclusion

The years 1952–63 represent a specific stage in the situation of sex and sexuality within the capitalist consumer culture of the long post-war period.

This was the start of an era where new theories and strategies – often directly influenced by psychoanalysis – were emerging in the corporate world to change and exploit attitudes towards sex. In the United Kingdom, innovations within popular culture, such as the pop charts, were among those lifted from American precedent by outsider entrepreneurs to arouse new, young consumers, claiming territory neglected by establishment institutions that believed mass appeal (and unvarnished capitalist marketisation) to be beneath their cultural mission. The outsiders were men – often Jewish, gay or both – and their influence can be seen in the increasing diversification of both musical style and lyrical themes on the subject of sex from 1956 onwards.

Behind the scenes their influence on marketing, visual presentation, business practices and studio production techniques were also pronounced, again more often than not using approaches pioneered in the USA. Sex and romance – both coded and literal within the pop text – came to be accepted as normal topics for youth consumption and this particular formulation of arousal gradually came to dominate representations of sex and romance across popular culture more generally. Traditional, literal representations of courtship ceded ground to passion, melodrama, introspection, abstraction and a sense of yearning for that which was forbidden. Male heterosexual desire remained the only truly permissible subject within the pop text. However, what grew during this phase was the sense of ambivalence, volatility or, for want of a better word, *queerness* within that subjectivity. Whether this was in the form of Little Richard's scarcely disguised drag act, Elvis's alpha male persona, the drift inwards represented by lonely dreamer acts, or The Beatles' realisation of the queer gaze, pop ascended into new echelons of commercial success by offering sexual desire – tangible, secure, multivalent desire – as a commodity. Personal possession of a favoured record allowed the listener to play and re-play sounds that projected otherwise incoherent or deeply buried desires into the world, resulting over time in the emergence of new, modern subjectivities defined by sexual preference. The drive of desire brought thousands of customers into shops to buy records: a mutually sustaining cycle of aroused consumption that, while by no means new at this stage, can certainly be witnessed here entering a heightened state that continues to this day. The first teenagers became perhaps the first pop subculture summoned and monetised in this way, but it would be far from the last.

Some lines of analysis fall outside the scope of this chapter. There is much more to be said about the strategies employed by organisations allied with the New Left to contend with pop culture's draw on the imaginations of young people. Left thinkers felt intensely then – as today – that the axis of youth culture, representations of sex and capitalism could be immensely damaging and counterproductive to positive socio-political change. From this perspective chart pop attained a central position within the rising hegemony of capital over representations of sex and sexuality, and the deliberate contestation of this hegemony by the left and emergent countercultures drove popular music into new and exciting territory in the years that followed. Resistance from within youth culture itself is also visible in nascent form here: the pull towards Black and gay subcultures (however unwitting) and the emergence of hyper-fandom suggest this. By the 1970s, second-wave feminism and poststructuralist histories of sexuality would begin to give a deeper theoretical framework to these critiques, and this intersection perhaps deserves its own longitudinal history.

In illuminating relationships between the psychological, aesthetic and economic aspects of sex in the post-war period, the pop charts have shown their value as a historical resource. They provide a timeline of the specific records people actually bought and listened to, making it possible to read closely, and reasonably reliably, the characteristics and evolutions of pop music over a given timespan. If we want to explore the inner lives and romantic desires of people in the later twentieth century the charts allow us to gain something approaching an objective understanding of popular taste, reducing the impact of the historian projecting their own taste on to music listeners of the past. Equally, it is important to acknowledge and gain an understanding of the means by which a high proportion of music listeners accessed music – that is, via commercial mainstream media. Analysing the marketing and industrial contexts in which pop was produced is essential given the evidently close psychosocial interdependencies of sex, music, consumption and commerce. Indeed, we can now see that the charts themselves are an expression – an originator, even – of that interdependency; an innocuous concept that grew to articulate broader social change and transform popular culture.

Notes

1. The phrase 'sex, drugs and rock 'n' roll' is so widely used as to have lent itself in some way to the title of dozens of academic and popular texts. Key among these is Simon Reynolds and Joy Press, *The Sex Revolts: Gender, Rebellion and Rock 'n' Roll* (Cambridge: Harvard University Press, 1996).
2. Jon Stratton, *The Desirable Body: Cultural Fetishism and the Erotics of Consumption* (Champagne: University of Illinois Press, 2001).
3. Anthony Giddens, *The Transformation of Intimacy: Love, Sexuality and Eroticism in Modern Societies* (Cambridge: Polity, 1993), p. 44.
4. Pat Long, *The History of the NME: High Times and Low Lives at the World's Most Famous Music Magazine* (Princeton, NJ: Portico, 2012), chap. 1.

5 Bob Stanley, *Yeah Yeah Yeah: The Story of Modern Pop* (London: Faber & Faber, 2013), pp. 1–2.
6 Quoted in Asa Briggs, *The History of Broadcasting in the United Kingdom: Volume IV: Sound and Vision* (Oxford: Oxford University Press, 1995).
7 Martin Cloonan and John Williamson, *Players' Work Time: A History of the Musicians' Union 1893–2013* (Manchester: Manchester University Press, 2016).
8 This proportion actually went up over time, as later rock and beat styles favoured male performers to an even greater degree, peaking at 89 per cent in 1960.
9 Lesley A. Hall, *Sex, Gender and Social Change in Britain since 1880* (New York: Palgrave Macmillan, 2012), p. 122.
10 Martin Aston, *Breaking Down the Walls of Heartache: How music came out* (London: Constable, 2016) Epub edn: chap. 5, sec. 8, para. 14.
11 Michael Billig, *Rock 'n' Roll Jews* (Nottingham: Five Leaves, 2000).
12 Judith R. Walkowitz, *Nights Out: Life in Cosmopolitan London* (New Haven, CT: Yale University Press, 2012), p. 175.
13 Most famously Richard Hoggart's *The Uses of Literacy* (Harmondsworth: Penguin Books, 1969) exemplified this position. See also Alan Sinfield, *Literature, Politics and Culture in Postwar Britain* (London: Continuum, 2011) and Keith Gildart, *Images of England through Popular Music 1955–76* (Palgrave, 2013) for a variety of angles on this tendency.
14 Quoted in Adrian Horn, *Juke Box Britain: Americanisation and Youth Culture, 1945–60* (Manchester: Manchester University Press, 2009), pp. 19–20.
15 Both Graham Smith in *When Jim Crow Met John Bull: Black American Soldiers in World War II Britain* (London: I.B. Tauris, 1987) and Mica Nava in *Visceral Cosmopolitanism: Gender, Culture and the Normalisation of Difference* (Oxford: Berg Publishers, 2007) explore cultural aspects of the American military presence in England.
16 Jim Tomlinson, *The Politics of Decline* (Harlow: Longman, 2000).
17 Ernest Dichter has been identified as a key figure in applying psychoanalytic principles – and therefore sexual allusion – in advertising and marketing campaigns: see 'Retail Therapy; How Ernest Dichter, an Acolyte of Sigmund Freud, Revolutionised Marketing', *The Economist*, 17 December 2011.
18 Claire Langhamer, *The English in Love: The Intimate Story of an Emotional Revolution* (Oxford: Oxford University Press, 2013), p. 93.
19 Aston, *Breaking Down the Walls of Heartache*: Ch. 5, Sec. 4, Para. 6.
20 Daryl Bullock, *The Velvet Mafia: The Gay Men who ran the Swinging Sixties* (London: Omnibus, 2021).
21 Langhamer, *The English in Love*, p. 108.
22 Lesley A. Hall, *Sex, Gender and Social Change in Britain since 1880* (New York: Palgrave Macmillan, 2012), p. 133.
23 Will Stos, 'Bouffants, Beehives, and Breaking Gender Norms: Rethinking "Girl Group" Music of the 1950s and 1960s', *Journal of Popular Music Studies*, 24:2 (2012), 117–54.
24 Aston, *Breaking Down the Walls*, Ch. 5, Sec. 10, Para. 12.
25 Aside from Hall and Langhamer, texts in this area include Jeffrey Weeks, *The World We Have Won: The Remaking of Erotic and Intimate Life* (London:

Routledge, 2007) and Frank Mort, *Capital Affairs: The Making of the Permissive Society* (New Haven, CT: Yale University Press, 2010).
26 Weeks, *The World We Have Won*, p. 8.
27 Hall, *Sex, Gender and Social Change*, p. 154.
28 Ibid., p. 138. See also Rosalind Watkiss-Singleton, 'Today I Met the Boy I'm Gonna Marry', in Subcultures Network (ed.), *Youth Culture and Social Change: Making a Difference By Making a Noise* (Basingstoke: Palgrave, 2017).
29 The initial outbreak seems to have occurred on 26 October 1963, where the sale of tickets for a Beatles concert in London caused a minor disturbance: 'everywhere the pattern was much the same. Youngsters struggled with police. Girls fainted. Those who could not get tickets wept openly': 'Beatle Crush', *News of the World*, 27 October 1963, p. 1.
30 Barbara Ehrenreich, Elizabeth Hess and Gloria Jacobs, 'Beatlemania: A Sexually Defiant Subculture?', in Ken Gelder and Sarah Thornton (eds), *The Subcultures Reader* (London: Routledge, 1997), pp. 523–36 (p. 527). See also Christine Feldman-Barrett *A Woman's History of the Beatles* (London: Bloomsbury, 2021).
31 For example, Russell J. Reising, *Every Sound There is: 'The Beatles" 'Revolver' and the Transformation of Rock and Roll* (London: Ashgate, 2002).
32 Sasha Geffen, *Glitter up the Dark: How Pop Music Broke the Binary* (Austin: University of Texas Press, 2020), Ch. 1, Para. 14.

2

The Jerry Lee Lewis scandal, the popular press and the moral standing of rock 'n' roll in late 1950s Britain

Gillian A.M. Mitchell

This chapter focuses on the brief, but intense, controversy caused by the abortive 1958 British tour of the American rock 'n' roller Jerry Lee Lewis, a venture which was brought to a premature conclusion when the British press discovered that the singer was married, apparently bigamously, to his 13-year-old cousin.

While concerned with the manner in which the British press covered – and exacerbated – the scandal, this chapter ultimately aims to reflect on the 'Lewis incident' as a means of measuring the status of rock 'n' roll music in Britain, specifically in the later 1950s, particularly with regard to its perceived moral and sexual risks for youth in the eyes of popular newspapers. Rock 'n' roll occupied a somewhat paradoxical position in British society during this time. Initial concerns over the genre had emerged during the so-called 'riots' of 1956, during which young people danced eagerly in cinema aisles and occasionally caused public disturbances during screenings of Bill Haley's *Rock Around the Clock*. However, these incidents had waned by the following year, leading some observers to suggest that the threats associated with the genre had been defused, and that the music was attaining a more settled position within the British scene. Nevertheless, this 'respectability' proved tentative and partial; the music had not lost its raw vitality on either side of the Atlantic, and its respectable status could still become threatened by, and linked to, other societal concerns regarding various aspects of youth behaviour, some of which seemed to intensify during the later 1950s. This was particularly the case with regard to anxieties over teenagers' sexual morality. Early concerns about rock 'n' roll in Britain had tended, overall, to emphasise its disorderliness, but by the end of the 1950s, some of the anxieties seemed more pointedly related to sexual issues. Worries about appropriate masculine behaviour surrounded the Lewis incident and would affect considerably those British rock 'n' rollers who forged careers within the domestic industry. The episode also illuminates contemporary concerns over the sexual morality of young British women; the portrayal of Lewis's juvenile wife in press accounts may be 'read', partially, as a reflection of rising anxieties about the perceived precocity, and corresponding vulnerability, of pubescent girls. These appeared to heighten markedly during the late 1950s as girls increasingly embraced freedoms offered by the 'affluent society'.

The scandal also, however, highlighted another phenomenon of the later 1950s – namely, the increasing readiness of the British popular press to promote sex-related scandals to boost sales. Lewis's story emerged during a time when discretion concerning reportage of personal lives was gradually eroding. This, coupled with the renewed concerns about youth, contributed to the brief yet feverish frenzy which the story generated.

The scandal had a disastrous short-term impact on Lewis's musical career. By the mid-1960s, the new generation of British 'beat groups' had inspired considerable national pride, and the press readily promoted 'Beatlemania' as an innocently vibrant outlet for youth. However, despite such changes to the musical landscape, Lewis returned to Britain on several occasions, managing to contextualise, if not to forget, the controversies which dogged his original tour. As the 1960s progressed, there was undoubtedly far greater recognition, if not exactly acceptance, of the fact that rock musicians – like other prominent figures – had colourful sex lives, as the press acknowledged (and profited from) the 'permissive society'.

Rock 'n' roll and the press in mid-fifties Britain

Prior to this incident, rock 'n' roll had arguably settled into a position of what might be termed precarious acceptability within mainstream British newspapers. The genre had certainly generated considerable concern in Britain. The press reported extensively on the 1956 'riots', arguably exaggerating the dangers and helping to fuel wider anxieties.[1] However, outraged or critical reporting of the incidents was intermingled with more balanced coverage which excused the harmless excitability of the 'rioters', and by late 1956 the shock-ridden headlines had largely disappeared as the incidents abated. It appeared, overall, that, particularly compared to the USA – where the music increasingly featured in public debates about Cold War security, morality and race relations – British fears concerning rock 'n' roll did not develop especially deep roots following this episode.[2] Certainly, the origins of the music, and its often overt sexual connotations, had tapped into established fears about the negative moral effects of American popular culture on British youth, with the hip-swivelling 'sexual suggestiveness' of Elvis Presley generating some concern.[3]

Nevertheless, sex-related anxieties did not dominate the early British coverage of the genre.[4] Furthermore, when Bill Haley himself toured Britain in early 1957, many columnists opined that this genial, wholesome American family man had managed simultaneously to delight youngsters and to quell lingering adult anxieties about his music.[5] After viewing one of Haley's concerts, the *Observer*'s Anthony Sampson heralded the new-found 'respectab[ility]' of rock 'n' roll, and arguably, beyond this point, responsibility for upholding such wholesomeness was placed increasingly on the shoulders of its American and British practitioners.[6] How Haley or Buddy Holly (who visited Britain in March 1958) – or their British counterparts such as Tommy Steele or Marty Wilde – behaved, both on- and off-stage, became a significant means of judging the music, with commentators assessing whether they constituted suitable role models for youth. Particularly significant in this regard was the readiness of performers and promoters to continue to minimise, or mediate, the original, American-derived associations between the music and sex. This would, they hoped, render it more acceptable to adults – perhaps particularly the parents of teenage girls who had become some of the most ardent rock 'n' roll fans, but whose forthright enthusiasm frequently caused concern.

The first generation of male British rock 'n' rollers generally cultivated images which, though not devoid of carefully crafted sex appeal, tended, overall, to conform to post-war ideals of romantic desirability rather than raw masculinity.[7] The shrewd rock manager Larry Parnes, keen to capitalise on the novel trend, duly renamed each of his signings; after Tommy Steele came, among others, Marty Wilde, Vince Eager and Billy Fury. Each Parnes artiste was given an innocent-sounding forename and a last name connoting 'sexual potential'.[8] However, this latter quality never dominated. While, reportedly, the private lives of certain early British rock 'n' rollers were not especially chaste, their premarital sexual exploits were never discussed publicly.[9] Marriage was also strongly discouraged, and serious romantic relationships were frequently concealed from fans.[10] The association between these musicians and the 'romantic ideal' was promoted further within girls' magazines, principally via 'pin-ups', sanitised features and picture stories 'inspired' by hit songs.[11] To appear romantically eligible and exciting, but never to a threatening extent, remained key requirements for British rock 'n' rollers during these formative years.

Despite their negative reportage of rock 'n' roll in 1956, the popular newspapers, anxious to enhance sales in an intensely competitive era, increasingly recognised, pragmatically, the profitability of the music.[12] Presenting it more positively could, thus, attract the readership of teenagers, whose perceived affluence made them a much-targeted market by the late 1950s. Of the major daily titles, the *Daily Mirror* was, ostensibly, the most supportive of the 'pop' scene; having sponsored Haley's first British tour, it sought to develop a particularly enticing style of musical coverage (penned principally by Patrick Doncaster) which matched its egalitarian ethic and desire to attract younger readers.[13] This disc column complemented other youth-centric aspects of the paper – most notably the 'Teen Page' which let youngsters air their views on various subjects. The ethos of the left-leaning *Mirror* tended to be irreverent and populist, and the paper had a reputation for being markedly open in its coverage of sexual matters – particularly via the inclusion of provocative 'pin-ups'.[14] Nevertheless, as Adrian Bingham notes, titles like these remained 'family newspapers', anxious not to 'alienate' any readers – and youth-orientated material tended to be vibrant, but seldom controversial or salacious.[15] Doncaster's breezy columns constructed a musical community in which rock 'n' rollers could happily coexist alongside practitioners of calypso, skiffle and longer-established jazz variants, and, amid this universalistic ethos, all generations could be satisfied, even as youngsters were generally prioritised. Key competitors, such as the *Daily Mail* and *Daily Express*, recognised the commercial perils of ignoring contemporary pop, and duly provided their own musical coverage; but the tendency of all such columns, by the late 1950s, was to depict the popular music world – rock 'n' roll included – as an acceptable, rather than threatening, facet of British life.[16]

In expressing tentative support for rock 'n' roll, however, many of the disc critics assumed that it was unlikely to endure as an autonomous genre. Parnes himself apparently concurred, informing *Melody Maker* that his ultimate intention was to oversee the evolution of his protégés into versatile entertainers, progressing to the established Variety and showbusiness worlds as the rock 'n' roll 'fad' declined.[17] The showcasing of early rock within traditional Variety-style shows has been widely noted, while novelty and children's songs duly became part of the repertoires of performers like Tommy Steele or Adam Faith, as they broadened their appeal.[18] This absorption into the adult-orientated commercial market was largely presumed by commentators to be inevitable – but for many admirers of the original American rock 'n' rollers, the British scene had seemed hopelessly diluted almost from the beginning.[19] George Melly presented a gendered reading of this situation in suggesting that the increase, and targeting, of ever-younger female fan-bases for rock 'n' rollers irrevocably alienated 'the [male] teenage rebels'. The increased softening of the images of these musicians he deemed a 'castrating process' for British rock 'n' roll.[20]

The persistence of anxiety surrounding youth culture

Some of the early British rockers undoubtedly felt lacking in control over their careers as their managers increasingly pursued such 'family friendly' routes. Nevertheless, it is possible to over-emphasise this apparent compulsion to 'tame' the music during the late 1950s. While much is made of the allegedly emasculating shift to 'family entertainment', some British promoters still evidently perceived plentiful vitality in the new sounds and sought to capture this more authentically. For example, the debut of Independent Television's *Oh Boy!* in 1958 marked a climactic point in an extensive quest by producer Jack Good to communicate the 'excitement' of pop on television, via slick staging and unhindered emphasis on the music.[21] That same year also witnessed the release of 'Move It', the debut single of Cliff Richard. This beat-driven song was widely considered a 'turning point', reinvigorating the British pop market, and generating fresh potential for a genuinely youth-orientated scene.[22] Indeed, despite predicting showbusiness careers for his charges, by the end of the 1950s Parnes himself had begun to develop musical 'package tours' which prioritised rock 'n' roll over Variety-style content.[23]

Just as the music remained more resilient than predicted, so too did the anxieties surrounding its suitability for youth prove impossible to quell altogether. The 'respectability' of rock 'n' roll seemed increasingly in doubt during the late 1950s as concerns about young people's behaviour re-intensified. Cliff Richard, whose sensual performance-style strongly evoked that of Presley, was forced to defend himself against charges, brought by the conservative *Daily Sketch* and *New Musical Express*, that he was 'too sexy' for young fans.[24] Richard was also implicated in concerns, expressed by the jazz-orientated *Melody Maker*, that rock 'n' rollers were encouraging a culture of violence within theatres, concerns which rapidly became entwined with heightened worries about young people's – and particularly girls' – sexual morality.

Consternation surrounding public performances of rock 'n' roll was undoubtedly rekindled during the late 1950s.[25] The showcasing of rock within Variety remained commonplace, and struggling theatre managers had little choice but to permit such performances, but both they and the older 'turns' were reportedly increasingly 'scared' by fan behaviour during what *Melody Maker* dubbed 'rock-'n'-riot shows'.[26] Reports often observed gender-specific reactions among the youngsters, and seemed uncertain as to which posed greater concern – the girls who 'scream[ed]' at the 'rockers', or the 'Teddy Boys' who 'boo[ed]' the idols who had captivated their girlfriends.[27] The latter practice presented considerable difficulties for performers like Richard, who was often pelted with improvised missiles while on stage. Amid the 'cat-calling' which was meted out to such performers were frequent implicit challenges to their masculinity; the 'pretty, smooth-skinned' Richard suffered particularly in this regard, as male spectators mocked his performances and derided his music.[28]

The behaviour of female fans, however, attracted particular criticism. In February 1958, *Melody Maker*'s Tony Brown condemned the 'fever[ish]' over-excitement of female concertgoers which seemed akin to the fervent adulation of a 'tin-pot ... dictator'. Such behaviour was first observed keenly in 1954 when the emotive American 'crooner' Johnnie Ray visited Britain. Nevertheless, it also manifested when the more sedate Haley toured the country – the example given by Brown was of a teenager who declared her longing to 'touch' the star.[29] Fan excitement could pose genuine safety risks – in May 1958, Tommy Steele was hospitalised after being injured by fans who rushed onstage during a concert in Dundee.[30] Commentators seemed to concur, however, that such behaviour from girls was disturbingly unseemly.

Teenage girls had, by the comparatively 'affluent' late 1950s, assumed vital economic significance via their status as consumers. The pop industry wished to encourage this; nevertheless, their greater visibility, and volubility, at concerts intensified adult concerns about threats to their safety and sexual welfare. In his report, Brown specifically commented upon those 'young viragos' who thronged stage doors desiring 'a few sordid moments' with their idols.[31] Indeed, the sexuality of teenage girls – perhaps particularly those who had barely, or not quite, reached the legal age of consent – became, if not a source of bona fide 'moral panic', then certainly a widespread cause for concern during these years.[32] Such worries predated this period, but the distinctive freedoms which leisure developments afforded girls, particularly, undoubtedly fuelled anxieties post war.[33] Girls also appeared to be maturing more quickly, both physically and emotionally – 'at thirteen ... using make-up' and 'by ... fifteen ... confidently expect[ing] to be "going steady"'.[34] As Louise Jackson demonstrates, police fears over delinquent and sexually precocious behaviour among young, and often under-age, girls became increasingly associated with their frequenting of 'beat (music) clubs' in Manchester during the late 1950s and early 1960s.[35] The risk of nocturnal leisure activities leading unchaperoned girls into grave moral danger was also discussed by the press; in January 1958, the *Mirror* cautioned 'dancing daughters' not to ignore parental advice on personal safety, following the disappearance (and murder) of two 17-year-old girls who had left home alone to attend dances.[36]

Some post-war newspaper reports and surveys had suggested that, contrary to traditional expectations, many young women were growing more sexually 'assertive'. Nevertheless, taboos surrounding premarital sex for girls, or extra-marital pregnancy, remained strong.[37] Concerns about female juvenile delinquency were often disproportionately focused on anxieties about 'disapproved sexual activity', and government investigations into youth problems advocated special protections for troubled girls who found themselves in sexual danger, particularly at the hands of predatory older men.[38]

The male delinquent – often labelled a 'Teddy Boy', regardless of his dress style – had, with his reputation for anti-authoritarian brutality, symbolised post-war socio-cultural disruption throughout the 1950s. He had been closely associated with the 1956 'cinema riots'– but, as with rock 'n' roll itself, the Teddy boy had undergone a partial reputational rehabilitation by the mid-1950s, with certain youth leaders endeavouring to replace condemnation with understanding.[39] However, in September 1958, anxieties were sharply reawakened when white youths in Teddy boy dress style became implicated in vicious, racially motivated attacks on Caribbean residents of Notting Hill in London.[40] Alongside challenging the complacency of many Britons concerning the nation's race relations, these violent episodes also provoked fears that juvenile delinquency, rather than abating, was in fact worsening, with crime rates rising and increasingly serious offences in evidence.[41] Press reports on such crimes could still incorporate rock 'n' roll into their coverage, demonstrating that the negative associations first established in 1956 were not entirely moribund.[42]

While the 'Teds' were feared principally for violent, rather than sexual, misdemeanours, allegations of 'promiscuity' did feature among charges brought against them by the early 1960s.[43] Frank Mort also notes that some Notting Hill-based Teddy boys perceived themselves as 'enforc[ing] informal codes of sexual honour' by targeting those involved in interracial relationships – a situation which 'catalys[ed]' the violence in 1958.[44] Possessive attitudes towards 'their' girls had also, arguably, influenced their harassment of the rock 'n' roll musicians.

As David Kynaston highlights, it was after the Notting Hill disturbances that the government commissioned the Albemarle Committee to investigate the dearth of appropriate youth leisure facilities, in the hope of reversing these immoral and delinquent tendencies.[45] All was not necessarily so 'respectable' regarding rock 'n' roll or the surrounding youth culture as the 1950s concluded, therefore – and, if anything, by 1958, anxieties surrounding these subjects seemed to be both increasing and evolving to reflect new societal preoccupations.

The press: scandal and morality

Amid such heightened concerns regarding youngsters and their 'idols', entertainers who failed to meet appropriate standards of professionalism and moral conduct could find themselves ostracised, and even pilloried, by the British press and authorities. Steve Turner suggests, in fact, that some journalists pointed the finger 'with great relish' at any such miscreants, enjoying the financially fruitful scandals while encouraging outraged responses.[46]

Such an assertion certainly corresponds with Bingham's contention that, by the late 1950s, the popular press was growing increasingly 'intrusive' regarding the private lives of celebrities, becoming ever 'more ruthless in exposing personal and sexual indiscretions' as competition intensified, and as attitudes grew less 'deferential'.[47] Publications like the *News of the World* explored such matters particularly luridly; its increasing emphasis on sordid sex stories culminated in the publication, in January 1960, of the highly 'salacious' memoirs of actress Diana Dors.[48] However, the 'dailies' also betrayed such tendencies, and, in 1959, the *Mirror* became embroiled in a lawsuit with the American pianist Liberace after the columnist 'Cassandra' made insinuations about his sexuality.[49] As Justin Bengry demonstrates, commentary on sexual practices which editors deemed distasteful tended to present an intermingling of moralistic and sensationalistic tones – a formula which proved commercially effective for the papers in question – and such dualities informed coverage of other prominent individuals whose morality was considered unpalatable in some way.[50]

The Jerry Lee Lewis affair undoubtedly represented a particularly vivid example of such sensationalising condemnation of an entertainer deemed unwholesome; the 'sexy' accusations subsequently made against Cliff Richard also illustrated such tendencies, although the singer swiftly quelled such concerns. His contemporary Terry Dene was, however, less successful in presenting himself as a good influence on youth. Amid the pressures of fame, the troubled Dene was arrested and fined for public disturbance in February 1958.[51] The following year, Dene faced fresh vilification for being discharged from National Service duties on medical grounds, an action which some authorities believed to have been a ruse to maintain his musical career.[52] However, when Dene resumed performing after departing the services, he reportedly fell victim to the contemporary trend for vocal audience judgement, finding himself viciously heckled by audience members who deemed him a coward.[53]

Dene's career was unable to recover fully from the scandal – a scandal which the popular papers had undoubtedly, and concertedly, helped to fuel. The collective coverage, overriding traditional tonal differences among newspapers, tended to adopt a notably unsympathetic, even condemnatory, tenor. Furthermore, although the Dene scandal had not been centred upon sex, in raking over the various facets of the case, the press often focused on elements which implied Dene's failure to comply with 'appropriate' masculine moral standards – such as the allegedly heated arguments, prior to the disturbances, between Dene and his girlfriend, the singer Edna Savage, or the scornful questioning, by audiences, of Dene's masculinity and bravery as he resumed touring in 1959.[54] Dene certainly discovered, to his distress and detriment, how journalists, in this era of shock revelations for profit, were inclined to treat those public figures – regardless of age or circumstances, or perhaps even particularly when they were 'teen idols' – who were considered to have breached imposed moral and masculine standards, thereby appearing inappropriate as role models for impressionable youngsters. When Jerry Lee Lewis – whose style of masculine sexuality would prove even more controversial to critical commentators – visited Britain merely months after Dene's initial arrest, he too would discover the destructive power of the popular press as it eagerly publicised another 'rock 'n' roll scandal' for moral and financial motives.

Jerry Lee Lewis in Britain

Despite arriving in Britain amid such ambivalent attitudes towards rock 'n' roll, and its practitioners and fans, Jerry Lee Lewis hoped for a positive reception in a country where his popularity was increasing. Born in Ferriday, Louisiana, in 1935, Lewis had forged a career as a distinctive rock 'n' roll performer principally via his onstage exuberance and his inventive, prodigious piano-playing. Lewis's singular abilities on this instrument demonstrated many influences, from blues to country music.[55]

Biographical works portray Lewis as a volatile man caught between the opposing forces of hedonism and Christianity.[56] A complex individual who had been twice married before reaching his twenties, Lewis contrasted considerably, musically and in image, to most of his peers in the mainstream American rock 'n' roll market. Alongside Presley, Johnny Cash and Carl Perkins, Lewis formed part of the 'million-dollar quartet' which recorded on Sam Phillips's Sun Records label, and his solo success had earned him 'the key' to his native Ferriday. However, prior to visiting Britain, the singer had participated, alongside Chuck Berry and Buddy Holly, in an American rock 'n' roll package tour, organised by the promoter Alan Freed. During a concert in Boston, serious violence erupted in and around the venue, leading city authorities to 'ban' rock 'n' roll. Controversies surrounding rock 'n' roll remained acute in America.[57] It was perhaps with this in mind that the singer's management had advised him not to publicise his recent (third) marriage to his young cousin, Myra, and to avoid taking her to Britain.[58]

Nevertheless, Lewis hoped that his first major international tour would capitalise on his growing popularity. His arrival at London Airport was certainly deemed worthy of a substantial press reception, as advance publicity declared him the successor to the rock 'n' roll 'crown' of army-bound Presley.[59] On disembarking, Lewis and his entourage – which included his sister, his wife, and her parents and young brother – were questioned good-naturedly, and a news agency reporter named Ray Berry apparently asked Myra Lewis to identify herself.[60] Caught unawares, she responded truthfully. Her youthful appearance had already attracted attention, and when pressed for further details, Lewis declared that she was 15.[61] This revelation was sufficient to generate several headlines as the 'scoop' filtered through the major titles.[62] However, as journalists probed further and discovered not only that Mrs Lewis was in fact 13, and thus well below the British age of consent, but that Lewis had also, apparently, married her before divorcing his previous wife, the scandal attained sensationalist proportions.[63]

As the Mayfair Hotel in which the Lewises were staying became surrounded by spectators – some overtly outraged, others merely curious – the Home Office was urged to 'check up' on the situation, and Sir Frank Medlicott MP questioned, in Parliament, how such a controversial individual could have been granted a British work permit.[64] After each of Lewis's London concerts culminated in heckling from scornful audience members, he was forced to abandon the tour, and the remaining prearranged dates were covered by The Treniers, a rhythm and blues group who had been the original supporting act, alongside the British artistes Chas McDevitt and Terry Wayne.[65] The disastrous nature of Lewis's first British visit has been widely recounted in rock 'n' roll histories; the ensuing scandal effectively ruined his musical career, which he steadily rebuilt over the next decades, but at considerable personal and financial cost.[66]

The uproar over Lewis undoubtedly reflected British concerns, particular to the late 1950s, about the moral standing of rock 'n' roll and its practitioners. As had occurred with Dene, the press coverage of Lewis became particularly personal, revolving predominantly around judgements of his morals and influence on British youth, with the calibre of his musicianship largely being assessed within this framework. The problematic sexual dimension of Lewis's situation, and his American nationality, only augmented the outrage in some quarters. The *People* called for the immediate deportation of the 'undesirable' singer, an instruction echoed by the *Daily Sketch* as these titles insisted that any right-thinking British youngster must now 'hate' this 'baby-snatcher'.[67] The *Mail*'s Eve Perrick, a long-standing critic of teenage culture, itemised the previous alleged wrong-doings of various idols – including Dene – and echoed calls for the 'irresponsible, arrogant and uneducated' Lewis's deportation 'before the Mississippi moral laws become the smart thing with our impressionable teenagers over here'.[68]

The unsettling implications of the marriage certainly intensified the attention accorded to Myra Lewis. Although marriages involving individuals who were significantly below the age of majority remained possible in certain US states, the practice was highly controversial, and the fact that Myra was the singer's cousin, and that he had not initially sought permission for the bigamous marriage, scarcely made the situation more palatable.[69] Some expressed sympathy for the girl who resembled 'a well-scrubbed fourth-former'; Myra recalled being described as her husband's 'girl victim', while the press reported on 'welfare checks' which had been conducted on the 'child bride'.[70] By her own account, Myra was inexperienced and naive, apparently unaware of the 'culture shock to the world' which she would inadvertently cause, and assuming that the ostensibly 'nice' reporters who had questioned her intended no malice.[71] The juvenility of the 'tiny, snub-nosed honey blonde' was emphasised in reports, as she outlined hopes for children of her own, and excitedly informed reporters of the 'red Cadillac' which her husband had bought her – comments which seemed, alarmingly, to blur the boundaries between childhood and womanhood.[72]

Much of the coverage certainly portrayed Myra as a product – or victim – of outlandishly 'primitive' Southern customs which were far removed from British experiences. Brian Ward observes that, some two years earlier, the *Mirror* had featured a photograph of a 12-year-old South Carolinian girl who had recently married a 21-year-old man.[73] Nevertheless, while both this bride and Myra could be dismissed by British commentators as products of a culture which seemed too 'other' to pose any domestic threat, the Lewis incident clearly emerged amid a period of heightened anxiety about girls' sexual welfare. Indeed, the concept of the British 'teenage bride' – particularly when the girl in question was only 16 or 17 – generated significant concerns during the late 1950s. Paradoxically, despite worries about promiscuity, early marriage – particularly teen weddings with especially youthful brides – became a distinctive feature of 1950s Britain.[74] The Albemarle Report recognised the singular status of the 'adolescent' bride and sought to support her appropriately.[75] The *Mirror* featured letters and debates, some during Lewis's visit, about whether marriage was an appropriate path for a teenage girl.[76] Some men who sought to marry younger partners became more sensitive to implications of unsavoury exploitation. The British singer Larry Page, when interviewed by the *Mail* in June 1958 about his whirlwind engagement to a 17-year-old fan, expressed 'nervous[ness]' as he admitted having received 'horrible' sidelong glances from judgemental onlookers. 'I haven't forgotten about Jerry Lee Lewis', he declared.[77] Therefore, Myra Lewis was portrayed by the press as decidedly un-British, but her story reflected wider concerns about increasingly early pubescence for women, and the potential vulnerability of girls who became sexually active at a young age, whether within or outside marriage. That an 'undesirable' type of rock 'n' roll musician was involved in Myra's situation would scarcely have eased anxieties at this juncture.

The practice of heckling male performers while implicitly challenging their masculinity, which had become a notable feature of the British live music scene by 1958, certainly reached a peak during Lewis's concerts, with 'Teddy boy'-style youths challenging the performer's treatment of Myra while crying 'go home, cradle-snatcher' and deriding his private circumstances. This ostensibly outraged, disruptive behaviour made the tour impracticable for Lewis. Combative by nature, he issued angry retorts in response – a reaction which critics deemed 'contempt[uous]' – and none of his rousing hits seemed capable of stirring enthusiasm from audiences.[78] Those performances which proceeded were halted prematurely, and this gave already lukewarm critics scant grounds to suppose that the performer deserved the acclaim which he had attained in America.[79]

However, although the story resonated with various contemporary concerns about youth, the extent to which the disgust which Lewis's situation evoked was widely or sustainedly felt in Britain remains debatable. Although critics like Perrick appeared genuinely repulsed by Lewis, and while some readers' letters echoed such sentiments, any press condemnation of the singer's morality was inevitably tempered by the realisation that a 'smashing scandal' invariably boosted sales.[80] The ambivalent mixture of tones and intentions which Bingham and Bengry observed in contemporary sex-related reportage was certainly present in features on Lewis. As Rick Bragg suggests, 'if outrage was unavailable, then feigned outrage would do just as well'.[81] Indeed, the behaviour and actions of those reporters who were cited in accounts of the unfolding story – from Ray Berry and the *Mail*'s 'Tanfield' who discovered Myra's identity, to the *Mirror*'s Iain Smith and John Rolls, who assiduously communicated the necessary details concerning her age – vividly illustrated the manner in which frenetic competition for exclusive 'scoops' escalated the scandal. Nevertheless, as had occurred with Dene, the collective actions of the press proved more significant than coverage within any one title; that the singer was 'targeted by Fleet Street, swiftly and efficiently' seemed evident to one biographer.[82]

Despite the shock-provoking headlines, several papers seized the opportunity to present the story titillatingly, blending ostensible disapproval with a prurient desire to communicate to readers how the Lewis party lived privately within their hotel rooms. Ward has noted the ready stereotyping of Lewis by the press, owing to his Southern roots. In their eyes, he embodied a type of American manhood which was not unthreatening (*People* implied this while issuing its marching orders to Lewis) but which could equally be scorned for its perceived primitivism. Imagery of Pentecostalism, 'gun-toting' and vigilantism, mingled with 'phonetic' transcriptions of Lewis's dialect ('Ah was a bigamist when ah was sixteen'), pervaded the coverage.[83] Negative perceptions of white Southerners had been evident in the British press, owing to awareness of the violence surrounding the 1957 school integrations of Little Rock, Arkansas.[84] However, as Ward notes, the Lewis scandal also evoked 'stereotypes about unsuppressed southern sexual appetites' alongside 'unhealthy regional predilections for incest and child brides', and the *Daily Herald* reported rather eagerly that Lewis had been unable to grant reporters an audience because he remained unclothed in his hotel room.[85] This 'feral' and 'primal' individual was exoticised as much as he was overtly condemned by journalists.[86]

The newspapers, naturally, could not ignore the wifely status of Myra. In observing the *Mirror*'s presentation of the South Carolinian child bride, who clutched a doll in her photograph, Ward argues that this superficially innocent image also indirectly evoked, for British audiences, the contemporary American film *Baby Doll*, which depicted a 19-year-old 'sexually precocious southern nymphet'.[87] While the childlike innocence of Myra was frequently observed by reporters, and although Lewis occasionally tried to defuse critics by presenting the marriage as a union between two God-fearing Pentecostalists, journalists remained aware that this young girl was nonetheless a bride.[88] Myra refused ever to disclose intimate details of her life as a young wife, which she recognised remained an 'elephant in the room' for uneasy outsiders, but the contemporary press could not overlook the possibility that such private realities existed.[89] Descriptions and photographs of the barefoot Mrs Lewis, described by her husband as being 'all woman', sitting on his knee while feeding him 'forkfuls' of peas, or lovingly 'stroking his arm', were by no means unprovocative.[90] Nevertheless, once again, her status as a product of 'exotic' Southern customs which were far removed from British experiences enabled the press to skirt around the sexual implications of her 'girl bride' status – and overall, the coverage of this most controversial and problematic aspect of the affair, though by no means absent, and while chiming with several contemporary British concerns, tended (perhaps because of such anxieties, and considering Myra's age) to remain suggestive rather than explicit.

The abortive British tour and negative reportage had a devastating impact on Lewis's career; he returned home to a storm of criticism, and, as Myra recalled, 'went from making $10,000 a concert to making $250 a night in a dive.'[91] Yet, curiously, despite the tales of press-led witch-hunts and jeering fans, and while, clearly, the moral backlash had tangibly devastating consequences for him, Lewis himself did not recall his first British experience as having been wholly negative. He apparently dismissed the perception that '[Britons] – or at least the rock-and-roll fans who had clamo[u]red for his visit there – suddenly turned on him en masse'.[92] The numerous return trips which Lewis made to Britain afforded him fresh chances, albeit amid an ever-changing scene, to allow audiences to focus on his music – for all that the original furore caused by his marriage could never be entirely forgotten – and, certainly, he won the admiration of various British performers, Cliff Richard and The Beatles included.[93] It is possible to overstate, or to misrepresent, the extent of the public outrage which Lewis engendered in Britain. Despite widespread reports of booing in concert venues, the reasons behind such behaviour were not necessarily straightforward. For all that this had become a discernible habit among some young men, it remained impossible to be certain whether 'patrons believe[d], semi-seriously or not, indignantly or with a half-grin', that Lewis constituted a moral menace.[94] During the 1956 'riots', it had been observed that press reportage of misbehaviour encouraged copycat incidents – whether this tendency was evident during Lewis's visit should be considered. Certainly, when Lewis revisited Britain in 1972, *Mirror* columnist Don Short observed that 'retired Teddy boys' appeared to be among his most ardent supporters.[95]

Post-war surveys had amply demonstrated that, while admitting enjoyment of sensationalist stories, newspaper readers seldom absorbed these unquestioningly or uncritically.[96] Even in 1958, some observers expressed sympathy for Lewis. One fan wrote to the *Mirror* that his personal life was irrelevant to his status as a performer, and that he should be judged on the latter alone.[97] There were some who – even if not especially enamoured of the singer's musical abilities – believed that the press had generated unnecessary distress for Lewis and his wife.[98] Nevertheless, regardless of the true nature of press or public reactions in Britain, the scandal proved very difficult for Lewis to overcome. Although he remained a volatile and controversial figure, and while he was certainly not the last male rock musician to associate with a far younger teenage girl, even positive reviews of subsequent British tours felt obliged to reference his ruinous debut visit to the country.[99] Myra Lewis Williams, meanwhile, has written candidly about her turbulent and challenging thirteen-year marriage to Lewis, which she recognises to be troubling for contemporary observers – although, in retrospect, she believed that her cousin had been motivated to marry her, first and foremost, by a desire to 'control' a far younger spouse. Forging a career as a writer and businesswoman, Lewis Williams ultimately restored agency to her life, eventually perceiving her former husband as no more than a 'distant tune in the background'.[100]

Conclusion

The Lewis scandal emerged in Britain at a time when anxieties about youth morality were heightened, and the images which it evoked of an aggressively sexualised American rock 'n' roller and a worryingly juvenile bride reflected, in various (albeit somewhat distorted) respects, some of the particular concerns of late 1950s Britain. Nevertheless, the episode is equally revealing of the practices of the popular press as, amid an era of changing standards, it increasingly tested the water regarding reportage of scandal involving celebrities while continuing to recognise the potential of rock 'n' roll to generate revenue in various ways.

Scandals like these emerged and disappeared routinely from the papers, just as, by the mid-1960s, worries about mods and rockers or beatniks had supplanted those concerning Teddy boys. Popular music, similarly, evolved, and there is no doubt that, once Beatlemania was in full swing, the newspapers recognised, afresh, the commercial benefits of adopting a supportive stance on youthful trends.[101] Managers like Brian Epstein understood, however, the importance of maintaining a wholesome public image and developing good relations with the press. Though impish and irreverent, The Beatles were carefully marketed as sexually unthreatening figures during the first phase of their popularity (while wilder stories of their formative Hamburg experiences remained concealed at this point). The expectations of moral 'respectability' for musicians with appeal for youth (particularly girls), which were visible in the late 1950s, remained prevalent into the mid-1960s, as did the scapegoating of those who unabashedly offered an alternative image – such as the Rolling Stones, who were frequently considered arrogant and sexually undesirable by the press.[102]

The exposure of scandal also, of course, became an increasing feature of newspaper provision – and as Bingham observes, the advent of the 'permissive society', in many ways, allowed the press to report ever more expansively on sexual matters.[103] The simultaneous experimentation with drugs and free love which rock groups were undertaking gave rise to more explicit and, at times, critical coverage of British musicians (including the post-*Sergeant Pepper* Beatles) as scope for sensationalism was widened. The Rolling Stones, whose relationship with the press had always been unsteady, were particularly targeted – the 1967 drugs raid on Keith Richards's home, which culminated in the arrest and (brief) imprisonment of Richards and Mick Jagger, had been triggered by an alert to police from a *News of the World* reporter. The resulting, superficially 'sanctimonious' coverage of the incident often focused intently upon Jagger's girlfriend Marianne Faithfull, who, despite being a singer in her own right, was interesting to reporters primarily via her status (and alleged 'wanton' behaviour) as the 'naked girl' at the raid.[104] Not unlike Myra Lewis, she became an inadvertent – albeit far more blatantly sexualised – target within the scandal, and both she and the Stones struggled to recover from the resultant publicity and harassment from authorities.[105]

Meanwhile, the pursuit by the tabloids of celebrity scandal grew ever more 'cut-throat' as the twentieth century ended.[106] The desire to shock and titillate readers simultaneously with intimate details about celebrities' sex lives certainly did not recede, with musicians remaining 'fair game' even as the pop business matured, and as readers themselves remained aware of the overblown and ethically questionable nature of some reportage.

Thus, while the Lewis episode belonged, in many ways, to a distinct moment in post-war popular culture, and reflected concerns about youth, gender and sexual morality which were quite specific to the late 1950s, it was also a significant step on a pathway towards increasing ruthlessness within popular newspaper reportage of celebrity sex scandals. As alleged 'role models' for young people, popular musicians often found themselves particular targets of such ostensibly moralising, yet simultaneously sensationalist, journalism, especially when they pursued sex lives which appeared lucratively controversial in the eyes of reporters.

Notes

1 I analysed this coverage in *The British National Daily Press and Popular Music, c.1956–1975* (London: Anthem Press, 2019), pp. 13–29. See also Simon Frith et al., *The History of Live Music in Britain, Volume I: 1950–1967* (Farnham: Ashgate, 2013), pp. 29–30.

2 Steven Lawson, 'Race, Rock 'n' Roll, and the Rigged Society: The Payola Scandal and the Political Culture of the 1950s', in William H. Chafe (ed.), *The Achievement of American Liberalism: The New Deal and its Legacies* (New York: Columbia University Press, 2002), pp. 205–42.

3 Dominic Sandbrook, *Never Had it So Good: A History of Britain from Suez to the Beatles* (London: Abacus, 2005), p. 461.

4 Although the *Daily Mail* deemed the music 'sexy' (in ibid.), one young woman told the *Mirror* that the music made her feel 'bubbly' but '[n]ot sexy'. 'The *Mirror* Throws a Rock 'n' Roll Party', *Daily Mirror*, 1 September 1956, p. 7.

5 Mitchell, *The British*, pp. 50–3.

6 Ibid., Anthony Sampson, 'Don't Knock the Rock', *Observer*, 10 February 1957, p. 10.

7 On post-war masculinity, see Laura King, 'The Perfect Man: Fatherhood, Masculinity and Romance in Popular Culture in Mid-Twentieth-Century Britain', in A. Harris et al. (eds), *Love and Romance in Britain, 1918–1970* (Basingstoke: Palgrave Macmillan, 2015), pp. 41–3.

8 Sandbrook, *Never Had It*, p. 473.

9 Apparently, Adam Faith was the first idol 'publicly to acknowledge his pre-marital sexual experience'. Brian Harrison, *Seeking A Role: The United Kingdom, 1951–1970* (Oxford: Oxford University Press, 2011), p. 238. Former

musicians discussed offstage behaviour in *Billy Fury: The Sound of Fury*, 02:30 07/04/2018, BBC4, 85 mins, https://learningonscreen.ac.uk/ondemand/index.php/prog/0C61501E?bcast=126460935 (accessed 7 October 2021), 57.00–57.24.
10 See Tommy Steele, *Bermondsey Boy: Memories of a South London Blitz Childhood* (London: Penguin, 2006), pp. 298–9.
11 David Kynaston, *Modernity Britain, 1957–62* (London: Bloomsbury, 2014), p. 592.
12 Martin Cloonan, 'Exclusive! The British Press and Popular Music. The Story So Far …', in Steve Jones (ed.), *Pop Music and the Press* (Philadelphia: Temple University Press, 2002), pp. 115–16.
13 Mitchell, *The British*, pp. 48–53.
14 Adrian Bingham, *Family Newspapers?: Sex, Private Life, and the British Popular Press, 1918–78* (Oxford: Oxford University Press, 2009), pp. 207–12.
15 Ibid., p. 203; A.C.H. Smith, *Paper Voices: The Popular Press and Social Changes, 1935–1965* (London: Chatto & Windus, 1975), p. 160.
16 Mitchell, *The British*, pp. 66–77.
17 Bob Dawbarn, 'The Man Behind Britain's Big Beat', *Melody Maker*, 29 August 1959, p. 3.
18 See Gillian A.M. Mitchell, *Adult Responses to Popular Music and Intergenerational Relations in Britain, c.1955–1975* (London: Anthem Press, 2019), pp. 138–9.
19 See *Billy Fury*, 18.50–19.20.
20 George Melly, *Revolt into Style: The Pop Arts* (Oxford: Oxford University Press, 1989), pp. 34, 50; Mitchell, *Adult Responses*, p. 137.
21 Norma Coates, 'Excitement is Made, Not Born: Jack Good, Television, and Rock and Roll', *Journal of Popular Music Studies*, 25:3 (2013), 306.
22 Steve Turner, *Cliff Richard: The Biography* (London: Lion Hudson, 2005), pp. 105, 118.
23 *Billy Fury*, 28.00–32.00.
24 Sandbrook, *Never Had It*, p. 474.
25 Mitchell, *Adult Responses*, p. 121.
26 'Stars, Theatre Staff Scared of … These Rock & Riot Shows', *Melody Maker*, 9 May 1959, p. 1.
27 Ibid.
28 Turner, *Cliff Richard*, p. 125. The issue of jealousy also discussed in *Billy Fury*, 58.00–59.16.
29 Tony Brown, 'Fan Fever: Pop Fans – You are Looking for Trouble', *Melody Maker*, 1 February 1958, pp. 2–3.
30 'Steele Looks Back in Anger', *Melody Maker*, 14 June 1958, p. 8.
31 Brown, 'Fan Fever', p. 3.
32 Bill Osgerby, *Youth in Britain* (Oxford: Blackwell, 1998), p. 46.
33 See Pamela Cox, *Gender, Justice and Welfare: Bad Girls in Britain, 1900–1950* (Basingstoke: Palgrave Macmillan, 2003).
34 Harry Hopkins, *The New Look: A Social History of Britain in the Forties and Fifties* (London: Secker & Warburg, 1963), p. 424.

35 Louise A. Jackson 'The Coffee Club Menace: Policing Youth, Leisure and Sexuality in Post-war Manchester', *Cultural and Social History*, 5:3 (2008), 293–4.
36 Mary Brown, 'Dancing Daughters!', *Daily Mirror*, 14 January 1958, p. 7.
37 On surveys, see Bingham, *Family Newspapers*, pp. 106–17. On under-age pregnancy, see the *Mirror*'s 'agony aunt' Marje Proops in *Dear Marje …* (London: Andre Deutsch, 1976), pp. 71–2.
38 Quote from James J. Cockburn and Inga Maclay, 'Sex Differentials in Juvenile Delinquency', *British Journal of Criminology*, 5:3 (July 1965), 304. See also Hansard: Juvenile Offenders (Accommodation) Volume 627: debated 29 July 1960, https://hansard.parliament.uk/commons/1960-07-29/debates/e7f95ce 3-de67-4830-b628-47196460114e/JuvenileOffenders(Accommodation) (accessed 1 December 2021).
39 "Hopeful Aspects of Teddy Boy', *The Times*, 5 May 1958, p. 6; 'From "Teddy Boy" to Scout', *Manchester Guardian*, 16 March 1959, p. 4.
40 Kynaston, *Modernity Britain*, pp. 170–4.
41 Sandbrook, *Never Had It*, pp. 445–8.
42 For example, 'Rock 'n' Roll Raid', *Daily Mail*, 13 January 1958, p. 5.
43 'A Generation in Revolt', *Guardian*, 11 September 1962, p. 3.
44 Frank Mort, 'Morality, Majesty and Murder in 1950s London: Metropolitan Culture and English Modernity', in Gyan Prakash and Kevin M. Kruse (eds), *The Spaces of the Modern City: Imaginaries, Politics and Everyday Life* (Princeton: Princeton University Press, 2008), p. 336.
45 Kynaston, *Modernity Britain*, p. 186.
46 Turner, *Cliff Richard*, p. 93.
47 Bingham, *Family Newspapers*, pp. 229–30.
48 See Kevin Williams, 'Bringing Popular Journalism into Disrepute: The *News of the World*, the Public and Politics 1953–2011', in Laurel Brake et al. (eds), *The News of the World and the British Press* (Basingstoke: Palgrave Macmillan, 2016), p. 219.
49 Justin Bengry, 'Profit (f)or the Public Good? Sensation, Homosexuality, and the Postwar Popular Press', *Media History*, 20:2 (2014), 157–8.
50 Ibid., p. 148.
51 '£155 Fine Against Terry Dene: Went Berserk', *Guardian*, 22 February 1958, p. 2; 'Terry Dene and the Army: Call for Enquiry', *Manchester Guardian*, 30 April 1959, 2.
52 Dan Wooding, *Terry Dene: Britain's First Rock & Roll Rebel* (London: Gonzo, 2013), pp. 84–7.
53 Ibid., p. 91; 'Ex-23604106 Reappears', *Manchester Guardian*, 27 April 1959, p. 1.
54 James Ure, 'Seven Day "Rock" Floors Terry Dene', *Daily Mail*, 20 February 1958, p. 7; 'Ex-23604106 Reappears'.
55 See Nick Tosches, *Hellfire: The Jerry Lee Lewis Story* (London: Penguin, 2019), pp. 56–8.
56 Ibid., p. 66.

57 Ibid., p. 146; Rick Bragg, *Jerry Lee Lewis: His Own Story* (Edinburgh: Canongate Books, 2015), pp. 253–7.
58 Bragg, *Jerry Lee Lewis*, p. 266.
59 This is depicted in the 1989 biopic *Great Balls of Fire!* (dir. Jim McBride, Orion Films).
60 On Berry, see Edwin Lawrence, 'Ray Put Prestwick Airport in World Headlines', *Daily Record*, 22 October 2010, www.dailyrecord.co.uk/news/local-news/ray-put-prestwick-airport-world-2421906 (accessed 10 October 2021).
61 Myra Lewis with Murray Silver, *Great Balls of Fire* (London: Mandarin, 1989), pp. 181–2.
62 On coverage, see Brian Ward, '"By Elvis and All the Saints": Images of the American South in the World of 1950s British Popular Music', in Joseph P. Ward (ed.), *Britain and the American South: From Colonialism to Rock and Roll* (Jackson: University of Mississippi Press, 2004), p. 206; John Rolls, 'Meet Myra from Memphis – Wife at 15!', *Daily Mirror*, 23 May 1958, p. 2.
63 Iain Smith, 'Police Check Up on Child Bride', *Daily Mirror*, 26 May 1958, p. 1.
64 Lewis and Silver, *Great Balls of Fire*, pp. 187–191; Bragg, *Jerry Lee Lewis*, p. 274.
65 Leslie Grade, 'Why I Dropped Jerry Lee Lewis', *Melody Maker*, 31 May 1958, p. 20.
66 Bragg, *Jerry Lee Lewis*, pp. 277–80.
67 Ibid., pp. 273–4; Ward, 'By Elvis', p. 209.
68 Eve Perrick, 'Send Them Packing', *Daily Mail*, 27 May 1958, p. 4.
69 On 'child marriages', see Thomas P. Monahan, 'State Control and Legislation on Marriage', *Summary of Proceedings: Officers, Committees (American Bar Association, Section of Family Law)* (1961), p. 62.
70 Myra Lewis Williams with Linda Hughes, *The Spark That Survived* (Atlanta: Deeds Publishing, 2016), p. 45.
71 Ibid., pp. 42–3.
72 Smith, 'Police Check Up'.
73 Ward, 'By Elvis', p. 208; 'The Bride – Aged 12', *Daily Mirror*, 9 March 1956, p. 1.
74 See Ronald Bedford, 'The Brides Get Younger: More Wed in 'Teens', *Daily Mirror*, 2 December 1958, p. 14.
75 *The Youth Service in England and Wales* (London: HMSO, 1960), p. 15.
76 'Viewpoint: Mrs Sixteen is So Happy!', *Daily Mirror*, 29 May 1958, p. 6; 'Teen Page', *Daily Mirror*, 9 December 1960, p. 13.
77 'Larry Page to Marry Fan of 17', *Daily Mail*, 9 June 1958, p. 5.
78 Bill Halden, 'Jerry Lee Produces Boos, Boredom', *Melody Maker*, 31 May 1958, p. 7.
79 Lewis and Silver, *Great Balls of Fire*, p. 193.
80 See 'Thanks Eve – but NOW let's go further', *Daily Mail*, 29 May 1958, p. 8.
81 Bragg, *Jerry Lee Lewis*, p. 268.

82 Joe Bonomo, *Jerry Lee Lewis: Lost and Found* (New York: Continuum, 2009), p. 25.
83 Ward, 'By Elvis', pp. 206–9.
84 Ibid., p. 208.
85 Ibid.
86 Ibid., p. 209.
87 Ibid., p. 208.
88 Smith, 'Police'.
89 Lewis Williams and Hughes, *The Spark*, p. 31.
90 See 'Meet Myra'; 'Jerry May Have to Cut his Tour', *Daily Mirror*, 27 May 1958, p. 10.
91 Lewis Williams and Hughes, *The Spark*, p. 46
92 Bragg, *Jerry Lee Lewis*, p. 269.
93 Don Short, *The Beatles and Beyond* (Bedford: Wymer, 2020), p. 57.
94 Bonomo, *Jerry Lee Lewis*, p. 25.
95 Short, *The Beatles*, p. 57.
96 See Mitchell, *The British*, p. 35.
97 'Private Lives' (Letters), *Daily Mirror*, 31 May 1958, p. 8.
98 Tony Brown, 'Pop Stars' Private Lives', *Melody Maker* 14 June 1958, p. 3.
99 For example, 'Jerry Lee Lewis: Rockin' Split Personality', *Record Mirror*, 9 March 1963, www.rocksbackpages.com.ezproxy.st-andrews.ac.uk/Library/Article/jerry-lee-lewis-rockin-split-personality (accessed 10 October 2021). On others, see Bill Wyman's account of his relationship with Mandy Smith in Wyman with Ray Coleman, *Stone Alone: The Story of a Rock 'n' Roll Band* (London: Viking, 1990), pp. 26–32.
100 Lewis Williams and Hughes, *The Spark*, pp. 142–5.
101 Mitchell, *The British*, pp. 77–81.
102 Derek Jewell reflected on this in 'Stones Start Rolling', *Sunday Times*, 24 May 1964, reprinted in *The Popular Voice: A Musical Record of the 60s and 70s* (London: Andre Deutsch, 1980), p. 74.
103 Bingham, *Family Newspapers*, pp. 117–24.
104 See Lindsay Zoladz, 'She's Marianne Faithfull, Damn It. And She's (Thankfully) Still Here', *New York Times*, 22 April 2021, www.nytimes.com/2021/04/22/arts/music/marianne-faithfull-she-walks-in-beauty.html (accessed 10 December 2021).
105 See David Dalton and Mick Farren (eds), *The Rolling Stones in their Own Words* (London: Omnibus, 1985), pp. 53–7.
106 Williams, 'Bringing', p. 224; Bingham, *Family Newspapers*, pp. 259–60.

3

'I'm different; I'm tough; I fuck': attitudes towards young men, sex and masculinity in Nik Cohn's *Awopbopaloobop Alopbamboom: Pop from the Beginning* (1969)

Patrick Glen

Published in 1969, Nik Cohn's *Awopbopaloobop Alopbamboom: Pop from the Beginning* bears all the hallmarks of an author who understood how the changing attitudes, behaviour and styles of young people, pop music and sex sold.[1] Through a history of pop music's movers and shakers, Cohn explored the stars, hits, forgotten heroes and moral panics of the time, showing a keen awareness of the scandals and perceptions of deviance that drove much of pop's hype. As is well known, scandal has long served to bring matters of gender and sex to the fore, negotiating new boundaries between the public and private. In public debate, in a society within which youth had grown more affluent and autonomous since the 1950s, scandal provoked ruminations on how sexual norms were changing.[2] This chapter analyses Cohn's book to understand pop music's role in shaping and reflecting the social lives of young men and their attitudes to sex.

Teenagers, for a variety of reasons, including a rise in birth rates but also due to increased personal income from work and parental generosity, became a significant market for cultural products post-1945.[3] Pop music was central to this. A sufficient quantity of young people gained a greater degree of discretion over spending to require a reaction from the music industry. Indeed, music and music-related industries developed in close vicinity to metropolitan subcultures described by Frank Mort as being at the forefront of the new consumer culture.[4] As a result, more varied and provocative music captured the attention of young people like Cohn, reaching a mass audience.

From the 1950s onwards, the music industry consolidated a reorganisation precipitated by shifts in the economies of Britain, Europe and the USA. The industry favoured a process of vertical integration which brought together manufacturing, recording, artist and repertoire (A&R), international distribution and marketing into larger corporations.[5] Competition between the major companies (Britain was dominated by EMI, Decca, Phillips and Pye) also resulted in a significant expansion of A&R expenditure, acquisitions and marketing outlays.[6] Through these changes, record companies presented and marketed new artists to sell records and generate income from publishing rights. Costs therefore increased but the rewards were significant. The number of younger A&R workers grew and, with their increased power, enabled new artists and trends that signalled a partial loss of control (in terms of public messages) for the more conservative tendencies of the music industry. As David Hesmondhalgh and Leslie M. Meier noted:

> Popular music's connections to emotion, sentiment and sexuality made it central to a new political economy based on individualism and consumerism. The links to sexuality and the breaking of boundaries between sacred and profane, and to complex trajectories of 'race' and youth, also made certain musical forms the object of a new politicization.[7]

This politicisation included aspects of 'personal' political thinking, such as what it meant to be 'a man', and about sexual encounters. The classic Frankfurt School analysis that popular music and culture exert a stultifying effect on the public that enforces dominant ideology still has some credence.[8] However, scholars such as Hesmondhalgh show how alternative uses and understandings of music could circulate. David Wilkinson has added that this could provoke a hopeful countercultural approach to developing new forms of political and personal expression, 'a forum for the exploration of alternative and oppositional freedoms and pleasures'.[9]

Such a focus on the politicisation of popular music and music fans relates to a broader historiographical project to understand gender relationships, masculinity and sex. Since the 1990s, social and cultural historians have more frequently approached masculinity or masculinities as an analytical category.[10] Two approaches sought to locate masculinity within relationships of structural power: one is an analysis of relationships between men and women, exposing and understanding patriarchy; the second differentiates representations of masculinity in relation to social status and class. Both approaches grapple with R.W. Connell's Gramsci-inspired concept of 'hegemonic masculinity' to understand the dominant forms of masculinity in culture and capitalism. These are then contrasted with femininity and men whose personal enactment of masculinity are 'subordinate', marginalised or 'complicit' in maintaining engrained relationships of power and domination.[11]

A third approach also developed, considering the lived experience of masculinity in terms of psychology, selfhood and subjective experience. Frequently influenced by Michel Foucault's contention that gender is discursively constructed and/or Judith Butler's theory of the performativity of gender, such analyses interrogated the concept of 'man' or 'men' as a site moulded by changing configurations of power and knowledge.[12] All three approaches offer much and this chapter draws from each as it reconsiders how Cohn's history related individual experience to enactments of masculinity, sexual display and sex.

A middle-class Ted in the Bogside

In August 1969, Weidenfeld & Nicholson published *Awopbopaloobop Alopbamboom: Pop from the Beginning* (*Awopbop.*). The book, which became commonly (if erroneously) known as the 'first book on rock 'n' roll', was a history of pop music written by Nik Cohn, a British journalist born in 1946. Taking leave from London, Cohn wrote the book from a cottage in rural Connemara during the late 1960s. Weidenfeld & Nicholson, the liberal-left publisher, established in 1948, had previously published works by the Russian novelist Vladimir Nabokov, Isaiah Berlin, the noted social and political theorist, and Eric Hobsbawm, the Marxist historian. Cohn's journalistic history of pop might therefore have seemed a curious choice considering the publisher's typical remit, but such was the contemporary interest in youth.

Cohn was also well placed to respond to the emerging social and popular cultural changes. At the time of the book's writing and publication, he wrote about popular music for the women's magazine *Queen* (later renamed *Harper's & Queen*) and freelanced for a handful of other publications, including *The Observer*. *Queen* aimed attention at the young women comprising West London's affluent 'Chelsea Set'. It was arguably one of the meeting points of the establishment and so-called 'swinging' London; the magazine even hosted a curious moment when Ronan O'Rahilly and Alan Crawford's pirate radio station, Radio Caroline, broadcast from its offices after Jocelyn Stevens, the magazine's editor, provided funding. By 1969, Cohn had also written two relatively obscure novels published by Secker & Warburg: the first, *Market*, written at the age of 19, was a modernist-inspired exploration of life in a market; the second, published in 1967, *I Am Still the Greatest Says Johnny Angelo*, was a fictionalised account of the life of an egotistical pop singer based on P.J. Proby.[13]

Cohn occupied a relatively unusual social position throughout his life, which clearly shaped aspects of his writing and views on music, culture and society. Born in London but raised in Derry, Cohn grew up in a predominantly working-class city with a majority Catholic nationalist population in the British-ruled North of Ireland. His father, Norman Cohn, took up a lectureship at Ulster University when Cohn was a child. His mother was Vera Broido, born in St Petersburg to a Jewish family, and historian of the Russian Revolution. Her Menshevik mother was executed for involvement in the post-revolution Social Democratic Party, meaning Broido lived through exile and escape from Siberia before meeting Norman and marrying in 1941. In between, she cohabited with the Dadaist photographer Raoul Hausmann and his wife in Berlin. Norman Cohn himself was from a mixed Jewish-Catholic background; a Londoner who worked as a historian of European fanaticism, millenarianism and anti-Semitism. Secker & Warburg, who later published Nik Cohn's books, published his father's most well-known history, *The Pursuit of the Millennium: A History of Popular Religious and Social Movements in Europe from the Eleventh to the Sixteenth Century*.[14] Nevertheless, as Montague Haltrecht observed when reviewing *Market* for *the Sunday Times*, Nik Cohn should not to be underestimated as a writer trading on parental connections:

> His nose is particularly keen, and he has no intention of letting us forget that urine and intercourse are of the essence of everyday life. The style is hip, hectic, American-orientated; but Mr Cohn's stumbling prodigality would make less than a warm response ungenerous.[15]

Such an attitude was palpable in *Awopbop*. The book celebrates the modern in style and attitude, encapsulated by Cohn's enthusiasm for a pop world viewed as intrinsically linked to aspects of US popular culture. Cohn was self-deprecating when, in 1972, he described the book as a 'cynical' attempt to 'buy freedom and a house in the country', knowing that 'slagging the Beatles and praising Presley would cause a mild sensation' in the late 1960s hippie-days of peace and love.[16] *Awopbop* demonstrates an affinity with – and an empathy for – outsiders and economically/socially marginalised people. It does not shirk from the visceral side of life and provides a relatively candid view of sex, lust and desire in young pop fans. His prose is not sensationalist and his worldview was later rationalised in the 2004 edition of the book, prefaced by Cohn's reflections on discovering pop music through watching working-class Derry Catholics listening to Little Richard's 'Tutti Frutti' in a 1950s coffee bar.[17] Impacted by the legacy of British colonialism and sectarianism, the Derry Teds were second-class citizens when it came to jobs and housing. These men, perceived by those in Cohn's immediate circles as 'losers', were to him 'made heroic by the power of Little Richard: rock 'n' roll'. The Teds in the Bogside's music, style and attitude provided articles of 'faith' that made Cohn a 'traitor' to his affluent origins.[18] Though he may be accused of exoticising the colonial 'Other', he saw this experience as 'my first glimpse of danger, and sex, and secret magic. I never got over it.'[19]

Cohn's understanding of himself and the narration of his putative escape from bourgeois norms and expectations resonates with accounts put forward by others in similar social positions. Their views could be understood in terms of what Bourdieu referred to as 'habitus': 'a subjective but not individual system of internalised structures, schemes of perception, conception and action common to all members of the same group or class'; or with regard to Raymond Williams's concept of a 'structure of feeling'.[20] Avid music fans, particularly those from middle-class backgrounds who became enmeshed in music scenes and the music industries, often tell a similar story, beginning with a musical encounter that fundamentally alters their life and worldview. For them, that moment is when pop *starts*.

In *Awopbop*, Cohn deems pop to start with Johnnie Ray in 1952, a man who's music, in spite of only moderate vocal abilities, caused riots.[21] In personal accounts, this music is typically African American but the conduit is often a white person from a marginalised background. This idea of musical epiphany could be seen to include traces of anecdotes offered by African American blues musicians explaining the disapproval they faced when their families discovered they were playing the blues – with profane lyrics about sex – instead of gospel music. Mick Farren, musician, writer and editor of *International Times*, recounted his 'origin story' during an oral history interview:

> I was eleven or twelve or ten or something when 'Heartbreak Hotel' came out and I managed to listen to it on the radio, Radio Luxembourg at seven o'clock. They used to have the top ten, sponsored by McDonalds biscuit bakery the makers of Penguin, after that they would have 'Dan Dare: Pilot of the Future', which was a dramatised version of what was in *The Eagle*. Prior to that they had Perry Como, Doris Day, 'Que Sera Sera', or something, then it's 'Heartbreak Hotel'! The hairs stand up on the back of my neck; after that Dan Dare was history and so was my job as a bank manager. I mean it was kind of coupled with an extra ethos. It was not just rock 'n' roll. There was James Dean and there was Brando; there were the changes that were going on at the cinema. There was the Beat Generation, but you know, if you want to take one crystallising moment it was hearing Elvis Presley for the first time and then Little Richard, and then Buddy Holly, and then Eddie Cochran, and after that there was no turning back … It is at that moment – I am kind of paraphrasing – almost one minute in to 'Heartbreak Hotel' my step-father yelled from the other room: 'What is that racket? Turn it off.' From that moment on it is an us and them situation.[22]

Like so many others, the sound of Black America carried by Elvis, a white working-class southerner, is taken to indelibly mark him. In Farren's autobiography, he explains his transition from a besuited 'bank manager' to a scruffy-but-handsome conduit for the styles of Gene Vincent, Miles Davis, Fidel Castro, Doc Holliday and Johnny Cash.[23] Where sex is concerned, Farren describes himself as sexually curious and experienced, but writes lovingly of long-term partners. Like Cohn, Farren's oral history interview and autobiography locate music as a rhetorical gateway to rebellion from 'straight' society. Farren's changes are entwined with attempts to be a different type of man from the norm; to deviate in cultural tastes, style and politics. But also to be a man more readily available for and open to sexual opportunities.

There is evidence to suggest that music's power to shape social attitudes had a broader effect on 1960s society. In September 1968, the University of Leicester's Centre for Mass Communication Research began a study of how school pupils adapted to a media-saturated society. The resulting book devoted a chapter to pop, arguing that music became 'a central part of many adolescents out-of-school activities'. The pupils' relationship to pop provided a means to 'explore their social and personal experience' in ways not provided in school, the report suggested.[24] Social class was a significant if not entirely determinant factor in young people's pop tastes and related behaviours. The report found that bohemian 'underground' music was favoured by middle-class pupils, whereas working-class pupils derived 'their alternative meanings from street peer groups rooted in the situational cultures of working-class neighbourhoods; and consequently, for them, pop music is likely to be either something which is part of the taken for granted background of group activities, or else part of the small coin of social exchange'.[25] Of course, understanding gender and sexuality was an aspect of this.

As candid as Cohn's account is in relation to sex, some limits must first be acknowledged. The culture of silence around sexual abuse in the music industry prevented any exposé of how changing sexual mores and the empowerment of younger people was exploited by the unscrupulous and abusive. *Awopbop* scolds the British press for negative reporting of Jerry Lee Lewis, an early rock 'n' roll musician who wrote 'Whole Lotta Shakin' Going on' and 'Great Balls of Fire', during his first UK tour in 1958. As Gillian Mitchell recounts in Chapter 2, the newspapers criticised Lewis for marrying a 13-year-old and, as Cohn puts it, 'cried babysnatcher'. Not dissimilarly, Cohn takes the imprisonment of Lewis's contemporary, Chuck Berry, for 'transporting' a 14-year-old girl across state lines for sex as merely the authentic inspiration for his song 'You Never Can Tell', a marker of the 'vicious, sly cynic[al]' lyrics that made 'him so funny, so attractive'.

Chillingly, now, Cohn also devotes around a page to the serial sexual abuser, rapist, paedophile and probable necrophile, Jimmy Savile. Cohn does offer some backhanded compliments in his description of Savile, noting that he 'isn't good-looking, smooth, or even very funny'. He explains that Savile, in lieu of talent or even looks, built a career on hard graft and 'outrage'. As the scandal broke in November 2011, it became clear that Savile was protected by friends in high places as a long-time donor to the Conservative Party and charity fundraiser, and was quick to threaten costly legal proceedings for slander or libel when accused. However, it is telling that Cohn's book is largely unconcerned with the darker side of power in the music industry and those who used changing codes of sexual behaviour to exploit women and less powerful men.

Silence towards the music industry's culture of abuse does not, however, mean that Cohn was entirely uncritical. *Awopbop* condemns the 'assorted greed, snidery and lunacy' of the pop business, noting how 'trousers dropped like ninepins'.[26] He twice describes music industry workers by making reference to Sammy Glick, the anti-hero of the novel *What Makes Sammy Run?*[27] The allusion is telling. The book was written by Budd Schulberg and published in 1941; it was inspired by the life of his father, B.P. Schulberg, who worked in the film industry and attempted to found a screenwriters' union. Glick is amoral, guided only by the accumulation of power and prestige in the film industry. He rejects the close-knit world of his impoverished orthodox Jewish family of recent migrants in the Lower East Side, treating women as if they are disposable and his colleagues awfully in trying to get ahead. He is a manipulative individualist who believes any empathy or solidarity to be a sign of weakness. Nevertheless, behind Glick's flaws is a cruel upbringing of poverty and brutal anti-Semitic abuse, which explains his will to earn security if not pardons his behaviour. The music industry workers in the pop era were less likely to be the high society tastemakers that came before them, but they wielded newfound power, which Cohn locates as a reaction to the privations of war and, for some, the trauma of persecution and the Holocaust.

Cohn's account also makes little explicit reference to homosexuality which, in spite of sexual acts between consenting men over 21 being decriminalised in 1967, remained deeply stigmatised by 1969. He made no comment on the queer symbolism, performance and styles of musicians such as Little Richard or Johnnie Ray, let alone their sexuality (although, in his defence, neither were 'out' at the time). He did note that 'most' of the new rock 'operators' in the music industry were gay, but did not name them in spite of making a passing claim of sexual exploitation: 'see some pretty young boy singing in a pub and fancy him and sign him up. Bed him and then they'd probably very quickly get bored with him.'[28] Cohn hinted at the sexuality of Brian Epstein, the Beatles' manager, using euphemisms throughout. His history of Epstein noted his training at the Royal Academy of Dramatic Arts and attempts to become an actor before turning to business.[29] He describes him as 'intelligent and loyal and neurotic, painfully sensitive, he was nobody's identikit of a hustler but he was civilized, basically honest, and he had capital'.[30]

'Sensitive' and 'neurotic' are terms sometimes used by Cohn to stand in for gay or queer. In one passage, he ascribes feminine traits to Epstein, describing him as a 'mother figure' who 'cared for them, reassured them, agonised on them, nagged them, and even wept for them'.[31] Of course, outing a person against their will or posthumously, in the case of Epstein, is ethically dubious and Cohn was writing in the prevailing register of the time.[32] Interestingly, however, the euphemistic terms used to describe Epstein and others are also used to describe heterosexual pop fans and musicians, particularly those from the middle class. Furthermore, in Cohn's later book on men's fashion, *Today There Are No Gentlemen* (1971), he made a more explicit link between popular music, youth culture and queer subcultures when describing the 'New Edwardians'. 'Bisexual' clothes and a general relaxation of sexual identity represented for Cohn the 'willingness of men to accept at last what was feminine in their own make up, so women were less tied down as well'.[33]

Another loser made palatable

When it comes to sex in Cohn's book, there is a recurring subtext: men involved in pop – and fans who give themselves up to its styles, symbols and attitudes – become sexier and have sex. They become more open to articulating and responding to emotions, anguish and desires; they find the symbolic, attitudinal and behavioural means to transform themselves. These individual changes fit with a broader realignment of sexual mores, through which some younger people question the values of their elders. Cohn attributed this to an opening up of expression in white popular music to include more fraught and raw, possibly even slightly discomforting, expressions of emotions. He deemed the music of Buddy Holly as the 'first time white popular music owned up to lust', grouping Holly with other rock 'n' roll artists including Little Richard, Chuck Berry, Eddie Cochran and Jerry Lee Lewis.[34] Each began their career in the late 1940s or early 1950s, coming to prominence after 1956. They helped develop what Cohn describes as the 'teendream' of sex and consumerism.[35]

However, the music made by southern US African Americans and whites was viewed by Cohn as too 'raw' for the industry. As such, their style and attitude was assimilated by artists more compliant and less personally flawed or problematic to satisfy a mass market. In their place, Cohn argued, came musicians like Elvis Presley (shaped by his manager 'Colonel' Tom Parker) and Bill Hayley (an older music industry chancer) who articulated Chuck Berry's 'endless teen romance' in a way that evoked high school desire rather than hinting at something darker.[36]

In Britain, Cohn observed how the career of the first British rock 'n' roll star, Tommy Steele, was driven (like Elvis) by a manager, John Kennedy, a

New Zealander then in his late 20s. Kennedy managed to kid a sufficient number of record buyers into thinking that Steele was akin to a British Elvis, rather than a slick showbiz performer who sought a break in the theatre.[37] At the start of the period, when popular music consumption and A&R expenditure intensified, the post-1945 music industry was concerned primarily with selling a 'respectable' form of dominant, patrician masculinity to a market dominated by women. For Gillian Mitchell, Steele served as a conduit between a conservative industry and a potentially racier music genre with its origins in African American culture.[38] Steele was fêted for his ordinariness; he was presented as polite, smartly dressed and having a good relationship with his family who he provided for with his newfound wealth. This presentation was worlds apart from the stereotype of an African American rock 'n' roll or blues musician. As Mitchell argues, Steele's example demonstrates how 'established interests tried to accommodate this new craze [rock 'n' roll] within established norms', absorbing 'rock 'n' roll into the existing structures of showbiz'.[39]

From viewing the meticulously stage-managed newsreels of Tommy Steele's public life, it is clear that Steele and his management collaborated with the press to convey a particular image of a man. This comprised a generally accepted sort of masculinity for a public figure, with Steele portrayed as the 'boy next door' becoming a 'family man'. One British Pathé reel from 1957 features Steele moving with his mother and stepfather from Bermondsey to Ravensbourne Park Road in Catford; he is presented as assured, well-kempt, successful, polite to his star-struck female fans, loyally family-oriented, economically successful and upwardly mobile. His next British Pathé newsreel came in 1960, when he married Ann Donoghue at St Patrick's Catholic Church in Soho. The short film shows how Steele graciously swerved a crowd made up of adoring female fans – and the sexual opportunities they may have presented – to meet his bride at the altar. They are filmed praying during the service before heading to the Savoy Hotel on the Strand to cut their wedding cake. (The reel did not show Steele's less aspirational wedding reception in The Bamboo Bar above the Carpenters Arms on Eltham High Street.) Steele was presented as deferential of his elders and their traditions; he was no sexual deviant. He and similar male British rock 'n' roll performers of the time encoded very little of the rebellious promise of rock 'n' roll to those watching these newsreels in cinemas across Britain.

By way of contrast, Martin Cloonan has noted – in agreement with Cohn – the erratic behaviour and mental health issues suffered by Steele's contemporary Terry Dene, which precluded him from similar presentation as an 'ordinary' man.[40] Cohn described Dene's talent and background as comparable to Steele, but he was timid and nervous.[41] He married Edna Savage, a fellow singer, in 1958, who Cohn notes was 'a few years older', and had a media-attended wedding like Steele. Yet, after getting called up for national service (which summoned comparisons to Elvis, who had won the respect of a previously scandalised adult America by serving in the US Army between 1958 and 1960 with no special privileges), Cohn describes Dene requiring a medical discharge within a matter of months. He was subsequently divorced by Savage, fell into obscurity and ended up 'standing on a Soho street corner, preaching the gospel with the Salvation Army'.[42]

Artists typically had to negotiate emotional performance, anguish and fragility without transgressing dominant codes of masculinity. Demonstrating conventionally masculine traits and a normative sex life was important to developing an 'acceptable' pop identity for a putative female audience. This reinforced broader social anxieties, in which a significant amount of people viewed boys and men of the late 1950s into the 1960s who enjoyed pop as being 'effeminate'. In 1964, for instance, forty people gathered for the National Association of Youth Clubs conference at Blue Coat School in Liverpool, which devoted two days to evaluating young people's 'compulsive interest in what they would call their type of music, "pop" and the "beat scene"'.[43] The *Guardian* reported a Liverpool-based youth leader proclaiming that music was 'tending to make boys more effeminate … and it's making young people suffer from "spectatoritis"'. However, he was given short shrift by other attendees who retorted: 'a boy's long hair does not make him less of a man'.[44] The general implication, however, was that they were indeed less of a man.

Of course, there were 'white' anxieties about 'blackness' as well. Dick Hebdige has noted how in later decades many cultural commentators viewed Black people as the 'quintessential subterranean', thereby aligning youth, music and 'blackness'.[45] White musicians achieved considerable commercial success by assimilating and adapting Black music for commercial performance and release (arguably even more so than those who had adapted jazz before them). The conventional narrative goes that Alexis Korner started the first charting UK blues band, Alexis Korner's Blues Incorporated, in 1961, and the genre was brought to prominence by the Rolling Stones after they formed in 1962 and took on a rebellious stance which provoked moments of public outrage. Along with the music, they often played with masculine roles in a manner that was informed by their interpretation of African American culture.

The equation between Black popular music styles, identities and masculinity that crossed the Atlantic to Britain reveals powerful perceptions of the relationship between gender and power in popular music. The supposed maleness and masculinity of the blues is centred at the expense of women's participation. Beyond a blindness to figures such as Sister Rosette Tharpe in *Awopbop*, Sean Lorre has noted that Ottilie Patterson, from County Down in the North of Ireland and a former student of Belfast College of

Art, released the UK's first blues album in 1961, not Alexis Korner. This was a full five years after she performed for the first time in Britain at the Royal Festival Hall in London on 9 January 1955. As Lorre argues:

> Based in part on Ottilie Patterson's elision from the historical record, academic and popular histories alike typically describe British R&B as stemming first and foremost from the actions of young, white, middle-class British men who turned to the sounds of Black American men for musical motivation. Many scholars relying on this narrative have argued that this articulation to the blues – particularly the 'downhome' blues of Mississippi circa 1930 and of early 1950s' Chicago – by white male Britons represented a desire to identify with and vicariously embody a romanticized representation of Black masculinity.[46]

In spite of music industry collusion with early rock 'n' roll musicians to foreground aspects of dominant masculinity, sexuality and sex, fans could interpret pop music to develop symbolic resources and attitudes to create partially or entirely different meanings and behaviours of their own. Cohn, certainly, framed popular music as vital to the formative sexual understandings and encounters of youth. As Adrian Bingham notes, the media was a significant driver of increasing sexual knowledge in society, and although music covered sex in less detail than newspapers, songs and performances expressed sex in more instinctive and emotional ways.[47] Cohn argued that although 17-year-olds might only imitate Elvis, younger fans around 14 years old were more impressionable. This is debatable, but the idea of affect and shades of influence is more tenable if coupled with complicated explanations.[48] The way Cohn weaved Elvis fandom into the lives and sex lives of young fans seems plausible and, as an avid Elvis fan himself, personal:

> Elvis is their great adolescent hero, he's central. They buy their first suit and have their first sex and promote their first hangover with him in the background. And then they have the five years in which they can distance him, get him into perspective and absorb him deeply.[49]

Not only was Elvis and pop the soundtrack to sex, Cohn noted that dancing was a prelude to courtship. He described people dancing alone to 'The Twist', the Chubby Checker song and accompanying dance that he supposes to start 'the hysterical adulation of pop singers by the rich and trendy all over the world', as 'nothing to do with romance … pure exhibitionism, a free platform for sexual display' where dancers could 'stand up and promote their ass'.[50]

Cohn is at pains to suggest that this new approach to sexual display opens, in turn, a new avenue to social acceptance, interaction and thus sex for individuals considered previously as 'outsiders'. To use a phrase Cohn reserved for Eddie Cochran, many musicians and fans were 'another loser made palatable' by pop.[51] This cuts across many of the men involved in pop music; their sexual attractiveness is seen by Cohn as related to their styles, attitudes and, in the case of musicians, aptitude for making music. The Derry Teds are understood in a similar way to Cochran, Phil Spector ('huge news for losers') and even The Beatles, who were described as 'anti-stars and superstars both'. In Cohn's later book on fashion, this mode of anti-hero attraction was described by Don McCullin, a photographer and Ted from Tottenham. McCullin reminisced about how as soon as he walked into the Tottenham Royal in the late 1950s, 'birds [women] would put a price on you', meaning they would take stock of the expense incurred in buying his outfit.[52] His account is shot through with a sexist subtext that women are especially materialistic, but this subcultural display responds to social attitudes towards the new economic and social opportunities for young people in the mid-to-late 1950s caused by full employment. However, McCullin further builds on this to explain how his style and attitude could be used to attract women:

> There was always a greasy comb around. This was a major instrument of attraction. Before you asked a girl to dance, you'd stand in front of her and comb your hair, staring right at her, with sort of hooded eyes.[53]

This form of subcultural courtship seems to celebrate a menacing persona that is starkly different to the boy-next-door and future husband image of Tommy Steele; young people had the intellectual resources to reconsider and respond to images and styles put forward by the music industry.

This sort of sexual menace and outsider image was later adapted by the Rolling Stones. The Beatles were often seen, in Cohn's words, as 'teenage property' who, in spite of signifying 'breaking loose, getting sex', appealed to almost everyone at a time of 'splintering tastes'. The Stones, meanwhile, were more provocative, sexualised and morally ambiguous.[54] Andrew August has argued there was a significant tension between the band's symbolic association with sexual freedom and their use of lyrics that were misogynistic and rejected women's 'claims to independence'.[55] In spite of these sexist messages, Cohn claimed the Stones were 'impossibly evil', 'sun gods' and 'creatures off another planet' who used post-Beat generation bohemianism to become 'the voice of hooliganism'.[56] Again, Cohn implied that outsider men – he describes Keith Richards's personality as 'insecure, neurotic', for instance – can attract women and sex by projecting menace; he describes screaming teenage girls as 'desperate' and claims that their female fans at a concert in Liverpool 'had screamed so hard and wet themselves'.[57] This pull on young people, he noted, 'made adults squirm'.[58]

Cohn notes that the Stones had closer intellectual ties to Black American blues than their white copyists, not to mention the notoriously misogynistic

'Beat Generation' of US writers. Beat Generation and white bohemian approaches to masculinity and sex were arguably shaped by a very reductive view of African American identity. During the 1960s, journalists and scholars tried to understand the relationship between Black masculinity and the blues, with one scholar from the State University of New York, Charles Kiel, writing a book on how the blues singer was a symbol for the Black community, embodying important attitudes and roles.[59] One such role was 'manhood', which Kiel wished to unbind from Freudian or Neo-Freudian ideas predominant at the time.

The Freudian interpretation argued that a combination of poor paternal relationships and 'loving but authoritarian' mothers resulted in 'Oedipal and identity complexes' which manifested in male working-class African American rituals to compensate for 'masculine self-doubt'.[60] It followed that these 'problems' were overcome by the attention of male siblings, which led to outlaw behaviour defined as street life, hustling and casual sex. Keil, who embedded himself into communities during his research, saw the emphasis of prior white scholars to be misguided, noting that most of the African American blues musicians he encountered had a 'lasting attachment and relationship with [their] wives', as well as living a more sexually free existence in the context of the sexual opportunities presented in the life of a peripatetic musician.[61] The dandyish clothes worn by blues musicians, Keil argued, did not signify a wrestling with masculine insecurity. Rather, they expressed 'prettiness and strength' that enhanced sex appeal, suggesting the masculinity of the bluesmen – and their attitudes towards women and sex – were in no way the product of a 'love-hate ambivalence towards women'.[62] The Rolling Stones ignored this more nuanced understanding, of course, living the myth and contributing to an enduring template of sexualised nastiness and rock star privilege that tainted later decades of popular music.

In time, the perception that middle-class and socially mobile working-class men were likely to use popular music as an intellectual resource led to a rejection of more macho forms of masculinity. For Cohn, at least, Bob Dylan 'expressed revolt through something more complicated than a big cock'.[63] Keith Gildart, too, argues that mod 'led to an inversion of existing notions of masculinity and femininity' through exploration of androgynous or unisex style.[64] This is touched upon by Cohn, who describes mods 'as small strange creatures' who made themselves 'look beautiful' but were, of course, 'neurotic' enough to fit into changing codes of sexual behaviour. Cohn also touches on art school students, who he deems 'more intellectual and altogether more soulful'. Simon Frith and Howard Horne's *Art into Pop* explains the place of art schools in British popular music cultures, one of the formative places that certain mods passed through and a hub for the formation of countercultures. Frith and Horne note how art schools and pop existed within a 'consumer world' where roles were learnt from popular performers; thus commodities shaped public selfhood and defined masculinity and femininity along 'lines of possession and desire'.[65] There was an acceptance within art school and associated bohemian cultures that masculinity was a subjective code and could be experimented with, using symbolism from popular cultural products. As this suggests, the myths of popular music served as significant inspiration for emerging values that, in turn, shaped approaches to gender and sex.

Conclusion

In *Awopbop*, Nik Cohn authored an effervescent and provocative account of pop and its impact on young people. Philip Tagg once commented that rock criticism by Cohn and his peers could 'degenerate into exegetic guesswork and "reading between the lines"' in their speculations about what musical texts meant.[66] Cohn's efforts to captivate as well as explain might have resulted in the occasional factual inaccuracy or flight of fancy in his book but preoccupation with its flaws belies something of real worth to those who seek to understand subjective responses to pop and representations of changing ideas about society, sex and masculinity. Popular music both contributed to and represented these changes; the narratives perpetuated by those like Cohn in books, magazines and music papers were, to some, influential in how they understood not just pop but society and their position within it. Cohn perceived pop music to be a broad response to the new consumer society, the tools and symbols of which could be used in varied ways to negotiate social attitudes and life. The ideas of dominant masculinity and sex in his account – and in light of contemporary attention to historic scandals – are coy, but correspond to a moment of social mobility and quick cash for those in the right place that coheres with changes in the economy and structure of the music industry. As we have learnt (or taken notice of) since Jimmy Savile's death in 2011, when he was exposed by those he abused, the social standing of men in the music industry enabled them to take advantage of fans who saw them as having special status. Cohn, following the discursive conventions of the time and industry, rarely confronts ideas of sexual abuse and at times makes light of it. Arguably, the social standing and power of youth signified by pop was still trumped by older men with power and influence.

A tension bound into the changing codes of masculine identity and sexual display transmitted by pop music was that 'outsiders', those who deviated from masculine or social norms, could be perceived as sexually attractive. This was radical and crossed established gender norms to approach unisex styles. Men with sex appeal in Cohn's text could be 'sensitive and neurotic', as he implies with queer men; they could dress decoratively, embrace emotion and express desire with raw abandon, even if limits were initially applied to those wanting to be 'a star' as sanctioned by the music industry. At the same time, in relation to heteronormative dynamics between men and women, menace and ironic detachment to conventional romance was defined as 'sexy', reinforcing notions of male sexual dominance (even if the menacing men wore unisex clothes or sang in a falsetto voice).

Despite such tension, Cohn's book demonstrates how, at the very least, popular music developed as a driver of social change. When supported by the more systematic research that followed, Cohn's breathless speculation is correct in observing pop music's contribution to a broader rethinking of sex, sexual display and masculinity, particularly for young people. *Awopbop* was often inflammatory, at times acerbic towards its subjects. But it was underpinned by an empathy for those who by their class or norms were different. As a result, it helps trace how emergent forms of being a man, of courting and having sex, were discovered at the 'beginning' of pop and in the 'golden age of rock'.

Notes

1 Nik Cohn, *Awopbopaloobop Alopbamboom: Pop from the Beginning* (London: Weidenfeld & Nicholson, 1969).
2 Adrian Bingham, *Family Newspapers?: Sex, Private Life, and the Popular Press in Britain* (Oxford: Oxford University Press: 2011); Frank Mort, *Cultures of Consumption: Masculinities and Social Space in Late Twentieth-Century Britain* (London: Routledge, 1996).
3 Mark Abrahams, *The Teenage Consumer* (London: London Press Exchange, 1959); Selina Todd and Hilary Young, 'Baby-Boomers to "Beanstalkers"', *Cultural and Social History*, 9:3 (2015), 451–67.
4 Frank Mort, *Capital Affairs: London and the Making of the Permissive Society* (New Haven, CT: Yale University Press, 2010).
5 Gerben Bakker, 'Adopting the Rights-based Model: Music Multinationals and Local Music Industries since 1945', *Economic History Working Papers* (London School of Economics and Political Science, 2012).
6 Ibid., p. 9.
7 David Hesmondhalgh and Leslie M. Meier, 'Popular Music, Independence and the Concept of the Alternative in Contemporary Capitalism', in James Bennett and Nikki Strange (eds), *Media Independence* (Abingdon: Routledge, 2015), p. 97.
8 Theodore Adorno, 'On the Fetish Character in Music and the Regression of Listening', in J.M. Bernstein (ed.), *The Culture Industry: Selected Essays on Mass Culture* (London: Routledge, 1991).

9 David Wilkinson, *Post-Punk, Politics and Pleasure in Britain* (London: Palgrave Macmillan, 2016), pp. 22–3.
10 Karen Harvey and Alexandra Shepard, 'What Have Historians Done with Masculinity? Reflections on Five Centuries of British History, circa 1500–1950', *Journal of British Studies*, 44 (2005), 274–80.
11 R.W. Connell and James W. Messerschmitt, 'Hegemonic Masculinity: Rethinking the Concept', *Gender & Society*, 19:6 (2005), 829–59.
12 Michel Foucault, *The History of Sexuality Volume One: An Introduction* (New York, NY: Pantheon, 1978); Judith Butler, *Gender Trouble: Feminism and the Subversion of Identity* (Abingdon: Routledge, 1990).
13 Nik Cohn, *Market* (Secker & Warburg: London, 1965). Nik Cohn, *I Am Still the Greatest Says Johnny Angelo* (Secker & Warburg: London, 1967).
14 Norman Cohn, *The Pursuit of the Millennium: A History of Popular Religious and Social Movements in Europe from the Eleventh to the Sixteenth Century* (London: Secker & Warburg, 1957).
15 Montague Haltrecht, 'Market', *Sunday Times* (21 November 1965), p. 33.
16 Steve Turner, 'My Book is Rubbish but it's the Best', *Beat Instrumental*, May 1972 (accessed through *Rock's Backpages*).
17 Cohn, *Awopbopaloobop* (2nd edn, 2004), pp. x–xiii.
18 Ibid., p. xiii.
19 Ibid., p. x.
20 Pierre Bourdieu, *Outline of a Theory of Practice* (Cambridge: Cambridge University Press, 1977), p. 86; Raymond Williams, *Marxism and Literature* (Oxford: Oxford University Press, 1977), pp. 128–35.
21 Cohn, *Awopbopaloobop*, p. 3.
22 Mick Farren, interview with author (2010).
23 Mick Farren, *Give the Anarchist a Cigarette* (London: Pimlico, 2001), pp. 64–5.
24 Graham Murdock and Guy Phelps, *Mass Media and the Secondary School* (London: Macmillan, 1973), pp. xviii and 143.
25 Murdock and Phelps, *Mass Media*, 109–10.
26 Cohn, *Awopbopaloobop*, p. 58.
27 B.P. Schulberg, *What Makes Sammy Run?* (New York: Random House, 1941).
28 Cohn, *Awopbopaloobop*, pp. 59–60.
29 Ibid., p. 136.
30 Ibid.
31 Ibid., p. 146.
32 Mort, *Capital Affairs*, pp. 114–15.
33 Nik Cohn, *Today, There Are No Gentlemen* (London: Weidenfeld & Nicolson, 1971), pp. 24–5, 114–15 and 153.
34 Cohn, *Awopbopaloobop*, p. 44.
35 Ibid., pp. 36–7.
36 Ibid., p. 35.
37 Ibid., p. 60.
38 Gillian A.M. Mitchell, 'A Very "British" Introduction to Rock 'n' Roll: Tommy Steele and the Advent of Rock 'n' Roll Music in Britain', *Contemporary British History*, 25:2 (2011), 219–21.

39 Ibid., 217.
40 Martin Cloonan, 'The Production of English Rock and Roll Stardom in the 1950s', *Popular Music History*, 4:3 (2009), 284.
41 Cohn, *Awopbopaloobop*, pp. 61–3.
42 Ibid., p. 63.
43 University of Birmingham Special Collections, Records of UK Youth, MS227/5/5/3 (File 3 of 4), Programme for 'The Beat Group in the Youth Club'.
44 *Guardian*, 15 June 1966, p. 3.
45 Dick Hebdige, *Cut 'n' Mix Culture, Identity and Caribbean Music* (Abingdon: Routledge, 1987), 44.
46 Sean Lorre, '"Mama, he treats your daughter mean": Reassessing the Narrative of British R&B with Ottilie Patterson', *Popular Music*, 39:3–4 (2020), 484.
47 Adrian Bingham, 'The "K-Bomb": Social Surveys, the Popular Press, and British Sexual Culture in the 1940s and 1950s', *Journal of British Studies*, 50:1 (2011), 156–79.
48 Cohn, *Awopbopaloobop*, pp. 76–7.
49 Ibid., p. 77.
50 Ibid.
51 Ibid., p. 55.
52 Cohn, *Today There Are No Gentlemen*, p. 30.
53 Ibid., p. 31.
54 Cohn, *Awopbopaloobop*, p. 151.
55 Andrew August, 'Gender and 1960s Youth Culture: The Rolling Stones and the New Woman', *Contemporary British History*, 23:1 (2009), 79.
56 Cohn, *Awopbopaloobop*, pp. 158–9.
57 Ibid., pp. 159 and 163.
58 Ibid., p. 161.
59 Charles Kiel, *Urban Blues* (Chicago: University of Chicago Press, 1966).
60 Ibid., pp. 20–3.
61 Ibid., pp. 26–8.
62 Ibid., p. 27.
63 Cohn, *Awopbopaloobop*, p. 179.
64 Keith Gildart, *Images of England through Popular Music* (Basingstoke: Palgrave Macmillan, 2013), pp. 97–8.
65 Simon Frith and Howard Horn, *Art into Pop* (Abingdon: Routledge, 1987), p. 17.
66 Philip Tagg, 'Analysing Popular Music: Theory, Method and Practice', *Popular Music*, 2 (1982), 43.

4

'We are no longer certain, any of us, what is "right" and what is "wrong"': *Honey*, *Petticoat*, and the construction of young women's sexuality in 1960s Britain

Sarah Kenny

'Everyone these days is talking about the Permissive Society', exclaimed journalist Christopher Ward in a July 1969 edition of *Petticoat* magazine.[1] In a tongue-in-cheek exposé of the rules of 'this unexclusive club' in his bi-monthly column, Ward outlined the society's strict policies on sex, drugs, pornography and marriage. 'Members are pledged never to condone or indulge in marriage or – worse still – sex within marriage', while 'pornography is also encouraged – indeed, it is insisted upon'. And the fate of those who defied the strict rules of the Permissive Society? According to Ward, all who transgressed could expect to be 'banished to a good, clean and upright life, such as was in wide existence before the formation of the Society'. Ward's column offers a fascinating insight into the way that the concept of the permissive society was narrated in the 1960s, and while the column's sarcastic tone is revealing in itself, the derision of the final line hints at the contradictions and hypocrisies inherent in debates about lifestyle and morality towards the end of the decade. Young women's sexuality in particular became a touchpoint for much wider discussions about societal change in the post-war period, accelerated in the 1960s by the introduction of legislative reform on divorce, abortion and oral contraception, and growing concern about rising rates of illegitimacy and venereal disease.

The magazine industry, one of the major benefactors of the post-war shift in youth lifestyle and consumer behaviours, was at the vanguard of much of this debate. This chapter draws primarily on material from two teenage magazines, both of which were new to the market in the 1960s: *Honey* (1960–86) and *Petticoat* (1966–75). It argues that their coverage of young women's sexuality in the 1960s shows that this was a moment in which a new sexual morality was being constructed, one that positioned young women as independent and ambitious, and was built on improving sexual knowledge and recognising young women's individual agency. It suggests that what was considered 'right' and 'wrong' remained, on the whole, a reflection of traditional principles that valued marriage and the nuclear family, but increasingly sought to provide young women with the knowledge and support to be able to make their own informed decisions about life, sex and love.

The launch of these publications, and their success in an increasingly crowded market, indicated the commercial and cultural power of young women in 1960s Britain. Magazines offered readers clear opportunities to explore a new world of youth-driven content, designed solely for them and their interests, yet were also a reflection of a new commercial marketplace: one in which young women's consumption and lifestyle choices were increasingly tied into the commercial interests of the publishing industry and advertisers.[2] They were read eagerly in bedrooms, shared between friends, provided sources of advice and information, and offered cultural scripts for how, in *Honey*'s words, the 'young, gay and get ahead' should behave.[3] As Joan Ormrod has argued, magazines for teenage girls provided a 'ready availability … because they were always on hand and could be reread, loaned, borrowed and discussed with friends'.[4] But they were also sites of agency for young women who, through letters pages and purchasing decisions, actively negotiated their thoughts, opinions and desires with writers, editors and publishers.[5] Young women's magazines were a unique and significant cultural space, and as such are a vital way for historians to access the changing ideals of girlhood and womanhood in 1960s Britain.[6]

This chapter focuses on the way that young women's sexuality was constructed and communicated in the 1960s, and in particular considers how these publications grappled with the growing opportunities that the industry presented to explore young women's sexuality. While the literature has considered the shifting portrayal of lifestyle, romance and relationships in the 1960s, less attention has been given to the construction and communication of sexual scripts in this period. This chapter therefore focuses on several key issues: sex, relationships and marriage, contraception, single motherhood and abortion, to consider how young women's sexuality was constructed and communicated. This was not, however, a simple case of progression away from the ideals of domesticity that characterised the 1950s towards a more critical feminist questioning of the status quo in the 1970s. Young women's sexuality was constructed as being at once a reflection of the growing social and cultural freedoms of the 1960s and a danger that threatened to disrupt those same freedoms.

Women's magazines and cultural change in post-war Britain

Honey and *Petticoat* were marketed towards girls and women in their mid-to-late teens and early twenties. Launched by Fleetway Publications in

1960 and 1966 respectively, they were among a raft of new publications aimed at the female teenage market, with other titles such as *Jackie*, *Fabulous* and *Boyfriend* all launching within the space of a few years. The early- to mid-1960s witnessed a boom in teenage magazines aimed at young women and reflected the magazine industry's realisation in the late 1950s that teenage girls and young unmarried women were an untapped and financially lucrative market.[7] By the 1960s these publications had a significant cultural reach and widespread readership, and *Honey* and *Petticoat* reached six-monthly sales figures of 190,000 and 200,000 respectively between 1966 and 1968.[8] Taken together these two publications reveal clearly the ways in which female sexuality was constructed and communicated to young wage-earning women in the 1960s. The many overlaps on issues such as dating and relationships, living and socialising independently, beauty, careers and sex can be read as providing a set of clear cultural scripts for young women's lifestyle choices in this period. However, as this chapter will show, there were multiple ways to read and interpret these, and engagement with the ideas presented in these publications were not consumed passively or without critique.

Scholars of youth culture have tended to view the popular magazine in the context of bedroom culture and the cultural construction of girlhood.[9] However, as other contributions to this collection clearly demonstrate, popular magazines were also an essential component of young people's wider lived engagement with youth culture. Their focus on music and pop icons, fashion and beauty meant they were firmly rooted in the growing commercial marketplace of youth culture. Similarly, their position as publications developed specifically for consumption by those in their teens and early twenties meant they were a regular feature of many young people's day-to-day lives. Magazines were ephemeral, consumed with and shared between friends, taken to work and school, read on buses and trains, in bedrooms and in bathtubs.[10] They were picked up and put down again, and not always read in one sitting. They were read, and then re-read, often multiple times. In short, magazines such as *Honey* and *Petticoat* were a prominent feature of many young women's spare time, and their consumption was part of the way in which youth culture infiltrated the everyday.[11]

This process of consumption, though, was by no means one-way. On the contrary, these publications were places where young women questioned and challenged social norms about sexuality and sexual behaviour. Magazines engaged in open dialogue with their audience about their wants and expectations, recognising the agency of their young readers.[12] *Honey*'s editor (and *Petticoat*'s founder), Audrey Slaughter, declared the July 1965 issue the 'I Hate Honey Month', following critique from readers about the content of the magazine. In her monthly letter to readers, Slaughter noted that readers had 'nagged and criticised' and the publication had taken its readers' 'letters to heart'.[13] Fan Carter's study of *Honey* demonstrates clearly how the publication operated as a commercial institution, remaking its relationship with readers following initial poor sales and fostering close relationships with advertisers.[14] Similarly, Elizabeth Lovegrove's work with *Honey* argues that paying attention to readers' interventions offers new ways of thinking about the relationship between young women and the magazines they read, and subverts the idea that young women had no 'critical faculty through which to filter these messages'.[15] What is clear is that young women wrote openly to publications to make their disapproval or disagreement with key topics known, and the magazines' publication of these critiques was an important commercial tool that gave readers an active stake in the industry. In addressing the changes made to *Honey* magazine, Slaughter closed her July 1965 letter by asking: '[I] wonder if you'll like it? One thing I do know. I'll soon hear about it if you don't!'[16]

The literature on young lives in the 1960s is extensive, and the breadth of this scholarship speaks clearly to the social and cultural significance placed on this period. Lynn Abrams categorises the young women who grew up in this period as being part of a 'transition' generation, sandwiched in the years between post-war domesticity and the women's liberation movement.[17] Such women, Abrams argues, have often been overshadowed by the 1968 generation whose legacies became closely entwined with the gains of 1970s feminism.[18] Within this landscape, young women's magazines were dismissed and criticised for their 'shallow materialism' and slated as cynical commercial projects that reflected traditional visions of femininity.[19] This dismissal was part of a much wider lack of interest in cultural products aimed at women, but also reflected the belief that popular young women's magazines were inherently conservative in both outlook and content. However, the emergence of cultural studies and feminist scholarship in the 1980s marked a material shift in the attention and focus given to women's magazines.[20] As a result, historians have increasingly challenged the image of women's magazines in the post-war period as containing a homogenised ideal of femininity. Penny Tinkler's work on the ideals of young womanhood, for example, demonstrates clearly that the 1960s was a significant moment in the shaping of new visions of femininity. Young women were, Tinkler argues, 'harbingers of social change', and were presented with new opportunities that were 'attractive, empowering … and fraught with tension'.[21] Fan Carter suggests that *Honey*'s launch in 1960 marked a new era in teenage magazine publishing, one that 'articulated a particular image of youthful femininity that was mobile, ambitious, fashionable and self-fashioning'.[22] Melanie Tebbutt's work with the magazine *Mirabelle* outlines a marked shift in advice given to young women between the 1950s and 1970s, suggesting that 'greater willingness to discuss sexual matters was accompanied by significant changes in how the dynamics of social and sexual relationships with boys were perceived'.[23]

Teenage girls and young women, often perceived to be in a liminal state between childhood and adulthood, were a central way through which anxieties and unease about the complex relationship between sexuality and adolescence were communicated. Sexual desire became, by the early twentieth century, an accepted part of childhood development, driven both by shifting ideas about childhood 'innocence' and the work of psychologists and sexologists such as Sigmund Freud, Havelock Ellis and Albert Moll.[24] However, the ways that sexual knowledge has been communicated to young people was, and continues to be, a topic of much contention and debate.[25] Lesley Hall argues that, from the outset, sex education in Britain was 'cast ... almost entirely within the framework of a strategy for damage limitation'.[26] In the 1960s, sex education in schools continued to promote a biological approach, 'with a strong emphasis on reproductive facts and relatively little about emotional development or moral questions'.[27] However, adult anxieties about the perceived shift in young people's sexual mores in this period also led to sex education and access to sexual knowledge becoming repositioned by moral traditionalists as a site of corruption, rather than as 'a public health solution'.[28]

As sites of open discussion about sex and sexuality, the publications themselves became a site of adult anxiety, and this anxiety was most clear in relation to young women's sexuality. Hannah Elizabeth has argued that some of this discomfort stemmed from the moral ambiguity of the mass media in relation to children and young adults, but that this was also a reaction to the 'proliferation of new knowing (often sexual) teenage femininities, where young women were constructed as active agents rather than innocents'.[29] Teenage magazines thus acted as a crucible within which anxieties about young women's sexuality were constructed, deconstructed and challenged. However, to characterise the presence of these anxieties in teenage magazines simply as a continuing moral panic about the state of youth in the post-war era, or as representing the moral threat posed by female sexuality, would be to do a disservice to both the publications and the young women who consumed them. Similarly, we should resist the characterisation of these publications as providing a homogenous message to teenage girls about the importance of striving for marriage, children and family life in the future. Topics such as abortion, adoption, consent and the difficulties of negotiating young relationships were often covered with sensitivity and insight. While this chapter suggests that there were clear limits in place regarding teenage magazines and their construction of teenage sexuality – these were, on the whole, shaped by traditional values and spoke to their dual commitment to reader and advertiser – it also argues that these were valuable spaces in which the narratives around young women's sexuality positioned education and individual agency as essential facets of their experience, and demonstrates the growth of sexual knowledges in the commercial leisure sphere.

Sex, contraception and marriage

Young women in 1960s Britain were presented with a seemingly ever-expanding range of options for their current and future lives. As Tinkler has shown, the new magazines for young women in their late teens and early twenties operated on the clear message that young women could and *should* pursue a range of life experiences; living independently, finding a fulfilling career, travelling and dating were just some of the options that magazines such as *Honey* and *Petticoat* turned their attention to.[30] This was also a period in which knowledges about heterosex were growing and, as Hannah Charnock argues, young women were increasingly willing to talk about and share their views on their, and their peers', sexual behaviour.[31] This growing openness about lifestyle choices, love, relationships and sex made its way, in various ways, onto the pages of young women's magazines.

Honey's January 1965 issue opened with the provocation 'How far will you go?' 1965, the publication argued, was a 'year for the daring'.[32] While the headline was designed to grab attention, the magazine's editor Audrey Slaughter was keen to emphasise the appropriate way to be daring. A 1965 *Honey* girl was, the editor's note explained, not somebody who makes headlines simply 'by doing something outrageous', but somebody who makes their mark by seizing 'all the exciting possibilities of 1965'.[33] In the themed issue, featuring sections on 'how far will you go' for fashion and careers, the article 'Dating Before Mating' provided readers with the opportunity to test their boyfriend's attitudes to sex and relationships. Dating, the article argued, was educational and, 'just as education in living would be limited if we were dependent on one teacher, so, too, would education for mating if our experience were tied up in only one boy'.[34] Dating thus gave young women a clearer sense of themselves by educating them about their capacity to cope with jealousy and irritation, as well as 'the more desirable qualities'. This education, though, did not extend to sexual experimentation. For young women it was acceptable, even expected, that a 'girl can enjoy sexual behaviour on the part of the man she loves', but that this behaviour would 'repel her if attempted by another man'.[35] While the essential message of this article maintained the clear moral signal that young women should abstain from sex before marriage, it also recognised the importance of sexual attraction and compatibility in making a successful partnership and, most importantly, that young women could be expected to want to act upon that sexual attraction.

Discussion of sex and sexual behaviour was a feature of young women's magazines – sometimes covertly, other times far less so – through the 1960s. Whether or not young women should have sex, who they should have sex with, how much they knew about sex and how they should feel about their sexual encounters were questions discussed regularly in these magazines, though this discussion was often far more explicit in *Honey* and *Petticoat* who were aimed at a slightly older readership than in other publications such as *Jackie*. Analysis of their problem pages, letters pages and advice columns reveal that oftentimes these discussions formed part of an ongoing dialogue between readers and the magazine's writers and editorial staff. While some of this communication was moralism masquerading as advice, there are clear examples of teenage magazines working constructively within the realities of their readers' lived experiences.

In *Petticoat*'s regular advice column Dr Roy Fraser, resident psychologist, offered guidance on relationships, family difficulties and careers. In March 1966, Fraser presented a frank conversation with reader Christine about sex and relationships. Christine felt pressured by her boyfriend to have sex, to which Fraser responded: 'What is unfair is the manner in which he is trying to force you into acceding his wishes.'[36] Most interesting in this exchange was the space given to Christine, and the open conversation between the two. 'Can't sexual intercourse help us to grow up and understand ourselves and others better?' asked Christine. Rather than warning Christine off sex with future partners, he replied: 'It certainly can, and it can make us more prepared for marriage. What's more a relationship need not to be permanent to be of value.' Fraser's advice for Christine was not that she should abstain from sex, or that she wait until she was sure she had found somebody whom she was likely to marry, but that she should engage in sexual intercourse only when she felt it was right. However, he was also clear to emphasise what he considered the dangers of acting on her sexual urges. 'You must guard against its dangers. Like most things in life, self-discipline and self-restraint are required, otherwise we have to pay far too great a price for immediate satisfactions – wonderful though those may be.'[37] What exactly Fraser meant by 'too great a price' is not entirely clear, but it is Christine who is given the final say. Responding to Fraser's advice that boys will respect her all the more 'for not cheapening yourself', Christina retorted with 'it isn't cheap if you're in love'. This final exchange between the two is just one point of tension exposed in the publication's coverage of sexuality. While Fraser presents an open but cautious attitude towards the sexuality of young women, space is given to Christine, somebody seen to be representative of, or at least relatable to, *Petticoat* readers, to vocally disagree and present her own vision of acceptable female sexuality.

The publication provided regular space for open and often frank discussion of sex and sexuality, with this featuring more prominently from 1967 onwards. In 1969, the journalist and author Peter Fryer, well known for his work on the Hungarian uprising of 1956 and later for his essential text *Staying Power* on the Black experience in Britain, wrote a series titled 'Sorting Out Your Sex Life'. While Fryer's work on the history of sexuality remains less well-known than his other works, Fryer had, by the end of the 1960s, published a number of texts on sex, censorship and pornography, making him a vastly qualified if rather unexpected commentator for *Petticoat*.[38] Seeking to write 'openly and with sympathy' on sexuality, Fryer set out in his first piece to reflect on a 'new morality'.[39] There is not, Fryer contends, 'any new morality, any single code of behaviour. We are no longer certain, any of us, what is "right" and what is "wrong".'[40] But Fryer's series was not a place for advice or musings on what individual readers of *Petticoat* should do – 'nobody in his right mind would give blanket advice, suitable for every reader of *Petticoat*'[41] – rather it was portrayed as a place for readers to reflect on the biggest challenges facing young women at the end of the 1960s. In part two of the series, Fryer grappled with love, contending that 'ignorance about sex produces an appalling amount of human misery'.[42] But knowledge about sex and the body was not a statement from Fryer that every young woman was, or wanted to be, sexually active. Rather, he contended that knowledge about how the body works, contraception, pregnancy and intercourse 'is important to you whether or not you decide to go with your boyfriend before marriage'.[43]

Perhaps one of the most significant markers of the shifting sexual landscape of youth in the 1960s were the growing opportunities to access information about contraception. Knowledge about contraception and available contraceptive methods was often patchy and inconsistent, and was only partially covered in formal sex education.[44] Michael Schofield's *The Sexual Behaviour of Young Adults* found in 1965 that sixteen per cent of boys and eighteen per cent of girls knew nothing about contraception, while many of the others surveyed 'had only a slight knowledge'.[45] The topic was a regular feature of letters pages and advice columns, and the services of the Brook Advisory Service (established in 1964) were advertised in a number of publications aimed at young women. Though birth control clinics were by no means new, having first been established during the birth control movement of the 1920s, the Brook Advisory Service was the first organisation established explicitly to provide advice and contraception to unmarried women 'openly and without subterfuge'.[46] In an interview with *Petticoat* in 1967, Helen

Brook refuted accusations that the clinics were making premarital sex 'socially acceptable'.[47] Rather, she explained to readers that 'there is no point in raising your hands in holy horror at the rise in illegitimacy rate, and confining practical help to preaching sermons to the young about self-control'.[48] The wider concern about sexual knowledge and contraception was driven by a number of factors: a moral panic about rising rates of illegitimacy; venereal disease; hastily organised marriages as a result of unintended pregnancies; and inadequate sex education in schools.[49] These concerns differed dramatically depending on the audience, but in the pages of *Honey* and *Petticoat* a concerted effort was undertaken to educate and inform young women, as well as to advise.

In the same vein, the November 1969 issue of *Petticoat* offered the short booklet *The Facts of Loving* free to readers. The fifteen-page supplement covered sexual relationships, venereal disease and contraception. This was not the first time that Slaughter's publications had provided sex education in this way. In 1966 she created the booklet *Birth Control and the Single Girl* which *Honey* readers could send for, leading to her being interviewed by the BBC about her 'permissive stance'.[50] It is here that we can see both *Honey* and *Petticoat* as situated clearly at the intersection between adult anxiety and the teenage consumer; the importance of education was framed explicitly within the sexual needs of young single women. Similarly, the presence of contraceptive advice reflected both the popularity of sexual advice among young readers and the realisation from publishers that this advice – often inconsistent and lacking in more formal settings – sold magazines and increased circulation. Importantly, this information was not presented as part of a formalised sex education, but interspersed between adverts for hairspray and articles on bedroom décor. The contraceptive advice in these publications is therefore representative of both the shifting sexual knowledge of the young and the many ways in which sexual knowledge became part of the everyday landscape of youth in post-war Britain.

While discussion of, and knowledge about, sex was no longer confined to those who were married or soon-to-be married, the topic of marriage itself remained high on the agenda for both *Honey* and *Petticoat*. Penny Tinkler has shown that both publications offered 'exciting new alternatives to the traditional route from school to marriage'.[51] Indeed, the question was no longer about the importance of marriage as the final destination for a young woman but instead became focused on the importance of building a successful marriage, one that didn't end in divorce. This was exemplified most clearly in August 1967 when the publication ran with the front page, 'Petticoat Test Paper on Marriage … Could YOU Pass or Should You Remain Single?'[52] The test quiz, featuring eight sections on topics including sex, home-making, budgeting and compatibility, was positioned clearly within the wider discourse on rising divorce rates among the young, but also interrogated why young women were choosing to marry. 'It seems to us', the magazine said, 'that if it were as difficult to marry as to unmarry, people might think more responsibly before promising their futures away in a rush of overpowering passion.'[53] The test paper's rejection of passion and romance in favour of level-headedness might seem out of place, particularly considering the overwhelming focus on dating and relationships elsewhere in *Petticoat*'s pages, and given Fleetway Publishing's wider commercial interests – *Honey* magazine launched a 'bride of the month' feature replete with targeted advertising and a new publication titled *Honey's Bride Guide*, for example – but their approach to young marriage was in line with a broader shift in attitudes towards companionate marriage.[54] For *Petticoat* writers, the concern for young women of the 1960s was not the importance of marriage, but the importance of marrying *successfully*.[55] Of course, the definition of a successful marriage was up for interpretation, but these publications were one of the central spaces in which young women were encouraged to think critically about their imagined future and what they wanted from it.

Sex, pregnancy and the single mother

While discussion of sex and sexual knowledge was becoming more common, and was increasingly separated from the institution of marriage, this was not presented as being without risk. It was in discussion about sex and the potential for pregnancy that young women's sexuality was exposed as a contradictory and malleable concept, one that offered both opportunities for freedom and adventure and posed serious and devastating risks.

Of all the issues tackled by young women's magazines in the 1960s, none were covered as seriously as unmarried motherhood. Despite the push by many of these magazines for young women to explore themselves and their potential through independent living, dating and the delaying of marriage, there were still clear ideas around the risks posed by female sexuality that they did not challenge. However, the narratives created around single motherhood were not simply communicated as a message for young women to abstain from sex. After all, the advertising pages of these publications regularly contained advice and information about contraception and family planning, while advice pages regularly spoke openly about premarital intercourse. Rather than present a single moralised narrative of single motherhood, both *Honey* and *Petticoat* situated their discussion of this topic within two key issues: young women's sexuality and their future lives, and the importance of education and informed decision making.

According to conventional narratives, argue Pat Thane and Tanya Evans, unmarried motherhood in Britain was associated with shame and stigma until the 1960s, when the dawn of the 'permissive society' signalled a major shift and cohabitation and childbirth out of wedlock became a far more common and accepted set-up.[56] The reality is, as they demonstrate, far more complex than this, and many young women were supported by close or extended family long before the 1960s. Similarly, the notion that the 1960s signalled a more open attitude to unmarried motherhood overlooks the continuing threat that the young unmarried mother was seen to pose throughout the period. However, Jeffrey Weeks has argued that the growing concern about single motherhood in the 1960s can be read as a representation of the growth in the number of women reaching childbearing age, as well as shifting practices around marriage and cohabitation, rather than a boom in single motherhood.[57] Despite this, the narrative of pregnancy and single motherhood as a threat was pervasive and had material consequences for young women. For many, sex became a 'process of fraught negotiation' between their sexual lives and imagined futures.[58] Hannah Charnock has shown clearly how young women navigated this, often inconsistently, and how the threat of pregnancy was a dominant factor in their approach to sex.[59]

In those publications aimed primarily at young unmarried women, the topic of single motherhood was a contentious one. In 1968, as part of their edition marking 50 years since the 1918 Representation of the People Act, *Honey* ran an editorial titled 'Free, young and female: but God help you if you have a baby and no husband …'[60] The byline, rather than reflecting the publication's judgement of single mothers, instead spoke to wider social attitudes about pregnancy, motherhood and young femininity. The editorial was a three-page spread featuring interviews with four single mothers, each of whom had different experiences when they discovered they were pregnant. Marian was a hairdresser, and her weekly £18 salary meant she was able to afford daily childcare for her daughter. Marian's experience was presented to readers as a challenging but not entirely negative one: her life had undoubtedly changed but was 'certainly not *dreadful* now'.[61] However, the financial and social implications of having a child out of wedlock were made clear. 'Life is', exclaimed Marian, 'what I would call un-normal. There is still a stigma attached to having a baby without a husband.' Indeed, Marian's story exposed the contradictions inherent in living in the 'permissive society'. 'Even among my crowd with few virgins in it', she explained, 'I'm looked on as someone – well, a bit fast. Of course, it's utterly illogical – but it's true.'[62]

Joanna, who lived in London with her two-year-old son, also felt her experiences as a single mother were marred by hypocrisy. Joanna stated that she had been 'led up the garden path'. In a powerful reflection on her own experiences, she argued:

> Everybody agrees that customs or morals, or whatever you call them – have changed. You're not punished for doing something you shouldn't, but simply for having been unlucky! You aren't chucked out of your youth club or job for sleeping with your boyfriend – or even for sleeping with several. But God help you if you have a baby and want to keep it – which the experts tell you is best for the baby![63]

The editorial shared a range of experiences, including a young mother who had originally considered adoption and later changed her mind, and a single teacher who had received advice from an adoption society before making the decision to have her child adopted. Through all four interviews, the publication presented a variety of experiences of young single motherhood. While all recognised the challenges that this presented, the editorial did not suggest that unmarried motherhood was either immoral or guaranteed to end a young woman's career or social life. Instead, the voice and experience of young mothers was presented to allow readers to form their own views on the subject. The piece ended with advice about the National Council for the Unmarried Mother and her Child, the lobbying group Mothers in Action, available financial support, and information about the adoption process and the potential implications for careers and work. Indeed, in focusing on the voices and experiences of young mothers, as well as ending the article with information about the support available for those in a similar situation, *Honey* positioned education and individual agency as essential, equipping its readers with the tools needed to make informed decisions about their lives.

Petticoat's coverage of pregnancy and single motherhood was, at times, more frank. In his column of March 1966, Dr Roy Fraser offered advice to 18-year-old Gwen who was three months pregnant. Gwen was reluctant to tell her parents about her pregnancy and felt she had let them down. Fraser's column made clear that he was a psychiatrist and 'not here to sit in moral judgement', and his advice was peppered with empathetic realism, as well a broader comment on the difficult situation in which young pregnant women were placed.[64] Fraser noted that he 'knew only too well the price she had to pay for her mistake would be an exorbitant one – out of all proportion to the reality of the situation'. Fraser's column presented young single motherhood as a challenge, but one that was manageable with the right support network – in this case, Gwen's employers and parents. Gwen had the full support of her employer, who had told Fraser 'there is no question of her losing her job … we will do all we can to support her'.[65] The column ends with Gwen's parents joining her at an appointment with

Fraser and, in telling them both, Gwen was presented as having 'got over the worst hurdle'.[66] The message communicated in Fraser's column was not that Gwen had been immoral or irresponsible, but that the secrecy she had placed around her pregnancy was only going to make her life more difficult. Finishing on an optimistic note, both in the context of Gwen's story and the wider message for those reading the column, Fraser argued that 'problems are far worse in anticipation: once they're faced, they're often cut down to size'. The portrayal of Gwen's pregnancy was therefore reframed as something that needed support rather than secrecy, and contextualising rather than catastrophising.

The discussion of teenage pregnancy was tied up closely within four key issues: young marriage, single motherhood, contraception and abortion. Within this, a central concern was the impact of pregnancy and motherhood on the future for young women. Both *Petticoat* and *Honey* recognised that raising a child was either not an option or a desired outcome for some pregnant young women, and both discussed support available to those who wished to terminate their pregnancy or place their child for adoption. The coverage of abortion in these publications was, on the whole, more divided and the language more emotive than discussions of premarital sex or contraception, and often centred on the lived experiences of young women. For readers, this was a vital way to access information about family planning, healthcare and support networks, in a society where single motherhood continued to be shrouded in secrecy and shame. Of course, not all young women who wished to access abortion were able to, and there were significant regional variations and imbalance.[67] While the coverage of abortion varied from young women who chose not to terminate their pregnancy, to those who suffered the trauma of 'backstreet' abortions, to those who successfully sought a termination, the importance of knowing how to prevent pregnancy and education on available contraceptive methods were central to these discussions.

In 1964, *Honey* ran a two-page spread on the topic 'What to do if you are going to be a single mother'. The piece ran three and a half years before the commencement of the 1967 Abortion Act and three years before the 1967 Family Planning Act, which extended the remit of those eligible for the oral contraceptive pill on the NHS. As such, the piece was focused on practical advice rather than prevention: 'no one achieves anything by moralising', the article argued in the opening paragraphs.[68] Between advice on speaking to parents, information on the National Council for the Unmarried Mother and Her Child, adoption organisations, financial and legal support, the piece outlined clearly the dangers posed by illegal abortions. Framing this within a discussion of what *not* to do (emphasis original), it argued that 'not being able to have children later is the least of the dangers. Quite possibly the pregnancy isn't even terminated, and all they may do is endanger the child's health.'[69] The article recognised clearly the terror felt by many girls and young women who found themselves in this position and sought to reassure them about both the support that many found in existing family networks as well as the organisations that could provide help and advice. This article was an early example of the coverage given to single motherhood in teenage magazines, which picked up pace dramatically from 1967, but was clear recognition that *Honey* saw its readers as being both sexually active and in need of practical advice that they were not able to access elsewhere.

In 1969, *Petticoat* ran a two-page spread on abortion, presenting 'one girl's true story'.[70] While it isn't clear whether this was in fact a true story, the piece followed other similar 'true life' formats by telling the story through the young woman's words. Helen, a 21-year-old from London relayed her experience to readers, writing 'for me, having the baby was just out of the question. It would have been disastrous as I didn't have any money, or very firm roots, and anyway, I couldn't have loved it, I'm sure.' Helen, unsure where to turn and who to talk to, visits a midwife on the advice of a work colleague 'who did occasional abortions', before finally having to borrow money for an abortion at a private clinic. Helen finishes her story by saying:

> Now I feel I must have been crazy to get pregnant. To run a risk like that, and to have to go through what I did. It is just *never* worth it. Really, I think every girl should realise this, and never let it happen to her.[71]

Helen's story is portrayed as a clear warning to other sexually active young women. The dangers of illegal procedures and difficulties in accessing safe abortion were made clear, as were Helen's own regrets. However, the medical and psychiatric advice that follows Helen's story reflect differently on her experience and focus on practical advice and information. While a doctor chastises Helen for not seeking a legal termination promptly, they do recognise that in some parts of Britain there 'is difficulty' in accessing abortion on the NHS due both to demand and the reluctance of some doctors to recommend this.[72] Information is provided on the Pregnancy Advisory Service, as well as information on contraceptives – 'this is *absolutely vital*' (emphasis original) the doctor concludes. A psychiatrist's view on Helen's experience is also presented, focusing on the potential for trauma and 'emotional disturbance'. However, reinforcing the importance of access to safe and legal abortion, the psychiatrist concludes:

> If a girl has decided she must have an abortion, I think an operation performed with as little fuss and sentiment as if it were the removal of a tooth, as some of them are, certainly cuts down on the trauma of the situation – which I personally consider a good thing.[73]

The focus on the emotional trauma and turmoil that an abortion could bring were central to much of the discussion. In a 1970 piece in the short feature 'Petticoat casebook', one doctor reflects on 'the problems of abortions'.[74] There is, the piece begins, 'so much talk about abortion these days yet little is said about what an unpleasant experience it actually is'. The piece presented a detailed description of many girls' experience in trying to access abortion on the NHS – reluctant doctors, delays, and difficulty accessing services in time – and argues that young women should 'try and avoid having an abortion if you can'. However, the doctor falls short of advising against abortions. Rather, they encourage young women to be educated about their options and, where an abortion is required, to 'persevere, whatever your medical advisor may say'.

The extended focus given to pregnancy and single and unmarried motherhood in teen magazines positioned young women's sexuality at a complex juncture. The attention given to this issue far outstripped the number of young readers who would experience either an unwanted pregnancy or single motherhood, and did not always recognise the inequities in young women's access to effective family planning. It is within the pages of young women's magazines that the tensions associated with the drive for freedom and independence were played out, where an active dating life and experimentation were celebrated, but where the risks of this freedom for young women were high. However, the portrayal of young single motherhood was not used solely as a warning against girls having 'too much fun'. Neither was it presented only in moral terms seeking to encourage young women to abstain from sex until marriage. The narrative constructed around single motherhood was complex, and in several cases was constructed in conjunction with young women who were single mothers. It intersected in important ways with changing ideas about adolescence, young women's freedom, ambition and sexual maturity, and complicated the accepted narrative that marriage or social marginalisation were the only possible outcomes of pregnancy and unmarried motherhood for young women in 1960s Britain.

Conclusion

Magazines published for teenage girls and young women in the 1960s were an important part of everyday ephemeral engagement with popular youth culture, and their coverage of issues including sex, marriage, contraception and abortion were central in constructing a new sexual morality. Young women growing up in 1960s Britain were subject to an increasingly visible sexual double standard, one where they were encouraged to pursue independence and freedom while maintaining feminine ideals of chastity and modesty.

However, within the pages of *Honey* and *Petticoat*, the construction of this new sexual morality increasingly replaced moralism with education, and advice with a recognition of agency. While this was, for the most part, still communicated in line with an imagined future centred on marriage and motherhood, and framed within the commercial interests of publishers, it recognised alternative versions of young womanhood and provided pathways to navigate this.

No single message of what constituted acceptable female sexuality was presented in the pages of these magazines, and the ideas discussed could be contradictory and complex; young marriage was not wrong, but was certainly not right for everybody, and marrying *successfully* was essential; the importance of sexual knowledge was spoken about openly, but uneducated sexual experimentation based solely on desire was framed as a threat; single and unmarried motherhood was no longer a guarantee of social exclusion, but was a difficult situation to be avoided through making educated choices. In short, *Honey* and *Petticoat* offered young women education and knowledge that was designed to enable them to navigate this new morality successfully, rather than attempting to definitively redefine feminine sexuality. While this has led some to conclude that young women's publications were essentially conservative reflections of dominant social norms, this chapter has shown that they responded clearly to the new landscape of youthful sexuality and could act as an essential site of sexual agency for teenage girls and young women.

Notes

1. Christopher Ward, 'The Permissive Society's Book of Rules', *Petticoat*, 5 July 1969, p. 4.
2. Brian Braithwaite and Joan Barrell, *The Business of Women's Magazines* (London: Kogan Page, 1988).
3. The concept of the cultural script has been explored in Laura M. Carpenter, 'From Girls into Women: Scripts for Sexuality and Romance in *Seventeen* Magazine, 1974–1994', *Journal of Sex Research* 35:2 (1998), 158–68.
4. Joan Ormrod, 'Reading, Production and Culture: UK Teen Girl Comics from 1955 to 1960', *Girlhood Studies*, 11:3 (2018), 20.
5. Penny Tinkler, 'Fragmentation and Inclusivity: Methods for Working with Girls' and Women's Magazines', in Rachel Ritchie, Sue Hawkins, Nicola Phillips and S. Jay Kleinberg (eds), *Women in Magazines Research, Representation, Production and Consumption* (London: Routledge, 2016), pp. 37–52.
6. For a discussion of how historians and feminist scholars have worked with magazines within this genre see Angela McRobbie, *In the Culture Society: Art, Fashion and Popular Music* (London: Routledge, 1999), pp. 46–61.

7 Penny Tinkler, '"Are You Really Living?" If Not, "Get With It!"', *Cultural and Social History*, 11:4 (2014), 599.
8 Ibid.
9 On 'bedroom culture' see Angela McRobbie and Jenny Garber, 'Girls and Subcultures: An Exploration', in Stuart Hall and Tony Jefferson (eds), *Resistance through Rituals: Youth Subcultures in Post-war Britain* (London: Routledge, 1993), pp. 209–22.
10 The ephemeral nature of youth magazines was aptly demonstrated by Elizabeth Frazer, 'Girls Reading *Jackie*', *Media, Culture & Society*, 9:4 (1987), 407–25.
11 The idea of spare time, as opposed to leisure, speaks to Claire Langhamer's work on young women's leisure in the early to mid-twentieth century. See Claire Langhamer, *Women's Leisure in England, 1920–1960* (Manchester: Manchester University Press, 2000).
12 See Frazer, 'Girls Reading *Jackie*'.
13 Audrey Slaughter, 'Dear Honeys', *Honey*, July 1965, p. 1.
14 Fan Carter, 'A Taste of *Honey*: Get-Ahead Femininity in 1960s Britain', Ritchie, Hawkins, Phillips and Kleinberg (eds), *Women in Magazines*, pp. 195–209.
15 Elizabeth Lovegrove, 'Interactions in the Text', *Logos*, 29:2 (2018), 38.
16 Slaughter, 'Dear Honeys', p. 1.
17 Lynn Abrams, 'Liberating the Female Self: Epiphanies, Conflict and Coherence in the Life Stories of Post-war British Women', *Social History*, 39:1 (2014), 15.
18 Ibid.
19 Rachel Ritchie, Sue Hawkins, Nicola Phillips and S. Jay Kleinberg, 'Introduction', in Ritchie, Hawkins, Phillips and Kleinberg (eds), *Women in Magazines*, p. 16.
20 The first notable, and still essential, text on women's magazines was Cynthia White, *Women's Magazines 1693–1968* (London: Michael Joseph, 1970). See also Janice Winship, *Inside Women's Magazines* (London: Rivers Oram, 1987); Angela McRobbie, *Feminism and Youth Culture: From Jackie to Just Seventeen* (Basingstoke: Macmillan 1991); Penny Tinkler, *Constructing Girlhood: Popular Magazines for Girls Growing Up in England, 1920–1950* (London: Routledge, 1995); Anna Gough Yates, *Understanding Women's Magazines: Publishing, Markets and Readerships* (London: Routledge, 2003).
21 Tinkler, '"Are You Really Living?"', 598.
22 Carter, 'A Taste of *Honey*', p. 205.
23 Melanie Tebbutt, 'From "marriage bureau" to "points of view": changing patterns of advice in teenage magazines: *Mirabelle*, 1956–77', in Alan Kidd and Melanie Tebbutt (eds), *People, Places and Identities: Themes in British Social and Cultural History, 1700s-1980s* (Manchester: Manchester University Press, 2017), p. 194.
24 Lutz D.H. Sauerteig and Roger Davison, 'Shaping the Sexual Knowledge of the Young: Introduction', in Lutz D.H. Sauerteig and Roger Davison (eds), *Shaping Sexual Knowledge: A Cultural History of Sex Education in Twentieth Century Europe* (Abingdon: Routledge, 2009), p. 2.
25 Sauerteig and Davison, 'Shaping the Sexual Knowledge of the Young', in Sauerteig and Davison (eds), *Shaping Sexual Knowledge*, pp. 1–18.

26 Lesley A. Hall, 'In Ignorance and In Knowledge: Reflections on the History of Sex Education in Britain', in Sauerteig and Davison (eds), *Shaping Sexual Knowledge*, p. 20.
27 James Hampshire and Jane Lewis, '"The Ravages of Permissiveness": Sex Education and the Permissive Society', *Twentieth Century British History*, 15:3 (2004), 294. See also Mara Gregory, '"Beamed Directly to the Children": School broadcasting and Sex Education in Britain in the 1960s and 1970s', *Transactions of the Royal Historical Society*, 25 (2015), 187–214.
28 Hampshire and Lewis, '"The Ravages of Permissiveness"', 292.
29 Hannah Elizabeth, '[Re]inventing Childhood in the Age of AIDS: The Representation of HIV Positive Identities to Children and Adolescents in Britain, 1983–1997' (PhD dissertation, University of Manchetser, 2017), p. 112.
30 Tinkler, '"Are You Really Living?"', 601.
31 Hannah Charnock, 'Teenage Girls, Female Friendship and the Making of the Sexual Revolution in England, 1950–1980', *The Historical Journal*, 63:4 (2020), 1032–53.
32 Audrey Slaughter, 'How Far Will You Go?', *Honey*, January 1965, p. 1.
33 Ibid.
34 Keith Cameron, 'Dating Before Mating', *Honey*, January 1965, p. 17.
35 Ibid.
36 Roy Fraser, 'How Far Should You Go?', *Petticoat*, 12 March 1966, pp. 38–9.
37 Ibid., p. 39.
38 See Peter Fryer, *Mrs Grundy: Studies in English Prudery* (London: Dobson, 1963); *The Birth Controllers* (London: Corgi, 1965); *Private Case – Public Scandal* (London: Secker & Warburg, 1966).
39 Peter Fryer, 'Sorting Out Your Sex Life', *Petticoat*, 15 March 1969, p. 8.
40 Ibid.
41 Ibid.
42 Peter Fryer, 'Sorting Out Your Sex Life, Part Two', *Petticoat*, 22 March 1969, p. 6.
43 Ibid.
44 See Hall, 'In Ignorance and in Knowledge'.
45 Michael Schofield, *The Sexual Behaviour of Young People* (London: Pelican, 1968, 3rd edn), p. 227.
46 Caroline Rusterholz, '"If we can show that we are helping adolescents to understand themselves, their feelings and their needs, then we are doing [a] valuable job": counselling young people on sexual health in the Brook Advisory Centre (1965–1985)', *Medical Humanities* (2021), advanced access: doi:10.1136/medhum-2021–012206, p. 2.
47 Ellen Graham, "I Was so Sick of Moralising, Something Practical had to be done', *Petticoat*, 4 November 1967, pp. 42–3.
48 Ibid.
49 See Jeffrey Weeks, *Sex, Politics and Society: The Regulations of Sexuality Since 1800* (Abingdon: Routledge, 2014, 3rd edn), pp. 325–30.
50 Carter, 'A Taste of Honey', p. 203.

51 Tinkler, '"Are You Really With It?"', p. 604.
52 Title Page, *Petticoat*, 26 August 1967.
53 'Marriage Test Paper', *Petticoat*, 26 August 1967, p. 16.
54 See Claire Langhamer, *The English in Love: The Intimate Story of an Emotional Revolution* (Oxford: Oxford University Press, 2013); Marcus Collins, *Modern Love: An Intimate History of Men and Women in Twentieth-Century Britain* (London: Atlantic, 2003).
55 This issue was dealt with at length in *Petticoat*. See Elisabeth Woolley, 'Unmarried Bliss', *Petticoat*, 2 September 1967, p. 12; Barbara Toner, 'Marrying Young: For Better? For Worse?', *Petticoat*, 22 February 1969, p. 13; Ethel Sherbourne, 'Hitch, Ditch, Which?', *Petticoat*, 22 February 1969, p. 4.
56 Pat Thane and Tanya Evans, *Sinners? Scroungers? Saints?: Unmarried Motherhood in Twentieth-Century England* (Oxford: Oxford University Press, 2012), p. 1.
57 Weeks, *Sex, Politics and Society*, p. 326.
58 Hannah Charnock 'Girlhood, Sexuality and Identity in England 1950–1980' (PhD thesis, University of Exeter, 2017), p. 258.
59 Ibid., 257–310.
60 Ruth Miller, 'Free, Young, and Female: but God Help You if You Have a Baby and no Husband ...', *Honey*, April 1968, pp. 114–20.
61 Ibid., p. 115.
62 Ibid., p. 117.
63 Ibid., p. 115.
64 Roy Fraser, 'Should She Tell?', *Petticoat*, 26 March 1966, p. 19.
65 Ibid., p. 18.
66 Ibid., p. 19.
67 Stephen Brooke, *Sexual Politics: Sexuality, Family Planning, and the British Left from the 1880s to the Present Day* (Oxford: Oxford University Press, 2011), p. 200.
68 Ruth Miller, 'What To Do If You Are Going To Be An Unmarried Mother', *Honey*, November 1964, p. 84.
69 Ibid.
70 Kate Morland, 'My Abortion: One Girl's True Story', *Petticoat*, 25 October 1969, pp. 30–1.
71 Emphasis original. Morland, 'My Abortion: One Girl's True Story', p. 30.
72 Stephen Brooke notes that in areas such as Birmingham, Sheffield and Leeds, abortions were far more difficult to access than in London and East Anglia. See Brooke, *Sexual Politics*, p. 200.
73 Morland, 'My Abortion: One Girl's True Story', p. 30.
74 Christine Pickard, 'The Problems of Abortions', *Petticoat*, 10 January 1970, p. 33.

5

Lovers' lanes and Haystacks: rural spaces and girls' experiences of courtship and sexual intimacy in post-war England

Sian Edwards

In the early 2000s, members of the volunteer panel of the British life-writing archive, the Mass Observation Project (MOP), were asked to reflect on their experiences of courtship, dating and sex in their lifetime. Collectively, the open-ended set of questions (directives) sent out by the organisation received 434 replies, with a significant number of responses coming from women who had reached adolescence during the 1950s and 1960s. Historians have used these replies to complicate the story of sex in post-war Britain.[1] They have critiqued the notion of an untrammelled 'sexual revolution' and instead demonstrated that the lives of young (particularly working-class) women in England continued to be restricted by traditional understandings of sexual morality and respectability, which shaped expectations of, and reactions to, girls' sexual behaviour.[2]

Despite the persistence of restrictions, girls' experiences of courtship and sex did undergo significant, if slow, change after the Second World War. Crucially, historians argue that girls themselves played a key role in actively shaping expectations of, and giving meaning to, sexual behaviour throughout the post-war period.[3] Hannah Charnock has argued that girls understood courtship and sex as one of the 'key markers of modern femininity',[4] while Stephen Brooke asserts that it was the sexual expression of young working-class women that became central to the remaking of working-class identity in the post-war years.[5] Notably, however, these markers of sexual change are often explored within a purely urban context; the romantic and sexual experiences of rural girls at this time are effaced within metro-centric narratives. As a result, urban spaces and the experiences of urban youth have come to dominate histories of post-war sexual change.[6] In her work on the memory of the 1960s, Helena Mills argued that the dominance of the urban in popular memory of the 'sexual revolution' shaped how women understood and narrated their experiences of sexual change, with women from smaller towns or rural villages perceiving themselves to have lived 'more conservative lifestyles' than their urban counterparts.[7] Such narratives reflect how rural communities are perceived as reinforcing normative and traditional sexual cultures, underpinned by an emphasis on heterosexuality and strict notions of morality.[8] Consequently, little is known about the romantic and sexual experiences of rural youth in the post-war period, even though, as Richard Byrne asserts, the countryside and symbolic sites such as the 'lovers' lane' are 'as much a part of British sexual culture and myth as the back row of the cinema'.[9]

This chapter builds upon our understanding of post-war sexual change by exploring rural, heterosexual teenage girls' experiences of consensual courtship and sex in the period 1950–70.[10] Utilising a study of advertisements, newspapers and the MOP archive, it seeks to consider how the rural was constructed as a romantic and intimate space within the context of post-war changes in emotional and sexual culture, as well as how rural contexts shaped the heterosexual sexual experiences of adolescent girls in a period of sexual change. In doing so, it challenges the predominantly urban understanding of post-war youth culture in which urban experiences have been taken as 'emblematic of youth as a whole'.[11] For example, in his study of post-war youth culture, Felix Fuhg emphasised the importance of changes to the built environment of the British city, and in particular 'swinging' London, in shaping young people's engagement with, and behaviour in, social spaces.[12] This emphasis is a result of the way in which post-war youth cultures are often associated with narratives of modernity; a concept in which the rural teenager sits uneasily, as they are considered to have been on the periphery of the 'modern' social and cultural changes that benefited youth after the Second World War.[13] For rural teenagers, access to leisure, well-paid work and freedom from parental control depended on their rural communities' extremely regionalised and localised nature; meaning that different levels of electrification, transport links and agricultural practice could dramatically impact the extent to which rural young people could engage in dominant post-war youth culture. These differences have led to a common assumption that rural adolescence was a period of isolation, boredom and frustration.[14]

Addressing this gap in our understanding of the experiences of youth in rural settings, this chapter considers what Julie C. Keller and Michael M. Bell have termed 'the rural sexual' and 'the sexual rural'. This is done through consideration of the importance of the space of the countryside in the social construction of rural sex and sexuality (the rural sexual), and through consideration of how the sexual practices and identities of rural youth are grounded in space and place (the sexual rural).[15] Through this framework, the chapter argues that rural spaces of courtship, and particularly the lovers' lane, were romanticised in the post-war popular press, reflecting the moral geographies in which contemporaries understood the sexual behaviour of post-war youth. However, in reality the specific context of country life and community could restrict rural girls' opportunities to experience romantic and sexual intimacy, challenging the dominant romanticism of rural courtship extolled in popular culture. Yet, despite these restrictions, the countryside could also provide the rural teenage girl with spaces to express their autonomous (hetero)sexuality away from parental control or community judgement. Moreover, post-war girls increasingly found themselves with opportunities to move between rural and urban spaces and move beyond their immediate locality for courtship. Thus, those with the opportunity to do so could take on the role of cultural navigators, working both within and outside urban models of romance and intimacy. Therefore, while MOP respondents often constructed their rural experiences as being different and outside of a perceived urban norm, their recollections suggest that meanings and experiences of rural girls were complex and sometimes contradictory, with opportunities shaped by the nature of the rural settings in which respondents grew up.

Romance, the rural idyll, and the moral geographies of courtship

Making only brief reference to the rural, both Claire Langhamer and Hannah Charnock have explored how post-war commercial spaces such as the cinema and coffee bar served as important sites of courtship, providing an acceptable public space for the display of heterosexual intimacy in the period after the Second World War.[16] At this time, courtship became central to the leisure experiences of post-war youth, as an ideology of romance permeated teenage culture, including advertisements aimed toward the newly identified 'teenage consumer'.[17] Advertisements, such as those for Player's cigarettes, Aristoc stockings and Burton tailoring, often emphasised idyllic and romantic depictions of the countryside, with the outdoors presented as a space of everyday companionate leisure, courtship and romantic intimacy.[18]

This romanticisation of the rural as a site of courtship was also evident in the post-war discussions of teenage courtship in the popular press, which, as Adrian Bingham has argued, 'found new ways of writing about sex' in the 1950s.[19] Indeed, despite the range of political agendas that shaped the tabloid press at this time, popular newspapers, including the *Daily Mirror*, *Daily Herald* and *Daily Express*, were united in their interest in teenage courting and sexual behaviour. In 1956, for example, the *Daily Mirror* investigated the 'Secrets of teenage lovers' including 'THE PETTING habits of teenagers and why it is the thing to do so much of it in public.'[20] It was the public nature of intimate activities that the tabloids found particularly fascinating. Subsequently, the idea of the 'lovers' lane', a quiet secluded space, often close to nature although not always rural, became ubiquitous in press reportage of teenage courting behaviour. In doing so, newspapers constructed a moral geography of courting and sex, in which rural spaces were romanticised and contrasted with deviant urban sites. This tendency was not new, yet in the context of the mass consumption of the teenage consumer market in the 1950s, rural spaces of courtship were consistently celebrated as sites of courtship for teenager in contrast to urban, commercial spaces, which came under much scrutiny in the post-war years from the popular press, adult youth leaders and even the police.[21]

Indeed, while the isolation of many lovers' lanes meant that they could often be reported as sites of illicit behaviour, both sexual and criminal in nature, press coverage of such incidents emphasised the legitimacy of lovers' lanes as sites of teenage courtship.[22] In May 1964, the *Daily Mirror* printed a 'Plea to Lovers' who may have witnessed the murder of 13-year-old Anne Dunwell, whose body was found in a South Yorkshire lovers' lane.[23] Similarly, in that same year, the *Daily Express* reported that, in their investigation of the murder of seven-year-old Kim Roberts, Scotland Yard would be appealing to 'Lovers' lane girls' in the East End 'to think back over the past few years and name every boyfriend who took them by car or scooter to "lovers' lanes" in the countryside around Southend'.[24] Such appeals reflected how the rural spaces and the more liminal lovers' lane were, despite their propensity to be spaces of danger, understood as a popular and legitimate site of courtship for increasingly mobile teenage couples.

This, in part, reflected the way in which the lovers' lane was considered a more traditional space for teenage courtship than 'modern' commercial spaces. In 1955, reflecting a distaste for teenage courtship, leisure and consumption habits of teenagers in Hammersmith, *Daily Mirror* columnist Keith Waterhouse declared: 'Lover's Lane ain't what it used to be!'[25] and informed readers that 'Young lovers don't need soft lights and birdsong any more ... Instead of trees carved with lovers' hearts there stands a row of shops, two cinemas, a milk bar, and an Underground station ... No nightingale sings. There is no grass either – BUT THERE ARE PLENTY OF LOVERS.'[26] While similarly, a 1956 investigation into courtship by the *Daily Herald* highlighted how modern youth were seemingly neglecting lovers' lanes for urban spaces of romance. Warning parents of their daughter's behaviour: Douglas Warth informed readers that: '*You'll find her "necking" in the backstreet behind your house OR ON YOUR DOORSTEP. LOVERS' LANE, 1956, is that short cut behind the cinema to the "caff" in the high-street.*'[27] However, compared to these urban spaces, lovers' lanes were represented as traditional courtship sites, in which generations of courting couples had fallen in love. In 1952, Mary Brown, a columnist for the *Daily Mirror*, described how:

'Old people look back gratefully in the sunlight and remember the days when spring meant long evening walks in Lovers' Lane.'[28] Meanwhile, in 1958, a member of the Burntwood parish council in Staffordshire remarked of the 'perils' of the local lovers' lane that: 'Couples still go down these paths and byways, as I did forty years ago.'[29] Coverage of lovers' lanes thus reinforced the moral superiority of the rural over the urban, with rural sites of courtship portrayed as traditional and desirable compared to urban spaces.[30]

Yet, urban youth culture was not the only threat to the lovers' lane. Other dangers included post-war rebuilding, stubborn farmers and the 'neglect' of the countryside, which could lead to the overgrowing of hedgerows and brambles that it was feared would put off the 'modern girl'[31] since the overgrowth could tear their nylon stockings. Animals might also pose a threat, as in the case of a 'spoilsport' bull named Tom in Kesteven, Lincolnshire.[32] As the *Daily Mirror* reported in 1967: 'The course of true love rarely runs smooth when Tom the bull roams Lovers'-lane'.[33] Subsequently, the post-war period saw numerous efforts by local councils to save or preserve their lovers' lanes, which were reported on positively by the largely sympathetic tabloids. In 1956, the *Daily Mirror* reported of Hexham in Northumberland that 'CUPID COUNCIL' PLAN A LANE FOR LOVERS',[34] while in 1964 it was reported: 'sentimental city saves lovers' lane', when a Birmingham new-build estate on the outskirts of the city had a 'treelined lovers' lane' incorporated into the plans.[35] This was partly about controlling the spaces in which young couples met and were intimate. In 1968, when West Bromwich borough council planned to develop a municipal lovers' lane, it was partly in response to worries of an 'unofficial' lovers' lane that existed in a nearby grassy alley and the 'goings on' that occurred there.[36] The local provision of lovers' lanes can therefore be understood as both an attempt to preserve what was deemed a legitimate space for courtship reflecting the nostalgic way that city planners were attempting to import idealised rural lifestyles into the urban, while also controlling and monitoring the behaviour of young people.

Indeed, the concerns about the sexual behaviour of couples expressed by the West Bromwich council in 1968 were evident in numerous other newspaper articles throughout the period. For example, in 1952, a *Daily Mirror* columnist warned teenage girls of the dangers of courting in the countryside. Drawing upon romanticised ideas of the countryside, she wrote: 'When you sit under a lovely tree with the wind making music in the branches … it is easy to believe that the boy who looks at you so ardently really is the one … If it is no more than spring in the blood you will be sorry afterwards.'[37] Meanwhile, in 1957, Durham youth were subjected to a 'petting patrol' to monitor the behaviour of youth in local lovers' lanes.[38]

Nonetheless, despite evidence of concern, the intervention of local councils also reflected continued support for perceived 'natural' spaces of courtship, which were deemed to be more traditional, healthy and (sometimes) innocent than their urban alternatives. Therefore, while Louise Jackson has argued that post-war authorities attempted to regulate the use of urban public space by young people, a study of discussions of lovers' lanes in the popular press suggests that rural areas remained part of an idealised understanding of romance, courtship and intimacy in the countryside.[39]

Idealised images of rural courtship were evident in many of the recollections of women recalling their experiences of their rural adolescence to the MOP in the early 2000s. As one retired nursey teacher and lecturer depicted her experience of her first date with her future husband: 'He took me to a very romantic setting … a walk on the Lickney Hills which looked like fairyland with the distant lights of Birmingham.'[40] Similarly, a caseworker from Disley, who grew up in a small country village, spoke of her interest in romance in her youth.[40] Talking of the local boys she wrote: 'I was romantic but had no idea about sex, and preferred to show them sunsets and sit in trees just talking. This was not their goal at all! A whole group of us went up Bredon Hill one night together and stood at the tower talking and looking at glow worms twinkling.'[41] Both recollections draw upon romanticised ideas of rural courtship, reflecting how constructs of the idyllic rural framed the courtship narratives of girls who grew up in rural England. Yet, despite the romanticisation of rural courtship sites, MOP testimonies also reveal how rural girls experienced several restrictions, which shaped their romantic and sexual experiences throughout the 1950s and 1960s.

Rural girls, courtship, sex and the negotiation of space in the post-war English countryside

The MOP has been celebrated as being a vital source in accessing individuals' lived experiences and memories, particularly with regards to personal or sensitive topics such as sexual behaviour. While the archive itself brings up numerous methodological issues, including those of representativeness and memory, it can provide historians interested in the twentieth-century with access to detailed accounts of lived experience, which often unavailable elsewhere.[42] Indeed, while it is impossible to come to general conclusions about girls' experiences, from a largely middle-class cohort of respondents, predominantly from southern England, the archive does provide historians of post-war youth with valuable insights into the ways in which women recall their experiences of courtship and sexual intimacy in a period of perceived sexual change. While narratives of rural experience tend to emphasise the sexual traditionalism of rural areas, the recollections of the respondents who identified as having gone through adolescence in parts of 'rural' England (broadly defined by the respondents themselves) in the 1950s and 1960s reveal that experiences of rural courtship and sex were more complex than narratives of 'missing out' or conservatism assume.

Testimonies from the archive tended to support traditional characterisations of rural society. For example, many respondents who identified growing up in rural areas recalled being late developers when it came to experiencing dating and sex. Narrating her adolescence living in a small village, one woman from Derbyshire informed the MOP that: 'I was rather late starting the dating game and didn't go out very much with living in such a small village.'[43] Another, who was in her fifties at the time of writing, recalled: 'When I first dated I lived in a small village in East Anglia … I think I probably first went out with someone when I was about 17. Dating would really be too strong a word for it!'[44] Here, by emphasising how living in a small village restricted their courtship opportunities, the respondents implicitly compared their rural experiences to a perceived urban norm of younger courtship. Subsequently, as Helena Mills has noted, MOP respondents often explicitly contrasted their experiences to urban narratives.[45] Writing of her experiences in the 1950s, one respondent added: 'It was a very unhappy time for a teenager who only wanted to keep up with her school friends who mostly lived in a more urban environment. At the time I longed to live somewhere with a bus stop outside the door!'[46] The notion of 'keeping up' with her school friends reflected how urban narratives of teenage experiences shaped the recollections of these respondents, who interpreted their limited experiences as being a product of their local environment. Meanwhile, another respondent told MOP in 2005 that she and her friends 'still debate the fact that none of us are sure where the "swinging sixties", in relation to sex, was taking place, outside perhaps Liverpool or London, because it wasn't anywhere that we hung out'.[47]

In shaping these narratives of isolation and difference, the respondents reinforced the findings of post-war sociological studies that emphasised the sexually traditional nature of post-war rural communities. For example, in his 1971 study *Sex and Marriage in England Today*, anthropologist Geoffrey Gorer concluded that: 'In general, living in a rural district seems to limit sexual adventurousness, compared with living in a town.'[48] This, he suggested in his earlier 1955 study, was partly due to continued religious practice in post-war rural English communities, which, in his words, was 'the strongest bulwark of austere English sexual morality'.[49] Indeed, while the perceived decline of religion in urban society is seen as being one of the critical drivers of sexual change in the 1950s and 1960s, according to Gorer, the continued importance of the church in the religious and social life of some rural communities provided the background to perceived sexual conservatism, which shaped rural girls' experiences.[50]

Such conservatism was strengthened when it came to girls' courtship activity. So, while William Morgan Williams noted that premarital sexual intimacy was 'quite common' amongst the youth of Gosforth, West Cumberland in the early 1950s, he also noted the significant gender differences in experiences of adolescent courtship and sex.[51] His conclusions are supported by the respondents' writings, as they frequently identified that the social and cultural make-up of village life, particularly the 'closeness' of the village community, could mean their romantic relationships were further monitored and regulated. Indeed, while girls' sexual behaviour was monitored closely in urban contexts, by parents, neighbours, religious leaders, teachers and even friends, MOP responses stressed the 'closeness' of their rural community as being the reason for delayed courtship, as it meant that, as teenagers, they could not receive the same perceived anonymity as in urban areas. The village, or in some cases suburbia, thus provided a framework through which the experience of romance and courtship were narrated and understood by respondents. As one ex-factory worker recalled of her courtship experiences at the age of 15 in Carlton Colville, a small village near Lowestoft during the 1960s: 'My Dad didn't like me going out with boys because he thought I was too young. So if I went out with a boy and we held hands we had to be careful because everybody knew everybody else in the village so they would tell my dad.'[52] While another respondent, who had in her own words 'proper sex' at the age of 19, recalled how it wasn't until the early 1970s, after moving from the Isle of Wight to London that: 'without the moral code of a small community, I found it easier to have sex with men than say no and it was generally an accepted thing'.[53] This is significant as, while Katharine Milestone identified parental control as being a more critical factor than geographical barriers in shaping girls' experiences of the 'swinging sixties', these responses suggest that the social closeness of village life meant that rural girls' behaviour was monitored closely and repercussions of sexual transgressions could be felt strongly.[54]

Moreover, if the 'moral code' of a small village gossip could inhibit their experiences of courtship and sex, it could also act as a form of punishment if they crossed acceptable boundaries of morality. For example, one woman who grew up in a 'little market town' recalled how, after having unprotected sex in the 1960s, she was publicly reprimanded and lectured on the importance of contraception by her local doctor, which left her feeling both 'relieved and embarrassed'.[55] While another respondent recalled how she was caught by a local villager having an emotional affair with a married man: '[we] were seen by someone from my village. (Yes, village life, everyone knows everyone else.) It became a nightmare. No sex as such ever occurred.'[56] The idea of 'getting caught' was thus a prominent theme in numerous women's recollections of their adolescent romantic experiences, revealing how a constructed view of the rural, as being 'close', rigid and traditional framed respondents' reflections of courtship and sex, despite the apparent sexual change of the 1960s.

Yet if the social make-up of rural areas could impact girls' sexual experiences, the physical isolation of some rural areas, particularly a lack of transport and leisure facilities, could further intensify feelings of difference among the respondents. For example, one ex-school inspector remembered her youth in the 1950s: 'I was living in a small town in Wiltshire at the time but went to grammar school in another small town eight miles away. To go on a date normally meant travelling by bus to a larger town where there was a cinema and coffee bar.'[57] A similar recollection was made by a married woman who noted of her teenage years in the 1960s that: 'There was nothing open late at night then, so a date was either a coffee bar, or a meeting in a pub, or going to the cinema, and then legging it to the station or bus stop to get the last ride home at 11 o'clock, as one had to go to Brighton from Steyning, for any entertainment.'[58] Of course, such restrictions depended on the nature and size of the village inhabited. While some areas of rural England became increasingly accessible as the post-war period went on, others remained remote. Class and financial constraints could also shape the extent to which rural isolation impacted girls' experiences. As with the previously quoted school inspector, grammar school – primarily a middle-class form of education in this period – could provide an 'escape' from the confines of rural areas and give the girls social and sometimes romantic opportunities unavailable in their small town or village.

The isolation in rural areas also impacted girls' relationships with their parents, with several MOP respondents recalling that they heavily relied upon parental support – both financial and practical – to ensure they could meet the opposite sex and engage in courtship activities. One woman, a writer and researcher from a North Lancashire village recalled her experience of growing up in a suburb of Liverpool in the 1950s: 'Our house was at the end of a dark, tree-lined road lit only by gas lamps. (It was an unadopted road.) It was a good seven- to-ten minutes' walk to the main road bus stop. My somewhat elderly parents were very strict with me, their only child, and living in such a dark and vulnerable place meant that my father would insist that the boy would see me home or father would (embarrassingly) meet the bus.'[59] Another respondent, who lived as a teenager in a small town on the Lancashire/Cheshire border, similarly recalled: 'Romance was frowned on slightly by my parents because even when I was seventeen my father used to come and escort me home from late dances.'[60] Such stories of parental interference were often recollected with embarrassment. Yet, a significant implication of the involvement of parents in courtship activities was that they often had more knowledge of whom their daughters were dating. This was significant because, as Williams found in his study of Gosforth, in agricultural communities, courtship was seen as an essential method of maintaining rural living through the merging of farming families.[61] Therefore, while parental control remained significant in shaping the lives of urban girls in this period, the specific context of rural society could demand that parents pay closer attention to the courtship habits of their daughters.

Despite these restrictions, numerous respondents' experiences did, in various ways, suggest that rural girls took part in, and actively shaped, changing sexual culture at this time. Importantly, responses suggest that rural girls did experience a variety of leisure and courtship activities during adolescence, including frequenting the theatre, the cinema, dances and coffee bars. Notably, many travelled significant distances to do so, suggesting that rural girls' sphere of social life was broader than once assumed. Therefore, while Angela McRobbie found in her 1970s study of girls in Birmingham that girls were 'firmly rooted in their home and local environment',[62] out of sheer necessity, many girls from rural areas navigated and composed a significant network of social contacts outside their immediate locality. As the ex-school inspector recalled: 'I rarely went out with someone from my hometown although I could, and did, meet boys at the Church social or at the Girls' Friendly Society's club night.'[63] This recollection is significant, as it reveals how the church, which in urban contexts is considered to have declined in importance after the Second World War in the lives of young people, continued to play a significant role in rural girls' experiences of courtship.

Additionally, experiences outside of the immediate locality were also gained by creating romantic attachments with boys who owned or had access to cars, which, according to one housewife, 'opened up opportunities'.[64] One retired library assistant recalled her experiences dating in the 1950s: 'I started going out with a man who was slightly older than myself when I was approximately twenty-three. He had his own car so it was easy to go to the theatre or cinema in Manchester and not have to worry about catching the last bus home. He also took me out for meals in the surrounding countryside which was such a new experience.'[65] Similarly, one woman recalled how her boyfriends provided her with the ability to socialise: 'Boyfriends (I had three before I met my future husband) would call at the house or pip their car horns. We would drive out to a pub in the country and meet up with a gang – there were 4 girls and 4 boys, we had a great time going to hunt meetings, assembly balls, camping in the lake district'.[66] Thus reflecting the popular media image of the 'modern' mobile girl in the

1950s and 1960s, for those with the means, courtship could provide them with a reason to legitimately travel outside their rural localities, meaning that for some rural girls, courtship experiences could be far-ranging and diverse.[67]

Yet, as Penny Tinkler has noted, not all girls had the means, meaning that 'spatial mobilities became a new axis of social differentiation' in the post-war period.[68] Nonetheless, for numerous respondents the ability to traverse the boundaries between urban and rural was informative and, in some cases, transformative. As one respondent, an artist who experienced adolescence in the late 1950s to early 1960s, recalled: 'Sex wasn't around when I was a child, I had no sex education from anyone. All knowledge was gained from friends, reading books and films.'[69] The latter of which would have most likely been accessed via the cinema in this period. The importance of the cinema in introducing girls to more open sexual cultures was explicitly identified by another respondent, a teenager in the 1960s who was living in a 'remote house' on the North Downs. She remembered that: 'As couples we went to see A or X rated films at the cinema and sat in the back row kissing.'[70] Such recollections are evidence of how, particularly for those who had access to a car or available public transport, urban spaces could be sites in which sexual knowledge and experience was gained, reflecting the way in which rural girls' experiences could traverse the boundaries of urban and rural.

Moreover, access to cars could provide an element of privacy away from the judgement of the local community, as it gave girls the ability to travel to secluded rural spaces to be intimate. Indeed, even for those who had little access to transport, rural spaces played a vital role in the developing sexual identity and sexual experiences of rural girls. Respondents frequently narrated sexual experiences in local rural areas and the countryside. Such activities began with kissing and 'heavy petting'. Speaking of her courtship experiences in the 1950s, one respondent told MOP that: 'In the summer we would play tennis, row on the park boating lake or river, go on picnics and kiss in the woods or behind hedges.'[71] This same respondent also recalled how an early boyfriend in the sixth form was 'more forward than previous boys and was very keen on walking in the countryside!!'[72] The exclamation marks here are suggestive of the implication that such walks included an expectation of sexual intimacy. While writing of her first love, one respondent from Bristol recalled: 'We did lots of walks in the country which of course progressed to heavy petting, usually lying in the heather.'[73]

Furthermore, while for these respondents the natural space of the countryside could provide romantic spaces for such activity, numerous others utilised rural spaces as spots for 'parking'. Although she remained a virgin until she went to university, the previous respondent recalled how: 'We also spent hours in his sports car writhing around the gear lever and steaming up the windows.'[74] Similarly, one respondent recalled her 'fumbles' with her boyfriend at 17: 'We would take a ride out into the countryside and park the car in a gateway and climb into the back seat. We sank into the mud once and had to get a farmer to tow us out and were very late home … it was all a bit fumbley and unromantic looking back – but very exciting.'[75] Such stories support Mimi Sheller and John Urry's assertion that, in modern times, the car has played a significant role in 'coming-of-age' rituals.[76]

The frequency with which the respondents discussed sexual intimacy in cars suggests that a level of independence was exerted by rural girls, who, faced with numerous restrictions on their courtship and sexual behaviour, engaged in sexual activity in a variety of rural spaces that provided privacy away from community judgement. In some cases, this could involve careful planning and consideration. As one woman recalled of her experiences in the 1960s:

> My boyfriend drove a Riley Elf so we decided we'd use my car, which was a Morris traveller which provided more room. The only problem was we normally used to take my boyfriend's car when we went out so it would have been rather odd to take my car keys. We had to wait until my parents had gone out before returning to the house to pick up keys. We then had to find a suitably private spot as there was a lot of window space in a Morris traveller. Even so we still had to try and drape the windows over as I was concerned about Peeping Toms.[77]

Notably, while the car may have become more frequent in the experiences of women who were teenagers in the 1960s, the use of rural spaces as sites of sexual intimacy was documented by Williams as early as 1950. His study found that secret meetings in outdoor spaces were popular in some sections of rural society, particularly adolescents from farming families. In Gosforth, the chosen spot was a lane at the top of a steep hill that was 'immune from interference by all but the most athletic of "Peeping Toms"'.[78] Williams's study thus further evidences how rural teenagers utilised rural settings as sites of intimacy away from the prying eyes of the community.

Yet, such examples are also evidence of the extent to which adults were aware of, and in some cases tolerated, adolescents' romantic and sexual behaviours in rural settings. Indeed, while the MOP respondents remembered the strictness of their parents and the need for subterfuge to meet lovers in isolated spaces, others suggested that adults may have been more conscious of adolescent sexual behaviour in the countryside. As one respondent recalled her first sexual experiences at the age of 15:

> We had sex in the open under the moon and stars, under haystacks and in fields and barns. It must have caused my parents some worry when I came

back after dark. Dad would be on his way to find me, coming up the road with a torch. My clothes were often semen stained and when I rinsed them out I would mutter something about falling in cow pat! Surely they guessed, or couldn't believe that their little girl would have done such things? My second cousin and great uncle at the farm warned me that the hay bales could fall and hurt me if I went in there – they were concerned too.[79]

The concern expressed by the family of this respondent is significant, as her recollections suggest awareness and tacit acceptance of teenage sexual behaviour. Williams's 1950s sociological study supports this. Writing of a local hillside in Gosforth where teenagers courted, Williams suggested that 'nearly all the adults in the parish are aware that such a meeting-place exists, and it is usually referred to with amused tolerance'.[80]

Such 'amused tolerance' was also evident in discussions of lovers' lanes in the popular press with which this chapter began, particularly in the 1960s, when (often through humour) newspapers acknowledged that isolated spaces were sites of sexual and emotional intimacy. In 1965, the *Sunday Mirror* joked: 'TWO old trees in Lovers Lane were being cut down by order of the council. Said the first old tree: "They say we encouraged young people to pet." Said the second old tree: "Maybe, but we are always more sinned against than sinning."'[81] Meanwhile, a 1969 cartoon that depicted a wrestling match and its audience highlighted a social awareness of lovers' lanes as sites of courtship and sexual intimacy, with an audience member declaring 'seen better wrestling in lovers' lane!'[82] Both examples reflect how knowledge of sexual activity was a cause of jest in the latter half of the 1960s, suggesting a more open discourse around sexual matters at the end of the period.

Of course, the public sexual behaviour of teenagers could also cause outrage – in 1969, for example, the *Daily Mirror* reported the 'shock' of a Devon country vicar who 'found a young couple among the tombstones'.[83] Yet, in general, discussions of restricting or policing the courtship of young people, such as through the aforementioned 'Petting Patrols' of Durham in the late 1950s, was more about distinguishing 'genuine courting couples' from those who were not.[84] This suggests that premarital sex, within the confines of love and the promise of commitment, was an accepted (albeit grudgingly) part of post-war youth culture. Indeed, while the presence of couples in lovers' lanes was reported more frequently by the more liberal *Daily Mirror* and *Daily Herald*, conservative tabloids such as the *Daily Express* included little concern or distaste for such behaviour. Moreover, throughout the period, local councils found themselves frequently having to cater to the demands of young people, who were asserting their right to frequent local 'lovers' lanes'. In 1969, for instance, in response to an 'unromantic light on the village lovers' lane' courting couples in Hampshire were reported as throwing bricks at the streetlights, leading to the installation of a light switch to 'please the courting couples – and save the council repair bills'.[85] This case is one among a number that reveals how, similar to the MOP respondents, post-war youth were demanding access to and control over spaces of courtship. The romanticisation of the rural romance, identified at the start of this chapter, was thus not the only factor shaping the acceptance of countryside spaces as a site of courtship and intimacy for teenagers, as the MOP responses and newspapers suggest young people played an active role in laying claim to and utlising rural sites for physical intimacy.

Conclusion

In the context of post-war cultures of intimacy in which, according to Claire Langhamer, love and sex became intertwined, the rural was continually romanticised as a site of youthful courtship, companionship and intimacy.[86] The importance of rural spaces of courtship and sex for both urban and rural youth was symbolised by the continued prominence of the 'lovers' lane' in contemporary understandings of teenage sexual behaviour. Importantly, although lovers' lanes were not exclusively rural, they were considered closer to nature and a more traditional space of courtship than urban commercial spaces, reflecting the moral geographies within which adolescent sexual behaviour was understood in a period of supposed sexual change, with rural sites being privileged over the urban.

Yet, while the rural was romanticised in post-war culture, a study of a select number of MOP respondents' writings reveals how, far from this idyllic image, rural living could restrict girls' ability to engage in courtship and premarital sex. Although Milestone argues that experiences of the 'swinging sixties' were not 'entirely contingent on geography',[87] this chapter has suggested that rurality played a vital role in shaping rural girls' experiences of love and sex after the Second World War and has supported Charnock's assertion that experiences and meanings of sex were framed by girls' relationship to their local community, which in rural areas was often close.[88] This is not to suggest that their experiences were completely distinct from their urban counterparts. Urban girls could also experience varying levels of restriction depending on numerous factors including class, religion, locality and parental control. Yet, as Mills has noted, the MOP respondents emphasised rurality as an essential factor in shaping their own romantic and sexual experiences and identified their experiences as being different from the urban norm.[89]

However, the responses also reveal the ways in which rural girls could actively navigate the difficulties of rural courtship. For those girls who lived close to urban conurbations, had the finances to travel frequently or, increasingly in the 1960s, had access to a car, their courtship activities could be wide-ranging. The urban and rural were thus not as clearly demarcated as narratives of rural difference may suggest, with the experience of some rural girls including urban models of courtship and romance, such as the cinema. Moreover, where rural girls were less mobile, they could exert independence and agency over their romantic lives, utilising rural spaces as sites of sexual intimacy and exploration. Importantly, although experiences were fractured by class and region, such life stories suggest that far from being dull sites of sexual traditionalism and conservatism, the rural was a space in which, like their urban counterparts, girls increasingly played a role in shaping sexual culture in the post-war period. The writings of the MOP thus allow us to challenge simplistic interpretations of rural sexualities and dominant narratives of rural conservatism in the post-war period.

Notes

Material reproduced with permission of Curtis Brown, London on behalf of the Trustees of the Mass Observation Archive © The Trustees of the Mass Observation Archive.

1 For use of these particular MOP responses see Hannah Charnock, 'Teenage Girls, Female Friendship and the Making of the Sexual Revolution in England, 1950–1980', *The Historical Journal*, 63:4 (2020), 1032–53; Helena Mills, 'Using the Personal to Critique the Popular: Women's Memories of 1960s Youth', *Contemporary British History*, 30:4 (2016), 463–83; Claire Langhamer, *The English in Love: The Intimate Story of an Emotional Revolution* (Oxford: Oxford University Press, 2013).
2 For discussion of the role of young women in the 'sexual revolution' see Arthur Marwick, *The Sixties: Cultural Revolution in Britain, France, Italy and the United States c.1958–1974* (Oxford: Oxford University Press, 1998), p. 527. See also: Callum G. Brown, 'Sex, Religion, and the Single Woman c.1950–75: The Importance of a "Short" Sexual Revolution to the English Religious Crisis of the Sixties', *Twentieth Century British History*, 22:2 (2011), 189–215. For a challenge to such work see Janet Fink and Penny Tinkler, 'Teetering on the Edge: Portraits of Innocence, Risk and Young Female Sexualities in 1950s' and 1960s' British Cinema', *Women's History Review*, 26:1 (2017), 10; Pamela Church Gibson, 'From Up North to Up West? London on Screen 1965–1967', *The London Journal*, 31:1 (2006), 86; Eleanor Simpson, 'Love, Marriage and Pleasure in Sex Education Textbooks and Manuals, 1950–1970', paper presented at the Centre for History in Public Health, London School of Tropical Hygiene and Medicine, 5 December 2019, www.lshtm.ac.uk/newsevents/events/love-marriage-and-pleasure-sex-education-textbooks-and-manuals-1950–1970 (accessed 3 December 2021);

Angela Davis, '"Oh no, Nothing, We didn't Learn Anything": Sex Education and the Preparation of Girls for Motherhood, c.1930–1970', *History of Education*, 37:5 (2008), 671.
3 Charnock, 'Teenage Girls', 1052; Caroline Rusterholz, 'Teenagers, Sex and the Brook Advisory Centres, 1964–85', in Sian Pooley and Jonathan Taylor (eds), *Children's Experiences of Welfare in Modern Britain* (London: University of London Press, 2021), p. 251; Penny Tinkler, '"Are You Really Living?" If Not, "Get With It!"', *Cultural and Social History*, 11:4 (2014), 612.
4 Charnock, 'Teenage Girls', 1052.
5 Stephen Brooke, 'Slumming', in Swinging London?, *Cultural and Social History*, 9:3 (2012), 439; Stephen Brooke, 'Bodies, Sexuality and the "Modernization" of the British Working Classes, 1920s to 1960s', *International Labor and Working-Class History*, 69 (2006), 119.
6 David Gilbert, 'The Youngest Legend in History': Cultures of Consumption and the Mythologies of Swinging London, *The London Journal*, 31:1 (2006), 1–14; John Griffiths, 'Rivalling the Metropolis': Cultural Conflict between London and the Regions c.1967–1973', *Contemporary British History*, 33:4 (2019), 524–47.
7 Mills, 'Using the Personal to Critique the Popular', 471.
8 Jo Little, 'Constructing Nature in the Performance of Rural Heterosexualities', *Environment and Planning: Society and Space*, 25 (2007), 851.
9 Richard Byrne, 'Beyond Lovers' Lane: The Rise of Illicit Sexual Leisure in Countryside Recreational Space', *Leisure/Loisir*, 30:1 (2006), 74.
10 Jon Binnie and Gill Valentine, 'Geographies of Sexuality – a Review of Progress', *Progress in Human Geography* 23:2 (1999), 178 and 183.
11 David Farrugia and Bronwyn E. Wood, 'Youth and Spatiality: Towards Interdisciplinarity in Youth Studies', *Young*, 25:3 (2017), 211. See also David Farrugia, 'Towards a Spatialised Youth Sociology: The Rural and the Urban in Times of Change', *Journal of Youth Studies*, 17:3 (2014), 301. For notable exceptions to this, see Laura Harrison, '"There Wasn't all that Much to Do … at Least not Here": Memories of Growing up in Rural South-west England in the Early Twentieth Century', *Rural History*, 31:2 (2020), 165–80; Selina Todd, 'Young Women, Work and Family in Inter-War Rural England', *The Agricultural History Review*, 52:1 (2004), 83–98.
12 Klaus Nathaus, '"All Dressed up and Nowhere to Go"?: SPACES and Conventions of Youth in 1950s Britain', *Geschichte und Gesellschaft*, 41:1 (2015), 43; Felix Fuhg, *London's Working-Class Youth and the Making of Post-Victorian Britain, 1958–1971* (Basingstoke: Palgrave Macmillan, 2021), p. 7.
13 See Rosemary Shirley, *Rural Modernity, Everyday Life and Visual Culture* (Oxon: Routledge, 2016); David Farrugia, John Smyth and Tim Harrison, 'Rural Young People in Late Modernity: Place, Globalisation and the Spatial Contours of Identity', *Current Sociology*, 62:7 (2014), 1038.
14 Sian Edwards, '"A Richness that is Lacking Now": Country Childhoods, Nostalgia and Rural Change in the Mass Observation Project', 104:363 (2020), 946; Mary Ann Powell, Nicola Taylor and Anne B. Smith, 'Constructions of Rural

Childhood: Challenging Dominant Perspectives', *Children's Geographies*, 11:1 (2013), 411; Robert Giddings and Richard Yarwood, 'Growing Up, Going Out and Growing Out of the Countryside: Childhood Experiences in Rural England', *Children's Geographies*, 3:1 (2005), 101–9.

15 Julie C. Keller and Michael M. Bell, 'Rolling in the Hay: The Rural as Sexual Space', in Conner Bailey, Leif Jensen and Elizabeth Ransom (eds), *Rural America in a Globalising World: Problems and Prospects for the 2010s* (Morgantown: West Virginia University Press, 2014), p. 506.

16 Claire Langhamer, 'Love and Courtship in Mid-Twentieth-Century England', *The Historical Journal*, 50:1 (2007), 193; Charnock, 'Teenage Girls', 1032–53. See also Charnock's 2017 PhD thesis for a discussion of rural experiences and spaces: Hannah Charnock, 'Girlhood, Sexuality and Identity in England, 1950–1980' (University of Exeter, 2017), 214 and 253–4.

17 Angela McRobbie, '*Jackie* Magazine: Romantic Individualism and the Teenage Girl', in Angela McRobbie, *Feminism and Youth Culture: From 'Jackie' to 'Just Seventeen'* (Basingstoke: Macmillan Education, 1991); Claire Langhamer, *Women's Leisure in England, 1920–1960* (Manchester: Manchester University Press, 2000), chapter 4.

18 Daniel O'Neill, '"People Love Player's": Cigarette Advertising and the Teenage Consumer in Post-war Britain', *Twentieth Century British History*, 28:3 (2017), 430. For examples, see: Burton Magazine Advertisement 1955, UK, Image number: 30532037 (accessed 18 October 2021), www.advertisingarchives.co.uk/en/asset/show_zoom_window_popup.html?asset=28286&location=grid&asset_list=28296,28295,28291,28287,28286,28285,7746,4567&basket_item_id=; Aristoc Magazine Advert 1968, UK, Image number 30542552. (accessed 1 September 2021), www.advertisingarchives.co.uk/?service=asset&action=show_zoom_window_popup&language=en&asset=38456&location=grid&asset_list=87524553,87522461,87522380,87522242,38457,38456,33334,29392,28497,28480,28474,28470,28441,28440,28439,7702,6247,361&basket_item_id=.

19 Adrian Bingham, 'The "K-Bomb": Social Surveys, the Popular Press, and British Sexual Culture in the 1940s and 1950s', *Journal of British Studies*, 50:1 (2011), 178.

20 Anon., 'How do you Woo? … It Begins Today', *Daily Mirror*, 6 February 1956, p. 1.

21 Little, 'Constructing Nature', 853 and 860; Louise A. Jackson, 'The Coffee Club Menace'; Marcus Collins, *Modern Love: An Intimate History of Men and Women in Twentieth Century Britain* (London: Atlantic Books, 2003), chapter 3. Sally Holloway has identified the romanticisation of spaces of courtship in the Georgian period. Sally Holloway, *The Game of Love in Georgian England: Courtship, Emotions, and Material Culture* (Oxford: Oxford University Press, 2019), p. 9.

22 *Express* staff reporter, 'Letter from Killer Threatens Victim No. 3', *Daily Express*, 18 August 1966, p. 7.

23 Anon., 'Anne: Plea to Lovers', *Daily Mirror*, 9 May 1964, p. 26.

24 Express staff reporter, 'Lovers' Lane Girls May Help Police', *Daily Express*, 20 April 1964, p. 7.

25 Keith Waterhouse, 'Lovers' Lane Ain't What it Used to Be!', *Daily Mirror*, 3 June 1955, p. 5.
26 Ibid.
27 Douglas Warth, *Daily Herald*, 10 May 1956, 'Concluding a *Herald* investigation into courtship', p. 9.
28 Mary Brown, 'A Time of Temptation', *Daily Mirror*, 21 May 1952, p. 2.
29 Anon., 'The Perils of Lovers' Lane', *Daily Mirror*, 14 April 1958, p. 9.
30 Little, 'Constructing Nature', 853.
31 Anon., 'The Perils of Lovers' Lane', *Daily Mirror*.
32 Ibid.
33 Anon., 'Ban-the-Bull Move in Lovers' Lane', *Daily Mirror*, Monday 19 June 1967, p. 12.
34 Anon., '"Cupid Council" Plan a Lane for Lovers', *Daily Mirror*, 27 April 1956, p. 6.
35 Ray Hill, 'The Sentimental City Saves a Lovers' Lane', *Daily Mirror*, 19 December 1964, p. 4.
36 Paul Connew, 'So Romantic ... A Stroll Down the Municipal Lovers' Lane', *Daily Mirror*, 2 August 1968, p. 3.
37 Brown, 'A Time of Temptation', p. 2.
38 Alan Price, 'Storm Over the "Petting Patrol"', *Daily Mirror*, 26 January 1957, p. 5.
39 Jackson, 'The Coffee Club Menace', p. 304.
40 Mass Observation Archive [hereafter MOA] (University of Sussex): Replies to Autumn 2005 directive [M3408, Female aged 59, Coventry]
41 MOA: Replies to Summer 2001 directive [T1843, female aged 56, Disley].
42 For a discussion of the MOP as a source, see Annebella Pollen, 'Research Methodology in Mass Observation Past and Present: "Scientifically, about as valuable as a chimpanzee's tea party at the zoo"?', *History Workshop Journal*, 75:1 (2013), 213–35.
43 MOA: Replies to Summer 2001 directive [H1703, female aged 53 from Derbyshire].
44 MOA: Replies to Summer 2001 directive [C2654, female in her 50s, Birmingham].
45 Mills, 'Using the Personal to Critique the Popular', 471.
46 MOA: Replies to Summer 2001 directive [G226, female aged 60, North Lancashire].
47 MOA: Replies to Autumn 2005 directive [M3408, female aged 59, Coventry].
48 Geoffrey Gorer, *Sex and Marriage in England Today: Study of the Views and Experience of under-45s* (London: Thomas Nelson and Sons, 1971), p. 54.
49 Geoffrey Gorer, *Exploring English Character* (New York: Criterion Books, 1955), pp. 117 and 237.
50 This is not to suggest that religiosity and moral frameworks did not continue to shape the lives of girls living in urban areas. See Charnock, 'Girlhood, Sexuality and Identity', 232–3.
51 William M. Williams, *The Sociology of an English Village: Gosforth* (London: Routledge & Kegan Paul Ltd, 1956), pp. 63–4.
52 MOA: Replies to Summer 2001 directive [C2579, female aged 56, Lowestoft].

53 MOA: Replies to Autumn 2005 directive [H1705, female aged 54].
54 Katharine Milestone, 'Swinging Regions: Young Women and club Culture in 1960s Manchester', *Film, Fashion* & Consumption, 7:2 (2018), 192.
55 MOA: Replies to Summer 2001 directive [T1843, female aged 56, Disley].
56 Ibid.
57 MOA: Replies to Summer 2001 directive [M1979, female aged 62, Tynemouth].
58 MOA: Replies to Summer 2001 directive [A1706, female aged 54, Shoreham-by-Sea].
59 MOA: Replies to Summer 2001 directive [G226, female aged 60, North Lancashire]
60 MOA: Replies to Summer 2001 directive [H2639, female aged 60, Ipswich].
61 Williams, *The Sociology of an English Village: Gosforth*, p. 62.
62 Angela McRobbie, 'The Culture of Working-Class Girls', in Angela McRobbie, *Feminism and Youth Culture*, p. 37.
63 MOA: Replies to Summer 2001 directive [M1979, female aged 62, Tynemouth].
64 MOA: Replies to Summer 2001 directive [W1923, female aged 62, Buckinghamshire].
65 MOA: Replies to Autumn 2005 directive [H2639, female aged 65, Ipswich].
66 MOA: Replies to Summer 2001 directive [R860, female aged 53, Stockport].
67 Penny Tinkler, 'Going Places or Out of Place? Representations of Mobile Girls and Young Women in Late-1950s and 1960s Britain', *Twentieth Century British History*, 32:2 (2021), 214.
68 Ibid., 237.
69 MOA: Replies to Autumn 2005 directive [A1706, female aged 59, Shoreham-by-Sea].
70 MOA: Replies to Summer 2001 directive [G2089, female aged 49, London].
71 MOA: Replies to Summer 2001 directive [M1979, female aged 62, Tynemouth].
72 Ibid.
73 MOA: Replies to Autumn 2005 directive [D826, female aged 55, Bristol].
74 MOA: Replies to Autumn 2005 directive [D826, female aged 55, Bristol].
75 MOA: Replies to Autumn 2005 directive [M3408, female aged 59, Coventry].
76 Mimi Sheller and John Urry, 'The City and the Car', *International Journal of Urban and Regional Research*, 24:4 (2000), 747.
77 MOA: Replies to Autumn 2005 directive [H1705, female aged 54].
78 Williams, *The Sociology of an English Village: Gosforth*, p. 62.
79 MOA: Replies to Summer 2001 directive [T1843, female aged 56, Disley].
80 Williams, *The Sociology of an English Village: Gosforth*, p. 62.
81 Paul Boyle (ed.), 'Your Joking', *Sunday Mirror*, 10 January 1965, p. 12.
82 Anon., *Daily Mirror*, 2 July 1969, p. 10.
83 *Mirror* Reporter, 'Naked Girl Shock for Vicar in a Churchyard', *Daily Mirror*, 7 October 1969, p. 23.
84 Price, 'Storm Over the "Petting Patrol"'.
85 Anon., 'For Privacy: A Switch on a Lovers' Lane Light', *Daily Mirror*, 10 February 1969, p. 3.
86 Claire Langhamer, 'Love, Selfhood and Authenticity in Post-War Britain', *Cultural and Social History*, 9:2 (2012), 288.
87 Milestone, 'Swinging Regions', 192.
88 Charnock, 'Teenage Girls', 1036.
89 Mills, 'Using the Personal to Critique the Popular', 471.

6

Queering modernism: social, sartorial and spatial intersections between mod and gay (sub)culture, 1957–67

Shaun Cole and Paul Sweetman

This chapter arises out of our shared interest in the interconnections and intersections between sexual and style-based scenes and subcultures, which, despite considerable overlaps, have tended in the academic literature to be treated as distinct. It has developed from initial discussions around this theme following a symposium at London College of Fashion in November 2019 – *Streetstyle: 1994–Now* – which revisited 1994's *Streetstyle* exhibition at the Victoria and Albert Museum. We noted the way in which sexual and style-based subcultures have tended to be approached differently – and as substantially distinct – at least since the development of the Birmingham Centre for Contemporary Cultural Studies' (CCCS) concern with post-war British youth subcultures, which broke from the deviancy studies tradition associated initially with the Chicago School.

In 1985, Michael Brake observed that youth subcultural studies rarely mention homosexuals, which he attributed to the 'masculinist' and 'heterosexist' emphases of subcultures.[1] Subsequent studies have begun to explore the role of subculture in queer youth identification and intersections between gay and straight subcultural participants, but it is still an area that is significantly underexplored.

Our focus, here, is on intersections between mod subculture and gay culture, particularly in London, during both mod's initial development and subsequent heyday in the mid-1960s, a period marked by social change and ideas of permissiveness.[2] We have bracketed our discussion in the decade 1957–67 because the earlier date anticipates the emergence of the first mods in around 1958 and saw the opening of gay/mod retailer John Stephen's first Carnaby Street boutique, as well as the publication of the Wolfenden Report, which recommended that 'homosexual behaviour between consenting adults in private should no longer be considered a criminal offence'.[3] In turn, 1967 was marked by the partial decriminalisation of male homosexual acts through the Sexual Offences Act, and the ongoing dissolution of mod (in its first incarnation) as the subculture diverged along the axes of psychedelia and the counterculture, on the one hand, and 'hard-mod'/skinhead on the other. This chapter looks first at the mod subculture and its partial associations with homosexuality and effeminacy, primarily to 'straight' observers. We then address sociological and subcultural studies accounts of mod, noting the partial and reductive aspects of Dick Hebdige's CCCS-type reading of mod style, which overlooks a host of wider influences and interconnections, before focusing on the intersections between mod and gay culture in social, sartorial and spatial terms. The penultimate section then considers how we might best conceptualise such interconnections, discussing both the idea of 'discourse communities' and the potential application of an Actor Network Theory (ANT) approach, to address and describe the overlapping networks of constituents involved. We conclude by summarising some of our key points and thinking a little about the broader implications of our discussion. We should note, at this point, that we are aware that our focus predominantly on male mod style and its overlaps with gay *male* culture in some respects reproduces the masculinist bias of subcultural studies for which the CCCS and others have rightly been criticised.[4] This reflects our source material and expertise. It should be noted, however, that female mods formed a key part of mod subculture as a whole.[5]

The mod subculture

Mod began in London in the late 1950s, when a relatively small group of young people calling themselves modernists, after their love for modern jazz, began drawing on a range of sources including Jewish tailoring, album covers by their favourite artists and the smart, preppy American look known as Ivy League, to create a new, self-conscious style of their own. The subculture grew in the 1960s, in part thanks to publicity from TV shows such as *Ready Steady Go!* (1963–66), and became increasingly influential, having a significant and lasting impact on the era as whole.[6] The 1960s mods were associated with smart suits for the men and up-to-the-minute styles for both men and women, with music such as soul, ska and R&B, and with a lifestyle that centred around shopping, nightclubs and dancing, sometimes fuelled by amphetamines.

Mods were fastidious about their appearance and mannerisms, drawing on influences such as French, Italian and American fashion, and wider developments in design and visual art. They were inspired by films from the French new wave, as well as Italian films such as *La Dolce Vita*, by the aesthetics of professional European cycling, African American culture and

West Indian style. Quintessential mod band The Who drew inspiration directly from pop-art, appropriating and popularising symbols such as the RAF roundel and the Union Jack and using them to decorate their clothes. The mods were keen on Italian scooters – Vespas and Lambrettas – and the men adopted American army-surplus parkas to keep their suits clean while they rode.

Predominantly working class, the mods were aspirational and keen participants in, as well as important progenitors of, the UK's emerging consumer culture. In the case of the men, their patronage of key figures such as retailer John Stephen helped to put Carnaby Street on the map as the ground zero of British style. That is not to suggest that they were passive consumers. In the case, specifically, of mod style, their creativity and innovation took the form of customising clothes from more mainstream retailers, designing them themselves, and also – equally importantly – combining and wearing them in new and interesting ways. And whilst influenced by popular and consumer culture, this exchange was also two-way; mods were inspired by retailers, artists and designers, but also influenced them in turn, the subculture's forward-looking ethos and aesthetic coming to be associated with and applied to a diverse range of fields in addition to fashion, including architecture and interior design, advertising, television, cinema, photography and visual art.[7]

The wider context for the emergence and development of the subculture includes a host of social, political and economic, as well as cultural, developments developments, not least increased affluence and social mobility, including among the young, but also more specific changes such as the creation of the National Health Service in 1948 and the phasing out of National (military) Service between 1957 and 1960, followed in the 1960s by 'the abolition of capital punishment, the [partial] decriminalising of homosexuality and abortion' and the increasing availability of the contraceptive pill, all of which 'was underpinned by' the waning influence of the church.[8] Not only did many young people have more money, they also found themselves living in, and themselves contributed to, an increasingly liberal, less deferential, apparently more egalitarian and aspirational environment. Despite its complex entanglements with media and consumer culture right from the start, the subculture was increasingly commercialised from the early 1960s on, including in the USA, with retailers, music promoters and others attempting to cash in directly on mod style.

Some of the early mods saw this as marking the death-knell of the subculture, but historian Richard Weight suggests it is also evidence of its growing popularity and accessibility, as well as its increasing influence in aesthetic terms.[9] It can be read as further complicating the relationship between subculture, media and commerce rather than signalling a shift from a pure or unadulterated subculture to one that subsequently existed only in a commoditised form. The subculture's status within the public eye also remained ambivalent, not least because of the 'moral panic'[10] generated around widely reported skirmishes between mods and their apparent rivals, the rockers, at seaside resorts such as Brighton, Clacton and Margate during the spring and summer Bank Holidays of 1964–65.

Many of the original mods decried the actions of those involved in the disturbances, who they saw as a distinct sub-group who failed to share the subculture's earlier ethos and intentions.[11] The so-called 'scooter boys' or 'hard mods' were later to develop into the more overtly masculine and working-class subculture of the skinheads, while other branches of the mod family fed into the psychedelic movement and, later, 1970s developments such as glam. 'Hard mods' and skinheads notwithstanding, 'There was', at least initially, 'something very gay about mod. Men were just checking each other', early mod Penny Reel acknowledged; a sentiment echoed by Mark Feld (later to become the bisexual glam rock singer Marc Bolan) who felt that 'mod was mentally a very homosexual thing, though not in any physical sense'.[12] Richard Barnes stated that 'There may have been a homosexual element' in mod subculture but that 'it wasn't particularly important'.[13] Elaborating, Ken Browne recalled that he 'never knew any gay mods'.[14] Barnes's and Browne's reactions may well have been down to the illegal nature of homosexuality at this time and the age of many involved in mod subculture; coming to terms with homosexuality and taking the brave step to come out would have been an issue in the visibility of young gay mods. Who vocalist Pete Townsend suggests that gay men were generally seen as older, but also as sharing affinities with the younger mods: 'Gays were different. They didn't behave like other adults; they were scornful of conventional behaviour; they mixed more easily with young people, and seemed to understand them.'[15] There certainly were gay mods, as noted in Peter Burton's recollections and by David Scoular: 'I was a mod then, shirts, cravats – I had a scooter … there were big changes going on, and it wasn't just about being gay.'[16]

That effeminacy in men was particularly associated with homosexuality at this time is relevant. Interviewed for *Town* magazine in 1962, Peter Sugar admitted: 'Some of our clothes are bit effeminate but they have to be. I mean you have to be a bit camp […] who cares', and Mark Feld conceded that 'if you wear something that's a bit different it's "Nancy" and "Look at that queer"', typical of homophobic taunts of the time.[17] Feld's friend and aspiring music business impresario Allan Warren recalled in relation to Feld's bisexuality, 'in the '60s it was practically compulsory to be bisexual! … If you weren't at least a little bit bisexual then you are [*sic*] not very trendy'.[18] The overt fastidiousness in attention to detail that mods paid to their dress style, highlighted in interviews with original mods and by commentators such as Kenneth Leech,[19] was conventionally seen as feminine and therefore queer. Many of the clothes mods were choosing were the same as those gay men had been wearing for some time. 'London clubs would have a lot of gays in them wearing outrageous white suits with big high heels. Mods took that influence', Ken Browne said of the early 1960s.[20] Steve Marriott of mod band Small Faces recalled that when he 'started turning to mod' he argued with his father 'for looking like a poof',[21] while his mother remembered that 'the first time he wore white trousers he was beaten up', emphasising violence against both perceived gay men and sartorial difference.[22] Mods such as Roland Kelly, Barry Fantoni, Penny Reel, Lloyd Johnson and Carlo Manzi all recalled the association of bright colours and the colour pink in particular with homosexuality, and wearing these colours led to homophobic name calling and arguments with parents and peers.[23] This queer association was confirmed by one Brighton-based gay man, who recalled: '[a] pink shirt was definitely queer, colourful clothes were definitely queer'.[24]

A short film released in 1964 called *Mods and Rockers*, directed by gay producer and director Kenneth Hume, features a gay mod dressed in pink, making a clear point about the overlaps between the subcultures. Nodding towards the media discussions about the bank holiday skirmishes between mods and rockers and the choreographed dance fights of the 1961 musical *West Side Story*, the film is set in a church basement youth club and featured members of Western Theatre Ballet Company.[25] The rival groups dance to instrumental versions of Beatles' hits played by a group called The Cheynes. Although the main plot centres around a mod girl dancing and leaving with a rocker boy, there is a parallel sub-plot involving the gay mod. Initially dancing alone in the background, this 'sad young man'[26] wears a cerise cardigan over a white T-shirt with bright pink trousers and black-heeled Chelsea boots. He stands out from the other mods in his brightly coloured outfit, almost monochromatically pink, the colour synonymous with homosexuality. His snugly fitting trousers are similar to those worn by Colin MacInnes's fashionable gay character, Fabulous Hoplite – 'a pair of skin-tight, rubber-glove thin, almost transparent cotton slacks' – which in turn were almost certainly based on garments sold by Bill Green at Vince or John Stephen.[27] The pink-clad mod's sexuality, symbolised through his clothing and mannerisms, is confirmed when he leaves the club with one of the rocker boys at the end of the film: hinting at a further off-screen sexual liaison and mirroring the cross-subculture departure of the mod girl and rocker boy earlier in the film.

Sociological and/or (sub)cultural studies accounts

More recent historical and other discussions aside, the primary accounts of mod from a sociological and/or (sub)cultural studies perspective come from two sources: Stanley Cohen's contemporaneously researched *Folk Devils and Moral Panics: The Creation of the Mods and Rockers*,[28] and Dick Hebdige's chapter 'The Meaning of Mod' in Stuart Hall and Tony Jefferson's *Resistance Through Rituals*,[29] as well as his discussion of mod, alongside other subcultures, in his subsequent *Subculture: The Meaning of Style*.[30] Cohen is not so much interested in the mod subculture per se, more the furore surrounding the 'mods vs rockers' events that took place at assorted UK seaside resorts on several bank holiday weekends from Easter 1964 on. His account shows how the media and 'control culture' (police, courts, legislature) response exaggerated and amplified these apparent disturbances, thereby helping substantially to create the 'folk devils' on which, in the media's case, it claimed simply to report. Early media accounts also helped to establish, or at least cement, the 'mod/rocker' distinction upon which their stories relied and, through a process of 'symbolisation', to solidify the association between the respective groups and their associated paraphernalia – including 'clothing styles, hair-styles and scooters', in the case of the mods.[31] These not only fed back to the wider public and to the 'folk devils' themselves, but were subsequently picked up on and further consolidated in the control culture response and commercial exploitation of mod in particular.[32] Although primarily concerned with demonstrating the establishment of a 'moral panic' and the way in which it subsequently unfolds, Cohen's account also shows how the mod subculture itself was co-created by a number of different constituents, most notably the media, not just by the 'subculturalists' themselves.

In contrast with Cohen, Hebdige provides us with a more conventional reading, from a subcultural studies perspective, of mod *style*, arguing that the mods, like earlier and later subcultures, engaged actively and creatively with a range of cultural commodities, the appropriation and recontextualisation of which constituted a form of *bricolage*, in which new uses were established and new meanings ascribed:

> Union jacks were emblazoned on the backs of grubby parka anoraks or cut up and converted into smartly tailored jackets [... and] the conventional insignia of the business world – the suit, collar and tie, short hair, etc. – were stripped of their original connotations [...] and transformed into 'empty' fetishes, objects to be desired, fondled and valued in their own right.[33]

All of this was important because, like other forms of subcultural bricolage, it denaturalised existing understandings, temporarily revealing 'the arbitrary nature of the codes which underlie' our discursive ordering of the world.[34] Hebdige's account emphasises the influence of Black culture on mod style, while noting, in passing, how the mods also drew on other influences, including 'indigenous British gangster style'[35] (although not, as is pertinent to this chapter, the influence of gay culture, nor the influence of Jewish culture as noted by contributors to Anderson's popular-historical account).[36] There are places, too, where Hebdige refers to particular aspects of mod practice and lifestyle.

Despite Shane Blackman's recent description of Hebdige's work as a form of 'scavenger ethnography',[37] however, his account is essentially textual or semiotic – a *reading* of mod style – which is also concerned primarily with mod in its originary moments or, in other words, its pure and supposedly unadulterated – *pre-incorporated* and *pre-commoditised* – form. This is also presented as an autonomous working-class response to wider structural issues or contradictions. In Hebdige's account, then, the relationship between subculture and commerce is one of incorporation and commodification; something that happens *to* the subculture and contributes subsequently to its dilution or demise. The original mods do engage with cultural commodities – including various consumer items – but this is presented as a process of selective and creative *appropriation* (at least in so far as any actual agency is involved), which changes once the style is subsequently commoditised. When commodities started being marketed to mods 'by a rapidly expanding pop industry', then 'Dress was no longer innovative – nobody "discovered" items like Levi jeans or hush puppies any more. Style was manufactured from above instead of being spontaneously created from within.'[38] In this respect, Hebdige's analysis is of a piece with the broader CCCS framework to which his initial work contributes and on which, despite its substantial emphasis on Black culture and its invocation of a broader range of theoretical and conceptual references, his later book substantially relies.[39] For the CCCS, post-war British youth subcultures were an autonomous working-class response to broader structural contradictions, the importance of which lay in the symbolic challenges they issued to hegemonic understandings of the world before these challenges were inevitably defused.

Paul Sweetman, along with others, has criticised the CCCS framework, arguing that its predominantly (Marxist realist) structural approach not only neglects lived experience, but makes its investigation unnecessary, and that in this context semiotic analysis, whatever its strengths, comes to the rescue by allowing the group to claim to attend to agency and creativity – as their more culturalist inclinations demand – whilst actually regarding it as a quasi-automatic response to broader structural conditions.[40] A magical attempt to resolve broader contradictions, which, because it only operates at a symbolic level is doomed, ultimately, to fail. For all the nods towards resistance and creativity, subculturalists are, in the final analysis, regarded by the CCCS framework as little more than ciphers, acting out a preordained response to wider realities, the specificities of which are unimportant to the broader theoretical analysis. Teds, mods, skinheads and punks are all doing essentially the same thing, despite variations in the details – and because the theoretical framework tells us, we know what that is in advance. In this context, the actual processes involved are unimportant, subordinate to the wider theoretical framework, and attending to lived realities is not only unnecessary but redundant, given the unlikelihood of subculturalists being either aware of, or able properly to articulate, the reality of the situation in which they find themselves.

This is important in that it overlooks subcultural practice, including where this relates to sexuality and gender, as well as failing to attend to subcultures' broader influences, connections and contributions. In the CCCS view, subcultures are seen as self-contained, spontaneous and autonomous in their originary moments (which are the only ones that matter), with incorporation and/or commodification occurring subsequent to their initial flowering. This is elitist in the sense that it only regards subcultures as interesting or authentic in their original manifestations. It is also problematic in that it ignores the potentially complex interplay between subcultures, media, commercial and other institutional interests from the start, as well as the input of other potentially important actors such as family members, those engaged with intersecting cultures and subcultures – including sexual (sub)cultures as we are concerned with here – and the various objects and artefacts with which subculturalists engage.

In his introduction to the second edition of *Folk Devils and Moral Panics*, Cohen is critical of CCCS-type approaches for their 'tendency [...] to see the historical development of a style as being wholly internal to the group – with commercialization and co-option as something which just happens afterwards'.[41] There are places where Hebdige presents us with a more complicated picture, acknowledging the ambiguities of the processes involved.[42] For the most part, however, he presents us with a fairly straightforward, linear model of 'recuperation', noting how: 'Each subculture moves through a cycle of resistance and defusion.'[43] In the case of mod, however, regarding the development of the style as 'wholly internal to the group' is to miss the range of actors and influences involved; the mods were not simply discovering and reworking 'straight' commodities, nor were they doing so alone.

Intersections between mod and gay culture

One of the complex sets of influences and interconnections that is overlooked in CCCS type accounts of mod is addressed in more recent historical accounts that attend to the voices of mods themselves.[44] In his autobiography, Peter Burton makes comparisons between mod clubs – such as the Scene in Ham Yard – and the gay coffee bars – including Le Duce in D'Arblay Street – in London's Soho. Both groups, he notes, were listening to the same music, including soul, ska, bluebeat and Motown, taking the same drugs, predominantly amphetamines, and wearing the same clothes, bought at Vince Man's Shop and John Stephen, in and off Carnaby Street.[45] Burton, who later became the manager of Le Duce, recalled that the music 'wasn't mass-produced music accepted by all and sundry' but instead more obscure recordings by Black artists and white artists 'influenced by Black American soul music', such as Dusty Springfield.[46]

Recalling his first visit to Le Duce in 1964, aged 16, gay DJ Tallulah recalled the same music as Burton, as well as men dancing alone to fashionable dances such as The Twist, the Madison, Buff Rug and The Shake, and in couples.[47] DJ Norman Scott similarly recalled: 'we used to go to Le Duce … you could dance with another guy, but you had to be about a foot apart'.[48] Artists Patrick Procktor, Derek Jarman and Keith Milow, and fashion designer Ossie Clark, also frequented Le Duce, mixing with young gay mods, with the latter three featuring in Procktor's 1966 painting *Shades*.[49] This large painting depicts the interior of Le Duce in tones of reddish-pink with 'apparition-like fragments of figures' dressed in a variety of mod-styled clothing and other gay styles of the period.[50] The upper part of the painting shows an area with a doorway that correlates with Barry Miles's description of the raised dimly lit area at the back of the basement where customers engaged in oral sex.[51] The shadowy basement of Le Duce was similar to the recessed archways of The Scene, where mods took breaks from dancing and heterosexual couples sometimes made out.[52]

Tallulah recalled that when he first visited Le Duce he 'was quite mod-y' and this was the first time he saw someone with 'the Small Faces hairdo – a mod hairdo. It looked like long sideburns, but they weren't sideburns … back-combed up'.[53] Terry Rawlins noted that mods backcombed their hair into 'flamboyant and feminine' hairstyles that were cut at women's salons rather than traditional men's barbers.[54] Wearing such hairstyles and eyeliner and face powder connected mods with effeminacy and thus homosexuality. Tight trousers were also historically associated with gay men.[55] Tallulah and Michael Brown recalled wearing tight, crotch-revealing trousers as a mode of attracting interest from other men and mod Dick Lawson remembered the offence his caused in respectable *straight* society.[56] While there was a similarity in the gay and straight adoption of tight trousers in the period, Vince Man's Shop's customer James Gardiner believes that gay men are 'conscious of their powers of sexual attractiveness in a way that straight men aren't'.[57] Such tight styles worn by gay men and prototype mods were drawn from Italian post-war tailoring and casual styles and sold at Vince and Stephen's boutique stores.

The history of Vince's Man's Shop has been covered in detail elsewhere[58] but its significance here is as a boutique with an initially predominantly gay male clientele. Editor of *Man About Town*, Colin Woodhead, recalled that 'Vince's catered to an extremely unconventional crowd',[59] while Vince shop assistant and catalogue model, John Hardy, confirmed that a high percentage of Vince's clients were gay.[60] The association of bright colours and tight-fitting clothing with homosexuality goes some way to explaining the shop's early gay clientele.[61] After working as a sales assistant at Vince, John Stephen was inspired to set up on his own as he saw the potential for 'really modern clothes for young men with a British label'.[62] Selling similar tight-fitting, brightly coloured clothes and opening his store close to Vince guaranteed that Stephen would attract the same customer base, but Stephen's advantage over Green was that he 'was young and … into pop music, so I gave kids something they could wear to complement that'.[63] Relating the styles and colours to ideas of sexuality and youthful rebellion, Nigel Waymouth, founder of Granny Takes a Trip, noted 'we didn't realise it then, but the John Stephen revolution was a very gay thing … It was self-consciously trendy and camp in the true sense of the word.'[64] After initially hesitating about entering Vince's because of its reputation as a shop for gay men, mod Martin Stone recalled buying a red-and-white gingham shirt.[65] Michael McGrath said, 'the clothes were initially too daring for "straights" to wear but as the 1960s went on they came to accept them', in part because of the shop's promotions. Here McGrath's use of the term 'straights' refers both to heterosexuals and to more conventional dressers who were not involved in mod subculture.

By 1963, Stephen owned eighteen shops all over central London. Dubbed the 'King of Carnaby Street' after his expansion into the USA, the *Observer* also referred to him as the 'Million-Pound Mod'. He shared the throne with singer Dusty Springfield, known as 'Queen of the Mods'.[66] That both were gay but did not publicly acknowledge their sexuality until later has a bearing on the queer aesthetics underpinning the popularisation of mod styles in the mid-1960s. Stephen was presented to the majority of his customers and the press as 'straight' and thus could be described as 'passing'. Stephen and his gay friends, including music producer Larry Parnes, frequented Le Duce and so mixed with gay and straight mods who were his customers[67] and, 'as a queen designing and cutting clothes that were tighter and tighter', Stephen was projecting a gay man's ideal of the 1960s male body 'on the straight boys'.[68]

Following Green's employment of the bodybuilder (and later actor) John Hamill as a shop assistant, Stephen and his gay interior designer Myles

Antony invited boxer Billy Walker to model for photographs for the shop windows. While this reinforced a queer presentation of men's clothing, as Nik Cohn observed, Walker was 'worshipped so much that not even pink denims could sully his manhood'.[69] Mike McGrath, who worked for Stephen, recalled Walker wearing 'daring' skintight trousers but because Walker was 'the epitome of masculinity', such clothes were not accused of being effeminate when Walker wore them.[70] Antony's use of camp referencing in his interiors and window displays provided a further gay sensibility in Carnaby Street. Mike Quinn, manager of Stephen's Male West One store, recalled that the majority of 'the window dressers were gay, and gay people are very creative. I ended up having gay mannerisms; it became quite trendy … even though I was straight.'[71]

There were significant intersections between gay culture and the mod music scene, too. Darryl Bullock's *The Velvet Mafia* explores in detail the careers of, and connections between, gay men who were responsible for producing much of the British popular music of the late 1950s and 1960s, including Larry Parnes, Lionel Bart, Joe Meek and Brian Epstein.[72] Bullock highlights the ways in which these managers and producers brought their sexuality and queer aesthetic to British music through their management of individual singers and groups, but also their sometimes unrequited relationships with, and sexual advances towards, these predominantly straight musicians. George Melly claimed that 'mods remained purists and for a time re-established their pre-eminence by quite coolly turning towards overt homosexuality and going with any showbiz queen who was famous and smart enough to reinforce their tottering egos'.[73] In such a statement, Melly acknowledged both the potential for homosexuality within mod subculture and the role that gay music impresarios had on the swinging London culture of the 1960s.

Richard Barnes acknowledged that it was Peter Meaden who was initially responsible for turning West London band The High Numbers into the first 'manufactured' mod group, The Who.[74] However, it was Kit Lambert, the gay son of a classical composer, and Chris Stamp, the straight working-class son of a tugboat worker (and brother of actor Terence Stamp), who subsequently took charge of the band, after wresting them away from Meaden and co-manager Helmut Gorden. Considering their partnership, Stamp recalled: 'We were both marginalised … me in my class, he in his gayness', a sentiment he echoed in relation to The Who: 'They were outsiders, man … They were misfits.'[75] Pete Townshend also reflected on the ways in which Lambert and Stamp influenced the group and its audience through innovative marketing techniques that resonated with Townshend's art school experience.[76]

Although The Beatles were not a band favoured by subcultural mods, the 'British invasion' of America and the mass popularisation of the term 'mod' by the mid-1960s included The Beatles within broader popular understandings of the term.[77] Relevant to this chapter's discussion is that their manager, Brian Epstein, was a gay man and responsible for their visual transformation from a leather and denim rock 'n' roll band to a slick, continental-styled pop group. Larry Parnes introduced Epstein to Soho tailor 'Dougie' Millings, who made the collarless jackets and tapered trousers that by 1962 became known as the 'Beatles Suit' (although based on a style originated by Pierre Cardin). Ann Shillinglaw notes the band's knowledge of Epstein's sexuality and the influence that his 'flair' had upon the queer sensibilities displayed in their 1964 film *A Hard Day's Night*.[78]

Conceptualising interconnections

How should we best conceptualise such interconnections? Shaun Cole has discussed how Ross Higgins's adoption of John Swales' 'discourse community' model in relation to gay fashion in 1960s Montreal – as a 'genre for the expression of knowledge and attitudes particular to its social viewpoint' – could be applied to both the gay and mod worlds of 1960s London.[79] Within both the overt and covert gay 'discourse community', discussions of fashions and styles allowed members to devise strategies and communicate with one another. Gay collective knowledge as a form of communication manifested in the 1960s in the underground language Polari, which despite its use by a knowing gay crowd was popularised on the BBC radio programme *Round the Horne*. Vince mail-order catalogues used Polari words as clothing descriptors, for example 'Butch' and 'Trade Wind' swimming trunks and a 'Sun Cruiser' jacket. Insider discourse could also be related to the ways in which the popular press attempted to understand subcultural communities. Overtly effeminate gay men were visible to, and vilified by, straight and gay communities and in the mainstream press, discussed in articles such as 'How to spot a possible homo' in the *Sunday Mirror* in 1962.[80] The language used in this, and others with headlines such as 'Evil Men', attempted to publicly identify gay men, often throwing up contradictions in descriptions of types or styles and creating a form of moral panic, particularly around perceived delinquency. The early mods or 'faces' also operated as a discourse community around fashion and style 'when a few teenagers emerged as utter clothes fanatics, obsessive to a degree that had been unknown before'.[81] As the style of the individual 'faces' evolved into the subculture of mod, so consensus on clothing and styles formed a key part of the discourse within this subcultural community: 'As with the mods later, you became a modernist by wearing the right kind of clothes … it was a group thing, a way of life interpreted by clothes.'[82]

Another way of exploring and describing such interconnections, which allows for the investigation of the full range of constituents involved, and encourages a focus on what they actually do, is provided by Actor Network Theory (ANT). ANT sees social phenomena as made up of heterogeneous networks of actors, human and otherwise, which act together to effect change of various kinds, thereby constituting and re-constituting – *in an ongoing and contingent process* – different aspects of the social world.[83] The job of the analyst is to look at how these processes unfold; at who, and what, does what, describing the ways in which social phenomena are assembled or enacted and the overlapping and co-constitutive networks of actors involved. Social phenomena, from an ANT perspective, are not fixed and decided, concrete and already existing frameworks or *containers* for social action, but are *contingent and provisional*, the ongoing outcomes of different actors doing different things. So, from this perspective, subcultures, like any other kind of social phenomena, would be seen as the contingent outcomes of overlapping networks of actors interacting in various ways. Which, in the case specifically of mod, would include not just the 'subculturalists', but similarly dressed gay men and gay retailers, films, books and other popular texts, the media and 'control culture', sociologists and other academics, and objects and paraphernalia such as scooters, clothes, music and drugs. All of which constituted important and active constituents in the overlapping and co-constitutive networks involved.

ANT is critical of standard sociologies – including various forms of structuralism – for putting forward as the explanation that which itself needs to be explained;[84] deploying concepts from *society* onwards to organise and explain the social world, instead of looking at how the concepts themselves and the networks they purportedly describe are actually constituted in contingent and ongoing assemblages. It takes as given exactly what needs to be unpacked and examined. And in the case of subcultures, structuralist frameworks such as that developed by the CCCS take a concept – subculture – and apply it to each and every subcultural group, imposing a one-size-fits-all 'explanation' onto the phenomenon in question, rather than examining it in its specific detail. So, mod is assumed to be a self-contained, autonomous working-class response to wider structural factors and conditions, the experiences and understandings of the mods and any other actors involved are ultimately unimportant,[85] and wider connections and contributions are, except where they support the broader theoretical framework, overlooked or ignored.[86] From an ANT viewpoint, the CCCS framework approaches things the wrong way round; it 'black-boxes' the concept of subculture and then deploys it as an explanation, rather than opening up the theoretical packaging and looking inside.

This also involves, to at least some extent, manipulating empirical realities to make sure they fit. In his chapter on mod in *Resistance Through Rituals*, Hebdige himself notes that mod is an 'umbrella term', and that 'groups of art-college students following in Mary Quant's footsteps [...] were technically "mods"', but he goes on, with no further justification, to note: 'But for our purposes, we must limit the definition [...] to *working-class teenagers* who lived mainly in London and the new towns of the South and who could be readily identified by characteristic hairstyles, clothing etc.'.[87] Not only is this classed and implicitly gendered in definitional terms, it also prioritises issues of class at the expense of other issues, including gender and sexuality. Having discussed an exaggerated account of the mod lifestyle in the *Sunday Times* in April 1964, Hebdige also goes on to note that the 'reality of mod life was somewhat less glamorous', referring to a survey of '43 Margate offenders' to support his claim.[88] As other accounts have indicated, however, the mods who took part in the mod vs rocker disturbances such as the one which formed the backdrop to the survey, were a specific subset of the broader subculture, who had already been disowned by some of their more style-conscious forebears.[89]

None of which is to say that Hebdige's description is not broadly correct, or that the majority of mods were not working class, but rather to point to the efforts to which he and others went to ensure that the subcultures they interrogated aligned with their conceptual framework as opposed to the other way round.[90] Which may also explain why Hebdige refers to some influences on mod but not others, including gay culture and, more specifically, gay retailers, as we have focused on here. From an ANT perspective, however, we need to start with the actors, not decide who they are and what sort of groups they comprise in advance. Groups, including subcultures, don't exist independently of the actors that make them up. As ANT proponent Bruno Latour points out during a hypothetical discussion with a student seeking to locate their study within a wider 'explanatory framework': 'what you are really telling me is that the actors in your description make *no difference whatsoever*. They have simply realized a potential – apart from minor deviations – which means they are not actors at all [...] Your fieldwork has been [...] wasted. You should have gone directly to the cause.'[91]

Starting with the actors, in the case of mod, means looking at the mods themselves, at who they were and at what they did, as well as at the range of other actors involved. This allows us to look at what actually happens – to see who and what plays a part – including gay men's retailers and gay mods as focused on here – rather than boxing the actors into a theoretical cul-de-sac and applying a blanket approach which does away with the actors except as the conduits of structural forces. Rather than forcing square pegs into round holes, assuming some sort of pre-commoditised state of grace and brushing middle-class subculturalists and broader influences under the carpet, it allows us to consider who and what makes up such formations, and actually to address issues of agency and creativity rather than approach them tangentially in semiotic terms.[92] Attending, in this case, to the initial importance of a particular subsection of retailers is not to suggest that subcultures are not, typically, commoditised, but rather to indicate that the relationship between subcultures and commerce may be complex, foundational and dialogic, as opposed to linear, consequential and unidirectional; a web of overlapping networks rather than an orderly or straightforward process that necessarily plays out subsequent to or consequent upon subcultures' initial popularity. It may also be mutually constitutive. In each case, however, how such relationships play out should be investigated rather than assumed.

Conclusion

This chapter has examined the intersections and overlaps between mod and gay culture in the UK from the late 1950s to the late 1960s. Having provided a brief description of mod and its partial associations with homosexuality and effeminacy, we went on to examine and critique existing accounts of mod from a sociological and/or subcultural studies perspective, before considering the intersections and overlaps between mod and gay culture in more detail. Having already indicated the difficulties of exploring such interconnections using a standard, CCCS-type model of subculture, we went on to consider how they might best be conceptualised, discussing both the idea of 'discourse communities' and the potential application of ANT to address and describe the networks involved. We hope that the chapter has gone some way towards acknowledging and describing such connections and, in so doing, addressed some of the difficulties of more structural accounts, as well as considering ways of conceptualising these. We conclude by briefly considering some broader implications.

Looking first at the use of ANT to think through such interconnections, we would argue that such an approach allows us to address what actually happens – to see who and what plays a part – rather than boxing the actors into a cul-de-sac and assuming 'one-size fits all'. It allows us to consider who and what make up such formations, and to address issues of agency and creativity in practice. In the case of mod, this includes gay mods and gay retailers from the start, suggesting – in the case of the latter – that the relationship between subcultures and commerce may be complex, dialogic and foundational, rather than linear, straightforward and subsequent to subcultures' initial popularity. It is also mutually constitutive. But in each case, how it actually plays out needs to be investigated not assumed. That is not to say that mod was not increasingly commoditised – and institutionalised – as the 1960s progressed, rather that this was not a case of a wholly autonomous subculture subsequently becoming incorporated or 'defused'. Nor is such an approach to downplay the agency of subculturalists themselves, but instead actually to examine it, *alongside* that of the other actors involved.

Second, the intersections and interconnections between mod and gay subculture in terms of shared space, style and a challenge to 'straight' lifestyles (understood here to refer both to heterosexuals and more 'conventional' members of society), suggests that mod and gay culture can be thought of as overlapping and partially co-constitutive networks of marginality. In this context, mod subculture might be considered as offering a relatively safe environment for the exploration of marginal or subversive forms of gendered or sexual identity (suggestive of Caroline Evans's 'model of subcultural identity as mobile, fluid; as a 'becoming' rather than a 'being'),[93] while gay style and space offered an existing underground milieu through which such identities could be further articulated. ANT reminds us that networks should be examined in their specificity. Nevertheless, similar connections may also be apparent in respect of other subcultures, not least punk, with its well-documented overlaps with gay and lesbian culture, as well as its stylistic links with BDSM and other scenes. We hope that future work will consider such overlaps and intersections, including between women subculturalists and lesbian and LGBTIQA+ culture, not just male subculturalists and gay culture as we have focused on here.

Notes

1 Michael Brake, *Comparative Youth Culture* (London: Routledge & Kegan Paul, 1985).
2 Marcus Collins (ed.), *The Permissive Society and its Enemies: Sixties British Culture* (London: Rivers Oram Press, 2007).
3 See British Library, www.bl.uk/collection-items/wolfenden-report-conclusion#:~:text=It%20was%20155%20pages%20long,to%20reach%20his%20conclusions%20impartially (accessed 15 June 2022).
4 Angela McRobbie and Jenny Garber, 'Girls and Subcultures', in Stuart Hall and Tony Jefferson (eds), *Resistance through Rituals: Youth Subcultures in Post-war Britain*, 2nd edn (London: Routledge, 2006).
5 As Stanley Cohen notes, 'in many ways Mod was a more female than a male phenomenon'. *Folk Devils and Moral Panics: The Creation of the Mods and Rockers*, 3rd edn (London: Routledge, 2002), p. 157.
6 Richard Weight, *Mod: A Very British Style* (London: Bodley Head, 2013).

7 Weight, *Mod*, p. 11.
8 Ibid., p. 3.
9 Ibid., p. 119.
10 Cohen, *Folk Devils*.
11 Weight, *Mod*, p. 87.
12 Cited in Nik Cohn, *Today There Are No Gentlemen: The Changes in Englishmen's Clothes Since the War* (London: Weidenfeld & Nicolson 1971), p. 80.
13 Richard Barnes, *Mods!* (London: Eel Pie, 1979), p. 15.
14 Cited in Terry Rawlings, *Mod: A Very British Phenomenon* (London: Omnibus, 2000), p. 50.
15 Cited in Weight, *Mod*, p. 73.
16 Peter Burton, *Parallel Lives* (London: Gay Men's Press, 1985), pp. 30–1; cited in Murray Healy, *Gay Skins: Class, Masculinity and Queer Appropriation* (London: Cassell, 1996), pp. 63–4.
17 Cited in Rawlings, *Mod*, p. 46.
18 Cited in Daryl W. Bullock, *The Velvet Mafia: The Gay Men who Ran the Swinging Sixties* (London: Omnibus, 2021), p. 162.
19 Kenneth Leech, *Youthquake: The Growth of a Counter-culture through Two Decades* (London: Sheldon Press, 1973).
20 Cited in Rawlings, *Mod*, p. 50.
21 Cited in Weight, *Mod*, pp. 40–1.
22 Weight, *Mod*, p. 74.
23 Paul Anderson, *Mods The New Religion: The Style and Music of the 1960s Mods* (London: Omnibus, 2103), pp. 25, 28; Jeremy Reed, *The King of Carnaby Street: The Life of John Stephen* (London: Haus Publishing 2010), pp. 224, 244; Paolo Hewitt, *The Sharper World: A Mod Anthology* (London: Helter Skelter, 2009), p. 54.
24 Brighton Ourstory Project, *Daring Hearts: Lesbian and Gay Lives of 50s and 60s Brighton* (Brighton: Queen Spark Books, 1992), p. 52.
25 Managed by the homosexual music entrepreneur Robert Stigwood, who was also in a relationship with Kit Lambert (manager of The Who).
26 Richard Dyer, *The Culture of Queers* (Abingdon and New York: Routledge, 2012), p. 116–36.
27 Colin MacInnes, *Absolute Beginners* (London: Allison & Busby, 1992), p. 51.
28 Cohen, *Folk Devils*.
29 Dick Hebdige, 'The Meaning of Mod', in Hall and Jefferson, *Resistance Through Rituals*.
30 Dick Hebdige, *Subculture: The Meaning of Style* (London: Methuen, 1979).
31 Cohen, *Folk Devils*, p. 73.
32 Ibid., p. 156.
33 Hebdige, *Subculture*, p. 104.
34 Ibid., p. 91.
35 Hebdige, 'The Meaning of Mod', p. 73.
36 Anderson, *Mods*.
37 Shane Blackman, 'Scavenger and Bricoleur: A Critical Analysis of Dick Hebdige's Repurposing of Subculture Through the Intersection of Biography and History',

in the Subcultures Network (eds), *Hebdige and Subculture in the Twenty-First Century* (Cham: Palgrave Macmillan, 2020).
38 Hebdige, 'The Meaning of Mod', p. 78.
39 Hebdige, *Subculture*, pp. 79–80.
40 Paul Sweetman, 'Structure, Agency, Subculture: The CCCS, *Resistance through Rituals*, and Post-Subcultural Studies', *Sociological Research Online*, 18:4 (2013), 227–36. https://doi.org/10.5153/sro.3246.
41 Cohen, *Folk Devils*, p. lvi.
42 Hebdige, *Subculture*, p. 95.
43 Ibid., p. 129.
44 Terry Rawlings, *Mod*; Hewitt, *The Sharper World*; Anderson, *Mods*; Weight, *Mod*.
45 Burton, *Parallel Lives*, pp. 30–1.
46 Ibid., p. 31.
47 Cited in Richard Smith, 'Do You Wanna Dance?', *Gay Times* (June 2000), p. 107.
48 Cited in Bullock, *The Velvet Mafia*, p. 188.
49 Barry Miles, *London Calling: A countercultural History of London since 1945* (London: Atlantic Books, 2010), p. 173. With thanks to Ian Massey for guiding us towards information on Patrick Procktor's painting *Shades*.
50 Ian Massey, *Patrick Procktor: Art and Life* (Lewes: Unicorn Press, 201), p. 82.
51 Miles, *London Calling*, p. 173.
52 See recollections in Anderson, *Mods*, pp. 81, 167–72.
53 Cited in Smith, 'Do You Wanna Dance?', p. 107.
54 Rawlings, *Mod*, p. 57.
55 Shaun Cole, *Don We Now Our Gay Apparel: Gay Men's Dress in the Twentieth Century* (Oxford: Berg, 2000).
56 See: Smith, 'Do You Wanna Dance?', pp. 106–7; Shaun Cole, 'Queers and Mods: Social and Sartorial Interaction in London's Carnaby Street', in Andy Reilly, Patricia Hunt-Hurs and Kimberley A. Miller-Spillman (eds), *The Meanings of Dress*, 3rd edn (New York: Fairchild 2012); Reed, *The King of Carnaby Street*, p. 241.
57 Cited in Cole, 'Queers and Mods', p. 218.
58 Cf: Cohn, *Today There Are No Gentlemen*; Cole, *Don We Now*.
59 Cited in Reed, *The King of Carnaby Street*, p. 18.
60 Cole, *Don We Now*, p. 72.
61 Cohn, *Today There Are No Gentlemen*; Cole, *Don We Now*.
62 Cited in Reed, *The King of Carnaby Street*, p. 16.
63 Cited in Paul Gorman, *The Look: Adventures in Rock and Pop Fashion* (London: Adelita, 2006), p. 53.
64 Cited in Gorman, *The Look*, p. 55.
65 Cited in Reed, *The King of Carnaby Street*, p. 11.
66 Patricia Juliana Smith, '"You don't have to say you love me": The Camp Masquerades of Dusty Springfield', in Patricia Juliana Smith (ed.), *The Queer Sixties* (New York: Routledge, 1999), p. 105.

67 Reed, *The King of Carnaby Street*, p. 118.
68 Peter Burton, cited in Cole, 'Queers and Mods', p. 215.
69 Nik Cohn, 'Carnaby Street', in Hewitt, *The Sharper Word*, p. 51.
70 Cited in Anderson, *Mods*, p. 37.
71 Ibid.
72 Bullock, *The Velvet Mafia*.
73 George Melly, *Revolt Into Style: Pop Arts Since the 50s and 60s* (London: Penguin, 1970), p. 169.
74 Cited in Rawlings, *Mod*, pp. 93–4.
75 Cited in Alastair McKay, 'Lambert & Stamp: The men who made The Who', BBC Arts (2015), www.bbc.co.uk/programmes/articles/2Ss51MfRT3lF4fRY2jxWCvg/lambert-stamp-the-men-who-made-the-who (accessed 4 February 2022).
76 Cited in McKay, 'Lambert & Stamp'.
77 See Rawlings, *Mod*; Weight, *Mod*.
78 Ann Shillinglaw, '"Give us a kiss": Queer Codes, Male Partnering and the Beatles', in Smith (ed.), *The Queer Sixties*, pp. 127–9.
79 Cole, 'Queers and Mods', p. 215.
80 Cole, *Don We Now*, p. 64.
81 Cohn, 'Mods', in Hewitt, *The Sharper Word*, p. 167.
82 Justin de Villeneuve, cited in Gorman, *The Look*, p. 37.
83 See, e.g., Bruno Latour, *Reassembling the Social: An Introduction to Actor-Network-Theory* (Oxford: Oxford University Press, 2005); John Law and John Hassard, *Actor Network Theory and After* (Oxford: Blackwell, 1999).
84 Latour, *Reassembling*, p. 238.
85 Sweetman, 'Structure, Agency, Subculture'.
86 Relatedly, in the context of this chapter, gay men might be seen as a homogenous and self-contained subcultural group, each responding to social factors in the same or similar ways, ignoring broader network connections and intersectional subject positional differences between individual gay men.
87 Hebdige, 'The Meaning of Mod', p. 71 (emphasis added).
88 Ibid., p. 74.
89 Weight, *Mod*, p. 87.
90 As indicated, there is also a gendered aspect to Hebdige's dismissal of those 'following in Mary Quant's footsteps'.
91 Latour, *Reassembling*, pp. 152–3.
92 Sweetman, 'Structure, Agency, Subculture'.
93 Caroline Evans, 'Dreams That Only Money Can Buy … Or, The Shy Tribe In Flight from Discourse', *Fashion Theory*, 1:2 (1997), 179.

7

'You just let your hair down': lesbian parties and clubs in the 1960s and early 1970s

Alison Oram

By exploring young lesbians' enjoyment of dancing and music, this chapter introduces some new perspectives on youth cultures of the 1960s and early 1970s. Excluded (at least as 'out' lesbians) from youth clubs and alternative youth subcultures, young gay women struggled to find community among other queer people where they could express their sexuality, make friends and seek partners. Some travelled to far-flung places in the deepest countryside for private parties, relishing the mobility of scooters, motorcycles and cars. They developed lesbian social networks and, in some cities, enjoyed the growing number of gay-tolerant clubs and bars. These pleasure-seeking women were not especially young. By the time they found congenial social circles through luck or persistence, many lesbians were in their thirties.

Lesley, who grew up in a village just outside Hull, remembered watching a short TV play in 1974, titled *Girl*.[1] The play addresses the aftermath of a lesbian relationship in the army, as one woman leaves the service and confronts her ex-lover. Lesley said:

> One thing I remember very strongly, and I remember being horrendously embarrassed but really wanting to watch it, and it was about these two women in the army, it was a television play [...] and my grandma was staying for some reason and she was there and my mum and dad and we were watching it [...] I think I must have been about 17 [...] I don't remember much about the play but I remember at one point they had Dusty Springfield singing 'This Girl's in Love With You' and they were dancing in the NAAFI, these two women, and I knew, you know, absolutely, that's what I was and where I wanted to be, and I did actually look at joining the forces at that point as well [...] as a way, [to find] a womanly environment as I saw it.[2]

The sensuality of the two women dancing together and kissing made vividly real Lesley's feelings about her own sexual desires. Her embarrassment highlights the potency of this TV story about lesbians and her understanding that same-sex desire was something that should remain hidden. A powerful mixture of emotions – a sense of shame, a sudden self-knowledge, her delight at seeing two women embracing and dancing, and the hope that there might be 'a womanly environment', a lesbian community beyond her village – are all at play in Lesley's recollection. Oral histories like hers, which combine memories of desire and identity with the emotional and physical charge of music and dance, open up fresh approaches to the history of youth and sexuality. Dusty Springfield, the iconic British soul singer whose hit song Lesley remembered, is also significant here. Her songs of love and heartbreak, and the rumours that she was gay herself, were an important soundtrack to lesbian cultures in this period and later: her song titles punctuate this chapter as sub-headings.

While sharing the pleasures of contemporary pop music, lesbian social spaces remained very separated from parallel mainstream youth cultures, and usually operated in semi-secrecy. To discuss the interplay of same-sex desires, music and dancing, I draw on some underused stories from a range of oral history collections, including the Lesbian Identity Project (2000s) in the north of England and the Brighton Ourstory interviews made in the late 1980s. The chapter seeks to move beyond London's lesbian bar and club culture, already discussed in detail elsewhere by Rebecca Jennings and Jill Gardiner.[3] Complementing these important studies, it drills down into the variety of social contexts that shaped lesbian cultures, emphasising the importance of private spaces for lesbian socialising and discussing regional experiences as well as those in the capital. Indeed geographic location played a major role in whether lesbians could access queer community. There was a stark distinction between those young lesbians who found their way to these convivial places and had a lot of fun in the 1960s and others, possibly the majority, who remained more isolated and outside them.

'I Just Don't Know What to do with Myself':[4] lesbians in the 1960s

Histories of youth culture, sexuality and pop music in the post-war years often emphasise their challenge to adult society. Yet despite this supposed transgressiveness, youth culture in this period was relentlessly heteronormative – as indeed the subsequent histories of it and their assumptions have also been. Post-war youth clubs were mostly mixed-sex. One explicit aim was to socialise teenage girls and boys into the wholesome courtship and gender complementarity thought necessary for successful modern marriage. Experts even argued that mixed youth clubs helped to prevent (male) homosexuality and made girls less tomboyish.[5] Alternative youth subcultures, from the Teds to the hippies, also emphasised heterosexuality. The popular music associated with them was based on boy–girl romance and sex as much as it was in mainstream pop.[6] Contemporary debates about 'sexual permissiveness' and the effects of the new rock 'n' roll music probably deepened assumptions about teenagers' heterosexuality. Despite the widening scope of youth cultures, there seemed to be no place for lesbians.

Lesley was lucky to catch a glimpse of lesbian sexuality on the TV. Contrary to popular belief, the first lesbian kiss on British TV was not in the 1994 Channel 4 soap *Brookside* but twenty years earlier in this 1974 BBC play *Girl*.[7] What is more, the lesbian sex was not confined to a kiss and a smoochy dance: the play includes a two-minute flashback to the couple in happier times, naked in bed together. Such representations were extremely rare, and indeed the play's transmission was preceded by a special announcement warning of its controversial subject matter.[8] Sexual relationships between women were heavily stigmatised in the 1960s and 1970s, but there was gradually increasing public awareness. The overwhelming social and moral emphasis on marriage and the family in post-war Britain meant that homosexuality was usually cast as a social problem.[9] Women's sexuality was viewed almost wholly in relation to men's, and their sexual independence criticised. Popular press stereotypes veered wildly between the predatory lesbian stealing wives 'over the teacups', to the sad and lonely 'odd girl out', living in a bedsit and excluded from family life.[10] But references to female homosexuality were so sparse that many women didn't come across the words or even the concept in their youth.[11] In this milieu of disapproval and near-invisibility, young women with same-sex desires commonly felt anxiety and shame.

Like Lesley, many young women trying to make sense of their lesbian desires were attracted to the women's military services as a way of leaving home, acquiring skills and finding same-sex companionship.[12] Indeed that is Chrissie's reason for joining up in the play *Girl*, and she refers cynically to the way that the women's corps are represented in army advertising as 'a dyke's dream'.[13] Homosexual relationships continued to be illegal in the services for both women and men until 2000, however, and many women were dishonourably discharged on these grounds. In civilian life, too, lesbians were usually firmly in the closet at work. Marriage rates boomed in the post-war years – by the mid-1960s 96 per cent of women were married by the age of 45 – and the average age at first marriage for women dropped to an astonishing 22 by 1971.[14] So powerful were the social pressures to marry and the lack of other alternatives that many young women who were already aware of their same-sex desires felt they had no other option but to follow their peer group up the aisle.[15]

Women who had found a same-sex partner often lived in coupled secrecy, knowing few other lesbians and fearing heterosexual prejudice. Some were isolated in regional towns, but even those in the major cities might have had no points of contact with other gay women. These experiences of isolation were very real and very common. But in the 1960s, an increasing minority of lesbians (though they might have preferred to describe themselves as 'gay girls')[16] found or created their own fun, and successfully sought friendships, sexual relationships and community in a variety of lesbian and gay subcultures. It is these places and positive changes that I want to focus on. The possibilities for same-sex dancing, courtship and socialising were expanding in the 1960s. Queer theorist Elizabeth Freeman emphasises the importance of celebrating the pleasures of the queer past and indeed of recreating them, rather than focusing only on the feelings of shame and hurt in the archives.[17] By exploring the playful elements of the lesbian past, the remainder of this chapter contributes to this approach, to what I've elsewhere referred to as 'the ludic turn' in queer history.[18]

Lesley came to a realisation of her sexual feelings while watching the two women in the TV play dance together to a Dusty Springfield record. For her, the fantasy of sexual expression and community was made real through the transcendence of dance and music. Her next thought was of how to find such places and such women. The earliest organised lesbian group, The Minorities Research Group (MRG) and its newsletter *Arena Three*, set up in 1963–64, strove for middle-class respectability and the social acceptance of lesbians. *Arena Three* was far more likely to review recent novels than to publicise the growing number of gay-friendly bars. It barely mentioned the established London lesbian club The Gateways, but it did encourage the formation of local groups and private socialising. A breakaway London-based group, Kenric, set up in 1965, put greater stress on meeting up and fun and quickly grew its membership, continuing to this day.[19] By the mid-1960s, then, there were two routes to lesbian community: first, through private parties in people's flats and houses, and second, via the limited number of clubs and bars that tolerated lesbians and gay men.

'In the Middle of Nowhere':[20] lesbian private parties

Both the MRG branches and Kenric organised lesbian parties (also called socials) in their localities. Others were organised more informally by friends. These private parties were very important for lesbians' social lives, for dancing, friendship and forming relationships.[21] The MRG was quickly successful in encouraging regional lesbian networks, at least in some cities. Doreen lived in 1960s London in her thirties and was involved in the MRG.

When she moved to Leeds she found other lesbians there and in West Yorkshire through those networks.

> when I came up to Leeds in '67 [...] there was a lass had a farmhouse outside Keighley and once a month we used to have a get-together there [...] we all became friends type of thing [...] [and] we danced.

These small, self-selecting groups of lesbians created their own community over time. Doreen explained the need to dissemble at work:

> then you had problems at work next day [...] the girls'd say to you, Oh what did you do at the weekend? and you couldn't say it, well you'd say you'd been to a party but you, you just … you couldn't say, you just had to gloss over who was there – 'cause then the next question was, Oh did you meet any nice guys? you know [...] I mean, you lived a lie… you had to … work was a lie … you couldn't be … you lived two lives.

At a lesbian party or social, in contrast, she could finally be herself, as a gay woman among other lesbians. Doreen acted as secretary of the Leeds group for about ten years: 'we used to put a supper on and we danced, talked, and you just let your hair down and you could relax completely and utterly and that was the whole idea of it'.[22] This metaphor of letting your hair down and being yourself was repeated by many other women in describing the relief of finding gay community.

For Doreen, this private socialising was much more congenial than the mixed gay pubs that were the alternative. In the late 1960s or early 1970s she once went to The New Penny, the long-standing gay pub in central Leeds.[23] 'I was dreading that I might meet somebody from work!' She and her friend felt very uncomfortable there and found its gay clientele 'coarse'.

Judith, a social worker, found community in Manchester through an unlikely route – her liberal psychiatrist. She moved to Rochdale aged 29 in 1963 while she was in the process of coming to terms with her lesbian feelings. Her psychiatrist told her that:

> one of his other patients was lesbian and was throwing a party the next day on the Saturday, would I like to go to it? And I thought, good GOD! you know. From what I've heard of psychiatrists since, I must have just fallen on my feet. So I was well tanked up with three sorts of drugs and then a lot of whisky [...] and I walked in and it was wonderful, I just felt immediately at home.[24]

Judith quickly found lesbian friends in the Greater Manchester area through this MRG group and became one of the founding members of the (mixed gay) Campaign for Homosexual Equality, which originated there.[25]

Lesbian parties were often held in far-flung places, and the oral histories suggest that many women were very mobile in their eagerness to seek community and lovers. Judith continued living in Rochdale, and said: 'I'd got friends obviously who were Manchester-centred ... the amount of petrol I spent travelling to, you know, Cheadle, and Cheadle overnight and back again and this sort of thing.' She also described the impetus to seek partners outside her home turf, for fear of being outed. 'I think a lot of professional women do that because I know a doctor who goes miles for her sexual life.'[26] Although they were not necessarily middle-class events, private lesbian socials were particularly important – indeed essential – for women who sought discretion, and were the only alternative to the more socially mixed but often seedy gay pubs of the 1960s. Doreen described how she travelled from Leeds to the parties in Keighley: '[short laugh] in those days I had a scooter then and I used to take the record player plus records on the back of it [laughs] to this place'. Her laughter evokes the fun of her youth. It is unlikely that the Keighley farmhouse was accessible by public transport. Yet: 'everybody turned up from – we had people from Newcastle came down ... Rochdale there were people, Manchester'. The portable record player and the willingness to travel symbolised their determination to have a good time and party.[27]

Barbara ran a South Coast MRG group in the Brighton area for about three years in the 1960s. The women met in each other's houses: 'We would do the rounds.'[28] These parties could be quite intimate, among a small group who knew each other, and clearly music was central to the fun. Barbara and her partner's home was the favoured venue: 'our house seemed to be the base where they could always come ... we used to periodically put on these dos, oh, they were lovely. We'd say to the neighbours, "Oh, I'm having a party tonight, we might be making a bit of noise but come and join us."' Barbara was lucky in having an understanding neighbour in the (relatively) open gay city of Brighton in the 1960s, although the precise nature of her friendship group was 'never, never openly discussed'.[29]

In Brighton and London, where there was a more developed lesbian social scene, other lesbian (and mixed gay) parties could be more spontaneous, as people spilled out of gay pubs at chucking-out time. Sheila said of Brighton:

> In those days we had a lot of private parties. You know, probably when you went to the loo in the club, you'd bump into somebody and say, 'If you'd like to bring a bottle and come back, we're having a party.' [...] There weren't that many places to go to so I think the tendency was that you went to private parties ... it would all be women.

The author Maureen Duffy bemoaned the English licensing laws, which meant that even the Gateways private members' club in London had to close at 'the sacred hour of eleven'.

For those who feel the night is just starting there is the problem of where to go. An impromptu party is the usual answer. Bottles are crammed into pockets, car doors slam, scooters are revved for the long run out to the edge of Essex or deep into Middlesex where someone has a large flat with accommodating neighbours. These are like any other parties with the one difference: men dance with men and women with women.[30]

Again, women's personal mobility appears to be essential for living a full lesbian social life. In a period when women's wages were still quite low it is striking how many lesbians, in very ordinary jobs, had scooters or a car. The level of harassment experienced especially by butch lesbians who wore male clothing and short hair was such that personal transport or a taxi was necessary to avoid comments or worse on the street or on public transport.[31]

'I'll Try Anything':[32] lesbian club cultures

By the 1960s, one or more pubs which tolerated queer people could be found in most major cities. Lesbians frequented some of these back bars and clubs, though in some the men froze women out. Some of these pub bars were rather shady and rough, where lesbians mixed – in a kind of radical conviviality[33] – not only with gay men but other marginalised people who were not welcome in more respectable venues, including people of colour, seamen in port cities and sex workers. Vito described:

> the first gay pub I went to in the mid-1960s when I was serving in the Women's Royal Naval Service in Lee-on-Solent. The Horse & Groom [in Southampton Docks] was extraordinary – it was a rough place that welcomed everyone – Black seamen, queer people and so on – people who wouldn't have been welcomed in ordinary places as themselves. Many women dressed as men and had men's names; often their girlfriends worked as prostitutes. I can still feel the excitement of being able to be there as myself for two hours of the day and be with a girlfriend.[34]

In west London, Carol's landlady warned her off the nearby Fiesta pub as being full of queers: 'she said it was a club where gay men and women went in drag, and not in drag, and there were criminals and convicts, blacks and everything [...] "you want to keep away from all them". So of course I wanted to go down there!'[35]

Many clubs were primarily drinking places, and often had longer licensing hours than pubs. Some had music, whether a piano or a jukebox, and a very few had a small dancefloor, providing the opportunity for the kind of romantic lesbian dancing to Dusty Springfield that Lesley remembered from the TV play. We have some evidence of the music that was favoured by patrons. Brighton's gay and lesbian-friendly clubs and bars were the most numerous and densely located of any urban area in the country; indeed the town was often referred to as the gay 'mecca'.[36] Its mostly mixed or men-only venues ranged from smart hotel bars to seedy basements. Many gay women and men interviewed for Brighton Ourstory's book *Daring Hearts* (1992) remembered piano music in several pubs and clubs and this traditional form of entertainment certainly continued until the mid-1960s at least. Sheila started to go to Pigott's in the 1950s, when she was in her twenties. She said:

> it was mostly girls [...] Dolly played the piano. This little lady used to play at the piano with her jangling bracelets, cigarette hanging on her mouth. And we used to have this sing-song, the old tunes, 'Don't laugh at me cos I'm a fool', that's right, 'Freight Train'. [...] Oh yes, they used to stand up at the piano. It's not a very big pub. [...] It was quite tatty, all really dark brown. It was just ordinary working class.[37]

As other clubs opened up, Sheila's crowd (and other lesbians) moved on to the back bar of the Spotted Dog, and Dolly followed. 'She liked the gay crowd so she always played the piano. She had a great following.'[38] Singing around the piano together in these pubs helped to forge bonds of community and friendship among their lesbian clientele.

Music also acted as background noise against which people could flirt and gossip. Grant described a venue at the classier end of the spectrum, the 'very ornate' Regina Club 'with a magnificent flight of stairs'. He started to play the piano there. 'The music had to be cover for conversation. It wasn't to be listened to. Although if someone wanted to convey something to someone else without going up and saying it, they would ask me to play whatever it was. [...] "Hold Me, Thrill Me" was a great favourite with the lesbians. So was "I Hate Men", from "Kiss Me Kate".'[39] Such songs could easily be retrofitted in this way for new gendered and sexualised meanings.

During the 1960s two or three of a new type of club opened up in Brighton, some short-lived, where women could dance as well as drink. Sandie, who arrived in Brighton in the early 1960s described 'a wonderful club', the mixed Variety Club in Middle Street: 'it was on three or four different floors, perhaps three. In the basement there was a disco. Ohh, that was wonderful. It was the first disco we'd ever been to, gay disco.' The Regency Club operated in another basement, with a clientele that 'was a third lesbian, a third gay men and a third straight but everybody was quite, quite happy. It was very working class, you'd get bus drivers of all three persuasions. [...] There was room for a small dancefloor, probably twelve feet by twelve feet, something like that and no-one would turn a hair at two boys dancing or two girls.'[40]

Being introduced to a lesbian or gay club could be an abrupt and intense experience of coming out. Vicky said: 'I didn't know what "a club" was.' Once she realised that the people in men's clothes there were women: 'Well, I couldn't believe my eyes. It suddenly began to gel that there were other women in this world that actually danced with women and they were kissing, and I couldn't believe this. I thought, "This is wonderful".'[41] In contrast, Janice, perhaps uneasy at confronting her sexual feelings in this way, felt rather shaken the first time she saw women dancing together at the Variety Club in Brighton. '[T]hat was the first gay club I ever went to. The first time also, I think, seeing two girls dance together in the way that they were. I have to say it shocked me. I know I drank a lot to cope with it.'[42] Even with just a few clubs in the town, class distinctions were remembered. Margaret discussed a short-lived gay women's night at the British Legion Club where she went in her thirties. 'You could have a drink, coffee, dance – that must have had a jukebox – just sit and chat.' She felt that 'that place was the best place of all. Because when you went in the drinking clubs there was an element of rough, tough girls but these were more sort of professional. They seemed to be nicer types of people.'[43]

Brighton's gay scene was known far and wide. Coach trips there were organised by the Robin Hood lesbian club in London, and carloads of women from the Gateways club or from Kenric groups would 'scream down what was then the A23'.[44] Valerie compared the Brighton and London clubs. The Queen of Clubs 'was quite nice but to me it wasn't quite like the London clubs, it was much sort of quieter and I was surprised to find a lot of older people there. […] it was much more like a social gathering than anything else, whereas the London clubs tended to have much more of an accent on dancing and picking people up'.[45]

'Come for a Dream':[46] The Gateways club

Frustratingly, we don't have much detail about the kind of music that was played in the Brighton clubs, beyond that it was vinyl records or from a jukebox, that is, contemporary pop music. Women enjoyed dancing in those clubs that had a dancefloor, and as Janice said, they danced together 'in the way that they were', in a sexual way. There are many more accounts of the Gateways club in Chelsea, London, the longest-running (until 1985) and best-known lesbian members club.[47] Dusty Springfield was definitely on the playlist here. Women describe the atmosphere on most nights as exciting, daunting and sexually charged. Vito described entering the club. 'There was something about the layout, you'd be at the top of these really high steps and you can look down into it and Smithy was on the door, quite a bulky tough woman, and that was pretty scary.'[48] Walking down into the dark and smoky club, being scrutinised first by the woman on the door and then assessed by the other women – 'everyone looked at you' as you went in – gave a feeling of entry to a secret and sexualised queer underground world. Former patrons described it as a pick-up place; in one woman's words: 'it was cruiserama'.[49] Cynthia found the Gateways intimidating on her first introduction to it: 'There didn't seem to be any people like me – sort of ordinary quiet shy middle-class girls. And everyone seemed to be so frightfully self-confident, knowing all the latest dances and the latest pop tunes.' Nevertheless, 'within a few months, I was going there quite regularly'.[50]

The novelist Maureen Duffy, also a regular, wrote a 1966 account of the club. On a weekend evening at the Gateways, at 8.30, she records: 'The juke-box is kept constantly fed but hardly anyone is ready to dance yet [...] Each new arrival peers round defensively for her group though there are a few walkers by themselves who stand on the edge of the dancefloor, coolly appraising. Soon the numbers will grow to fifty and then a hundred.' An hour or so later, 'the floor is rocking under the dancers' feet'. Later still: 'The floor becomes so crowded that it is impossible to do more than gyrate on the spot and by half-past-ten nearly two hundred people will be packed between the bulging walls. Eyes smart and water in the smoke.' Duffy described the popularity of 'the beat numbers [...] because of the opportunities for display like the dancing of cranes and for sheer physical response to rhythm. Neither partner is committed except to the music.'[51] The sexual charge of contemporary rock and pop songs could clearly be appropriated for lesbian enjoyment, despite the ostensibly heterosexual nature of the lyrics.[52] Duffy's description evokes the physical delight of movement and the visceral sense of losing oneself in the crowd on the packed dancefloor. This dynamic enjoyment of dance and music can be a kind of *jouissance*, a sexual pleasure of abandonment within a crowd of other women.[53] Like the communal singing in some of the Brighton bars, 'dancing to the same tune' created a feeling of shared identity and belonging with other gay women.

For the individual or couple, dancing was also a performance directed at other people. In a medium-sized gay club like the Gateways, where one wouldn't know all the other 200 women, dancing was a means of flirting, of meeting and picking up potential sexual partners. And it might be a way of asserting the coupled relationship of two women, in an embrace displaying sexual desire. 'Lovers dance locked together to the slower records', wrote Maureen Duffy.[54] Many of the regulars put it more bluntly in describing 'the Gateways Grind'. 'That was the only dance most people knew', said Vito, who rather disparaged the Gateways. 'One leg goes between the [other woman's] legs so that your hips are adjoining and it's a sort of a swaying movement, usually to a slow dance, so you're really in a clinch [....] and just rubbing yourself against each other basically!'[55]

Lesbian nightlife and sexuality gained considerable publicity in 1968 with the release of the feature film *The Killing of Sister George*. Around fifteen minutes of the film took place in the Gateways club and the precise street address of the club was given by the lead characters as they prepared to go to a fancy dress party there. The real life managers of the club played a part, and its lesbian patrons were recruited as extras, in the eight minutes of scenes of the club's crowded dancefloor with women dancing very closely together.[56] Although the film has been much-criticised for portraying stereotypes of lesbians, it was immensely important in advertising the existence of lesbian clubs, which were otherwise mainly found through word of mouth.[57]

Although the Gateways and other clubs paralleled heterosexual youth culture, there were some important differences. While some patrons may have been teenagers, the majority were a lot older than their counterparts at straight dances. Doreen was in her thirties by the time she came out and went to the Gateways in London, subsequently moving up north to Leeds in 1967.[58] Lesbian and gay clubs were conducive to same-sex pairing up, but not necessarily to longer-lasting relationships. Some couples might settle down, 'set up home together [and] drift away from the club'.[59] But the clubs were seen by some lesbians as places where women might go through strings of successive girlfriends and return for the next one.

'Girls will be Boys, and Boys will be Girls':[60] lesbian courtship

In most clubs in the 1960s, dancing and courtship were regulated by the dynamic of butch and femme role-playing, which added further complexity to the way young lesbians could access the culture.[61] Women new to the club scene often expressed their shock when the people they'd initially believed were men turned out to be women. At the Variety Club in Brighton, Janice said: 'There were two definite types of gender. There was the sort of shirts and ties brigade, with very cropped hair, and there was the frilly frock brigade. And I found this very hard to hack because I didn't fit into either.'[62] Newcomers often found it was easiest to conform to the dress codes of being either butch – expressing various degrees of masculinity in clothing, haircut and appearance – or femme, which often meant a hyper-, almost a camp, femininity. In terms of dancing and flirting, if someone wanted to dance with a femme, they were supposed to ask the butch woman whom she was with, otherwise 'people used to get smacked around'.[63] Jocelyn said: 'A very butch little number came up to me and said, "I'd like to ask you to dance but first I must know whether you are butch or fem". I said, "It depends on who I'm in bed with!" … I always found that a bit strange. I thought, you know, you were both women, that's what it's all about.'[64]

There were certainly regional differences in how much emphasis was placed on butch and femme identities. Jan and her four friends from Essex 'piled into a car, an old Vauxhall Viva' to drive down to Brighton one Saturday, having heard that it was 'a real swinging town'. At the Queen of Clubs, she said 'that was when I realised that there were such things as butch and fem, because in Clacton we all just used to wear trousers and sort of sloppy sweatshirts. These women really looked like men, you know. I could never actually understand it. And these very, very feminine women … But it was fun, it was good … It was the dress that I couldn't get over. I mean there were a few in Clacton that used to wear ties and suits but nothing quite so outrageous as there was down in Brighton.'[65] From the mid-1960s, however, fashions began to change and 'people didn't wear suits and frocks so much, it was more unisex'.[66]

The butch-femme dynamic might also be evident at private parties. When Judith went to her first lesbian party in Manchester she said: 'I didn't even consider what to dress in, I just put on an ordinary little dress … when I walked into the room I realised that there were about five women in dresses and the whole damn lot of them, about another twenty more, were in trousers, I was absolutely staggered.' Wearing dresses brought Judith a lot of attention when she hung out with the 'New Group' in Manchester, an offshoot of the MRG. '[I]t was more butch or middling than femme […] I used to enjoy it because I had pretty dresses, had a whale of a time.'[67] Other kinds of flirting and pairing off might go on at parties, in comparison to the slightly more formal rules about who asked whom to dance in the semi-public world of the clubs. Sandie described the parties in Brighton, after the clubs shut. '[W]e used to play party games too, like spin the bottle and all that rubbish but it was fun. We used to play murder and sardines and all those sort of screaming games, where everyone has an hysterical time […] You got around to kiss the person that you wanted to kiss that you would never normally get the opportunity to.'[68]

'I Close my Eyes and Count to Ten':[69] lesbians' music choices

The stories these lesbians told of the music they heard, danced to and made love to gives us new histories of courtship culture among young people in this period and the ways that mainstream pop blurred across these private and semi-public spaces. At the Gateways, the music came from a juke box, so patrons chose what they wanted to hear. Mary recalled how 'it gave me a huge buzz to be there when it was crowded and there was just a sea of women like us. We danced to a lot of Dusty Springfield. Roy Orbison's "Only the Lonely (know the way I feel tonight)" was the one that people really danced to. That kind of yearning theme was very popular, and the whole Dusty Springfield attitude of unhappy love. It seemed to correspond to some sense that most of the world didn't understand [us].'[70] As Maureen Duffy wrote: 'The tunes are those popular in the charts at the moment but there is a distinct preference for songs to and about girls. Some catch on because they can be very equivocally interpreted.'[71] But as Jill Gardiner makes clear, Gateways patrons also enjoyed more upbeat dance tunes. One woman said: '"Walk Right Back", the Everlys, that was a great favourite. In the '60s the floor was packed with people dancing the twist, usually very well. Helen Shapiro was just coming in – "Walking Back to Happiness"'.[72]

Not all gay women happily followed this Gateways diet of music. Carol disdained the 'posers' at the club and thought 'the music was naff'. She preferred a decidedly downmarket venue, the Casino, off Wardour Street in Soho. In the early 1960s, it was popular with gay girls 'from all over the country'. The Casino was a late-night coffee bar, and like similar places in regional cities including Brighton and Plymouth: 'felt comfortable because everyone accepted everybody', the clientele including gay people, runaways, sex workers, touts, crooks and drug dealers. Alcohol was not served, but this was far from being a respectable venue for young people. 'It was like American style, coffee, teas, Coca-Cola and drugs. Lots of heroin going around and dope. You name it, it was there. But it was a great place to be.' This, for Carol, was also because of the music played there. 'They played all reggae, Blue Beat it was called in those days, it was like a Jamaican reggae.'[73] Blue beat, also known as ska, was probably also played in the Notting Hill pubs and clubs that had a mixed gay, lesbian and local Black clientele.

It was the great British 'white queen of soul', Dusty Springfield, who was most often mentioned by lesbians. Her heyday was the 1960s, though for gay women her iconic status continued into the 1970s when one of her hits, 'This Girl's in Love With You', featured in the TV play remembered by Lesley, as the two women kissed in the barracks. Indeed, one of the lovers comments to the other that the song is 'top of the gay girls' hit parade'.[74] Dusty's glamorous image, her emotionally super-charged soul music and the rumours that she was gay herself all contributed to her aura. With her blonde beehive and heavy eye make-up she was a hugely successful icon of the 1960s. Her amazing voice conveyed a depth of feeling – especially about lost love – that resonated with gay women as well as straight fans. Dusty Springfield's performance of an absurdly over-the-top camp femininity spoke to femme identity among lesbians, while also queering conventional gender categories, as indeed those more ordinary femmes were also doing. She has been described as a female drag queen, playing herself as if she were a Black woman singer in her vocal style and as a femme gay man in her soul anthems and melodramatic torch songs.[75]

Many lesbians were Dusty fans without being aware of the increasing rumours that she was gay herself. Others enjoyed the extra thrill of believing, or knowing, that she inhabited the same world as they did. This shared fantasy, myth-making and knowingness helped to cement a shared lesbian culture around the star.[76] There was widespread gossip that Dusty sometimes went to the Gateways.[77] 'I wasn't there but a girl I knew who worked there told me that when Dusty used to come down they'd shut it [to members]. Dusty would go in about twelve or one o'clock with a crowd and they'd open it up for her. So no-one really saw her.'[78] Janice, one of the Brighton contributors to *Daring Hearts*, strongly hinted at an affair with the singer. The relationship 'was with quite a famous person who was in the charts at that time'. After a night at a club, she was invited to a party. 'So we ended up in this beautiful penthouse flat in Hove and there I met this lady who I had a very brief liaison with for about three months or something but I'm not going to say anything about it, it's not really fair because they are still performing today.'[79]

Dusty Springfield's sexuality was for years an open secret in the pop music world, but from the late 1960s her public image as a 'bachelor girl' started to crumble. Press articles began to note that she shared her home with another woman musician (in fact her lover) and she evaded personal questions in interviews.[80] She effectively outed herself, at least as bisexual, in a 1970 interview with the *Evening Standard*:

> Many other people say I'm bent, and I've heard it so many times that I've almost learned to accept it … Girls run after me a lot and it doesn't upset me. I know I'm perfectly as capable of being swayed by a girl as by a boy. More and more people feel that way and I don't see why I shouldn't.[81]

On the cusp of the 1970s, the tabloids' increasing obsession with pop performers' sexuality was partly driven by the publicity given to the gay liberation movement as well as by the androgynous appearance of the new glam rockers.

'Little by Little':[82] change in the 1970s

Dusty Springfield's media coming-out took place during a few years of major expansion in lesbian and gay cultures and politics. While it did not alter lesbians' legal position, the 1967 Sexual Offences Act (which partially decriminalised sex between men) made it easier for gay venues to flourish. The counterculture had been deepening the idea of sexual permissiveness in the mid–late 1960s, though this remained largely heterosexually focused. Fuelled by these political and cultural changes, the Gay Liberation Front (GLF) rapidly took off in Britain from 1970, organising demonstrations, zaps, new publications to promote liberation and new forms of lifestyle. It staged large-scale dances and discos – to show that gay people would no longer hide away in seedy commercial clubs – and in the early years of the GLF, lesbians were certainly a part of these activities.[83] But the politics of out and proud gay liberationists clashed with the earlier more discreet cultures. Lesbians from the GLF got into a fight with the management of the Gateways after trying to sell tickets for their own GLF dance there. They subsequently leafleted and critiqued the club as a commercial venue designed to make money out of lesbians, and for its attitude that lesbians were best off staying in the closet.[84]

The growing number of commercial gay and lesbian bars and clubs could now be found more easily through the rapidly expanding lesbian and gay press, through listings magazines and via gay switchboards (set up from 1974 onwards).[85] *Sappho* magazine, which followed directly on from the MRG and *Arena Three*, placed more emphasis on social events, and by 1972 had made a deal with the Gateways to allow subscribers to become instant members of the club. *Sappho* began to organise its own lesbian discos in London, for Christmas and Valentine's Day, for example.[86] In some university cities, student societies provided venues for lesbian and gay social events and organisations from the early–mid-1970s.[87] These alternative discos – often fund-raising for political campaigns – offered a third kind of social space alongside the commercial scene and the private parties. The latter continued to be important for many lesbians who needed discretion in relation to their work or family lives.

Despite this expansion in the early 1970s, many young women in small towns and cities, like Lesley in Hull, remained isolated and far from any 'scene'. Into her early twenties Lesley stayed out late at nightclubs with her straight friends and made a pretence of being 'normal', wearing 'lots of make-up' and dresses. Her story can be replicated thousands of times. She said: 'I did try going out with men for a while but as a total front, I mean I knew it was *a total front*.' Lesley eventually made a more congenial group of 'oddball' friends at college but it was only in the later 1970s, when she went to Bradford University aged 20 as a mature student, that she first met other women who identified as lesbians: *'that was the first time I knew anything about lesbians'*.[88] Lesley's story, which is fairly typical, shows the continuing difficulties faced by young lesbians in finding others like themselves with whom to make friends and party, and how lesbian and gay social networks remained very constrained in the late twentieth century.

Janice said of the 1960s: 'Everything was new, wasn't it? [...] certainly, from the lesbian point of view, it was the start of a whole new era for lesbians to actually come out as being like that, more so than ever.'[89] This period saw a gradual expansion of places where young lesbians could meet, with more private parties and lesbian and gay clubs as alternatives to the traditional but often seedy queer pubs. Like their straight peers, lesbians could enjoy the new styles of pop music and dancing – the twist, rock 'n' roll, close couple dancing – in these still semi-secret venues.

But lesbians' experiences call into question many generalisations about young people in these years. Histories of youth culture which focus on the teenage to early twenties age group, and conceptualise it as either a bridge between childhood and heterosexual marriage or as a time for performing rituals of resistance against stifling mainstream conventions, miss out on the complex alternative cultures of sexuality and music which were pivotal in bringing social change to Britain. Young gay women needed knowledge, persistence and a measure of luck to overcome the social barriers of shame and exclusion and find their way to the shared pleasures and community of lesbian and gay venues. By the time they discovered these places, with a sense of relief and homecoming, lesbians were often significantly older than their heterosexual peers, often well into their twenties or thirties. Once found, their convivial gay networks were not abandoned lightly. This was less about 'youth' culture than about more mature and independent women painstakingly finding community.

Their experience also tells a different story about *where* change happened in the long 1960s – both in types of meeting places and also in terms of geographies. Lesbian club spaces and bars began to grow in many larger cities but, importantly, so did social networks which could materialise as parties and socials in smaller towns and rural areas. These places, though relatively few, were quite varied. While distinctions of social class and age were more fluid in lesbian cultures than among young straight people – the significance of a common gay identity overrode many of these differences – they were not unimportant. These sub-groupings among lesbians, including some sharp divergences in musical tastes and in politics and identity, would develop further in the 1970s.

Reusing already gathered oral histories to ask new questions about social and sexual pleasures and glean stories of gay women partying also breathes new emotions into the lesbian history of the period.[90] Highlighting the lesbian delights experienced in the past, even in otherwise difficult social contexts, adds to the ludic turn, the turn to playfulness in queer history.

These sources show how the sense of freedom, abandonment, sensuality and desire expressed through music and dancing contributed to both the individual discovery of sexual identity and the social processes of forming lesbian community.

Notes

My warm thanks to the people who commented on earlier drafts of this chapter: Justin Bengry, my History Girls writing group (Lucy Bland, Caroline Bressey, Carmen Mangion, Clare Midgley, Katherina Rowold and Cornelie Usborne) and Lucy Robinson.

1. *Girl*, BBC Birmingham for Second City Firsts, BBC 2, broadcast 25 February 1974.
2. Lesley, Lesbian Identity Project (LIP) interviews, no. 2. c.2008.
3. Rebecca Jennings, *Tomboys and Bachelor Girls: A Lesbian History of Post-war Britain 1945–71* (Manchester: Manchester University Press, 2007), chapter 4. Jill Gardiner, *From the Closet to the Screen: Women at the Gateways Club, 1945–85* (London: Pandora, 2003)
4. A 1964 UK top ten hit for Dusty Springfield.
5. Marcus Collins, *Modern Love: An Intimate History of Men and Women in Twentieth-Century Britain* (London: Atlantic Books, 2003), chapter 3, especially pp. 77, 80.
6. For the influence of mainstream pop music, see Rosalind Watkiss Singleton, '"(Today I Met) The Boy I'm Gonna Marry": Romantic Expectations of Teenage Girls in the 1960s West Midlands', in Keith Gildart et al. (eds), *Youth Culture and Social Change* (London: Palgrave, 2017), 119–46.
7. 'Myra Frances', obituary, *The Guardian*, 24 April 2021. Michael Blyth, BFI Viewing Notes for 'Girl'. BFI, n.d.
8. Blyth, BFI Viewing Notes.
9. Lesley Hall, *Sex, Gender and Social Change in Britain since 1880* (London: Palgrave Macmillan, 2013), chapters 9 and 10.
10. Alison Oram, '"Love Off The Rails" or "Over the Teacups"?: Lesbian Desire and Female Sexualities in the 1950s British Popular Press', in Heike Bauer and Matt Cook (eds), *Queer 1950s: Rethinking Sexuality in the Postwar Years* (London: Palgrave, 2012), pp. 41–57.
11. See, for example, Jane Traies, *The Lives of Older Lesbians: Sexuality, Identity and the Life Course* (London: Palgrave Macmillan, 2016), chapter 4.
12. A high proportion of lesbians had spent time in one of the military services between the 1950s and 1970s. Traies, *Older Lesbians*, chapter 5.
13. *Girl*, BBC Birmingham.
14. Jeffrey Weeks, *The World We Have Won* (London: Routledge, 2007), p. 66. Claire Langhamer, *The English in Love* (Oxford: Oxford University Press, 2013), pp. 4–5.

15 Amy Tooth Murphy, '"I Conformed; I got Married. It Seemed like a Good Idea at the time": Domesticity in Post-war Lesbian Oral History', in Brian Lewis (ed.), *British Queer History: New Approaches and Perspectives* (Manchester: Manchester University Press, 2013), pp. 165–87. A high proportion of narrators in any collections of older lesbians' life stories had been married during the 1960s and 1970s.

16 Maureen Duffy, 'Lesbian London', in Hunter Davies, *The New London Spy* (London: Anthony Blond, 1966), p. 237.

17 Elizabeth Freeman, *Time Binds: Queer Temporalities, Queer Histories* (Durham, NC: Duke University Press, 2010).

18 Alison Oram, 'Making Place and Community: Contrasting Lesbian and Gay, Feminist and Queer Oral History Projects in Brighton and Leeds', *Oral History Review* 49:2 (2022), 227–50.

19 Jennings, *Tomboys*, chapter 5. Alison Oram, 'Little By Little?: *Arena Three* and Lesbian Politics in the 1960s', in Marcus Collins (ed.), *The Permissive Society and its Enemies* (London: Rivers Oram; New York University Press, 2007).

20 A 1965 UK top ten hit for Dusty Springfield.

21 See Matt Cook and Alison Oram, *Queer Beyond London* (Manchester: Manchester University Press, 2022), chapter 6.

22 Doreen, Lesbian Identity Project (LIP) interviews, no. 7.

23 Named the Hope and Anchor until *c.*1971, the New Penny still flourishes as a gay pub.

24 Judith, LIP interviews, no 3.

25 See Cook and Oram, *Queer Beyond London*, for more on 1960s Manchester.

26 Judith, LIP interview.

27 Alison Oram, 'The Portable Lesbian Party', in Chris Brickell and Judith Collard (eds), *Queer Objects* (Manchester: Manchester University Press, 2019).

28 Brighton Ourstory, *Daring Hearts: Lesbian and Gay Lives in 50s and 60s Brighton* (Brighton: QueenSpark Books, 1992), p. 87.

29 Ourstory, *Daring Hearts*, p. 87. Also see Matt Cook, 'Local Matters: Queer Scenes in 1960s Manchester, Plymouth and Brighton', *Journal of British Studies* 59 (2020), 32–56.

30 Duffy, 'Lesbian London', p. 236.

31 Ourstory, *Daring Hearts*, p. 38 and passim.

32 A 1967 UK top twenty hit for Dusty Springfield.

33 I have borrowed this lovely phrase from Caroline Bressey.

34 Vito, recorded for 'Pride of Place: England's LGBTQ Heritage' (2016), https://historicengland.org.uk/research/inclusive-heritage/lgbtq-heritage-project/meeting-and-socialising/lesbian-clubs-and-pubs/ (accessed 22 December 2021).

35 Carol in Clare Summerskill, *Gateway to Heaven: Fifty Years of Lesbian and Gay Oral History* (Machynlleth: Tollington Press, 2012), p. 67.

36 Cook and Oram, *Queer Beyond London*.

37 Ourstory, *Daring Hearts*, p. 62. 'Freight Train', recorded by Chas McDevitt, was a skiffle chart hit in the late 1950s in the UK.

38 Ourstory, *Daring Hearts*, p. 70.

39 Ibid., pp. 63–4. Mel Carter's version of 'Hold Me, Thrill Me' was a hit in 1965.
40 Ibid., pp. 72, 74.
41 Ibid., p. 23.
42 Ibid., p. 72.
43 Ibid., p. 78. Also see Rebecca Jennings, *A Lesbian History of Britain: Love and Sex Between Women since 1500* (Oxford: Greenwood World Publishing, 2007), pp. 137–40 for a discussion of Brighton's bars.
44 Ourstory, *Daring Hearts*, pp. 59–60.
45 Ibid., p. 79.
46 A track from the Dusty Springfield album 'Come for a Dream' (1972).
47 The most detailed account of the Gateways is Gardiner, *Closet to Screen*. Also see Jennings, *Tomboys*, pp. 114–17.
48 Summerskill, *Gateway to Heaven*, pp. 68–9.
49 Discussion during 'The Gateways' online event for Queer Britain, 27 April 2021, www.queerbritain.org.uk/history-2021-the-gateways.
50 Quoted in Jennings, *Tomboys*, p. 125.
51 Duffy, 'Lesbian London', p. 232.
52 Barbara Bradby, 'Lesbians and Popular Music: Does it Matter Who is Singing?', in Gabriele Griffin (ed.), *Outwrite: Lesbianism and Popular Culture* (London: Pluto Press, 1999), pp. 148–71. Andrew August, 'Gender and 1960s Youth Culture: The Rolling Stones and the New Woman', *Contemporary British History* 23:1 (2009), 79–100.
53 Richard Middleton, *Studying Popular Music* (Milton Keynes: Open University Press, 2002), pp. 257–87. William Danaher, 'Music and Social Movements', *Sociology Compass* 4:9 (2010), 811–23.
54 Duffy, 'Lesbian London', p. 232.
55 Summerskill, *Gateway to Heaven*, p. 69. Also see Gardiner, *Closet to Screen*, p. 60.
56 For a nuanced analysis of the film and its reception, see Lizzie Thynne, '"A Comic Monster of Revue": Beryl Reid, *Sister George* and the Performance of Dykery', in Robin Griffiths (ed.), *British Queer Cinema* (London, Routledge: 2006), pp. 91–103.
57 Gardiner, *Closet to Screen*, chapter 7.
58 Doreen, LIP interview.
59 Duffy, 'Lesbian London', p. 233.
60 A line from 'Lola', a UK top ten hit in 1970 by The Kinks.
61 For a detailed discussion of butch-femme see Jennings, *Tomboys*, pp. 119–25.
62 Ourstory, *Daring Hearts*, p. 72.
63 Ibid., p. 73.
64 Ibid., p. 79.
65 Ibid., p. 58.
66 Ibid., p. 54.
67 Judith, LIP interview.
68 Ourstory, *Daring Hearts*, p. 114.
69 A 1968 UK top ten hit for Dusty Springfield.

70 Gardiner, *Closet to Screen*, p. 79.
71 Duffy, 'Lesbian London', p. 232.
72 Gardiner, *Closet to Screen*, p. 80.
73 Summerskill, *Gateway to Heaven*, pp. 68, 70.
74 *Girl* (1974). And see Blyth, BFI Viewing Notes.
75 Patricia Juliana Smith, '"You Don't Have to Say You Love Me". The Camp Masquerade of Dusty Springfield in Patricia Juliana Smith (ed.), *The Queer Sixties* (New York: Routledge, 1999); Gardiner, *Closet to Screen*, p. 86.
76 Bradby, 'Lesbians and Popular Music'.
77 Gardiner, *Closet to Screen*, pp. 86–8.
78 Summerskill, *Gateway to Heaven*, pp. 70–1.
79 Ourstory, *Daring Hearts*, p. 116. The interviews were carried out 1988–91 – Dusty Springfield died in 1999.
80 Annie J Randall, *Dusty!: Queen of the Postmods* (Oxford: Oxford University Press, 2009).
81 *London Evening Standard*, 6 September 1970.
82 A 1966 UK top twenty hit for Dusty Springfield.
83 Lisa Power, *No Bath, but Plenty of Bubbles: An Oral History of the Gay Liberation Front 1970–73* (London: Cassell, 1995), pp. 34–5, 61, 75.
84 See Gardiner, *Closet to Screen*, pp. 178–84 for a detailed account. Power, *No Bath*, pp. 119–22.
85 Jennings, *Tomboys*, p. 127. Alison Oram and Justin Bengry, 'The LGBTQ Press in Twentieth-Century Britain and Ireland', in Martin Conboy and Adrian Bingham, *The Edinburgh History of the British and Irish Press, Volume 3: Competition and Disruption, 1900–2017* (Edinburgh: Edinburgh University Press, 2020), pp. 483–501.
86 *Sappho* 1:7 (September 1972), p. 2 for the Gateways offer. *Sappho*, 1:8 (November 1972), p. 11; 1:9 (December 1972), p. 18; pp. 2:1 (April 1973), pp. 4–5 etc. for notices and reviews of their own discos.
87 See Cook and Oram, *Queer Beyond London*, chapter 5.
88 Lesley, LIP interview. Emphasis in the original.
89 Ourstory, *Daring Hearts*, p. 88.
90 April Gallwey, 'The Rewards of Using Archived Oral Histories in Research: The Case of the Millennium Memory Bank', *Oral History* 41:1 (2013), 37–50.

8

Singing Elton's song: queer sexualities and youth cultures in England and Wales, 1967–85

Daryl Leeworthy

As the age of lesbian and gay liberation, the period between the passing of the Sexual Offences Act in 1967 and the advent of the HIV and AIDS pandemic in the mid-1980s, the long 1970s was a distinctive period in the development of queer sexualities and identities in post-war Britain.[1] The 1967 Act, which partially decriminalised male homosexuality in England and Wales, established a legal age of consent (twenty-one years) substantially different from that which governed heterosexual relationships, namely sixteen years. Parliament had also insisted that homosex take place 'in private' according to a strict – and keenly policed – definition of that term.[2] These new conditions, together with a sharply drawn boundary between what was, and was not, considered legal (and therefore tolerated as socially acceptable), quickly led to the creation of radical activist movements seeking further reform: either equality before the law, as in the case of the homophile Campaign for Homosexual Equality (CHE), or a more determined overthrow of heteronormativity, as in the Gay Liberation Front (GLF).

One of the unintended consequences of the permissive legislation of the 1960s was the construction, in the 1970s, of a distinctive identity: that of the queer teenager. Here was a young person under the age of consent, aware of their sexuality, who had perhaps come out, but who was not yet legally permitted to engage in homosex and unable to fully integrate into queer life.[3] Their experiences were therefore qualitatively different from those of heterosexual teenagers in the same period and thus ill-fit such normative understandings of post-war adolescence that have been the subject of considerable scholarly discussion since the 1990s.[4] As an embattled minority deprived of rights, the teenage act of leaving the closet had both personal and collective implications: personal because it affirmed the veracity of one's individual desires, collective because it invoked solidarity with other queer

Singing Elton's song

people. But how to provide a safe and expressive environment in which a young person could successfully find their place in queer society – that was the concern of the queer civil rights movement.

My purpose in this chapter, then, is to examine the making of the queer teenager in the long 1970s using the interactions between the liberation and homophile movements, queer young people, and musical subcultures as my guide. In other words, I want to understand how young people used music to navigate sexual desire at a time when physical expression, even for those who had reached the age of consent, was legally curtailed, especially in public. The historic experiences of queer young people are vastly understudied, a situation which has prevailed despite scholarly interest in the apparent 'delayed adolescence' of queer people.[5] In 1990, behavioural scientists Ritch Savin-Williams and Rand Lenhart observed pointedly that 'a forgotten, largely invisible minority in twentieth-century society is the gay adolescent'.[6] The British sociologist Ken Plummer made a similar point in his 1989 chapter, 'Lesbian and Gay Youth in England'. He wrote, even then, of a 'voluminous literature on youth in England, but an almost total absence of any reference to youthful same-gender desire'.[7] Historians of popular music and associated subcultures, such as Keith Gildart and Lucy Robinson, on the other hand, have added considerably to our knowledge of the queer teenager, as has an emerging generation of queer historians who are in the process of realising a regionally aware and much less London-centric 'post-New British Queer History'.[8]

In fact, as Matt Cook has written of 1960s London, 'what was happening there was … distinct and was not necessarily replicated in other parts of the country; London's queer story cannot stand in for that of other places and was in any case itself multifaceted'.[9] What was true of the 1960s was no less true of the decades either side: the 1950s and the 1970s.[10] The functional, developmental dynamics, I suggest, following this recognition of difference, lay in the interactions between smaller communities and regional centres (such as Bristol or Manchester), and between those regional centres and London – the latter as a real place and as an imagined utopia of queer adventure and possibility. This bottom-up sensibility forms part of an ongoing response to, and revision of, the historiography of 'cultural change in post-war Britain as a largely metropolitan phenomenon' and thus firmly top-down.[11] Charlie Lynch rightly suggests, drawing on his research into changing attitudes towards heterosexuality in post-war Scotland, that this was much a more diffuse process than previously claimed.[12] In what follows, I have sought to tease out even subtle regional distinctions, such as of musical taste, to illustrate the importance of a bottom-up, extra-London approach to the history of sexuality in modern Britain.

Your Disco Needs You: tracing the local scene

Open the pages of the Reading *Evening Post* in the mid-1970s and adverts for the 'gay disco club' at the Railway Tavern or for Camps in nearby Basingstoke are easy to spot.[13] Discos and dances were an essential part of the culture of queer liberation. As one Sheffield campaigner has pointed out, it was through these activities that 'the concept of "gay community" was born'.[14] The experience of going out and coming together helped to build individual and collective understandings of queerness. This was not an organic process, however, but a deliberate one. Activists took on the challenge of building a community, they thought about what sort of facilities were required, and they theorised how queer people could openly lead lives liberated from a heterosexual norm. They founded newspapers, publishers, and bookshops such as London's (now iconic) Gay's The Word; they created theatre, art and scholarship, notably Jeffrey Weeks's landmark history *Coming Out* published in 1978; they set up advice lines such as FRIEND and Switchboard; they occupied squats such as those at Brixton in South London.[15] Of course, not all these phenomena were apparent in every locality. The specific activities of queer liberation in places like Reading was often distinctive, but most places had a pub – even if it served queer customers only on a part-time basis – and they provide our starting point.

There are two components to explore: first, where the pubs (and clubs and discos) were located; second what music was played and how was it facilitated. A useful example can be drawn from circumstances along the northern coastline of Wales, stretching from the university city of Bangor in the west through the ageing coastal resorts of Llandudno, Prestatyn and Rhyl, and into the industrial zone of Alyn and Deeside in the east. Belying the modesty of local homophile activism – at the end of January 1976 the combined membership of CHE across North Wales was just six people – there was an everyday queer scene.[16] Men and women danced and cruised, got drunk and hooked up in such (relatively) safe social spaces as had emerged. These included Llandudno's Washington Hotel, which was advertised as gay-friendly in the American *International Guild Guide* as early as 1968; the Orme Bar at the Alexandra Hotel; and the Queen's Hotel. The Washington was one of the first venues in North Wales to run a discotheque, which may explain its early appeal, and by the late 1970s it was even hosting discos on behalf of the Gwynedd branch of CHE.[17]

The most immediate, regional competitors for the Washington Hotel were to be found in Bangor, Rhyl and Chester. The latter, with its active branch of CHE and popular nightclub, Oliver's, served as a hub for an area stretching as far west as Anglesey. Liverpool and Manchester were more distant metropolitan centres and London very far away. The cornerstone of Rhyl's burgeoning queer scene was the Hotel Morville, one of several hotels and guesthouses situated along the resort's seafront boulevard. It was first identified as having queer patrons by *Gay News* in the spring of 1975.[18] Within a couple of years, even the decidedly non-pink local press had noticed that Saturday night at the Morville was 'GAY NIGHT'.[19] The hotel capitalised on its increased revenue and soon opened a cabaret room, which became the venue for a resident gay disco called Lil's and for the peripatetic Moving Violation. Based in Manchester and with regular sessions in Preston and Wigan, Moving Violation described itself as the 'North's largest gay disco roadshow experience'.[20] Adding Rhyl to the list was one way in which North Wales was firmly integrated into the wider 'Northern' (that is, North of England) networks of queer entertainment and subculture.

Towards the end of the 1970s, the regional popularity of gay discos at the Morville meant that it was now too small a venue and activity switched instead to the 1520 Club, situated opposite the funfair in Rhyl's west end. Closely associated with the alternative music scene, including the punk band The Toilets, whose members would go on to form The Alarm in 1981, the club was known by its queer patrons as both 'North Wales' No. 1 Strictly Gay Venue' and as 'North Wales' first gay club'.[21] Both epithets were seemingly correctly applied by *Gay News*: the club even poached Lil's gay disco from the Morville. The 1520's association with a queer clientele, as well as with the punk and new wave scenes remained active until at least 1980. The club then underwent a shift in identity becoming, in succession, The Buccaneer and the Welsh-language Clwb Mic a'r Meic, neither of which were especially queer in orientation. Following the loss of the 1520, Rhyl's openly queer scene shrank – growth had proven to be fragile. The NUTZ disco opened at the Queen's Hotel in the autumn of 1980 as an alternative-cum-replacement. But by 1983, Rhyl's only advertised gay bar was to be found in the cellar of the Westminster Hotel, a short walk from the Morville where the scene began in earnest ten years earlier.

Camp revamp: music for liberation, part one

If establishing the role of the disco in a local queer scene is straightforward, identifying what music was played is a more difficult task. Pen portraits of pubs and clubs are frequently tight-lipped. Only occasionally does memoir bring back the noise of a venue. The fashion designer Simon Doonan (b. 1952), who attended Reading's Railway Tavern as a young man, recalled that the pub was 'aimed at the local homosexuals, the majority of whom were shockingly provincial and gin-soaked. *Tragic* is another adjective which springs uncharitably to mind.'[22] These older queers, the 'pre-Wolfendens' as Doonan nicknamed them, were no more comfortable with the latest David Bowie moves than Doonan and his friends were with learned habits of respectability. They shuffled uneasily in their seats as 'the very instant we heard "Suffragette City" we went completely bonkers, strutting onto the postage stamp-size disco floor and posing in imitation of our god'.[23] The youngsters were soon banned from the Railway Tavern as a disruptive influence and forced to try their luck in London. 'The pre-Wolfendens were not ready', Doonan concluded, 'for our particular brand of hip sophistication, nor would they ever be.'[24] Where it can be identified, then, music nuances our appreciation of regional queer scenes and reveals several points of intersection and contestation including age and gender.

CHE's musical tastes could be very old-fashioned: seemingly absent queerness or, to the casual observer such as Bob Phillips of the *Liverpool Echo*, outwardly 'respectable'. Phillips wrote of a CHE disco in New Brighton on Merseyside that he had 'suffered far more dubious and less stimulating conversations at hale-and-heart rugby club stag parties and heard less melodious communal singing there, too'.[25] It was true even in London. A 'Gay 90s Evening' held at Fulham Town Hall in February 1972 offered dramatic monologue, a conjurer and 'all your favourite music hall songs'.[26] This was unlikely to appeal to those raised on 1960s pop music, but it was in line with the enthusiasms of CHE's cultural sections. They tended to favour classical music, fine art, wine making, even train spotting – activities reflective, perhaps, of an older generation.[27] Respectability may have reflected generational tastes and class-based attitudes, but it may also have reflected the need to maintain friendly relationships with those hotel bars and pubs which opened their doors to queer events. Respectability enabled a form of social safety.

By contrast, there was a more contemporary or youthful feel amongst GLF groups. An advert placed in the *International Times* for a GLF People's Dance at Fulham Town Hall in July 1972 offers an indication of countervailing taste.[28] The booked acts were Bristol-based rock band Squidd, with the artist and illustrator Rodney Matthews (b. 1945) on drums, and the more widely known blues-rock group Uncle Dog led by vocalist Carol Ann Grimes (b. 1944). Uncle Dog had appeared the previous year at Glastonbury, sharing a stage with Fairport Convention and David Bowie. A few years later, a fundraiser for Switchboard held at Hammersmith Town Hall was headlined by Tom Robinson's Late Night Extra.[29] This was early in Robinson's career and before he had established a permanent line-up for the punk/new wave Tom Robinson Band. The liberation-inspired single '2–4–6–8 Motorway' was eighteen months away. Robinson (b. 1950) had arrived in London in 1973 seeking to make his way as a musician with the acoustic band Café Society but also, as he later explained, 'trying to make a name for myself as an activist on the London gay scene'.[30] For him, the two went hand in hand.

As ever with analysis of CHE and GLF, it is possible to exaggerate the differences between the two wings of the queer civil rights movement. Musical gatherings generally followed a set formula: there were to be two bands and a disco. This model was quickly regarded as stale by some critics, one of whom complained to *Gay News* in the summer of 1972 that the People's Dances 'are held more and more frequently … disco, light show and two heavy rock groups. Not everyone digs rock music or dancing. Why not one group and a drag artist, or one group and a film.'[31] The disco portion was dominated by soul music rather than rock. As a manager of a gay disco in London in the early 1970s explained, 'soul music is definitely THE music of the gay scene, Black and white. You go to any club where there are gays, and that's what you'll hear.'[32] This association lasted into the early 1980s before giving way, in the clubs, to HiNRG and Eurodisco. Such longevity was, in part, argued one music critic, because of regular revivals of the 'oldies due to the lack of good new gay product'.[33]

Whether DJs played soul as in the 1970s or HiNRG as in the 1980s, the tempo was always upwards of 120 beats per minute. Speed was a hallmark of the queer discotheque. 'For one reason or another, music in gay clubs has always had to be fast', observed *Smash Hits* in a profile of HiNRG's mainstream crossover in 1984: 'speedy stuff by people like The Ritchie Family, The Four Tops and, even then, Gloria Gaynor'.[34] A nightclub's soundscape was primarily the responsibility of the DJ. It was they who curated sets to appeal to audiences, with music designed to encourage interacting, dancing (according to local rules, which in some areas specified a clear distance between partners), drinking and self-expression. There were two different types of DJ: the resident, who played the same venue week after week, and those who took to the road as 'travelling' gay discos or 'disco roadshows'. As one newspaper had it in 1970, 'if you are fed up with going to the same discotheque at the same place every week, why not bring the discotheque to you?'[35]

The most important and influential DJ working on the queer scene in London in this period was Richard Scanes, a thirty-something former public health inspector inspired to come out following the advent of gay liberation. Better known by his tradename Tricky Dicky, 'disc jockey with a difference', Scanes and his 'Dicks Inn' business, launched in the summer of 1971, provided discos at various venues around the capital.[36] Soon his was the 'best-known gay disco' in London.[37] Scanes's playlists inspired DJs working elsewhere in England and Wales: he supplied a regular top ten chart for *Gay News* detailing the music guaranteed to be heard on nights out. Occasionally, he delivered set lists to James Hamilton at the *Record Mirror*, as well. In an interview with Hamilton in 1979, Scanes complained that 'gay discos are playing too many formula "disco" sounds these days', and then detailed a top ten including Shirley Bassey ('This Is My Life'), Antonia Rodriguez ('La Bamba'), and Diana Ross ('No-One Gets The Prize'). 'Most jocks will hate them', Scanes said of his choices, 'though their punters won't'.[38]

Tricky Dicky's aim was to create a queer alternative to straight nightclubs, in keeping with his liberationist beliefs. In an interview with *Gay News* in 1972, he explained that he wanted to 'entertain my fellow gays, and to play my favourite sort of music – soul music, which has a very strong following among gays'.[39] Although he drew little distinction between metropolitan and regional tastes, the available evidence suggests that there were subtle variations in the music heard in Bristol or Cardiff, for instance, or in more provincial pubs and clubs.[40] 'I was taken to the Moulin Rouge in Clifton by my very first boyfriend … in 1972', recalled one Bristol resident. 'I was sixteen years old. I loved the music, and it was great to see guys dancing together.'[41] *Top of the Pops* was Barry Blue's 'Dancin' (On a Saturday Night)' from 1974 and Donna Summer's 1975 single 'Love to Love You, Baby'. The latter seemed to another Moulin Rouge regular like the club's unofficial anthem. 'It was definitely THE place to go – especially for disco', he added.[42] In Cardiff, by contrast, club-goers eschewed Shirley Bassey, despite outside expectations, on the grounds that she was 'too dramatic'. Instead, as journalists from *Gay News* were told on a visit to the city's queer scene in 1976, 'people prefer Aretha Franklin and Diana Ross'.[43]

Dance to the radio: music for liberation, part two

Music played in nightclubs was an important form of representation, but it was not the only option available to those searching for sonic echoes of their identity. A radio or a record player – with appropriate music choices – could transform a room, even momentarily, into a subcultural environment. Artists and songs stressing 'the weakening of the traditional male role or a sense of androgyny' were especially prized, hence Plummer's identification of 'the early mods, the hippies, "glamrock", [and] punk' as having had a particular appeal to queer youth.[44] For members of the London Young Lesbian Group, which was established in 1979, a 'bring your own' policy adopted for meetings meant that music was both an individual and collective means of expression. Choices ranged from reggae to new wave, soul, blues and cabaret, with 'women singers favoured!'[45] This mirrored the soundscape of women-only discos and nightclubs, such as at the Gaslight Club in Ashton-under-Lyne. As the Queer Noise project has noted, the

Gaslight employed women DJs whose most played hit in the mid-1970s was 'When Will I See You Again?' by The Three Degrees. Cardiff, too, had its women-only events featuring feminist punk-rock bands such as Moira and the Mice.[46]

Radio was the more challenging medium, particularly on those stations operated by the BBC, given the dominance of a popular and normative mainstream sound. Thus, for Karl, an 18-year-old from South Wales, who wrote to *Gay Youth* magazine in the spring of 1984, the difficulty faced by queer youth was getting queer music played on radio stations at all. He complained about the absence of queer artists from the playlists of the BBC's youth-orientated Radio One. As he put it:

> The only audience Radio One wants to please is straight, apathetic persons who are only interested in Duran Duran's latest single or who's going to appear on *Top of the Pops* tonight. OK there are a few exceptions like John Peel, David Jensen, [and] Janis Long, but on the whole the majority of Britain's DJs are a bunch of wallies who never know when to shut up and use their airtime to spread their bigoted and stereotyping views about gay people.

Six years earlier, Radio One had refused to air Tom Robinson's liberationist anthem 'Glad to be Gay' during its run down of the week's music charts. The record was banned from *Top of the Pops* as well.[47] Even in 1984, Karl pointed out, it was possible to ask, 'when was the last time Radio One played Tom Robinson's "Glad To Be Gay" [or] any serious record'. He felt that the fault lay with 'obnoxious' and 'reactionary' presenters who played 'boring, uncontroversial records'. The young man added,

> Chris Ransome sums up what I am trying to say in his song 'Advertisements for Heterosexuality' on the excellent 'Coming Out – Ready or Not' album, which I don't suppose will get much airplay on the Steve Wright Show.

Karl's letter is usefully indicative. Historians are generally agreed that, per Jon Savage, 'pop's relationship to different ideas of sexuality and gender is … deep and intricate'.[48] The point is echoed by Gildart and Catterall. 'Music provide[s] a sonic backdrop, a source of knowledge and a way of making sense of private and public relationships', they observe, it was 'a coping mechanism and a soundtrack to the ebb and flow of everyday life for British youth in the 1970s'.[49] But what if normative accessibility was restricted, as it was for queer youth seeking a sonic representation of themselves on the radio?

One useful and widely accessible avenue was the music magazine. The teenage-orientated *Smash Hits*, which regularly engaged with questions of representation in the music industry, published the lyrics of 'Glad to be Gay' in its request-spot pages in 1979, for example, apparently in response to a young woman from Surrey.[50] A few years later, young fans debated whether 'most good singers are either bisexual or gay'. The list included 'David Bowie, Tom Robinson, Elton John. I wonder who will be next? Bob Geldof maybe, or even Sting – but then I said good singers!'[51] There are even coded hints at the threat of 'a nasty form of cancer'.[52] Discussion was not always so positive or jocular – George Michael's weariness about being asked his sexuality was evident and one reader's speculation about Gary Numan was dismissed as irrelevant – but it was nevertheless present and occasionally allowed artists to be visible in their support of queer sexualities.[53] Bronski Beat, whose commercially successful and soulful 'Smalltown Boy' was a mainstream hit in 1984, were amongst those who stood up. 'You have to make a stance', explained Jimmy Somerville (b. 1961) in an interview published in June 1984. 'We just want to wake people up to what's happening'. His bandmate Larry Steinbachek (1960–2016) added, 'what we're dealing with is how the big, mad world is treating people like us'.[54]

It was the record shop which provided the most important mechanism for identity formation through music. Although many were geared towards the heteronormative mainstream, record shops were a key part of youth culture in post-war Britain.[55] Entrepreneurial DJs like Richard Scanes took advantage of this queer gap in the market: Disco Music, Scanes's first record shop, opened on London's Mile End Road at the end of the 1970s.[56] There he stocked and sold (including via mail order) the latest American and European imports, including the 12-inch records used by DJs. Disco Music's success led to a more central store, the Record Cellar, being opened near Leicester Square in 1983.[57] It was a popular haunt for artists such as Culture Club's Boy George. With the offer of substantial discounts for fellow DJs, Scanes used his shops to exert further influence over what music was played in clubs.[58] This had a subsequent impact on wider queer musical taste. For instance: having acquired an American edition of Gloria Gaynor's 'I Will Survive' in the summer of 1978 – the track would not be released in Britain until January 1979 – Scanes added it to his nightclub sets and encouraged his colleagues to do the same. None of them were surprised when it reached Number One in the charts.

Elton's song: queer youth and homosex

Having considered the availability of space and musical tastes, at this point in the chapter I want to relate these elements more directly to homosex. The nightclub, after all, was not only a venue for dancing and listening to music, but it also provided a sexual environment quite different from the public toilets and cruised streets which had served as the mainstay of an older generation. Lingering in the air was often the smell of amyl nitrate, colloquially called poppers, which mixed with alcohol and sweat.[59] 'The cloakroom chemist does a roaring trade', observed a journalist in an exposé of Cardiff's queer scene published in 1985. 'Amyl's use would be frowned upon in ordinary clubs but with the gays it is all part of the atmosphere.'[60] There was even talk, repeated anecdotally to younger scene goers decades later, that poppers were added to the smoke machines at the city's Tunnel Club. Certainly, 'its strong smell floats around', as the journalist added, telling readers that the odour 'is reckoned to be of pear drops but to this untutored nose reeks of a rugby XV's socks left in the dirty bag for a few days too many'. The smell and the instant high fused with the jazz-funk heard 'bouncing off the walls' to create a heady experience and the frizzante anticipation of a sexual encounter.[61]

Club-goers were coded, and read, according to an elaborate social vocabulary of desire: defined tastes, positions of dominance or submission, and availability.[62] 'I seek out men who are going to be good at sex', explained one younger member of the Gay Left collective in 1979, 'sometimes at Bangs disco I stare at men who are classic stereotypes: tall, slim, moustaches, beards, check-shirts and keys, because I know, or think, that they will be good'.[63] Appearance was especially important. 'By wearing a white T-shirt and a black motorcycle jacket, faded blue jeans and short cropped hair I know I present a very "masculine" image', added another member of the collective, 'I want to attract men who are not as powerful as me'.[64] Casual observers noted a range of stylistic divisions. These included 'Mr Macho' who dressed in 'lots of leather and denim'; 'Mr Casual' who turned out in 'comfortable clothes, nice open-neck shirts in soft colours, well-cut trousers'; the 'Goth', with their 'hang-over[s] from punk-style fashion'; and the 'semi-skinhead'. What each had in common was a need – and a desire – to be read as masculine rather than effeminate, since 'the old music hall image of … dressing up in women's clothes is long gone'.[65]

This was masculinity inflected by an idealisation of youth: a system of power and desire which some liberation activists associated with the 'sexism of the gay world'.[66] It could lead, especially in metropolitan centres with larger queer scenes, to 'social moulding' and to a 'stress on lookin' "good" – according to that place's particular sexual stereotype, e.g. young and dolly or butch and tough'.[67] In the more limited scenes of provincial towns and cities, there was more mixing: 'no single "look" dominates', noted one Welsh observer, 'the several different sects of gays mingle together, unlike the factionalised life of London'. All the same 'to the outsider, it appears the crowd fall into several camps'.[68] When Cardiff's scene had slightly more variety, as it did in the 1970s, some division by venue was evident. The Showbiz Club, which always admitted women, was known for its younger, mixed crowds, and generally embracing atmosphere, whereas the men-only 'Sir's' club, which only admitted women reluctantly following the passing of the 1975 Sex Discrimination Act – and then insisted that they be served half pints – was home to older, 'plastic' gays.[69]

The emergence of coded camps within queer culture was itself a process. In the 1960s, there was more ambiguity about image, physical and sartorial, coinciding with the challenges to boundaries of gender and sexuality apparent in contemporary mod subculture. Certain London clubs, such as the Kandy Club, 'attracted working-class mods and elements of London's gay subculture'.[70] Sartorial style, too, was common, since 'their clothes came from the same shops'.[71] The arrival of David Bowie's androgynous, bisexual characters, Ziggy Stardust and Aladdin Sane, in 1972 and 1973, respectively, prefigured by the Pre-Raphaelite-inspired album cover for *The Man Who Sold The World* (1970), featuring the singer in long blond curls and a colourful 'man's dress' designed by Michael Fish (b. 1940), fuelled something new. Bowie's characters were images of youth, of what was increasingly termed the twink in queer male slang, and not easily established as above or below the legal age of consent which remained 21.[72] Was Ziggy Stardust 18, 21, 25, or even 15? That ambiguity was important in the context of queer demands for equalisation of consent at 16.

In short: Bowie symbolised the intersections of youth, sexuality and music in an age of queer liberation. Whereas those of a more conservative nature insisted that his changing identities were all in service of a concept or a gimmick, a cynical means of making vast sums of money, *Gay News* proclaimed him a 'potent spokesman' for the cause.[73] How much it was, in fact, a commercial posture of Bowie's part, is open to question. As he was writing the Ziggy Stardust album, he immersed himself in London's gay nightclubs, played benefit gigs for the nascent GLF, and even famously came out in an interview with *Melody Maker*, although he assiduously avoided becoming too closely associated with or active in the GLF and eventually backtracked on his emergence from the closet.[74] Bowie's androgyny appealed to those searching for role models and guides to fashioning non-normativity. The premium applied to youth in queer (male) subcultures enabled some to gain access to nightclubs at a much younger age than the law intended. 'I had to pretend to be twenty-one', recalled one Bristolian of his early visits to the city's Oasis club, 'even though I looked about fifteen'.[75] Dressed the same as everyone else with elaborate make-up, a wardrobe of camp drag including skin-tight jumpsuits, flares, feather boas, platform shoes, and a vibrant range of jewellery, who could really tell the difference?

But how to safely integrate young people into this aspect of queer culture? That question ran in parallel with the burgeoning nightclub scene of the 1970s. The answer provided by the queer civil rights movement had two elements: the campaign to lower the age of consent and the creation of a queer youth movement. Initially, the legal situation seemed to be in direct conflict with the desire to integrate. Trevor Locke, an influential figure in the CHE's youth movement, and one of the founders of that movement's newsletter *Youth News*, noted in the autumn of 1974 that:

> It does not at this stage seem sensible to set up gay youth clubs where young gay people can meet each other socially; it could be argued that this could lead to sexual contacts, and it is within the power of the law to prosecute anyone running a gay youth club either for conspiracy to corrupt or for procuring. Yet, such facilities would be of great value in helping confirmed homosexuals (of which there are a large number) to lead a happier and mentally more healthy life.[76]

There were a small number of youth groups already in existence by this point including Manchester Young People's Group, the Bristol Youth Group, and a student branch attached to the Liverpool CHE, but it was also true that 'some local groups [were] not ready to integrate their young members' and the CHE generally avoided active recruitment of young people because of the legal concerns Locke identified.[77]

With a year or so, the situation had changed. The Labour government's Policy Advisory Committee on Sexual Offences was launched in December 1975 by the then Home Secretary, Roy Jenkins, and tasked with considering changes to the age of consent.[78] This public debate focused attention on queer young people and prompted a reconsideration of what could be done to support their social development within the limitations of the existing law and with a view to reform. For its part, CHE established its Manchester-based Youth Services Information Project (originally the Young Gays Campaign) in late 1974 and published a leaflet *Young Homosexuals* (1975) not long afterwards.[79] The language used was indicative: these organisations were about advice, guidance and counselling, about fostering an inclusive culture, one of self-awareness and self-acceptance.[80] But they did not shy away from recognising a duty of care and it was at this point of intersection that homosex was brought within the experience of being a queer youth. Young people, recorded *Young Homosexuals*, 'should not and CANNOT be protected from sexual experiences which they freely enter into'.[81]

Conclusion

Queer youth emerged as an identifiable social category in the long 1970s, then, precisely because the law was concerned about homosex, about where it should occur, and about who should be able to enjoy it. A young queer person, distinguished from their straight compatriots by an age of consent which differed by five years, had to find ways of navigating their sexual identity and sexual desires, making choices which either broke the law directly or otherwise transgressed. As we have explored in this chapter, music was a central component of the latter: it provided meaningful representation of identity and desire, the icons to imitate, the sartorial style to follow, and the rhythms which gave meaning to queerness. Since 'we are everywhere', as liberationists chanted, this was a process of cultural change experienced in every part of Britain. It was neither exclusive to London nor fully directed by circumstances in the metropolis. Regional cities and small local towns had their own facilities including pubs, clubs and record shops, and they offered up their own soundscapes. Some found this restrictive and yearned for an imagined queertopia, a place apparently free of respectable (boring) pre-Wolfendens; others made the most of what was available and, in so doing, fashioned a subculture with subtle regional variations.

Given ongoing marginalisation of Britain's queer minority, many of the debates about the place of young people, about the identities of queer youth, about their sexuality and sexual desire and so forth, were conducted within the context of the queer civil rights movement. To that extent, young people had to seek change from within (what was not yet called) 'the community' before amplifying those demands in the normative mainstream. As the long 1970s gave way to the homophobia of the 1980s, fuelled by Thatcherism and anxieties surrounding the HIV and AIDS pandemic, there was a backlash against those calls for change – however modest they had been in practice. 'I have nothing against freedom of gays to be what they want to be, or to do what they want to do', insisted one reader of *Smash Hits* in 1987, 'but that doesn't give [you, the magazine] the *right* to propagate homosexual ideas to ignorant young people. Some of your readers tend to think in simplistic naïve terms accepting that it is actually quite *nice* to be gay.' The magazine's editorial team was then rebuked for their 'irresponsible free for all gay campaign'.[82]

Thatcherism swept away the possibilities of greater permissiveness which had been hinted at in the previous decade. In place of liberation and progressive liberalisation of attitudes, there was a tightening of the law and a strident emphasis on protecting young people from danger – especially from that supposedly posed by queers – and instilling, in the infamous words of the Prime Minister, 'traditional moral values'. Some even called for homosexuals to be locked up in the name of public safety.[83] The introduction of Section 28 in the wake of the Conservative election victory in 1987, with its ban on the 'promotion of homosexuality' as a 'normal family relationship' by local councils, ensured that discussion in schools, libraries, museums and archives was minimised. What remained, what could not be eradicated or effaced, was music and its subcultural queer meaning. This was the great continuity. When the age of consent was equalised, belatedly, in 2000 and Section 28 was removed in 2003, both by the Labour government of 1997–2010, it was found that queer young Britons still sang Elton's song.

Notes

1 Jeffrey Weeks, *Coming Out: The Emergence of LGBT Identities in Britain from the Nineteenth Century to the Present* (London: Quartet, 1977); Jeffrey Weeks, The World We Have Won: The Remaking of Erotic and Intimate Life (London: Routledge, 2007); Matt Cook, *A Gay History of Britain: Love and Sex Between Men Since the Middle Ages* (London: Greenwood World, 2007); Rebecca Jennings, *Lesbian History of Britain: Love and Sex Between Women since 1500* (London: Greenwood World, 2007); Daryl Leeworthy, *A Little Gay History of Wales* (Cardiff: University of Wales, 2019).
2 Equivalent legislation was passed for Scotland in 1980 and for Northern Ireland in 1982, albeit in the latter case following intervention by the European Court of Human Rights in 1981. See: Jeffrey Meek, *Queer Voices in Post-War Scotland: Male Homosexuality, Religion and Society* (Basingstoke: Palgrave Macmillan 2015); Paul Johnson, *Going to Strasbourg: An Oral History of Sexual Orientation Discrimination and the European Convention on Human Rights* (Oxford: Oxford University Press, 2016), pp. 77–82; Tom Hulme, 'Out of the Shadows: One Hundred Years of LGBT Life in Northern Ireland', in Marie Coleman, Paul Bew and Caoimhe Nic Dhábhéid (eds), *Northern Ireland, 1921–2021: Centenary Historical Perspectives* (Belfast: Ulster Historical Foundation, 2022).
3 Abigail C. Saguy, *Come Out, Come Out, Whoever You Are* (Oxford: Oxford University Press, 2020).
4 Jon Savage, *Teenage: The Creation of Youth, 1875–1945* (London: Faber & Faber, 2007); David Fowler, *The First Teenagers: The Lifestyle of Young Wage-Earners in Interwar Britain* (London: Routledge, 1995); Melanie Tebbutt, *Making Youth: A History of Youth in Modern Britain* (Basingstoke: Palgrave Macmillan, 2016). LGBTQ+ youth activism in London is examined in archival detail in Clifford Williams, *Courage to Be: Organised Gay Youth in England, 1967–1990* (London: Book Guild, 2021).
5 Eli Coleman, 'Developmental Stages of the Coming Out Process', *Journal of Homosexuality*, 8:2–3 (1982), 31–43, p. 38.
6 Ritch C. Savin-Williams and Rand E. Lenhart, 'AIDS Prevention Among Gay and Lesbian Youth: Psychosocial Stress and Health Care Intervention Guidelines', in David. G. Ostrow (ed.), *Behavioral Aspects of AIDS* (New York: Springer, 1990), pp. 75–99.
7 Ken Plummer, 'Lesbian and Gay Youth in England', in Gilbert Herdt (ed.), *Gay and Lesbian Youth* (London: Routledge, 1989), p. 195.
8 The term is my own. Keith Gildart, *Images of England Through Popular Music: Class, Youth and Rock 'n' Roll, 1955–1976* (Basingstoke: Palgrave Macmillan,

2013); Lucy Robinson, *Gay Men and the Left in Post-War Britain* (Manchester: Manchester University Press, 2007); Lucy Robinson and Ben Jones, 'Queering the Grammar School Boy: Class, Sexuality and Authenticity in the Works of Colin MacInnes and Ray Gosling', in Nick Bentley, Beth Johnson and Andrzej Zieleniec (eds), *Youth Subcultures in Fiction, Film and Other Media: Teenage Dreams* (Basingstoke: Palgrave Macmillan, 2017), pp. 23–40. An indicative summary of 'New British Queer History' can be found in Brian Lewis (ed.), *British Queer History: New Approaches and Perspectives* (Manchester: Manchester University Press, 2013). The classic statement in the field is Matt Houlbrook, *Queer London: Perils and Pleasures of the Sexual Metropolis, 1918–1957* (Chicago: University of Chicago, 2005). On the regional turn see the chapters in Matt Cook, Alison Oram and Justin Bengry (eds), *Locating Queer Histories: Places and Traces in the UK* (London: Bloomsbury, 2022) as well as Tom Hulme, 'Queer Belfast during the First World War: Masculinity and Same-sex Desire in the Irish City', *Irish Historical Studies* 45:168 (2022), 239–61.
9 Matt Cook, 'Local Matters: Queer Scenes in 1960s Brighton, Manchester and Plymouth', *Journal of British Studies*, 59:1 (2020), 32–56, p. 33.
10 Heike Bauer and Matt Cook (eds), *Queer 1950s: Rethinking Sexuality in the Postwar Years* (Basingstoke: Palgrave Macmillan, 2012); Matt Cook, 'Gay Times: Identity, Locality, Memory, and the Brixton Squats in 1970s London', *Twentieth Century British History*, 24:1 (2013), 84–109.
11 Charlie Lynch, 'Moral Panic in the Industrial Town: Teenage Deviancy and Religious Crisis in Central Scotland, *c*.1968–9', *Twentieth Century British History*, 32:3 (2021), 371–91; the classic casting of London as the motor of post-war cultural change is Frank Mort, *Capital Affairs: London and the Making of the Permissive Society* (New Haven, CT: Yale University Press, 2010).
12 Lynch, 'Moral Panic', p. 374.
13 *Reading Evening Post*, 26 January 1974, p. 4; *Reading Evening Post*, 6 August 1977, p. 4.
14 Terry Sanderson, 'Faltering from the Closet', in Bob Cant and Susan Hemmings (eds), *Radical Records: Thirty Years of Lesbian and Gay History* (London: Routledge, 1988), p. 88.
15 Matt Cook, '"Gay Times": Identity, Locality, Memory, and the Brixton Squats in 1970s London', *Twentieth Century British History* 24:1 (2013), 84–109.
16 Gwynedd CHE, Newsletter No. 3 (February–March 1976), p. 1.
17 Gwynedd CHE, *Newssheet* No. 19 (October 1977), p. 1; *Newssheet* No. 2 (November 1977), p. 1. The music was provided by Rumaz Disco, a local business which otherwise provided entertainment to rugby clubs and the Llandudno Catholic Parents' Association. *North Wales Weekly News*, 9 March 1978, p. 26; *North Wales Weekly News*, 16 March 1978, p. 25.
18 *Gay News* 66 (13 March–26 March 1975), p. 16.
19 *North Wales Weekly News*, 27 January 1977, p. 18.
20 *Gay News*, 123 (14–27 July 1977), p. 35.
21 *Gay News*, 111 (27 January–6 February 1977), p. 4; *Gay News* 116 (7–20 April 1977), p. 4.

22 Simon Doonan, *Beautiful People: My Family and Other Glamorous Varmints* (London: Simon & Schuster, 2009), p. 11.
23 Ibid., p. 12.
24 Ibid., p. 13.
25 Bob Phillips, 'A Race Apart? The Night I Went to the Disco with a Difference', *Liverpool Echo*, 4 December 1974, p. 6.
26 *Lunch*, 5 (January 1972), p. 5.
27 See the notices in *Lunch*, 18 (March 1973), 28–30.
28 *International Times*, 132 (19 June 1972), p. 47.
29 *Acton Gazette*, 25 March 1976, p. 21.
30 'Interview with Tom Robinson, 8 October 2009', https://gladtobegay.net/interview-tom-robinson/part-1/ (accessed 5 December 2021).
31 David Seligman, 'Come Dancing Together', *Gay News* 1 (*c*.May 1972), p. 4.
32 Keith Gildart and Stephen Catterall, *Keeping the Faith: A History of Northern Soul* (Manchester: Manchester University Press, 2020), p. 235.
33 James Hamilton, 'Gay Days', *Record Mirror*, 2 May 1981, p. 30.
34 'High Energy', *Smash Hits*, 20 June 1984, pp. 22–3.
35 *Long Eaton Advertiser*, 23 January 1970, p. 16.
36 *The Stage*, 13 April 1972, p. 9.
37 Ibid., 16 December 1976, p. 5.
38 James Hamilton, 'DJ Top Ten', *Record Mirror*, 30 June 1979, p. 27.
39 Peter Holmes, 'Tricky Dicky – The Gay Liberator', *Gay News*, 12 (December 1972), p. 8.
40 As the band Pauline Black with Sunday Best put it in 1984: 'different places have different vibes'. *Smash Hits*, 29 March–11 April 1984, p. 16.
41 Comment by 'Alan Parish', Out Stories Bristol, Moulin Rouge entry, 29 January 2014, https://outstoriesbristol.org.uk/places/pubs-clubs/moulin-rouge/.
42 Comment by 'Charlie', Out Stories Bristol, Moulin Rouge entry, 18 November 2017. As above.
43 Keith Howes and Bob Workman, 'Gay Britain: Cardiff', *Gay News*, 4–17 November 1976, pp. 13–14.
44 Plummer, 'Lesbian and Gay Youth in England', p. 197; Matthew Worley, *No Future: Punk, Politics and British Youth Culture, 1976–84* (Cambridge: Cambridge University Press, 2017).
45 London Gay Teenage Group, *Annual Report 1982* (London, 1982), p. 18.
46 Glamorgan Archives, DWAW6/1: *Cardiff Women's Newsletter Christmas Edition 1981* (Cardiff, 1981). The original is unpaginated; Lucy Delap has usefully considered the role and recovery of sound in the women's movement in her *Feminisms: A Global History* (London: Pelican, 2020), chapter 8.
47 *Daily Mirror*, 20 May 1978, p. 15.
48 Jon Savage, 'Tainted Love: The influence of male homosexuality and sexual divergence on pop music and culture since the war', in Alan Tomlinson (ed.), *Consumption, Identity & Style: Marketing, Meanings, and the Packing of Pleasure* (London: Routledge, 1990), p. 104.
49 Gildart and Catterall, *Keeping the Faith*, p. 221.

50 *Smash Hits*, 13 December 1979, p. 27.
51 *Smash Hits*, 17 April 1980, p. 35; 15 May 1980, p. 34.
52 James Hamilton, 'Odds 'n' Bods', *Record Mirror*, 27 November 1982, p. 27. The cancer had claimed the life of Patrick Cowley (1950–82), an American disco and HiNRG artist known to be an early victim of the AIDS pandemic.
53 *Smash Hits*, 2–15 August 1984, p. 65. Occasionally young people turned to music magazines for agony advice, too. For instance: 'Help: Gay Despair at the Baths', *Record Mirror*, 25 November 1978, p. 33.
54 *Smash Hits*, 21 June 1984, pp. 8–10.
55 Andrew Flory, 'Tamla Motown in the UK: Transatlantic Reception of American and Rhythm and Blues', in Brett Lashua, Karl Spracklen and Stephen Wagg (eds), *Sounds and the City: Popular Music, Place and Globalization* (Basingstoke: Palgrave Macmillan, 2014), pp. 113–27.
56 James Hamilton, 'Disco News', *Record Mirror*, 25 November 1978, p. 51.
57 James Hamilton, 'Odds 'n' Bods', *Record Mirror*, 26 March 1983, p. 38.
58 Ibid., 14 August 1982, p. 31. Scanes had reportedly told Hamilton, to the latter's apparent discomfort, of his long-running in-store offer that 'if you're gay and a DJ you get an extra special kiss!'
59 The cultural history of poppers is explored in Adam Zmith, *Deep Sniff: A History of Poppers and Queer Futures* (London: Repeater, 2021). Use of amyl nitrate in nightclubs was first subject to public debate in the early 1960s. 'Exhilaration Drug Warning', *Liverpool Echo*, 17 November 1962, p. 19. By the late 1970s the association with disco was the stuff of tabloid scaremongering. 'Danger in a Disco Sex Drug', *Daily Mirror*, 4 May 1979, p. 5; Gillian Frank, 'Discophobia: Antigay Prejudice and the 1979 Backlash against Disco', *Journal of the History of Sexuality*, 16:2 (2007), 276–306.
60 Paul Horton, 'Cardiff After Dark: City Club Where Boy Meets Boy', *South Wales Echo*, 20 November 1985, p. 12.
61 Paul Horton, 'Cardiff After Dark: It's Saturday Night Fever!', *South Wales Echo*, 18 November 1985, p. 8; Paul Burston, *Queens' Country: A Tour Around the Gay Ghettos, Queer Spots and Camp Sights of Britain* (London: Little Brown, 1998).
62 David Halperin, *How To Be Gay* (Cambridge, MA: Harvard University Press, 2014).
63 Gay Left Collective, 'Self and Self Image', *Gay Left*, 9 (Winter 1979), p. 5.
64 Ibid., p. 3.
65 Horton, 'Boy Meets Boy', *South Wales Echo*, 20 November 1985, p. 12.
66 Gay Left Collective, 'Within These Walls …', *Gay Left* 2 (Spring 1976), p. 2.
67 Ibid., p. 3.
68 Horton, 'Boy Meets Boy', p. 12.
69 Howes and Workman, 'Cardiff', *Gay News*, 4–17 November 1976, pp. 13–14.
70 Gildart, *Images of England*, p. 126.
71 Ibid., p. 96.
72 Bruce Rogers, *The Queens' Vernacular: A Gay Lexicon* (San Francisco: Straight Arrow, 1972); William Stewart, *Cassell's Queer Companion* (London: Continuum, 1995), p. 259.

73 Peter Holmes, 'Gay Rock', *Gay News*, No. 5 (July 1972), p. 7.
74 The *Melody Maker* interview with Bowie was published on 22 January 1972.
75 Bristol City Council, Museum Collections, Outstories Bristol Oral History Project: OH440, Interview with 'Martyn (b. 1972)'.
76 Trevor Locke, 'Counselling Homosexuals Under 18, 6 October 1974', London School of Economics, Hall-Carpenter Archive, Campaign for Homosexual Equality Records, HCA/CHE/9/50.
77 *Lunch*, 5 (January 1972), p. 21; *Lunch*, 6 (March 1972), p. 26; Campaign for Homosexual Equality, *Annual Report for 1975* (London: Campaign for Homosexual Equality, 1976), p. 8.
78 Matthew Waites, *The Age of Consent: Young People, Sexuality and Citizenship* (Basingstoke: Palgrave Macmillan, 2005).
79 Campaign for Homosexual Equality, *Annual Report for 1975*, p. 8.
80 Tel Airs, 'Teenage Movement', in Campaign for Homosexual Equality, *Annual Report, March 1975–March 1976* (London, 1976). The original is unpaginated.
81 Campaign for Homosexual Equality Youth Services Information Project, *Young Homosexuals* (Manchester: Campaign for Homosexual Equality, 1975), p. 1. The leaflet was originally published in February 1975.
82 'Letter from Terry Burns', *Smash Hits*, 24 February 1987, p. 60.
83 Leeworthy, *A Little Gay History of Wales*, p. 123.

9

'Nothing like a little disaster for sorting things out': *Blowup* (1966) and the free hedonism(s) of Swinging London

Marlie Centawer

My greatest difficulty was to reproduce the violence of reality.
Michelangelo Antonioni[1]

While the 1960s saw the exploration of new lifestyles related to youth and sex, Michelangelo Antonioni's first English language film, *Blowup* (1966), ushered in these new representations on the cinematic screen parallel with the rise of Swinging London as a media spectacle in larger popular culture.[2] Following the pursuits of a photographer's daily encounters between the worlds of high fashion and pop, the film offers a frictionless visual passage between the fantasies and potential realities of youth culture in spaces relating to music and sex. Widely regarded as the first arthouse–mainstream cinema crossover, *Blowup* toys with sexual tension throughout: from the first screen revealing of pubic hair (via Jane Birkin) to David Hemmings languid coital photoshoot with model Verushka, forever immortalised as the film's iconic image.

As a film, *Blowup* effectively has 'everything': sex, murder, lust, intrigue. Yet these acts are never fully realised but rather hinted at in a larger cultural and visual tableau. In many instances, violence is used as the push-pull between the subtle nuances of such experiences, creating an unease about 'the opportunities for sexual fulfilment opened up by the permissive society […] It is a film constructed like a poem of thematically related images, about the way in which perceptions can be tampered with, undermined, and finally broken down.'[3] Interestingly, these images also relate to music: from The Yardbirds' combative performance of 'Stroll On' at the Ricky Tick (featuring Jimmy Page) to Herbie Hancock's jazz score soundtrack. This burden of representing Swinging London through 'the David Bailey-like hero, the guitar smashing, the casual sex, the dope-smoking party, the mime troupe with which the film begins and ends – combines with the faster rhythm of cutting imposed on the film […] to disrupt the mysterious quality which makes [Antonioni's other films] enigmatically complex'.[4]

While *Blowup* remains an 'influential, stylish study of paranoid intrigue and disorientation' and 'a time capsule of mod London, a mini-scape of the era's fashion, free love, parties [and] music', sex and desire appear in many instances as unfulfilled by the film's end.[5] Looking to recognisable signs, symbols, sounds and iconography of the counterculture, Antonioni both captures and posits a new, free hedonism of youth and the desire for excess, a thread of 'fantasy, reality, vice and versa' that later continued in Donald Cammell and Nicolas Roeg's *Performance* (1970) and his own *Zabriskie Point* (1970).

Swinging London and youth culture

Loosely based on a short story by Argentinian writer Julio Cortazar[6] and Francis Wyndham's *Sunday Times Colour Magazine* article 'The Modelmakers' (10 May 1964),[7] *Blowup* follows the pursuits of main protagonist Thomas[8] (David Hemmings) and his daily encounters with so-called Swinging London life as a photographer-observer. These activities manifest as rituals of voyeurism, including photographing models in his studio, cruising the city in his Rolls Royce and exploring London's cityscape in states of progress and renewal. The film culminates in Thomas's encounter and image-mapping of a potential murder that may or may not have occurred in a park central to the mise-en-scène of the film (filming location: Maryon Park, Woolwich) through the magnification, or 'blow-up', of his photographs.

Blowup portrays a fluid and seemingly spontaneous portrayal of youth excess, including sex and music, yet the film was scripted with attention to detail and a sense of ambiguity. Hemmings's portrayal of the photographer character draws on his personal experience of making the film and interpreting the script, as well as Antonioni's style of direction: 'it's always been a surprise to me that Antonioni thought of me as the epitome of the 1960s', he remembered. Antonioni thought of Hemmings, then aged 23, as both 'too blonde and too young', to which Hemmings responded: 'I look older on film.' *Blowup* was Hemmings thirty-seventh film, and although his best-known role, Hemmings initially 'hated it, hated it! I didn't understand it at all [...] because I didn't know what was going on. It had a script of fourteen pages originally.'[9] The scripted chaos of the film reflects a similar feeling that permeates throughout: *Blowup* both captures elements of an emerging youth counterculture and critiques it through its reflected cinematic representations. *Blowup* uses familiar referents, signs and symbols from the larger media spectacle of Swinging London, one that attracted Antonioni to use London as the backdrop of his film, 'the dazzle and the madness of London today [...] seen through Antonioni's camera. [This is] his London.'[10] Hemmings clearly was an interesting choice, and one that the actor took pleasure in throughout the rest of the decade: he had subsequent roles in the sexually charged *Barbarella* (dir. Roger Vadim, 1968), amidst the violence of The *Charge of the Light Brigade* (dir. Tony Richardson, 1968), and later recorded his debut album of psychedelic folk-pop (featuring The Byrds' Roger McGuinn, Chris Hillman, Gene Clark, and produced by their manager Jim Dickson), released as *David Hemmings Happens in* September 1967.[11]

As Peter Ackroyd notes, 'London has always been an ugly city. It is part of its identity. It has always been rebuilt, and demolished, and vandalised. That, too, is part of its history.'[12] With post-war refurbishments to the city, London was subject to multiple reconfigurations in which

> vast swathes were demolished in order to make way for what became known as 'comprehensive redevelopment'. What it represented was a deliberate act of erasure, an act of forgetting, not so dissimilar in spirit to the mood and ambience of the 'Swinging Sixties' elsewhere in London. It was as if time, and London's history, had for all practical purposes ceased to exist. In pursuit of profit and instant gratification, the past became a foreign country.[13]

The reconstruction of London as a cinematic city in *Blowup* serves to propagate Antonioni's critique of Swinging London and youth culture from an outsider-observer perspective, utilising the unique possibilities of film. According to Michael Dear, the exploration of space and time in film as a medium creates a distinct cinematic geography. This construction also reiterates the 'cinematisation of contemporary life – representations of the real have become stand-ins for actual, lived experiences'.[14] Further, Dear claims there are three broad attitudes toward cinematic representations of cities: first, the city is simply 'there' as background; second, there is a celebratory, utopian view of the city; or third, the city exists as a dystopia.[15] The appearance of these three elements in *Blowup* further elucidates Dear's assertion that 'the cinematic landscape is not [...] a neutral place of entertainment or an objective documentation or mirror of the "real", but an ideologically charged cultural creation whereby meanings of place and society are made, legitimised, contested and obscured'.[16]

The film depicts the city in a state of perpetual flux with Thomas exploring the urban landscape in various states of renewal and progress. While the city is simply 'there' as background and an integral component of the mise-en-scène, it also serves as a social space in which the photographer interprets and encounters the boundaries of 'the real' in his surroundings. Similar to the mapping of Swinging London in *Time*'s feature article from 1966, Antonioni charts the film's narrative with a topographical premise where actual locations are not made explicit.[17] What results is a reconstructed London that unfolds on the peripheries and edges of the city in the form of non-spaces. As Ian Buchanan asserts, non-space involves 'a kind of travel that is to be written under erasure – one has gone there, without having been there [...] we swim through places more than we dwell there and consequently a new type of social space has emerged whose precise purpose is to facilitate a frictionless passage – airports, train stations, bus terminals, fast food outlets, supermarkets and hotels. Because they do not confer a sense of place, [Marc] Augé calls these places non-places.'[18] Thomas drifts through a constructed yet fragmented cinematic city, and although provoked to confront the reality, or hyper-reality of this construction, he encounters various forms of social spaces that facilitate a 'frictionless passage' of a misconstrued experience of the 'real'.[19]

The pop photographer and the pop lifestyle

Throughout *Blowup*, Thomas experiences both 'real' and 'non-real' London (mirroring Swinging London as a media spectacle) made manifest in his role as a photographer, which also defined the public's image of the 1960s fashion photographer.[20] Influenced in part by the career and romantic pursuits of top Swinging London photographer David Bailey, age 28 in 1966, Antonioni's film also depicts Thomas's pop lifestyle, one involving the consumption of and sexual disposability of women for the male gaze, and the voyeuristic pleasures of image-making.[21] According to George Melly in *Revolt Into Style*, '[in the context of Swinging London,] the personification of the photographer as pop hero is undoubtedly David Bailey [...] the openly sardonic historian of his time elevating a narrow circle of his own friends and acquaintances into a chic but deliberately frivolous pantheon; hard-working but ruled by pleasure'.[22] Melly claims that '[the pop photographer] is in the position to move between two worlds', that of high fashion and the pop world, carrying the ideas and rage for the new form from one to the other.[23] He connects this to his discussions on pop: 'side by side with the idea of the photograph as pop medium has arisen the concept of the photographer as pop hero. Every idea about pop favours this myth: the balance between technical expertise and intellectual indifference, the camera's amorality, the availability and disposability [of the medium]'.[24]

One of the film's main themes, the division between reality and fantasy, also sets up a sense of duality in how sex and music operate in the film as expressions of youth culture, both acting as worlds of surface through which Thomas moves. The ways in which sex and music are produced and consumed by youth culture in the film are also integral to the pop lifestyle, one in which style obsolescence, change and expendability were seen by the young not as a means but as ends in themselves: as a 'natural and desirable' condition; an affirmation of life in the post-war era, a period in which Britain entered its own high mass-consumption stage and one in which new youth industries emerged relating to sex, music, fashion and photography.[25]

As a Swinging London flaneur, Thomas embodies the pop lifestyle with an outlook immediate to things, consumption and sensations; yet he eventually becomes disillusioned with the city ('I've gone off London this week, it doesn't do anything for me') and ultimately questions some of the starker realities of post-war London captured through his lens.[26] Thomas's stature as a photographer is unveiled throughout the film's seemingly fluid narrative. Upon his first introduction in the film, Thomas emerges from a doss house where he has 'been up all night' photographing the harsh truths of its derelict, homeless inhabitants. Initially displaying a dishevelled appearance, Thomas's higher-class status is revealed once he drives his Rolls Royce convertible towards his photography studio.

The relationship between image and spectacle is explored further in Thomas's encounters with an apparent murder, which he experiences through his blown-up photographs of the park. Thomas's description of the murder as 'fantastic' to Ron on the phone reinforces both the desire of the image and what Guy Debord calls 'the society of the spectacle [...] the entire life of societies in which modern conditions of production reign announces itself as an immense accumulation of spectacles. Everything that was directly lived has moved away into a representation.'[27] Similarly, the film's topographical premise of mapping an alternate Swinging London uses elements of psychogeography, a later tenet of the student riots and activities of May 1968 in Paris. Thomas drifts and wanders, at times aimlessly, through a fictionalised London, and it is this unplanned sense of direction that leads him to discover a potential murder in the park. However, Thomas's discovery of the murder through images further confuses and dislocates his actual experience, for he did not witness the murder at first hand and creates a reconstructed sequence of events through the mechanics of photography.[28] Despite revisiting the actual space of the murder at night, Thomas stays consumed with the power of the image of the murder and the ability to construct narratives and potential meanings through the juxtaposition and magnification of images in his darkroom and studio.[29]

Blowup and the counterculture

As Adam Scovell notes, '[Antonioni's] London may be a fiction but one that also holds a very powerful communal truth.'[30] This sense of community, a basis of the counterculture, is inherent to the expression of youth throughout the film. The film opens to a group of mimes (described as 'shouting students' in a version of the film's script) in youthful, anarchic revelry; there are comparisons to be made here between Antonioni's use of the mimes as references to American signifiers of youth culture from the time period, including the Merry Pranksters and their bus 'Furthur' to the San Francisco Mime Troupe and their form of radical guerrilla theatre championed by founder R.G. Davis in his text 'Guerilla Theater' (a title inspired by Mime Troupe actor Peter Berg, later co-founder of the San Francisco Diggers in 1966).[31] Interestingly, R.G. Davis discusses his Guerilla Theater Manifesto in *Revolution* (1968), a film that also features future *Zabriskie Point* actor Daria Halprin as part of her mother Anna Halprin's San Francisco Dance Workshop collective, which was based in Haight Ashbury, San Francisco. As noted by David Talbot, 'the 1960s was essentially a cultural dialogue between San Francisco and London'.[32] With London as a cultural backdrop, future Mime Troupe actor and Digger founder Emmett Grogan lived briefly in Hollywood Road, South Kensington in 1965, and other members of The Diggers stayed at the Prince of Wales Mansions in Battersea when they visited The Beatles at their Apple Offices, Savile Row in December 1968.

With the appearance of a top hat worn by one of the mimes, further connections between the two cities, and signifiers of the counterculture emerge: the top hat as stovepipe as costume hat (variations on a theme) features heavily in youth imagery and fashion of the era, from the insignia for Chet Helm's Family Dog collective at the Avalon Ballroom circa 1963 onwards, to The Orkustra founder-guitarist Bobby Beausoleil and his trademark 'Cupid' top hat, which also features in his performance as Lucifer in *Invocation of My Demon Brother* (dir. Kenneth Anger 1969). The youthful 'top hat' character also features in the mercurial last episode of *The Prisoner* (1967), demarcating insanity (the Mad Hatter?) and playful youth reverie at the same time. American connections to the film also include the original plot and its loose threads to J.F. Kennedy's assassination in 1963 and the Zapruder film, particularly in its blow-up images capturing a tragedy shrouded in mystery.

Together, the mimes disrupt the everyday silences of London's West End Economist Plaza and their frenetic energy combats the expectations of the silent mime as archetype.[33] Seeking monetary donations as Rag Day students, the mimes fill the street with spontaneity and chaos yet become somewhat antagonistic in their approach to wealthy Londoners who drive extravagant automobiles. Here, class and social status becomes further apparent in the film's opening scenes, with cut edits between two settings. During the mimes' romp through the streets, two nuns dressed in white proceed down the sidewalk and a lone Buckingham Palace Queen's guard marches in full uniform. The scenes of Thomas emerging from being 'up all night' photographing in a doss house are cut with visuals of revelry, offering a stark contrast between the harsher realities of London that are far from swinging. Thomas's power is not made fully apparent in the doss house; rather, his role as a photographer is only revealed when certain symbols and signs are in place, such as the flashy Rolls Royce, the hidden camera in a paper bag and the folded paper money bills. Acting as bookends to the film, the mimes reappear in the film's concluding tennis court scene in the park. Thomas's confrontation of perception and reality climaxes here and he is both centre and at the periphery of his surroundings. As an outsider, Thomas observes and then participates in the mimes' imaginary tennis match by picking up the imaginary tennis ball and tossing it back to the court; his gaze follows the imaginary ball's fall to the court and, by doing so, Thomas engages in a suspension of disbelief in his surroundings. By joining in on their unexplained and silent ritual, Thomas experiences a dislocation of previous beliefs (perhaps the tennis game is 'real'?), subsequently disappearing into celluloid as the film's final moments acknowledge his presence as a fictional construction.

Sex, models and image

References to Swinging London images and iconography of youth are revealed in the opening credits of the film, which feature live action footage of model Donatella Luna objectified and photographed by a group of male photographers. In this construction, the model is positioned as an object of fascination for the male gaze and made into a spectacle and icon of Swinging London. The introduction of the photographer as a prominent image maker in this context foreshadows the central focus on Thomas's experiences throughout the film. The value of images as symbols is made further apparent during the photoshoot scene between Thomas and Verushka, a prominent Swinging London model who plays an unnamed model in the film. Before he enters the studio, Verushka is without value or presence. As a model manipulated in front of the camera, she is an attractive source of power in the context of the photoshoot, yet is otherwise discarded.

As evident in the scene featuring Verushka's photo session, models are an integral component of the photographer's pop lifestyle, his business and romantic affairs. Verushka's performance in the film reinforces her professional modelling career during the Swinging London era.[34] Her appearance in the film is initially fragmented. Sitting between a male and female set of bust sculptures and reflected in plastic plexiglass against a wall in Thomas's studio, she announces 'here I am', introducing her pent-up desire for the photographer and increasing anticipation of the photoshoot. Verushka thus adopts two roles: that of a top model and, presumably, Thomas's lover.

While she is discarded by Thomas's gaze during the photoshoot, Verushka later appears briefly in the party sequence (actual location, Christopher Gibb's house at 100 Cheyne Walk, Chelsea), which offers another portrayal of hip insiders integral to London's youth scene, complete with an uncredited appearance of Rolling Stones friend and associate Stash De Rola. Thomas's enquiry that she is 'supposed to be in Paris' is met with 'I am in Paris.' Her response is in keeping with the 'photography, rock and pot [...] foci of London's mod world', but also the film's interest in exploring the metaphysical boundaries of fantasy and reality.[35]

According to Antonioni scholar Peter Brunette, the director's social critique in *Blowup* is made primarily evident in his 'exploration of gender issues that now, for the first time, focus on a principal male character rather than a female one [...] examining the relationship between an individual and reality, rather than interpersonal relations central to his previous films'.[36] *Blowup* showcases a predominantly male point of view, both from Antonioni's standpoint as a director and Thomas's position as a photographer who offers an intrusive male gaze on models and other female characters. Brunette claims that *Blowup* is concerned with 'perception, specifically, artistic perception, and even more specifically, male artistic perception'.[37] Thomas is surrounded by desiring female characters who are delegated to such roles as wife, 'birds', models and, in the case of Sarah Miles's character Patricia, a quiet and domesticated dolly bird.

The relationship between Thomas and his models is a site of conflict; his career depends on capturing their image and promoting the clothing they wear, yet he manipulates the female models as objects of purpose for a photographer and image maker. The models' lack of agency and objectification is enhanced through their inability to speak and Thomas's instructions to 'close their eyes' and his reference to one of the models as 'Stripes', the pattern on her clothing. The use of clothespins gives the illusion of form-fitting clothing in fashion photography, enhancing the models' disposability as throwaway objects.

Thomas exercises his male power through the manipulation of the camera, as evidenced in his commanding presence during the group modelling photoshoot and his role as image maker pursued and desired by two aspiring models, the Blonde One (Jane Birkin) and The Brunette (Gillian Hills). He is later rendered powerless by Jane (Vanessa Redgrave), whom he first encounters in the park with the man he later believes to be a murder victim. Jane demands the photographs ('I'll pay you'), to which Thomas replies, 'I overcharge ... there are other things I want on the reel', creating an erotically charged banter between the two characters, as Jane grovels at his feet in an attempt to dismantle his camera and the roll of film from his grasp ('don't let's spoil everything, we've only just met'). During their next meeting at Thomas's studio, Jane attempts to obtain the photographs again. Here, Thomas's discussion of his 'wife' (who may or may not be 'real'), coupled with his patronising treatment of the female sculpture whose head he pats lightly and on which he extinguishes his cigarette, extends a patriarchal, oppressive view. His claim that 'even with beautiful girls, you look at them and that's that [...] I'm stuck with them all day long', further reveals a disregard for women. Jane and Thomas's attempts to seduce one another creates an additional layer of desire to the scene but also a unique struggle for power over 'the image'. Her abrupt departure during their erotic encounter in his studio leaves him desiring her through anonymity and absence, coupled with the incorrect phone number she gives him, leaving him all the more dissatisfied. In bearing witness to the apparent murder in the park, Thomas is rendered both powerful and powerless, in that the image offers him the possibility of power, yet Jane's stealing of the photographic images from his studio leaves him with no evidence to prove the murder, and another instance in which he disdains a female character.

The emphasis on youth permissiveness and a free sense of sexuality is heightened in Thomas's interplay with particular female characters; when The Brunette and The Blonde One visit Thomas's studio for a second time, they are treated to an assortment of dresses and eventually partake in a scandalous romp with the photographer on a purple paper backdrop. While exploring the studio, The Brunette whispers to The Blonde One, 'Psst! look at all these clothes', upon which the two young girls frenetically look through the poster dresses. Here, the girls' overtly emphatic desire for the latest in mod fashions is countered with the anonymity of female identity when Thomas first enquires about The Brunette's name. 'What do they call you in bed?' Her response: 'I only go to bed to sleep.'

From rock to jazz

In *Blowup*, music plays a significant role in shaping the viewers' experience of youth culture within the context of Swinging London. Herbie Hancock first recorded his score for the film in London with British musicians but found the results lacking and re-recorded the music in New York with American jazz musicians.[38] With jazz helping to define the sounds of the beat generation a decade prior, the use of the genre in *Blowup* acts as background to an emerging youth culture taking influence from the previous into the formation of the new. Interestingly, the main riff from Hancock's track 'Bring Down the Birds' would later be sampled for 1990s dance culture in the form of 'Groove is in the Heart' by Dee-Lite, the reverberations of the film and its soundtrack heard in the city, and its youth spaces, some twenty-five years later.

In the film, the interactions between Jane and Thomas in his studio are interesting in that they evoke a variety of youth cultural rituals of the time, such as drugs (smoking), music, dance and fashion in a curious pop interior. While the couple are conversing in the sitting area, Thomas instructs Jane to listen to a jazz record in a particular way; in doing so, he introduces her to particular 'hip' modes of consuming youth music – 'have a listen to this!' – upon which the non-diegetic music of Herbie Hancock's original jazz score becomes diegetic, emanating from a revolving turntable. Jane participates in this ritual, yet her actions are allowed and informed by Thomas's instructions to 'listen, keep still. You can smoke if you like … slowly, slowly! Against the beat.' Her interpretation of the music through erratic dance moves is ultimately tamed by Thomas's vocal demands and seductive, come-hither stare. While Hancock's jazz score is paramount to the film, sounds of rock and pop music weave in and out of the film similar to radio waves of the era. A cover version of the Lovin' Spoonful's 'Did You Ever Have to Make Up Your Mind' plays quietly in the background of the 'close your eyes' model scene but interestingly was not included as part of the film's final soundtrack release. Released as a single at the end of April 1966, the song would have been played consistently on the radio, and its inclusion in the film stands out not only apart from Hancock's jazz score but also as a mimetic device, weaving together the realities of Swinging London with Antonioni's cinematic version.

The use of rock as a site of transgression for youth comes to fruition during The Yardbirds' performance of 'Stroll On' in the Ricky Tick nightclub. Situated besides a prominent window display featuring female mannequins and examples of mod fashion, the Ricky Tick represents the nightclub music scene in mid-1960s Britain. Initially, Thomas encounters the club after following a woman he believes to be Jane, yet her 'image' vanishes in front of the Permutit Leisure boutique. Thomas proceeds down a back alleyway and wanders into the club, encountering The Yardbirds on stage in front of an audience of motionless youths. The club is positioned as a hidden site of youthful expression, tucked away from busy London streets. As an interstitial space, then, Antonioni emphasises the Ricky Tick as a meeting space for youth; reconstructed images are featured on the interior door to the performance area and reference then-contemporary events and figures associated with a larger cultural context of Swinging London. The images included references to Harold Wilson (featuring the phrase, 'I Love Harold'), Hitler (a portrait with the word bubble, 'It was either this, or a milk round'), and Bob Dylan's 'death' ('Here Lies Bob Dylan: Passed Away Royal Albert Hall, 27 May 1966 R.I.P.'). In particular, the Dylan image refers to his infamous concert at the Albert Hall (actually the Free Trade Hall in Manchester on 17 May), during which his use of an electric guitar caused controversy with his dedicated folk audience, leading part of his audience to proclaim his 'death'.

Juxtaposed with The Yardbirds' raucous performance, the Ricky Tick serves as a place in which youth culture meets and consumes, albeit statically apart from Janet Street-Porter and her dance partner's rhythmic moves which break up the straight lines of the audience. As Roland-Francois Lack notes, 'the original Ricky Tick Club was in Windsor, with branches in other areas outside London [...] The relocation of this club to central London off Oxford and Heddon Street is one of the film's manipulations of reality, though considerable effort is made to make the displacement feasible, down to producing posters for this staged event at the new location.'[39] The juxtaposition of Thomas's fluid movement through the static audience (strolling on ...?) imparts a sense of critique in which youth culture can be viewed as static, empty and vacuous and not in keeping with the implicit tones of destruction in The Yardbird's performance. According to writer and cultural historian Paul Drummond, 'Jimmy Page refused to believe that the scene he was in with The Yardbirds was heavily scripted, including the whole bit when Jeff Beck bangs the guitar into the amp (more of The Who than The Yardbirds anyways). Page's impression was that Michelangelo [Antonioni] hadn't a clue what he was doing. He couldn't believe it. That whole club scene looks a bit despondent, there is no direction from the camera.'[40]

Interestingly, The Yardbirds were not Antonioni's first choice; he toyed also with the Velvet Underground, The Who and The In Crowd (later known as Tomorrow). The Yardbirds offered a darker window into the era's penchant for rock 'n' roll and become representative of the youthful hedonism suggested by the music.[41] The Yardbirds' re-working of 'Train Kept A Rollin' highlights a style of songwriting for blues rock compositions of the time, one that Page would continue with Led Zeppelin. The Yardbirds' performance also captures the band at an interesting point in their history, with two lead guitarists, Page and Beck, after Eric Clapton's departure. During their performance, filmic time and space is further displaced with the 'give em' the song again' cut towards the end of the scene, in which Beck smashes his guitar all the more against his Vox amp and then the stage floor before hurling the debris into the crowd. This extends the group's performance and musical interlude in the film, noting also the moment when the audience comes alive into constructed violence: collectively crowding the stage to obtain a piece of Beck's guitar, an emblematic symbol of rock 'n' roll power in the context of the Ricky Tick but outside in the street at night, discarded.

'Sometimes reality is the strangest fantasy of all': *Blowup* conclusions

With *Blowup*'s eventual success, 'Antonioni reached a broader public than ever before or since in his career, and the film's success led to a contract for three more English-language films with MGM (only two were ever made: *Zabriskie Point* and *The Passenger*)'.[42] Continuing an exploration of the relationship between youth culture and violence in *Zabriskie Point*, the blowup of the image became the violent and material blowup of the American dream. This cultural fascination with youth permissiveness made manifest through new rituals of sex and music offered a voyeuristic type of seduction into new modes and ways of being. For many within the counterculture, *Blowup* presented a way out of the mundane: both Ethan Russell and Baron Wolman, noted rock photographers of the era, have cited the film as their inspiration, the latter quipped in 2010, '*Blow-Up* was my inspiration; with the exception of the Bentley and the murder, that was pretty much my life, too.'[43] With an emphasis on 'the image' and practices of looking, Antonioni suggests a critical stance for interpreting the media myth of Swinging London as well as its representations of youth culture. As Antonioni suggests, 'the young people among whom my film is situated are all aimless, without any drive but to reach that aimless freedom. Freedom from that for them means marijuana, sexual perversion, anything ... What you get at the end doesn't interest me ... It's that conquest of freedom that matters. Once it's conquered, once all discipline is discarded, then it's decadence. Decadence without any visible future'.[44] While much of the mystery in the film is by compromise and not design, the free hedonism explored in *Blowup* interweaves with moments of sex and music to present a sordid youth culture in which London is not Swinging but caught in a moment on the verge of collapse.

Notes

1. Antonioni quoted in Carlo di Carlo (ed.), *My Antonioni* (Cineteca di Bologna/Istituto Luce: Cinecitta, 2017).
2. This chapter uses the original 1966 UK release title for the film, rather than the hyphenated *Blow-Up*, which is used on subsequent US releases for the film.
3. Quoted Robert Murphy, *Sixties British Cinema* (London: BPI Publishing, 1992), p. 148.
4. Ibid.
5. *Blowup* DVD notes (2004).
6. Cortazar's original title is 'Las Babas del Diablo' (literally translated as 'The Droolings of the Devil'), although Peter Brunette asserts in the 2004 DVD

commentary that Antonioni's film is 'only very loosely based' on the short story. Nevertheless, the success of the film influenced Cortazar's career, and his 1967 collection of short stories was subsequently titled *Blow-Up and Other Short Stories*.
7 According to Peter Lev, 'Wyndham's article is a long interview with three successful young photographers – Brian Duffy, Terence Donovan, and David Bailey – which describes the milieu of British fashion photography circa 1964 [...] Their professional and personal innovations included a more directly sexual approach to fashion, photography and art photography, and a similar coming together of documentation of an event and creation of an event. The photographers observed the London scene but also helped to create it.' See Peter Lev, "Blow-up, Swinging London and the Film Generation," *Literature Film Quarterly*, 17:2 (1989), 134.
8 This chapter uses the names of the characters Thomas, Jane, The Blonde One and The Brunette, as noted in the original screenplay of the film. There is no mention of specific names for characters throughout the duration of the film, apart from Ron, who can perhaps be determined as representative of the older generation owing to his more established position as Thomas's business partner. The aura of anonymity that pervades youth in the film ultimately enhances the characters' fluid explorations of Swinging London.
9 Criterion Collection, 'Blowup: Interview with David Hemmings', 2017, www.youtube.com/watch?v=SsVdGr9yNjg (accessed November 2021).
10 *Blowup* trailer (1966).
11 Also in 1967, Hemmings founded Hemdale Film Corporation, which he left in 1971. After directing David Bowie in *Just a Gigolo* (1978), Hemmings was asked to film footage of the singer performing at Stafford and Earl's Court London that same year; the saga perhaps too long for this footnote. A few minutes of this footage have resurfaced in the David Bowie documentary *Moonage Daydream* (dir. Brett Morgen, 2022).
12 Peter Ackroyd, *London: The Biography* (London: Vintage, 2001), p. 760.
13 Ibid.
14 Michael J. Dear, *The Postmodern Urban Condition* (Oxford: Blackwell Publishers, 2000), p. 179.
15 Ibid., p. 184.
16 Ibid., p. 182.
17 Entitled 'The Scene', *Time*'s map of the Swinging London scene delineates such districts as South Kensington, Belgravia, Chelsea and Mayfair as youth-oriented consumer spaces. Boutiques such as Hung on You, Bazaar, Top Gear and Countdown are also noted.
18 Ian Buchanan, 'Space in the Age of Non-Place', in Ian Buchanan and Gregg Lambert (eds), *Deleuze and Space* (Toronto: University of Toronto Press, 2005), p. 28.
19 Ibid., p. 29.
20 Martin Harrison quoted in Hilary Radner, 'On the Move: Fashion Photography and the Single Girl in the 1960s', in Stella Bruzzi and Pamela Church Gibson

(eds), *Fashion Cultures: Theories, Explorations and Analysis* (London: Routledge, 2000), p. 129.
21 In his autobiography, David Hemmings claims, 'originally, it was the idea of Antonioni's producer, Carlo Ponti, that he should make a film that reflected the new breed of unorthodox and independent fashion photographers like David Bailey, Terry O'Neil and Terry Donovan. However, nothing had come of it until Ponti heard that Antonioni was adapting a Julio Cortazar story about a photographer and planning to shoot it in Milan, at which point he suggested that the Maestro should set it in London. Antonioni had come to London over the winter specifically to see if the media portrayals of the city were real'. See David Hemmings, *Blow-Up and Other Exaggerations* (London: Robson Books, 2004), pp. 8–9.
22 George Melly, *Revolt into Style: The Pop Arts* (London: Penguin Press, 1970), p. 160.
23 Ibid., p. 161.
24 Ibid., p. 160.
25 *Blowup* theatrical trailer (1966).
26 Swinging London, with its fashion models, music clubs and playful parties is tempered with the images of the harsher realities of London. Thomas's freelance photography project has him visit the doss house at the beginning of the film and show the photographs to Ron (Peter Bowles) later during the restaurant scene (actual restaurant location: 8–9 Blacklands Terrace, just off the King's Road, Chelsea).
27 Guy Debord, *Society of the Spectacle* (Detroit: Black and Red, 1970), p. 2.
28 Interestingly, the murder photographs, along with Thomas's portfolio photographs of the doss house and scenes of London life, were taken on set by British photojournalist Don McCullin, known also for his war photography and scenes of downtrodden life. See John Cowan, *Through the Light Barrier* (Munich: Schirmer/Mosel, 1999).
29 This 'mirroring' of reality and fantasy is also apparent in the use of actual Swinging London photographer John Cowan's studio as a principal set for Thomas's studio at 39 Princes Place, as well as Cowan's photography throughout the film. See Cowan, *Through the Light Barrier*.
30 Adam Scovell, 'Blowup: In search of the Swinging London locations', 3 May 2017, www2.bfi.org.uk/news-opinion/news-bfi/features/blowup-michelangelo-antonioni-london-locations (accessed November 2021).
31 For further information see R.G. Davis, 'Guerrilla Theatre', www.diggers.org/guerrilla_theatre.htm.
32 David Talbot, *Season of the Witch: Enchantment, Terror, and Deliverance in the City of Love* (New York: Free Press, 2013), p. 90.
33 The Economist Plaza also features in the opening scenes of the Swinging London film *I'll Never Forget What's 'is Name* (1967), starring Oliver Reed and Carol White, directed by Michael Winner.
34 Born Verushka von Lehndorff in East Prussia, 1939, Verushka began modelling in the mid-60s. Interestingly, her family history adds impetus to the class myth

which pervades the Swinging London era; her mother was the former Countess Gottliebe von Kalnein, and her father, Heinrich Graf von Lehndorff Steinort was a member of the German Resistance. Her involvement in London during the mid-1960s also enhanced the increasing European stylistic influence on fashion, music and modelling.

35 George Slover, 'Isolation and Make-Believe in *Blow-Up*', in Roy Huss (ed.), *Focus on Blow-Up* (London: Prentice Hall, 1971).
36 Peter Brunette, *The Films of Michelangelo Antonioni* (Cambridge: Cambridge University Press, 1998), pp. 110–12.
37 Ibid., p. 111.
38 *Blowup* soundtrack liner notes to 2000 CD release.
39 See Roland-Francois Lack, 'London Circa Sixty-Six: The Map of the Film', in Gail Cunningham and Stephen Barber (eds), *London Eyes: Reflections Intext and Image* (New York: Berghahn Books, 2007), p. 162.
40 Personal communication, 2021.
41 After filming *Blowup*, The Yardbirds appeared later that year as signifiers of 'the new youth music' in *Go Go Go Said The Bird* (aired 26 October 1966), a film that aimed to 'pinpoint the attitudes that have contributed to the phenomenon of 'Swinging London' through four vignettes of Swinging London movers and shakers: John Dunbar, Pauline Fordham, David Cammell and Simon Napier-Bell.
42 Lev, 'Blow-up, Swinging London', p. 135.
43 Personal communication, 2010.
44 Antonioni, Michelangelo, 'Antonioni Talks About His Work: "First I Must Isolate Myself"', *Life*, 27 January 1967, p. 66.

10

'Everything gets boring after a time': *Deep End* and swinging sex

David Wilkinson

Jerzy Skolimowski's *Deep End* deals stylishly with the seductions and dangers of sexual desire, accompanied by a hip soundtrack featuring Can and Cat Stevens. The film depicts the volatile and ultimately murderous sexual awakening of its baby-faced teen protagonist Mike in his first job as a pool attendant at a decrepit London swimming baths. Beset with various difficulties upon its release in 1970, *Deep End* was consigned to obscurity for four decades. To revisit this film is to encounter a cultural document that asks some difficult questions of the much-mythologised sexual liberation of the 1960s; a myth encapsulated first by the mediatised phenomenon of Swinging London and later by its more radical countercultural outgrowth.

In this chapter, I argue that *Deep End* undertakes a kind of autocritique that is as much formal as it is content-based, drawing like the counterculture upon a boundary crossing jumble of modernist and popular cultural sources. It does so in a manner that participates knowingly in the transgressive allure of youthful 'sexual liberation' quite as much as it undermines this sensibility. Ideologically complex and suggestive, appearing to critique youthful alienation, consumerism and sexism even as it is tinged with a certain pessimistic conservatism, *Deep End* is significant not only for the structures of feeling it captures from its own era but also for the ways the film's themes continue to resonate in a fractious present of ever more commodified sexual desire.

Why Deep End?

It is worth asking why my focus is on film, given that this is a collection focused on youth culture and popular music. As Patrick Glen's ethnographic research has confirmed, there was a two-way process at work in the 1960s and 1970s, whereby film viewing both fed the critical perspectives of participants in the British counterculture and was itself understood through these perspectives.[1] Film, therefore, was a key element of the diverse range of cultural production and consumption through which countercultural attitudes to sex were explored.

Furthermore, it is important to clarify why I concentrate on *Deep End* in particular. First, this is a collection that wants to look again at the post-war era, youth culture and sex. The cult status of *Deep End*, long difficult to view until its eventual appearance on a BFI DVD in 2011, fits nicely such an aim of revisiting.[2] There is also a strong intertextual link between *Deep End* and Michelangelo Antonioni's more canonical *Blowup*, addressed elsewhere in the collection. Both feature a European auteur turning their attention to sexual liberation in the anglophone world. With the Polish Skolimowski in particular, we are getting an outsider's perspective at least partly informed by the Eastern bloc – though a dissident one, it must be said. Skolimowski quite literally acts as a curious observer, at one point granting himself a brief non-speaking cameo playing a passenger on a London Underground train in which the film's two main characters Mike and Susan argue.

As also above, the film prominently features music associated with the counterculture in its soundtrack: Cat Stevens's 'But I Might Die Tonight' at its opening and conclusion, along with Can's 'Mother Sky' in a frenetic after-dark sequence occurring amidst the backstreet porn cinemas, brothels and clubs of Soho. This is neither a historical coincidence nor a purely commercial decision designed to attract a particular audience. Rather, both songs were written specifically for the film and are central to its examination of sexual desire and countercultural values.[3] *Deep End* cements this connection to the counterculture through its casting of the actress Jane Asher in a leading role as Susan. Between 1963 and 1968, Asher had been in a relationship with Paul McCartney and accompanied the Beatles on their famed journey to Rishikesh to study transcendental meditation. As I have already suggested, there are significant formal similarities between *Deep End* and other instances of countercultural production, most noticeably in the fusion of 'high' and popular modes that marked everything from the novels of Michael Moorcock to the underground press. Finally, and crucially, the confused and volatile sexual awakening of adolescent youth is the central theme of the film.

The following analysis begins by reflecting briefly on the social and sexual conjuncture of Britain at the dawn of the 1970s, noting key countercultural perspectives on it while situating *Deep End* in relation to these perspectives. From here, I turn to Skolimowski's habitus as a means of framing the film's thematic concerns, formal strategies and ideological positions. I then consider Skolimowski's formal strategies and their implications in more detail, before moving to a close reading of the film that notes the ways in which it addresses three important themes in relation to sexual liberation: youth, commodification and gender.

Overall, I claim that *Deep End* draws shrewd parallels between the 'permissive' liberalism of the dominant culture in the late 1960s and the more radical or transgressive positions adopted by the counterculture. This is an ideologically ambiguous critique, mirroring the structural and historical vacillations of the new middle class when it comes to political allegiance. Looked at from one angle, *Deep End* is *kulturkritik* in pop-cultural disguise; an elitist, pessimistic aesthetic recoil from advancing modernity.[4] From another angle, however, the film offers a kind of immanent critique, taking the eros of sexual liberation at its word while compellingly exploring the thanatotic contradictions of generational conflict, commodity fetishism and patriarchy. In concluding, I think through the implications of *Deep End* in the contemporary conjuncture – including the film's use of death as a metaphor for commodified sexual desire.

Swinging London, the counterculture and sex

As Yvonne Tasker has argued, despite the 'significant liberalisation of sexual mores' in the years leading up to *Deep End*'s release, 'it is easy to overstate the pace of social … change'. Tasker notes that surveys throughout the 1960s revealed a tenacious conservatism regarding sexual matters; that 'the highly marketable image of the Swinging Sixties was centred on and largely derived from a metropolitan elite rather than reflecting the norms of British men and women's experience'; and that 'the very phrase "permissive society" encapsulates the contradictions of the moment, incorporating as it does a degree of doubt as to what should be permitted in a modern society'.[5] Nevertheless, something of note was going on. Raph Samuel has characterised the '"liberal hour" of the 1960s' as 'the moment when the repressed energies of [the new middle class] were released, when it began to move freely across the face of society, and to see in itself, culturally if not politically, society's natural leaders'.[6] Such perceptions of leadership were accompanied by inevitable ambitions toward hegemony, including in matters of sex. Where the new middle class went for kicks, others were expected to follow.

This is the situation of *Deep End*'s characters – confronted with, and partly interpellated by, what David Alderson has theorised as 'repressive incitement': a provocation of sexual desire which commodifies, fetishises and alienates it in the pursuit of profit, freeing it from the fetters of hidebound morality yet subjecting it to capital's relentless logic of production and growth.[7] 'We are encouraged to believe', Alderson argues, 'that we can always have more and better sex.'[8] This is a situation that makes contentment impossible while rendering frustration and disappointment endemic. Early in the film we see the phrase 'I'm not getting enough' graffitied upon the wall of a bathing cabin, setting the mood for what transpires.

The sexual liberalisation of the dominant culture is not the only pressure explored in *Deep End*. Arriving in the wake of the counterculture's blossoming, the film engages too with countercultural affirmations of sex as a wayward, irrational and disruptive force. Jeff Nuttall wrote of 'a particular kind of fucking, no gracious domestic coupling of dam and sire, but the hot, intense act of desperate moments … of self-affirmation for people … whose selves seem often to be wandering some way off'.[9] Meanwhile Germaine Greer railed against 'dull sex for dull people' and the 'statistically ideal fuck' advocated by mainstream sexology. 'The sexual personality is basically anti-authoritarian', Greer asserted, advising women that 'they must hold out not just for orgasm but for ecstasy.'[10] Such claims evoke the frenzy that Mike becomes caught up in as his pursuit of Susan becomes ever more obsessive and unhinged, leading to behaviour that seems completely at odds with his otherwise amiable and innocent temperament.

Habitus

In what social milieu, though, was *Deep End*'s investigation of sexual liberation rooted? Against the doxa of the death of the author, it is especially important to consider the work of Skolimowski in this manner, given that he is 'a compulsive autobiographer who uses film to tell different versions of his own story'.[11] The son of an architect father and a mother who was a cultural attaché in Prague, he attended the famed Lodz Film School and was thus caught up in the expansion of the cultural industries that took place in the Eastern bloc just as in the West in the post-war period.[12] Like many of his generation globally, such experiences disposed the young Skolimowski to countercultural participation. He travelled with, and made lighting for, the dissident jazz ensemble of Krzystof Komeda, which soundtracked the films of Andrej Wajda and Roman Polanski.[13] Skolimowski was also involved with the alternative student theatre movement in Poland, which, as Joanna Ostrowska and Juliusz Tyszka have argued, was 'an important part of the world countercultural art movement' of the 1960s and beyond.[14] His early films dealt with 'young people disenfranchised from society', leading to a reputation as the cinematic 'voice of his generation'.[15] Importantly with regard to the way in which *Deep End* investigates sexual desire, this was a generation that, according to Ewa Mazierska, 'was more individualistic, even self-centred and consumption-oriented than their predecessors' – a statement as true of the Western audience of *Deep End* as it is of Skolimowski's native Poland to which Mazierska here refers.[16]

All this meant that the director's outlook was dissident, anti-authoritarian and 'non-conformist' as Mazierska puts it. Skolimowski clashed with the Polish Communist authorities over the content of his film *Hands Up!* and became an émigré to the West, settling first in London between 1970 and 1984 before moving to California. He would not return to Poland until the fall of communism.[17] As a result, Skolimowski maintained a political and artistic hostility toward socialism and communism, perceiving them as inherently totalitarian.[18] Along with this went a resentful 'contempt' for the working class, motivated by the way in which the 'official discourses' of the Communist state portrayed it as 'the nation's elite, at the expense of the intelligentsia'.[19] Though determined by different national and political circumstances, such contempt echoed those middle-class factions of the British counterculture competing to occupy the role of social vanguard, which dismissed the working class as 'authoritarian xenophobic hardhats'.[20]

On the face of it, such a habitus might suggest an affinity with Western liberal sexual mores, along with countercultural responses to them, rather than a radical critical investigation. Yet an insightful observation by Mazierska complicates this picture somewhat. She argues that in Skolimowski's films that are set in the capitalist West, characters are often somewhat socially decontextualised and one-dimensional. Mazierska puts this down to two factors: first, the director's lack of interest in the 'politics and culture of those countries where he lived as an emigrant'. Second, she claims that despite Skolimowski's opposition to communism, his interviews and films frequently demonstrate the belief that for Westerners, 'there is no more to life than work and consumption. Consequently, they are defined by where they work and what they can afford to buy'. This is a belief inculcated by the Polish state propaganda of the era.[21]

I would argue, however, that what might seem to be potential formal weaknesses may actually be strengths. Presented in uncanny isolation, wage labour and consumerism are defamiliarised, conveying starkly their undeniably powerful determining force on young people's lives in post-war capitalist societies. This is certainly the case with Mike, Susan and various other characters in *Deep End*, whose sexual desires are without exception presented squarely in the context of work and consumption. Furthermore, though Skolimowski's habitus predictably led him to break with state-sanctioned socialist realism, his use of surrealist and expressionist tropes meant that the potentially subversive features of these modes were deployed in films such as *Deep End*.

Form

It is important to discuss the issue of form in more detail. As Fredric Jameson has argued, particular means of representing the world entail both opportunities and limits as to how we are able to imagine that world and what might be possible both within and beyond it.[22] Ultimately, though, the possibilities and limits of cultural forms can only be evaluated by what Perry Anderson has evoked as 'a sense of culture as a battlefield ... the plane of politics'.[23] It is therefore important to reflect not only on the significance of form for the way Skolimowski handles the theme of sexual liberation in *Deep End* but also on the specific ways that the effects of such formal decisions resonate in our contemporary conjuncture.

Beginning his career as a poet before moving to cinema, Skolimowski's eclectic approach to cultural form matched his 'indifferen[ce] to the laws of genre'.[24] His utilisation of both 'high' and popular formal resources within *Deep End* was typical of the counterculture more broadly. A large body of scholarship has documented the way in which post-war trends of expanded education, the growth of mass media and the increasing commodification of culture acted to partly democratise aesthetic practices and knowledges that had once largely been the preserve of the leisure class and the dissident bourgeoisie.[25] This is a phenomenon that Mark Fisher has called 'popular modernism'.[26] As much as this popularisation of the avant-garde may be viewed as part of a more general postmodern collapsing of 'high' and 'low' in the wake of 'an immense dilation of [the cultural] sphere' by way of the market, it is important to think this process through further in terms specific to Skolimowski's habitus.[27] Discussing modernism and the avant-garde, Raymond Williams notes that their formal origins lay frequently in the phenomenon of 'immigration to the metropolis'. Thus the frequent strangeness, hybridity and self-consciousness of modernist and avant-garde cultural forms often have their roots in the experiences of figures displaced from their roots in large, multicultural cities.[28] These are experiences that Skolimowski would retread over half a century later, accounting for the unsettling atmosphere of *Deep End* and its treatment of sexual desire.

In particular, Skolimowski explicitly borrows from the legacy of surrealism.[29] Metaphor; juxtaposition; black humour; the uncanny; and inanimate objects acquiring significance are all consistent features of his *oeuvre*.[30] For Mazierska, the surreal effects of Skolimowski's films occasionally derive from the straitened circumstances in which he made them.[31] This is clearly the case with *Deep End* – its uncanny, dreamlike feel is in part a result of expedient filming and casting, with many scenes being shot in Munich and a majority of the supporting actors being German, despite the film's setting in London. Expressionism, too, is a common resource.[32] The use of colour, lighting and setting, as well as camerawork, to evoke emotion and subjective states all feature in *Deep End*. Surrealist and expressionist tropes coexist in the film with the use of popular forms – notably psychological horror and countercultural rock.

All in all, there is a curious continuity between the film's hybrid form, its ideological ambiguity and Skolimowski's professional middle-class background. Alex Callinicos notes with regard to the professional 'new' middle class that it 'is a collection of heterogeneous social layers who have in common an ambiguous and intermediate position with respect to the fundamental contradiction between capital and wage-labour'.[33] Because of this, Val Burris adds, 'nothing definitive can be inferred about their political orientation other than it is likely to be varied and changeable'.[34] In the following sections, I examine how this variability plays out at the level of form and content with respect to *Deep End*'s presentation of sexual liberation.

'But I Might Die Tonight': youth

As the introduction to this collection notes: 'The sexual liberation of the late twentieth century, however contested and awkward and incomplete, was bound to a cultural "youthquake" that tested how far the freedoms promised by capitalism, consumerism and democracy could go.'[35] In a more explicitly countercultural register, Jeff Nuttall claimed that from the late 1960s, 'young people … made war on their elders, and their elders made war on them'.[36] The issue of sexual freedom was only one facet of a conjuncture in which, as the Centre for Contemporary Cultural Studies argued, youth became a metaphor for the tensions and upheavals of post-war social change more broadly.[37]

Deep End, like much of Skolimowski's output, is intensely focused on the trials of youth. Its amorphously aquatic atmosphere draws on another Skolimowski staple – the use of water as a surrealist metaphor for a transitional state.[38] Echoing the broader conjuncture, the director both celebrates youth as an intoxicating, disruptive force and presents it as a problem – an arrested phase between a lost childhood and an undesirably corrupt, conformist adulthood. The use of Cat Stevens's 'But I Might Die Tonight' to open the film captures this exquisitely. Its delicate introduction, led by acoustic guitar, piano and wistful, wordless vocals treated with echo, beautifully conveys the film's sympathy with youthful rebellion and the rejection of adult responsibility, which is crystallised in the song's first lines: 'I don't want to work away/ doing just what they all say/ Work hard boy and you'll find/ one day you'll have a job like mine.'[39]

This has a number of resonances at the level of sexual desire and freedom. In line with the film's celebration of youth as rebellion, Mike's increasingly obsessive and irrational pursuit of Susan is the alluring narrative hook of the film, drawing on psychological horror's ability to compellingly manifest unconscious or socially inappropriate desire in a pleasurable way.[40] This is not just a narrative phenomenon but a visual one. As viewers, our identification with the desires of the main characters is encouraged through their frequent objectification. Interestingly, this is not just the case with Asher as Susan but also John Moulder-Brown as Mike. The camera lingers on his angelic features and his slim teenage body is depicted semi- or fully nude a number of times in a manner that allows not only for heterosexual female desire but also for a transgressively queer gaze.

Yet the potentially lethal consequences of youthful lust are also the film's seeming moral message. Some viewers and critics were apparently shocked and dissatisfied with *Deep End*'s conclusion. Mike, overwhelmed with shame and rage after experiencing nervous impotence or premature ejaculation (it is not clear which), swings an overhead pool light at Susan, which catches her on the head and kills her. Skolimowski responded to claims that this turn of events was incongruous by stating, 'I made the film for that last five minutes.'[41]

In fairness, there are more than enough premonitory hints throughout the film that things are not going to end well. The very first image we see in the title credits is a luscious drop of vivid red blood – and what gives Stevens's song its power is the way its gentle verses build to the chorus's impassioned, existential climax line: 'But I might die tonight!' As the plot develops, too, *Deep End* makes use of surrealist juxtaposition via the growing contrast between Mike's innocent appearance and his increasingly dangerous behaviour (riding his bicycle in front of the car of a teacher with whom Susan is having an affair, caressing her from a seat behind her in the cinema where she is sitting with her fiancé and so on). Following the repetitive logic of the recurring dream, both Mike's humiliation and Susan's death are repeatedly prefigured in symbolic form. For example, Mike is knocked into the pool by a group of teenage boys whom he challenges after they cat-call Susan and tease him by crudely asking if he has 'been up there' – and the first scene in the pool manager's office has Mike dazedly fixating on a dangerous looking light patched up with red electrical tape that occupies the space between him and the manager.

The threat posed by deranging desire is also conveyed through expressionistic means. *Deep End* makes frequent symbolic use of the colour red and its connotations of passion, aggression and danger – from Susan's hair and the pool's interior railings to the scene in which Mike slips a mirror under a door to observe her having sex, which he then drops. He responds by smashing the pool's red fire alarm in a jealous fury (which has a red 'danger' sign next to it), his hand shown bleeding from the broken glass. The shattered fire alarm panel and the broken mirror may also convey the definitive fragmentation of his stable state of mind. The film's setting, too, works powerfully to convey psychological disquiet. Two thirds of *Deep End* is shot within the confines of the pool and many other scenes take place in the dark, generating an intense and claustrophobic mood.

Skolimowski's accentuation of youthful lust as a problem does not, however, result in an affirmation of adult sexual maturity and social conformity. In line with the director's countercultural anti-conformism, the adults of *Deep End* are frequently presented as expressionistic sexual grotesques, damaged by repression or hypocrisy. The decrepitude of the pool itself seems a further extension of this portrayal. The first scene features an absurd close-up of the pool manager's gnarled face and stained teeth, his desk surrounded by pin-up girls as he echoes Cat Stevens ironically, saying to Mike, 'if you work hard you may end up behind this desk one day'. Susan's workplace nemesis, the receptionist, is portrayed as jealous, seething and repressed; the closest she gets to release is running down the corridor wielding an ejaculating fire extinguisher after Mike sets off the alarm. Most notoriously, Diana Dors has a cameo as a middle-aged bather, all peroxide and polka dots, who flirts campily with Mike. Shortly afterwards, she pretends to faint in her cabin as a pretext for performing a sexual assault on him that is as hilarious as it is distressing, culminating in her shoving Mike's head between her legs as she fantasises about George Best: 'Dribble, dribble … shoot! … Get out. I don't need you anymore.' The film is shot through with such black humour, which in a further instance of juxtaposition contrasts sharply with the seriousness of Mike's obsession, thus accentuating the latter. It is not just adult sexuality that the film decries either. In an uncanny moment, Mike bumps into his former girlfriend in the baths, who attempts to seduce him. Fixated on Susan, though, he is forever detached from what might appear to be a safe, familiar option. Rebuffing her, he remarks 'the old scene seems so strange.'

Mike, then, is stranded, caught between a lost childhood and a corrupt older generation in an arrested youth marked by destructive sexual frustration and insecurity. Unlike the more radical elements of the counterculture, which elided *amour fou* with social revolution, or the humanistic dialogue established in Cat Stevens's 'Father and Son' (from the same LP as 'But I Might Die Tonight'), the film will not or cannot suggest a productive way out. Symbolically, 'But I Might Die Tonight' plays at the conclusion of the film as well as the opening credits, rejecting any wholesome, *Bildungsroman*-style suggestions of development and maturity.

As a means of evaluating *Deep End*'s treatment of post-war youth and sexual liberation, we might do well to start by recalling György Lukács' critique of the modernist and avant-garde cultural forms that the film draws upon:

> both emotionally and intellectually they all remain frozen in their own immediacy; they fail to pierce the surface to discover the underlying essence, i.e. the real factors that relate their experiences to the hidden social forces that produce them.[42]

It is a critique that could with some justification be levelled at *Deep End*. The film's camerawork, in particular, frequently simulates the fleeting and often confused perceptions of its central characters. By using external settings to symbolise subjective states, it could be said that the film's expressionist techniques collapse the social world into its immediate apprehension by individuals. Meanwhile, the reliance of surrealism on a Freudian model of the unconscious risks reducing social conflict to purely psychological conflict, an impression that is strengthened by Mazierska's willingness to interpret Skolimowski's cinematic depictions of youth in psychoanalytical terms.[43]

Nevertheless, as Yvonne Tasker observes, one of the notable features of the film is its resolute avoidance of private, domestic space. Instead it depicts a 'public sexual culture' in which sex is 'insistently present'.[44] Thus *Deep End*'s evocations of Mike's sexual frustration and confusion come to seem applicable at a broader social level. Furthermore, the temptation to view the film in eternalised, Oedipal terms is undermined by the fact that Mike's parents hardly feature and we have little sense of his relationship with them or his historical subject formation. This is a film about work and consumption, not the family, according with Herbert Marcuse's observation that in the post-war period, capitalist reproduction has increasingly relied upon libidinised commodification rather than familial authority.[45] Indeed, *Deep End* is far from blind to the socially determining influence of consumerism on youthful sexual desire.

'Ten bob, she takes everything off!': commodification

As with the theme of youth, *Deep End* makes full use of avant-garde formal elements to convey the linkage of sex and consumerism. One such device is the surrealist attention to 'dream objects' – random features of material culture that seem to possess a greater significance than might first appear.[46] Mike's red bicycle is especially significant in this respect, especially when set against the teacher's red car. The film establishes an identity between Mike and his bike from the beginning – close-ups of it feature in the title sequence, as does a short clip of Mike riding it to his first fateful day at work. Throughout the film, these commodities come to symbolise sexual and generational competition and inequality, with a hint of castration anxiety when Mike's bicycle is run over as he tries to block the car's path, or when in the concluding scenes Mike punctures the car tyres to ensure that the teacher cannot pursue Susan and himself. Likewise, Susan and the middle-aged receptionist enact their mutual resentment of one another by way of consumer items. Suggestively eating whipped cream from the top of a hot chocolate, Susan says to the receptionist 'you'd like some of this, wouldn't you? I'm lucky I don't have a weight problem' – to which the receptionist responds by petulantly spraying the cream with the bottle of perfume she has been primly dousing herself with. In this way, the film can be read as a wry comment on the inherent alienation and competition of commodified sexual 'permissiveness'.

The comic spite and frustration of this scene lead on to another resonance of *Deep End*'s metaphorical 'dream objects'. This is the way in which the commodification of sexual desire ironically puts the apparent gratification promised by such 'liberation' tantalisingly out of reach by absorbing sexual pleasure into capitalism's logic of endless reproduction and growth – and through the inequality of access to sex once it is subjected to a pricing structure. 'Everything gets boring after a time', Mike says to Susan as they discuss money and her fiancé. Denied what he presumably believes to be the ultimate satisfaction of sleeping with Susan, Mike affixes his desire to a range of substitutions with predictably unfulfilling results. Receiving his first pay packet, Mike stalks Susan and her fiancé to a club in Soho where it turns out he cannot afford the cost of membership. He ends up lingering for hours outside, consuming endless hot dogs from a stall and briefly winning the affections of two young Liverpudlian girls by buying them one too. Encountering a life-size cardboard cut-out of the nude model 'Angelica from Manchester', Mike is first shocked to see that it appears to be Susan – then quickly steals it. In a further instance of the endless deferral of gratification transposed to the level of narrative, we never find out if the cut-out is 'really' Susan or if we are simply perceiving it through the deluded eyes of Mike. Hiding from the angry peepshow proprietor, he stumbles into a middle-aged prostitute's boudoir. With her garish make-up and her leg in cast, she is presented as another grotesque figure, one who openly acknowledges that her value has declined due to her condition. She nevertheless attempts to seduce Mike, saying 'you can't imagine the things we can do for three bob' as she offers to hold the cardboard cut-out over herself to fulfil Mike's fantasy.

The whole chaotic sequence is soundtracked by the avant-rock band Can's 'Mother Sky'. Its use of insistent rhythmic and lyrical repetition thrillingly conveys Mike's obsessive yet fruitless pursuit. So do the wild, improvisatory guitar parts, which vary just like the barrage of titillations Mike is subjected to by peepshow hustlers: 'Ten bob, she takes everything off!' Like those titillations, though, they go nowhere, repeatedly building and dropping in intensity. There is no climax, no ultimate satisfaction, to be had here, and no straightforward linear path through it all; the song opens mid- guitar solo and its structure does not conform to the standard pop song format. 'Tell me what's the price of your life?', the band's vocalist Damo Suzuki repeatedly murmurs, in an encapsulation of the commodification of desire.[47]

Returning to the pool under cover of night, Mike swims naked with the cut-out, miming sex with it and fantasising the real Susan. It is a sinister moment; one that turns out to be darker still, given that it acts as another of the repeated forewarnings of her death in the concluding scene. When Susan collapses into the pool after having been struck twice by the heavy overhead light, Mike's first response is to swim underwater, caressing her nude body in the film's disturbing final image. This necrophilia is no cheap, provocative horror film transgression – or rather, it is not only that. At the same time, surrealist metaphor is drawn upon: the reifying power of commodity fetishism as literal death. This, the film seems to suggest, is the source of youthful sexual frustration; of an obsessive pursuit of fulfilment that never materialises, resulting in an inability to flourish and profoundly morbid consequences. The price we pay is the pure madness that Suzuki sings of in 'Mother Sky'.

Deep End, therefore, does not stop at critiquing the commodified sex and sexualised consumerism of permissive 1960s Britain. In a further move, the film appears to suggest that the apparent social transgression of countercultural *amour fou* may actually have a direct connection with this dominant liberalism. It is Mike's pursuit of the glamorous and upwardly mobile Susan, after all, that sends him mad. An irrational aggression underpins the libidinised 'commodity wars' between Mike and the teacher and between Susan and the receptionist. The poster of the pregnant man on the notice board of the baths, designed to encourage the use of male contraception ('Would you be more careful if it was you that got pregnant?'), was a real-life campaign by Saatchi and Saatchi.[48] Produced for the Health Education Council, it signifies the extent of the crossover of sex and the market by this point, in that even the staid post-war welfare state was beginning to make use of the shock tactics of advertising. Yet it too becomes a 'dream object', bound up with the wilder fringes of sexual desire. Flirting with Mike, Susan lays the poster over him – and when Mike smashes the fire alarm after witnessing Susan's infidelity with the teacher, he wraps the same poster around his fist as a (failed) prophylactic against cutting his hand.

Finally, Susan's death is anticipated by sex-as-transaction: the only way Mike finally manages to have sexual contact with her is by finding the lost diamond from her engagement ring, which he proffers to her on his tongue.

Is countercultural sexual excess, then, just the furthest reach of modernising 'permissiveness' according to *Deep End*? Is Susan's death an extreme but 'logical' conclusion of such a society? Looked at this way, the film seems to presage those pessimistic critiques of the counterculture and the youthful libertarian energies of the 1960s more broadly that see them only or mainly as a forerunner of destructive free market fundamentalism.[49] Furthermore, Skolimowski's critique is by no means unequivocally progressive when considered in relation to habitus. Rather, given his opposition to socialism, it is more likely informed by the high-minded anti-philistinism of *kulturkritik*, able to perceive modernity only as the shallow materialism of the masses.

Yet this is not the whole picture. There is something compelling, intoxicating even, about *Deep End*'s portrayal of *amour fou*, suggesting a sympathy with it that keeps open the potential of sex as socially disruptive in more ways than simply the anarchy of the capitalist market. This is not an obviously didactic, puritanical film. Nor does it display straightforward contempt for its main characters in the way that we might expect from an elitist cultural cleric. The humour of *Deep End*, along with Mike's winning bashfulness and Susan's mischievous self-possession, lends it a humanity that allows us to identify rather than condemn. Asher and Moulder-Brown recall that Skolimowski involved them, giving them freedom to improvise and rewrite lines.[50] Susan's characterisation, in particular, as well as *Deep End's* representation of women more generally in relation to sexual liberation, is worth dwelling on in more detail before concluding.

'What am I supposed to be like?': gender

As Mazierska has identified, many of Skolimowski's films focus on young male protagonists trying to find a place in the world.[51] Predictably, this gives them a masculinist, even sexist, bent.[52] In this, they resemble much countercultural output before the advent of women's liberation. For Mazierska, 'Skolimowski seems unable to perceive women as autonomous beings, existing outside male perceptions. Connected with this narrative marginalisation of women is the fact that they come across as belonging to a specific type, rather than being unique individuals.'[53] She goes on to elaborate a taxonomy of female types in the director's *oeuvre*, categorising Susan as a 'broken lily', a woman 'whose experience with men has made her bitter and sometimes cunning'.[54] Because Mike is the protagonist with whom the film encourages us to identify most directly, Mazierska goes so far as to argue that Susan's death 'appears a just punishment ... a warning to women who attempt to elude male control and imagination'.[55] There is some evidence for a reading of Susan as unsympathetic and manipulative, a young woman whose sexual self-possession makes her cruel and dangerous by definition. When she asks her fiancé to get the manager after Mike touches her in the cinema, she waits for her fiancé's absence before leaning round and kissing Mike passionately, smirking to herself afterwards. Towards the end of the film, surrealist metaphor is employed when Susan coaxes a dog toward her, only to pelt it with a snowball.

Another category of female types in Skolimoski's films according to Mazierska is the 'withered rose' – 'women who have lost their youthful charm, but not their appetite for sex'. Such women are 'wretched ... pathetic ... undignified'. Including Diana Dors's portrayal of the female bather in this category, Mazierska believes that 'the clear message ... is that older women should stay away from young men'.[56] Again, there is some plausibility to this interpretation; Dors is an absurd figure of fun and a passing cameo rather than a fully developed character. Formally speaking, Raymond Williams observed that modernist and avant-garde revolts against dominant sexual and familial conventions often misogynistically scapegoated women.[57] Such sexism has been repeatedly documented, too, in the 'popular modernism' of the counterculture, such that feminist scholarship has long since moved on from simply identifying it to investigating women's troubling and complicated hegemonic investment in it.[58]

Deep End, however, is not as straightforwardly, obnoxiously misogynistic in its portrayal of women and sexual desire as Mazierska makes out. Another way to read it might be as an illustration of the very real dangers and problems faced by young women negotiating the apparent sexual liberation of commodified 'permissiveness', whose social position is still contradictorily determined by patriarchy. Confronting Susan with the nude cut-out he believes to be her, Mike pleads 'you're not like this', to which Susan tellingly responds, 'what am I supposed to be like?'

In a queasily disconcerting moment indebted to the film's use of psychological horror tropes, the largely incidental character of the pool's boilerman remarks exasperatedly of Susan, 'one of these days I'm really going to give her one' before returning to composed amiability. It is a line that implies the normalisation of a pervasive and aggressively domineering masculine desire with which women are forced to contend at every turn, accompanied by a spiteful victim-blaming sensibility that suggests women provoke such desire by embracing their own sexuality. Susan, too, is presented not only as a mean-spirited tease but also a victim of patriarchal dominance via her relationships; the older teacher with whom she is having an affair is portrayed as an exploitative pervert via a series of rapid and distressing cuts in which he interferes with the young teenage girls whose swimming lesson he is supervising, groping them and peering down their swimming costumes. Shortly before her death, Susan rejects him decisively, with a verbal assault that suggests a disturbing history of grooming. It is a moment that foregrounds her as an independent character, since Mike's only connection to the relationship between Susan and the teacher is one of jealousy. Class, too, conditions Susan's unenviable position: Tasker points out that she is often listless and bored, caught between the reality of a 'class ridden society' and the ideological perception of late 1960s liberal Britain 'as a site of opportunity'.[59] This boredom may also be interpreted as the alienating effect of the commodified sexual desire that the film critiques.

Finally, the stock type of the 'withered rose' can be denounced easily. Yet Dors's fervid, sweatily overwrought performance may also be seen as a critical comment on the dominant association of sex, youthfulness and leisured consumption that attempts to portray older people, especially women, as ridiculous and disgusting if they attempt to participate. There is a strong element of camp to the scene, suggesting ironic awareness more than unselfconscious complicity. If *Deep End* is not quite an example of the sexually affirmative countercultural feminism that would develop in the early 1970s, neither is it purely a sour spectacle of woman-hating.

Conclusion

Reflecting on *Deep End* upon its DVD release in 2011, Skolimowski opined, 'it still seems very fresh to me'. Asher concurred, claiming, 'I don't think it's dated at all.'[60] One reason for such perceptions may be that the themes the film deals with are more pervasive than ever. *Deep End*'s recognition of arrested youth and the sexual expression of this as compelling but problematic is far more insightful than the straightforward celebration of 'stretched out adolescence' as a supposedly radical subcultural challenge to bourgeois adult heteronormativity, which has developed from the work of cultural theorist Jack Halberstam on 'queer temporalities'.[61] The film's acknowledgement that Mike's increasingly outlandish behaviour is a product of the dominant conventions of the social world that he inhabits resonates with our contemporary conjuncture. These days, 'stretched out adolescence' is less a deliberate subcultural challenge and more the unchosen result of the economic precarity and weakened labour movement inherited by young people in the first decades of the twenty-first century.[62]

What Mark Fisher once called 'depressive hedonia', defined as 'not … an inability to get pleasure so much as an inability to do anything *except* pursue pleasure' in the eternal present of late capitalism, seems as prevalent as ever among many young people: sociological research suggests that overwhelming precarity conditions not just work but leisure time too.[63] At the level of sexual desire, such a situation is illustrated by commonplace addiction to dating and hook-up apps like Tinder and Grindr.[64] The grisly consequences of youthful *amour fou* in *Deep End* are not even necessarily metaphorical in the current conjuncture – Google searches for 'Tinder murders' and 'Grindr murders' bring up a horrifying number of news stories.

Deep End's recognition of the proximity between countercultural and dominant values regarding sex is also astute. Today's sexual avant-gardes, such as polyamory and the endless proliferation of sexual identities, are quite clearly bound up with the rhetoric of consumer choice rooted in expanding commodification and with the reification of selfhood demanded by digital platform capitalism, even as they offer utopian hints of a transformed future. As Christian Klesse has argued, they are also marked by divisions of class, echoing *Deep End*'s portrayal of the way that access to commodified sexual liberation is determined by class inequality.[65]

The connections that the film establishes between commodification, sexual desire and death are also relevant to contemporary gender relations. Susan's body is commodified through the earning of tips by swapping male bathing clients with Mike. He increasingly perceives her as an object to be possessed, culminating in the murderous reduction of her to one. The mortal danger faced by women in today's expanding sex industry is at least partly determined by the dehumanising effect of bodily commodification and its effects on consent, that is, the potential for the client to perceive that they can do what they want to the seller of sex, since that seller has become their 'property'.[66] As Karen Ingala Smith notes, 'a market of women ... commodifies women. It makes us into objects. As objects we become "less than", less than fully human, not equal ... interchangeable and disposable.'[67] This is an issue that should not be side-stepped by contemporary feminist thinking on sex work.[68]

Beyond gender, *Deep End*'s concern with the connections between commodification, sexual desire and death have more existential resonances. If the post-war period was a 'bomb culture', pervaded with a sense of underlying dread at the perpetual prospect of nuclear annihilation, we are now also contending with the 'anthropocene': a geological era in which the world's climate and ecosystems are now predominantly determined by the ruinous power of 'fossil capital'.[69] We would do well to consider that sexual liberation need not be bound to the insatiable and ecologically destructive drive of capitalism, just as many other aspects of a post-capitalist 'good life' may well be less subject to what Herbert Marcuse called the 'performance principle ... of an acquisitive and antagonistic society in the process of constant expansion', and what Theodor Adorno referred to as the 'confused compulsion to the conquest of strange stars'.[70]

Notes

1 Patrick Glen, 'Freak Scene: Cinema-going Memories and the British Counterculture of the 1960s', *The Sixties: A Journal of History, Politics and Culture*, 12:1 (2019), 45–68.
2 The filmmaker David Thompson attributes this to a limited art house cinema release and subsequent legal rights issues. David Thompson, 'Deep End', accompanying booklet to DVD re-release (BFI, 2011), p. 5.
3 Stevens (famously known as Yusuf Islam since his religious conversion in 1977) confirms that the song was written for the film on his website: https://web.archive.org/web/20110721094956/www.yusufislam.com/lifeline/10/a45dd1dc1476115ceb7fa21a45cbcd0f/ (accessed 16 May 2022), while 'Mother Sky' first appeared on Can's 1970 LP *Soundtracks*, a compilation of the band's work for films.
4 See Francis Mulhern, *Culture/Metaculture* (London: Routledge, 2000), pp. 18–21 for a discussion of the historical discourse of *kulturkritik*.
5 Yvonne Tasker, 'Permissive British Cinema?', accompanying booklet to DVD re-release of *Deep End* (BFI, 2011), p. 8.
6 Raph Samuel, 'The SDP and the New Middle Class', in Alison Light, Sally Alexander and Gareth Stedman Jones (eds), *Island Stories: Unravelling Britain* (London: Verso, 1999), p. 259.
7 David Alderson, 'Postmodernity, Hegemony, Sexuality', *Theoretical Studies in Literature in Art*, 33:1 (2013), 116.
8 Ibid., 114.
9 Jeff Nuttall, *Bomb Culture* (London: Strange Attractor, 2018 [1970]), p. 9.
10 Germaine Greer, *The Female Eunuch* (London: Paladin, 1970), pp. 43–4.
11 Ewa Mazierska, *Jerzy Skolimowski: The Cinema of a Nonconformist* (Oxford: Berghahn Books, 2010), p. 15.
12 Ewa Mazierska, 'Jerzy Skolimowski 1938 –' accompanying booklet to DVD re-release of *Deep End* (BFI, 2011), p. 15; Eglė Rindzevičiūtė, 'Transforming Cultural Policy in Eastern Europe: The Endless Frontier', *International Journal of Cultural Policy*, 27:2 (2021), 149–62.
13 Mazierksa, *Jerzy Skolimowski*, p. 3.
14 Joanna Ostrowska and Juliusz Tyszka, 'Alternative Theatre in Poland After 1989', *Journal of Applied Cultural Studies*, 2:1 (2016), 57–66.
15 Mazierska, *Jerzy Skolimowski*, pp. 6 and 3.
16 Ibid., p. 19.
17 Ibid., p. 4; Mazierska, 'Jerzy Skolimowski 1938 –', pp. 16–17.
18 Mazierska, *Jerzy Skolimowski*, p. 37.
19 Ibid., p. 28.
20 Richard Neville, *Playpower* (London: Paladin, 1971), p. 224.

21 Mazierska, *Jerzy Skolimowski*, p. 44.
22 Fredric Jameson, 'Cognitive Mapping', in Michael Hardt and Kathi Weeks (eds), *The Jameson Reader* (Oxford: Blackwell, 2000), p. 287.
23 Perry Anderson, *The Origins of Postmodernity* (London: Verso, 1998), p. 134.
24 Mazierska, *Jerzy Skolimowski*, pp. 108 and 73.
25 See, for example, Simon Frith and Howard Horne, *Art Into Pop* (London: Methuen, 1987).
26 Mark Fisher, *Ghosts of My Life: Writings on Depression, Hauntology and Lost Futures* (Winchester: Zero, 2014), p. 22.
27 Fredric Jameson, *Postmodernism or the Cultural Logic of Late Capitalism* (London: Verso, 1991), p. x.
28 Raymond Williams, 'Metropolitan Perceptions and the Emergence of Modernism', in *The Politics of Modernism* (London: Verso, 1989), p. 45.
29 Mazierska, *Jerzy Skolimowski*, p. 72.
30 Ibid., pp. 72–3.
31 Ibid., p. 77.
32 Ibid., p. 79.
33 Alex Callinicos, 'The New Middle Class and Socialist Politics', *International Socialism*, 2:20 (1983), www.marxists.org/history/etol/writers/callinicos/1983/xx/newmc.html (accessed 11 January 2022).
34 Val Burris, 'The Discovery of the New Middle Class', *Theory and Society*, 15:3 (1986), 317–49.
35 Matthew Worley, Keith Gildart, Anna Gough-Yates, Sian Lincoln, Bill Osgerby, Lucy Robinson, John Street and Pete Webb, 'Introduction', in *Let's Spend the Night Together: Sex, Pop Music and British Youth Culture, 1950s–80s* (Manchester: Manchester University Press, 2023).
36 Nuttall, *Bomb Culture*, p. 3.
37 John Clarke, Stuart Hall, Tony Jefferson and Brian Roberts, 'Subcultures, Cultures and Class: A Theoretical Overview', in Stuart Hall and Tony Jefferson (eds), *Resistance Through Rituals: Youth Subcultures in Post-War Britain* (London: Hutchinson, 1976), pp. 9–74 (p. 9).
38 Mazierska, *Jerzy Skolimowski*, p. 103.
39 Cat Stevens, 'But I Might Die Tonight', *Tea for the Tillerman* (Island, 1970).
40 Brigid Cherry, *Horror* (London: Routledge, 2009), pp. 99–101.
41 Ryan Gilbey, '*Deep End*: Pulled from the Water', *The Guardian*, 1 May 2011, www.theguardian.com/film/2011/may/01/deep-end (accessed 24 May 2022).
42 György Lukács, 'Realism in the Balance', in Rodney Livingstone, Perry Anderson and Francis Mulhern (eds), *Aesthetics and Politics: Debates Between Bloch, Lukács, Brecht, Benjamin, Adorno* (London: Verso, 1980), p. 37.
43 Mazierska, *Jerzy Skolimowski*, p. 47.
44 Tasker, 'Permissive British Cinema?', p. 10.
45 Herbert Marcuse, *Eros and Civilisation* (London: Routledge & Kegan Paul, 1956), pp. 94–105.
46 Chris Fite-Wassilak, 'Objects That Speak For Themselves', *Tate Etc*, 5 March 2018, www.tate.org.uk/tate-etc/issue-42-spring-2018/chris-fite-wassilak-objects-speak-themselves (accessed 25 May 2022).

47 Can, 'Mother Sky', *Soundtracks* (United Artists, 1970).
48 Tasker, 'Permissive British Cinema?', p. 9.
49 See for example Luc Boltanski and Eve Chiapello, *The New Spirit of Capitalism*, trans. Gregory Elliott (London: Verso, 2018); Thomas Frank, *The Conquest of Cool: Business Culture, Counterculture, and the Rise of Hip Consumerism* (Chicago and London: The University of Chicago Press, 1997); Jim McGuigan, *Cool Capitalism* (London: Pluto, 2009); Slavoj Žižek, 'The Ambiguous Legacy of '68', *In These Times*, 20 June 2008, http://inthesetimes.com/article/3751/the_ambiguous_legacy_of_68 (accessed 26 May 2022).
50 Gilbey, '*Deep End*: Pulled from the Water'.
51 Mazierska, *Jerzy Skolimowski*, p. 32.
52 Ibid., p. 48.
53 Ibid., pp. 56–7.
54 Ibid., p. 58.
55 Ibid., p. 59.
56 Ibid., pp. 61–3.
57 Raymond Williams, 'The Politics of the Avant-Garde', in *The Politics of Modernism* (London: Verso, 1989), p. 57.
58 See for example Rhian E. Jones and Eli Davies (eds), *Under My Thumb: Songs That Hate Women and the Women Who Love Them* (London: Repeater, 2017).
59 Tasker, 'Permissive British Cinema?', p. 9.
60 Gilbey, '*Deep End*: Pulled from the Water'.
61 Jack Halberstam, *In a Queer Time and Place: Transgender Bodies, Subcultural Lives* (New York: New York University Press, 2005).
62 Craig Berry and Sean McDaniel, 'Young People and the Post-Crisis Precarity: The Abnormality of "the New Normal"', LSE Blogs, 20 January 2020, https://blogs.lse.ac.uk/politicsandpolicy/young-people-and-the-post-crisis-precarity/ (accessed 27 May 2022).
63 Mark Fisher, *Capitalist Realism: Is There No Alternative?* (Winchester: Zero, 2009), p. 22; Susan Batchelor, Alistair Fraser, Lisa Whittaker and Leona Li, 'Precarious leisure: (Re)imagining Youth, Transitions and Temporality', *Journal of Youth Studies*, 23:1 (2020), 93–108.
64 See for example Sophie Riise Nors, 'Fuck Dating Apps: How Tinder Addiction Nearly Ruined My Life', *Fizzy Mag*, 2019, https://fizzymag.com/articles/fuck-tinder (accessed 27 May 2022); Jack Turban, 'We Need to Talk About how Grindr is affecting Gay Men's Mental Health', *Vox*, 4 April 2018, www.vox.com/science-and-health/2018/4/4/17177058/grindr-gay-men-mental-health-psychiatrist (accessed 27 May 2022).
65 Christian Klesse, 'Poly Economics – Capitalism, Class and Polyamoury', *International Journal of Politics, Culture and Society*, 27 (2014), 203–20.
66 Maya Oppenheim, 'Growing Numbers of Women Turning to Sex Work as Covid Crisis Pushes them into "Desperate Poverty"', *The Independent*, 8 January 2021, www.independent.co.uk/news/uk/home-news/sex-work-coronavirus-poverty-b1769426.html (accessed 27 May 2022).
67 Karen Ingala Smith, 'A Tale of Six Johns', 16 August 2015, https://kareningalasmith.com/category/commodification-of-women/ (accessed 27 May 2022).

68 For a key example of such thinking, see: Juno Mac and Molly Smith, *Revolting Prostitutes: The Fight For Sex Workers' Rights* (London: Verso, 2020), which rightly and insightfully considers violence against sex workers through the lenses of legal, police and other forms of state power, racism, border control, homophobia and transphobia but not the commodification of the body.
69 Nuttall, *Bomb Culture*, p. 17; Andreas Malm, *Fossil Capital* (London: Verso, 2016).
70 Marcuse, *Eros and Civilisation*, p. 45; Theodor Adorno, *Minima Moralia: Reflections From Damaged Life* (London: Verso, 2005 [1951]).

11

Run the track, but no bother chat slack: overstanding the relationship between slackness and culture within the reggae dancehall, 1960s–80s

William 'Lez' Henry

The relationship between 'slackness' and 'culture' within the dancehall arena is one of the oldest and perhaps most overly misunderstood aspects of reggae. My approach is from the perspective of an inveterate reggae fan, a dancehall deejay,[1] DJ and former sound system owner. When speaking to the forms of popular cultural artefacts that one recognises as crucial to their everyday livity,[2] reggae is foremost in my world. This means my discussion here is derived from my epistemologically privileged position within the reggae dancehall space. Moreover, being born of Jamaican parentage and raised by elder siblings who came from Jamaica, my knowledge of what represents slackness goes beyond sexually explicit lyrics that often debase the feminine whilst extolling the virtues of hyper-sexual 'badman' masculinity. Yet those who believe they can interpret the culture second hand will not share my perspective; and this explains why reggae culture is often misunderstood, as aptly demonstrated by the horror of a white schoolteacher who bore witness to an 'openly sexual' method of Black dancing. 'It's disgusting', cried the woman teacher at a school dance, 'they're masturbating in there'.[3]

Seemingly in contrast to the lewd lyrics and movements of slackness, 'culture' is regarded as the epitome of righteous and conscious lyricism; that which represents the ultimate form of 'reality', heavily investing in an ideal or natural, normative heterosexuality. Ergo, to be known as a conscious singer or deejay is to be the deliverer of 'culture lyrics' that are designed to educate and uplift the people premised upon truth, rights and justice. Equally, as the antithesis of the slackness deejay, the culture deejay frames their lyricism through the lens of Pan Africanism and Black Nationalism, usually through the lens of Garveyism.[4]

'Lie down gal mek mi push it up, push it up, lie down'

From as long as I can remember there has been debate and discussion about reggae and its association with slackness, which on the surface seems to be antithetical to the conscious aspects of Rastafari-inspired 'roots and culture' music. Yet, as will be evidenced here, this is a false dichotomy that simplifies what the culture represents, because a focus on a literal translation of the words 'slackness' and 'culture' serves more to obscure than illuminate. I begin the discussion with a slackness song by the Jamaican singer Max Romeo (Maxwell Livingston Smith), who was a popular vocalist with The Emotions in the later 1960s. Rather ironically, he is not regarded as a slackness performer within the reggae world, and his case speaks to how problematic it is to equate the lyrical content of a song with an established reputation. I state this because it was his slackness tune 'Wet Dream', released in Jamaica in 1968 and in the UK in 1969, that opened the door for this type of music in the white-dominated, British/European popular music scene.[5] In fact, 'Wet Dream' was so popular it 'stayed in the UK charts a full six months, despite a radio ban', with BBC radio DJs allowed only to refer to the song as 'The Dream'.[6] This was also the title it was promoted under in the Netherlands, where it reached number 11 in the charts. Unsurprisingly, then, Max Romeo was subsequently banned from appearing live at many white-owned/controlled venues on his UK tour, which was essentially the first time a Jamaican performer had had this experience. Despite such censorship, my elder siblings shared their experiences with me of seeing him perform 'Wet Dream' live in Black-owned/controlled venues. What was excluded from one space found presence in another.

The differential treatments, censorship and unmitigated control of alternative public arenas is significant here, as white-owned venues operated an unofficial 'colour bar' in Britain. This was in line with many other racialised exclusionary practices the Black community faced during that moment, which even extended to entering churches.[7] The 'colour bar' partially explains why Max Romeo would be invited to perform only at Black-owned venues. Yet, with this said, it is easier to understand the banning of Max Romeo within the wider, white-dominated public arena when consideration is given to the lyrical content of his song:

> Every night me go to sleep, me have wet dreams/ every night me go to sleep, me have wet dreams.
>
> Lie down gal let me push it up, push it up, lie down/ lie down gal let me push it up, push it up, lie down.
>
> You in your small corner, I stand in mine/ throw all the punch you want to I can take them all.

> Lie down gal let me push it up, push it up, lie down/ Lie down gal let me push it up, push it up, lie down.
>
> Look how you're big and fat, like a big, big shot/ give the crumpet to big foot Joe, give the fanny to me.
>
> Lie down gal let me push it up, push it up, lie down/ lie down gal let me push it up, push it up, lie down.

I recall my older Jamaican-born siblings playing this record, obviously when our parents were not around due to its explicit content. It was therefore not unusual to hear white and Black people of all ages, including primary and secondary school children (I was 11 years old at the time), singing 'every night me go to sleep, me have wet dreams. Lie down gal let me push it up, push it up, lie down.' Did we as young children have a clue about what Max Romeo was describing? Even being overly generous to the rudest and slackest amongst my peers, I sincerely think not, but we knew enough to appreciate that we could not sing it in front of adults, especially Black ones.

The song 'Wet Dream' is a slack tune, but what is also of interest is Romeo's use of the words 'crumpet' and 'fanny'. These were/are very white/ British ways of describing the vagina and did not have the same currency in 1960s Jamaica, where terms such as 'pum pum', 'pussy', 'cratches' or 'punaany' were far more common. Furthermore, the rest of Max Romeo's music is not known for this type of lascivious lyricism, as borne out in two of his aliases, 'Rasta Pickney' and 'Son of Selassie'. These names firmly place him in the culture camp, as do two of his most famous tunes, 'War Ina Babylon'[8] and 'Chase The Devil',[9] which you are guaranteed to hear at any reggae roots session to this day. Take the following extract from the former into consideration:

> War inna Babylon, tribal war inna Babylon
> Let me tell, it sipple[10] out deh/ So wha' fe do? We slide out deh, oh yeah
>
> War inna Babylon, let me tell, tribal war inna Babylon
> So wha' fe do? It sipple out deh/ So wha' fe do? Make we slide out deh, oh yeah
>
> Marcus Garvey prophecise, say/ 'One mus' live ten miles away, yeah, in this time'
> I-man satta at the mountain top/ Watching Babylon burning red hot, red hot.

Max Romeo is conscientising listeners to the continuous struggle against the forces of Babylon in a profoundly unequivocal way, exposing what appears to be a 'lived' contradiction. When measured against the slackness of 'Wet Dream' this may seem illogical, a conscious performer singing slackness (or vice versa), but it speaks to the argument here that to reduce reggae, or any of its artists to one camp or the other, is problematic. Max Romeo's reputation as a culture performer was not affected then nor since by the release of 'Wet Dream', which was aberrant but never the yardstick by which he is measured within the culture. His position as Rastafari is the foundation his reputation is built on, evidenced in the extract when he states 'Marcus Garvey prophecise, say. One mus' live ten miles away', perfectly capturing the notion of overstanding a system that is your enemy.[11] This is the cultural performer explaining to the audience the need to recognise that the system is designed to fail you and as such, wherever possible, you should remove yourself from its deadly and decadent ways: 'I-man satta at the mountain top/ Watching Babylon burning red hot.' His conscious perspective resonates with me as an insider who has lived, grown up with and thus experienced the various iterations of reggae music today. Equally, I am in an epistemologically privileged position on an experiential level and thereby endorse his suggestion that for Black people, globally, we constantly face a hazardously 'sipple' 'War ina Babylon', which is why he makes this ongoing, lived reality known through the medium of reggae music.

Slackness vs culture a false dichotomy: reflections from an insider perspective

My privileged insider position is drawn from being a 'box bwoy'[12] on the late, great, Jah Shaka's Sound System in the early 1970s, beginning my own deejay career on Saxon Sound System in 1982.[13] In the same year, I was a co-owner of Ghettotone Sound System. I have the experience of performing on major UK-based sound systems, including Frontline International, Diamonds The Girl's Best Friend and Jam Down Rockers; on Small Clothes in Grenada and Metro Media with Peter Metro at Stand Pipe in Barbican, one of the most iconic Jamaican reggae dancehall venues. I here bring these insider knowledges to the table, while also drawing upon the A~Side–B~Side conceptual framework designed during my time as a doctoral researcher to make sense of the differences between an 'insider' and an 'outsider' perspective when analysing slackness and culture.[14] In other words, the types of reggae lyricism and performances I consider here represent known values that affect how a commonality of condition is rendered as a textual analysis. This is especially the case when viewed through the lens of what Paul Gilroy dubbed in 1993 an Africentric perspective that encourages the embracing of alternative modes of interpreting cultural phenomena in thought-provoking ways.[15]

The A~Side–B~Side framework is premised upon the fact that without the 45-inch singles produced in Jamaica, played on reggae sound systems, packed in 'Grips'[16] and traversing Gilroy's 'Black Atlantic' to the UK, there would be no content for this piece. Spreading the reggae message, in the form of 'vocals' on the A~Side and a toaster/deejay 'version' on the B~Side, is what makes reggae culture unique. Moreover, in line with my thinking here, the A~Side generally contains the performance of another artist, the 'vocal', which is immutable. The vocals tell their story before you have the opportunity to tell your own as a singer or deejay once the record is 'pull-up an tun' (turned over). The B~Side, the 'version', is the dub *tabula rasa* upon which the performer delivers their lyrical contribution in the most original, imaginative, fluid and flexible way. Therefore, slackness versus culture is a false dichotomy that obscures the specificities of cultural ways of knowing, based on appreciating the profundity of what you are experiencing first-hand, because:

> Cultural refers to the organisation of experience shared by members of a community, a process which includes the standards and values for judging or perceiving, for predicting and acting.[17]

This speaks to how the 'cultural' can be historically and intergenerationally transmitted by those who have an awareness of, and familiarity with, the society from which the artistic expression manifests, as in the case of my direct learning from my older siblings. The concern would therefore be to make 'sense' of 'organised' differences which may not be apparent and can be overlooked, dismissed or misinterpreted by cultural outsiders. The A~Side 'Wet Dream' firmly places Max Romeo in the slackness camp. Yet, this is an incomplete picture as evidenced in Romeo's interview with David Katz, where he states:

> 'I started moving with Striker', Max continues. 'That's a "Wet Dream" come into play, the first song with Bunny Lee. He came with this idea about doing this dirty song'. When Romeo had written something suitably suggestive, he found that Slim Smith, Roy Shirley, John Holt and Derrick Morgan all refused to sing it, forcing Romeo to do the honours on a session at Studio One.[18]

Katz names some of the luminaries in the reggae world who refused to be associated with a slackness record that was arguably quite tame when compared to others. Yet the exchange demonstrates at least two things that are contextually dependent to overstand what I am suggesting here. The first is that Max Romeo was asked by the famous producer Bunny 'Striker' Lee to write 'Wet Dream' and, after he had crafted something 'suitably suggestive', the luminaries mentioned were approached to sing it. This means Max Romeo had no intention of doing so himself. For him it was just another piece of work as a singer songwriter. Second, when asked why he wrote and sang the song he replied, 'Ah Satan mek mi dweet.' Thus, the citing of the role of the devil in everyday life, as an influencer of people, captures my second point, which is you cannot separate, let us say, many Jamaicans from the Judeo-Christian sensibilities that still dominate their worldviews.

Utter condemnation of the culture readily comes from many who embrace a Judeo-Christian worldview, wherein reggae is generally regarded as antithetical; it is what such Jamaicans dismiss as a 'worlian' pursuit[19] – a perspective that only makes sense when consideration is given to the major role that white Christianity, in various guises, played in the suppression of African cultures, worldviews, languages, cosmologies and so on, within Europe's New World. Unsurprisingly, the socialisation and indoctrination into Christianity of the chattel-enslaved African was as the inferior/godless/heathen 'other' to the European superior/godlike/Christian 'self'. The demarcation between what is 'slackness' and what is 'culture' must therefore be measured by this yardstick. Moreover, before the 'imposition of Christianity', African peoples across the continent had various philosophical, social, cultural and religious systems that provided them with a collective sense of rightness, wrongness, acceptable and non-acceptable behaviour:[20] not just to each other as members of the human family, but also to the divine and to the land of their birth, in myriad indigenous ways, that included performativity.

The cultural phenomenon known as 'twerking', which is often attributed to the 1980s New Orleans 'bounce' music scene, can assist here as it provides a prime example of how African performativity is repackaged as something else. More importantly, that style of dancing is generally regarded as slackness bordering on the pornographic, due to its evocative nature and focus on the female buttocks. However, this type of movement was/is historically known within African, and African diasporic, cultures, evidenced and celebrated in musical genres like calypso, soca, rumba, samba, reggae, zouk and dancehall. Unsurprisingly then, hearing the MC or deejay encourage females to 'wine up dem batty' or 'flash dem big batty' or 'show wi di winery' and so on, across a range of musical styles within the dancehall space is commonplace and not necessarily associated with the European, Christian view of slack cultural expression. Indeed, the Eurocentric separation of the sacred and the profane is an aspect of their religious assault on the 'African psyche'.[21] It should therefore be noted that according to Marimba Ani:

> The Christian statement, as an established aspect of European culture, is, after all, a nationalistic ideology (in that it is an expression of the ideology of a particular culture just as any religious statement is), and its function in this regard is to serve the interests of that culture.[22]

Ani suggests the ideological systems that underpin religious belief necessarily impact on the way acceptable and non-acceptable forms of artistic expression are received within the cultural frame of reference. It therefore makes sense to consider what that frame of reference is determined by when judging African expression through a European lens. 'Wet Dream' is a tame record when placed up against some of the other Jamaican songs that were popular within the 1960s and 1970s Black British community. For instance, Prince Buster (Cecil Bustamente Campbell) was renowned for the rawness of his slackness songs. The most explicit was arguably 'Big Five' (1970) that I only heard by chance a couple of times as a child, but I suspect at 'big people dances' this was not the case. This was an unequivocally, unmistakably, slack tune:[23]

> Gonna be a wet, wet night, in Big Five/ Screaming, screaming night, in Big Five.
> It will be pussy versus cocky tonight/ Gonna be pussy versus cocky tonight.
>
> Right now I'm feeling sexy/ Want a big, fat pussy to spend night.
> Today I smoke an ounce of weed/ Tonight I'm gonna plant a seed/ In her womb, alright.
>
> Spunky, spunky night in Big Five/ Spunky, spunky night in Big Five.
> Oh, there'll be squeaking all over the bed/ There'll be water all over her head.

In this extract, Prince Buster leaves nothing to the imagination; thus most of what he suggests is self-explanatory and I was told as a child that 'Big Five' was a famous hotel, which Jamaicans often call a 'Sex Shop'. However, it was Prince Buster's 1969 version of Katherine Kennicott Davis's popular Christmas song 'The Little Drummer Boy' (1941), entitled 'Wreck a Pum Pum', that is one of the most recognisable slackness tunes from the era.[24] This song was immediately versioned on Buster's record label, as is the reggae way, by the Soul Sisters' 'Wreck a Buddy', and both tunes dominated the reggae world for a considerable time.[25] It was not often you had a balance between the male and female perspective when it came to sexuality in the reggae world, because for a woman to openly partake in such lascivious public displays was frowned upon.

Of interest here is how slackness, within the cultural framework, mirrors the wider normative, hyper-masculine, cross-racial/cultural dominant 'ideal' of what it means to be a sexualised human being. Men with multiple partners are lauded and applauded as 'studs' or 'Casanovas', and this, in many ways, is seen as a 'natural' aspect of being heterosexually male. But women who openly display such behaviour are in many cultures branded as 'slack' or 'loose women', 'sluts', 'whores' or 'leggobeasts'.[26] Yet, this is not the case in these two tracks where the sexual intentions are clearly stated and balanced, firstly, by Prince Buster and followed by the Soul Sisters. So, Prince Buster:

> Tonight I want to wreck a pum pum/ A fat, fat girl to wreck a pum pum
> And if she's ugly, I don't mind/ I'm feeling fit and fine to wine/ So I want to grind, I want to grind, Lord/ When you go tear a pum pum

> My dick is in a terrible state/ Oh Lord, good Lord, give me the fate
> I want to sit and wait till it/ Because if she's ugly, I don't mind
> It's not her face, her bodyline, boy/ When you go tear a pum pum …

Then, Soul Sisters:

> I need a man to wreck 'im buddy/ A big, strong man to wreck 'Im buddy
> And if he's ugly, I don't mind/ He has a dick and I want to grind/ I want to grind, I want to grind, oh/ A wreck, a wreck 'Im buddy

> My skin is in a terrible state/ Oh lord, good lord, give him the fate
> I want to lie and wine 'till eight/ And if it's big, I do not mind
> I want to grind, I want to grind, oh/ Me a go crash 'Im buddy …

The overtly sexualised and celebratory nature of 'wrecking a pum pum' or 'wrecking 'im buddy' evidenced on these tracks enables us to reconsider slackness as merely describing heterosexual behaviour that generally takes place in private. The lyrics may be explicit, or – as the former slackness female deejay Lady Saw suggests – 'dutty reality'.[27] During the time Lady Saw was regarded as a slackness performer, one of her most popular recordings was 'Glory be to God'.[28] Thus, when she performed a Christian song, Lady Saw would be regarded as a cultural rather than a slack artiste, which interestingly speaks to how Max Romeo was a slackness performer for his own seminal song. Both takes on how one can be regarded in the culture may be explained through the lens of the performer or sound system's ability to cater for different audiences within their own frames of reference. In the next section, I highlight how the culture shape-shifts, explaining why the dichotomy between slackness and culture is often a false one, misrepresenting what happens within the reggae dancehall as an alternative public arena.

Here come I play some breast to chest, or chest to breast, cau no guy test!

In a recent film about lovers' rock, the British comedian, performer and writer Angie Lamar remembered:

> Sometimes the light would turn on and you would see this guy, ugly, looking at you. 'Oh my god, oh my god, sorry about that. Were we scrubbing? I'm sorry. My bad.' Then you would be outside, and he would be following you like. 'So, so what, we can?' And you would be like 'no, no, no, no, no. Let me just break it down to you. What was going on there was in the dark, so let's leave it there yeah'. You can almost feel sorry for them as you were doing an intimate dance. For half the dance […] he saw love. And we saw the light, so it had to stop.[29]

The Jamaican Rastafari deejay Charlie Chaplin makes a crucial point when he states: 'Every Deejay have a message fi give, whether them chat slackness or culture.'[30] This can only be really understood from an insider perspective. The title for this section captures a call from the deejay on the mic, encouraging attendees to ready themselves for the most intimate part of the dancehall session. This is when the style of music changes and one can readily experience intimacy, often with a total stranger, in an invariably darkened space. That is why Angie Lamar's shock at her dancing partner's appearance when the 'light went on' during a lovers' rock session is humorous but poignant.[31] Within this space a dance is a dance, no matter how much evocative, provocative, sweat-inducing wining takes place. An insider, those who live and experience the culture, will appreciate this. To add further context here, when I was deejaying on West London's Diamonds The Girls' Best Friend Sound System, during the mid-1980s, it was rumoured that I was a homosexual. The rumours abounded because I would rarely 'scrub up' with women during dancehall sessions and would just chill and 'hold mi corner' until I was called to the mic to chat. However, during a Diamonds session I decided to dispel the rumours and dance with a young lady, who was notorious for 'bending up' any man she danced with. After that experience, as is the deejay way, I wrote and performed an account of what happened:

> Little girl over there, Daddy Lezlee over here,
> Say come dance with me we would ah make a nice pair,
> nuff of the Diamonds posse talk bout Lezlee is ah queer,
> bout me no dance with woman me only stand up and stare,
> so me go fi rub down ah big fat beef named Clare,
> Benji fraid fi the gal through something him hear,
> how she hold man tighter than ah grizzly bear,
> how she bend up Desi B and rub away him pubic hair,
> but when it come to woman Lyrix don't have no fear,
> when Tyrone fling the rockers that's when me draw near,
> me home in like the missile weh them call nuclear,
> me pull her fi ah dance she whisper in me ear,
> 'if you back no make ah rubber bwoy you better beware',
> but that no frighten me cause me no easy fi scare,
> she fling her two hands round me neck me put me two hands pon her rear,
> she fling the first wine I believe what Benji hear,
> because she take me down slow,
> she take me down so low,
> that if you never know you would ah swear we disappear,
> the way me under pressure man me trousers batty tear,
> me try fi come up she just ah hold me down there,
> me a to Massa God fi make me life get spare,

> while me a wonder to myself when we ah come back up fi air,
> as the rhythm done me run go sit down pon a chair,
> ah wipe the sweat and ketch me breath and ah drink ah cold beer,
> when me see the gal ah laugh me say 'come over here',
> she say 'you ah the first man me ever rub down and no feel him hardware!'[32]

The dance we engaged in epitomises the 'breast to chest' or 'front to front' liaison within the dancehall space, which could perhaps be construed as partaking in utter slackness: 'you ah the first man me ever rub down and no feel him hardware!' Clare's suggestion is overtly sexual and speaks to the normative hetero-erotic nature of the culture, particularly during that historical moment; that which was regarded by the white teacher mentioned before as 'masturbation'. I am not reducing this misrepresentative viewpoint solely to the white gaze. Rather, detractors of this cultural form are legion, as expressed in my reasoning on the role of Judeo-Christian sensibilities within the Jamaican worldview. The point is, despite three to four minutes of 'breast to chest' intimacy, there were no expectations on either's part this would constitute anything other than a dance. Of equal importance, as Lezlee Lyrix I am renown as a 'conscious deejay' who does not chat slackness, yet what is presented here can comfortably fit into that camp on a surface level. This paradox demonstrates the intricacy of the politics involved in the deejay performance, meaning that 'slackness' and 'culture' as generic constructs, are context dependent and aligned with specific musical moments.

The act of being 'conscious' cannot therefore be ascribed to the performer as a total cultural or political being; slackness is perhaps idiosyncratic in this way. The suggestion is that ontologically, being 'cultural' or 'slack' is in the 'doing' and often occurs in that critical moment during the performance – an aspect missed by a mainstream white reggae DJ in the UK when he refused to play 'Blind Date', a record I released in 1985 on the Greensleeves UK Bubblers label.[33] His refusal was based on construing the lyric as 'slack', whereas for me it was at best risqué. Yet, the supreme irony here is that he also refused to play the other track on the flipside, recounting my experiences at the hands of the racist police force in Britain, entitled 'Put Back You Truncheon'. I also walked away from an album deal with the said record company because they wanted me to chat slackness and I refused. I told them unequivocally at the time: 'I will never record a track I cannot play to my mother and my daughter', because disrespecting women is slackness and not my thing. The point here is not to place myself on a pedestal as a paragon of virtue. What I am suggesting is that the makers and doers of the culture should have the foremost voice in what is, and is not, acceptable.

The same paradox is exemplified in the performances of Jamaican deejays such as General Echo and Earl Anthony Robinson, aka 'Ranking Slackness'.

Before his murder in 1980, General Echo released one of the most cultural albums during that moment entitled *Rocking and Swing*. The tracks on the album feature General Echo addressing social, cultural, global and political issues such as 'Oil in a Babylon (dem seh it soon done)', 'Armageddon' and that featured the tracks 'Bathroom Sex', 'Know Everything About She Pum Pum' and 'It's My Desire to Set Your Crutches on Fire'.[34] Even more tellingly, within reggae music circles, General Echo is credited as the one who revolutionised the live deejay performance during the mid-1970s until his death in 1980. He was renowned as both a slackness and culture performer, because according to Manzie:

> General Echo, The Teacher Fi The Class, has come a long way in a short time. The year 1976 brought about a revolutionary change in DJ music. The General's Disco Sound 'Echo Tone Hi FI' stopped playing soul music and started to play strictly Rockers. At this time the General decided to DJ the rhythm tracks at dance halls all over Jamaica. This was the beginning of the road to success ... By 1977 the General Sound became the No. 1 Sound in Jamaica. General Echo was now on top of the dance hall scene. Everywhere he played the crowd followed ... The Sound was playing every night and most times the crowd was so large that patrons had to fight to get inside. Others simply stayed outside and enjoyed 'The General sound'.[35]

This extract, from the sleevenotes to *Rocking And Swing*, provides an insight as to why, even after his death, he is to this day regarded by many reggae-dancehall fans as the 'Teacher Fi The Class'. Crucially, in the aftermath of his death, Jamaica's most cultural Rastafari performer, Briggy (aka Brigadier Jerry), offered a poignant reflection on Echo's murder, using the melody from Queen's 'Another One Bites The Dust'.[36] He lamented:

> Uh uh uh slackness (Echo) bite the dust,
> uh uh uh culture must come fuss,
> I used to walk with them, I used to taak to them,
> but culture must come fuss (first),
> I used to eat with them I used to reason with them,
> but culture must come fust,
> I seh uh uh uh slackness bite the dust,
> I seh uh uh uh slackness bite the dust.
> I don't know if it's Big John, Echo or Flux,
> they was going in ah car man it wasn't ah truck,
> when all of ah sudden man them run out ah luck,
> last ting mi hear is that them life mash-up,
> uh uh uh another one bite the dust.[37]

Briggy suggests there was a closeness between himself as a 'culture' and Echo as a 'slackness' performer when stating that he used to 'eat' and 'reason with them'. Anyone who is familiar with Jamaican culture will be aware that they do not generally 'reason' with, much less 'eat' with, people they do not respect. This is particularly so with those who embrace Rastafari, meaning the lyric is a profound statement for Briggy to make about a deejay who *should* have been his antithesis. Echo was mourned across the reggae world, and in Britain we were all geared up to watch him perform live at Christmas 1980. I recall, after hearing Briggy's lyric on a Yard-tape[38] within weeks of Echo's death, being inspired to pen my own tribute, because Echo's murder was a massive blow to deejay fans in Britain. He was due to begin his tour of Britain the same week he was killed, which explains why I wrote:

> Dem kill Papa Echo in ah Half Way Tree,
> dem murder Papa Echo in ah Half Way Tree,
> dem kill Big John and them murder fluxy,
> me never know the breddah them personally,
> me used to hear them pon the tapes weh me breddah give me,
> an when me listen them me feel Irie.
> Mi hear bout Echo from me bredrin Everton,
> him seh him used to cork dance in ah Skateland,
> him seh there was ten woman to each an every man,
> him chat slackness and sing church song,
> Papa Echo was a champion.
> Him chat nuff lyrics pon Stereophonic Hi Fi,
> give people joke til man an woman start cry,
> whether him a chat slackness or praise the Most High,
> papa Echo was a one away bwoy,
> why di wicked haffi kill him don't ask me why,
> an left him mummah and him puppah wid not a dry eye,
> di wicked shoulda give him a bligh.[39]

Penning these lyrics speaks to the influence that General Echo as Ranking Slackness had beyond the shores of Jamaica, captured in Paul Gilroy's suggestion that we 'took the confidence of the Jamaican slackness toasters', using it as a template for our British deejay style.[40] Indeed, I state that 'me never know the breddah them personally', as I was introduced to them by my 'bredrin Everton'. Everton was an entrepreneurial character who was born in Jamaica, came to live in London during the 1970s, and would often fly back and forth to Jamaica as part of his involvement in the Sound System business. As a result of his constant travelling, he was like a living library stacked with knowledge about the shifts in the culture and, more importantly, he was initially the main source of our exposure to the 'freshest' Yard tapes. It was Everton who informed us during the mid-1970s about General Echo/Ranking Slackness and his Sound System 'Echo Tone' (the name inspired me to call our set Ghettotone), which was redefining the deejay performance in Jamaican reggae dancehalls. By providing Yard tapes, Everton enabled us to experience the 'live' reggae dancehall deejay performance in an unexpurgated fashion, unlike anything we experienced on vinyl releases. General Echo's unique performances epitomised that 'hidden' dimension, whilst embodying the difficulty we encounter when trying to conveniently locate slackness and culture as oppositional within the reggae world.

Conclusion

I have argued here that an analysis of the relationship between what is construed as 'slackness' and 'culture' within the reggae dancehall arena must be appreciated within its own frames of reference. That is why I have explained when interpreting meaningful behaviour, gleaned from observing relationships with popular cultural artefacts such as reggae music, an insider perspective is crucial. The role of language in specific, racial, social, political and cultural contexts explains why Max Romeo was not a slackness performer, but it was a slackness record that made him a household name in Britain. Equally, there are contestations over language. The way Jamaicans use terms like 'slackness' and 'culture' within the reggae dancehall world are qualitatively different from what they represent in a British context and slackness was not the only reason reggae music was banned or censored.

An embracing of Rastafari challenges whiteness as rightness and speaks to the imposition of Judeo-Christian sensibilities that are in essence Eurocentric and therefore ethnocentric. Thus, dichotomising slackness and culture in an unproblematic way is largely premised on a misunderstanding of the worldview of those who created reggae music in the first place. This explains why I located myself here as being epistemologically privileged, drawing upon my Jamaican cultural heritage in juxtaposition to being born on these shores, explaining my unique position within the reggae dancehall space. For my knowledge of what represents slackness and culture is beyond the way we use such terms in a British context, and my positionality as a performer and an academic have assisted my take on this aspect of reggae musical culture.

Notes

1 Deejays chat lyrics on the mic whereas DJs play records. For a fuller explanation see William 'Lez' Henry, *What The Deejay Said: A Critique From The Street!* (London: Learning By Choice Publications, 2006).
2 Rastafari use the word 'livity' to capture the philosophical, holistic experience of everyday living as a member of the human family, premised upon the recognition

of the presence of the Almighty Creator of all things, in and at all times, that dwells within I and I. I = God and I = human.
3 Ian Chambers, *Popular Culture: The Metropolitan Experience* (London: Methuen & Co., 1986), p. 150.
4 Marcus Mosiah Garvey was born in Saint Ann's Bay in Jamaica (17 August 1887–10 June 1940) and is credited with being the foremost Black nationalist leader of all time. He was the founder of the UNIA, Universal Negro Improvement Association and African Communities League (UNIA-ACL) and his philosophy is known as Garveyism. For an insight see Tony Martin, *Race First: The Ideological and Organizational Struggles of Marcus Garvey and the Universal Negro Improvement Association* (USA: The Majority Press, 1986).
5 Max Romeo, 'Wet Dream' (Unity Records, Jamaica, 1968).
6 David Katz, *Solid Foundation: An Oral History of Reggae* (London: Bloomsbury, 2004), p. 110.
7 See the extensive work done in this area by Robert Beckford, including *God of the Rahtid: Redeeming Rage* (London: Darton, Longman & Todd, 2001).
8 Max Romeo and the Upsetters, *War ina Babylon* (Island Records, 1976)
9 Max Romeo, 'Chase The Devil' (Upsetters, 1976).
10 'Sipple' is slippery in Patwa, Jamaican language.
11 The idea of 'overstanding' is taken from a Rastafari worldview within which the word 'understand' is taken to mean you 'stand under' the thing you are discussing; as such your view of it is limited by merely looking up. To overstand means to 'stand over' the thing in question from the vantage point of seeing it from all possible angles, thus remaining conscious, circumspect, awake and aware.
12 A 'Box Bwoy' loads up the sound-van with the equipment, then unloads and carries the speakers into the dancehall, assists in the 'stringing up' of the 'Set' (another name for a sound system), which includes running the wires from the speaker boxes to the amplifier etc. This guarantees free entry to the session and free travel (usually in the back of the van amongst the speakers) to and from the venue. After the session you 'string-down' the Set, unload the equipment and go home. See Henry, *What The Deejay Said*, pp. 216–20) for a more detailed account of the division of labour in the sound system world.
13 Clarendon, Jamaica, born Neville, 'Knocky' Powell, AKA Jah Shaka transitioned 12 April 2023.
14 The A~Side-B~Side conceptual framework was developed in my PhD thesis (1998–2002) and more fully explained in Henry, *What The Deejay Said*.
15 Paul Gilroy, *The Black Atlantic: Modernity and Double Consciousness* (London: Verso Books, 1993).
16 'Grips' are what people from Jamaica and other parts of the Caribbean call suitcases.
17 Eric. R. Wolf, *Europe and the People Without History* (Berkeley: University of California Press, 1982), p. 387.
18 Katz, *Solid Foundation*, p. 110.
19 In Jamaican language, patwa, a 'worlian' is the antithesis of a Christian, because they worship the world and Christians worship God.

20 See Yosef Ben-Jochannan, *Africa: Mother of Western Civilization* (New York: Alkebu-lan Books Associates, 1971).
21 See Chinweizu Ibekwe. *Decolonising The African Mind* (Lagos: Pero Press, 1987).
22 Marimba Ani, *Yurugu: An African-Centred Critique of European Cultural Thought and Behaviour* (Trenton: Africa World Press, 1994), pp. 143–4.
23 Prince Buster (1970) 'Big Five' 7" single. 4prong Centre label, Jamaica.
24 The popular version was sung by Harry Simeone Chorale (1958) and released on the 20th Century Fox Label. For the Prince Buster version, 'Wreck A Pum Pum', *Prince Buster And The All Stars*' (Blues Label, UK, 1969).
25 Soul Sisters, 'Wreck A Buddy', *Prince Buster And The All Stars*' (Blues Label, UK, 1969).
26 The Jamaican term 'leggobeast' literally translates in English as 'let go beast'.
27 Lady Saw was baptised in 2015 and is now ordained Minister Marion Hall, who no longer performs dancehall music due to her embracing of the gospel music scene.
28 Lady Saw, 'Glory Be To God' (Sampalue, Jamaica, 1996).
29 Angie Lamar in *The Story of Lovers Rock* (produced by Menelik Shabazz, 2011).
30 Charlie Chaplin, Creation Sound System, Jamaica (1983 cassette tape recording).
31 Lisa Palmer, 'Men Cry Too: Masculinity and the Feminization of Lovers' Rock', in Jon Straton and Nabeel Zuberi (eds), *Black Popular Music in Britain since 1945* (Abingdon: Ashgate, 2014); William 'Lez' Henry and Les Back, 'Reggae Culture as Local Knowledge: Mapping the Beats on Southeast London Streets', in William 'Lez' Henry and Matthew Worley (eds), *Narratives from Beyond the UK Reggae Bassline: The System is Sound* (Basingstoke: Palgrave, 2021).
32 Lezlee Lyrix, 'Clare and Present Danger', Diamonds Sound System (1984 cassette tape recording). Also performed in *The Story of Lovers Rock* (2011).
33 Lesley Lyrics 'Blind Date' b/w 'Put Back You Truncheon' (Greensleeves, UK Bubblers, London, 1985). Interestingly, myself and the dearly departed singer Deborah Glasgow were the only non-Saxon Sound System performers to feature on that label.
34 General Echo, *12" of Pleasure* (Greensleeves Records, UK, 1980).
35 Manzie, sleevenotes to *Rocking and Swing* (Rock-it Records, Jamaica, 1980).
36 Brigadier Jerry, Cassette tape recording, Black Star Sound System. Jamaica, 1980.
37 6 Ibid.
38 Jamaican Deejays featured on the 'Yard-tapes', cassette recordings that were critical to our development as performers and social commentators in Britain, because they came from 'Back A Yard', a popular name for the island of Jamaica. Reggae recordings from other parts of the globe, including Britain and the USA are known as 'session tapes', or 'sound tapes'.
39 'Bligh' in Jamaican language means to give someone a chance or a pardon. Lezlee Lyrix, cassette tape recording, Ghettotone Sound System, UK, 1982.
40 Paul Gilroy, *There Ain't no Black in the Union Jack: The Cultural Politics of Race and Nation* (London: Hutchinson Education, 1987), p. 190.

12

'This could be a night to remember': authenticity, historicising and the silencing of sexual experience in the northern soul scene

Sarah Raine and Caitlin Shentall

Frenetic music, 'rare' records and the timeless euphoria of sweaty dancefloors, northern soul events have brought together young women and men from across the UK for over five decades. The 1970s golden era of the scene is remembered by ageing attendees as a time of unity through music and the rejection of all distractions: nights dedicated to the music. For those who recount this time, sexuality had no place on the dancefloor; sexual orientation was irrelevant to a musical community which welcomed all new devotees, evoking a utopian epoch of tolerance and equality. This, too, is a story replicated in academic attempts to document and analyse the historic northern soul scene, a valuable 'inside' of meaningful action placed in stark opposition to the contemporaneous mainstream 'out'. Extending previous work, this chapter considers this positioning of the scene as part of wider processes of historicising, an authenticating and mythologising narrative which works to facilitate the power dynamics of an ongoing and multigenerational community.[1] We explore how men and women remember their gendered and sexualised subjectivities in the 1970s northern soul scene, and we reflect upon what and who is lost through the silencing of sexual experience.

Northern soul is both a canon of music and a continuing multigenerational and retrospective music scene, active within the UK and beyond. As a music- and event-focused community, elements were evident in the clubs and youth clubs of the late 1960s, developing into an identifiable form in the early 1970s. The use of the term 'northern soul' has been attributed to the activities of journalist and music aficionado Dave Godin as a record shop owner and key writer for *Blues & Soul* magazine. While the term was in common parlance before Godin used it for the first time in writing, Godin played a central role in mythologising the scene, both in the 1970s and since.[2] Equally, the northern soul scene has been emplaced within the north of England – by its very name, through the words of Godin (a southern music writer), and by subsequent processes of historicising – although key events did occur in the Midlands and North Wales, and trickled down into the south of England and up into Scotland. The central practices of the northern soul scene were (and continue to be) dancing, record collecting, event organising and DJing. Each practice takes a particular form and they have since been formalised through interconnected discourses of authentic participation, tradition and knowledge. Dancing and DJing at public events now offer original and continuing participants a means to publicly claim belonging and to demonstrate insider knowledge, dedicated participation and respect. However, the act of storytelling, too, plays a central role in demonstrating insider status, creating and sharing a collective history and differentiating the scene (and its members) from a perceived 'outside'.[3]

These stories – both oral through interviews and written in fan-penned and published scene memoirs (including Godin's regular *Blues & Soul* column) – are also the core material for academic work which attempts to understand the northern soul past. Much of the earlier scholarship relied upon uncritical reference to these fan-penned self-documenting histories and the 'expertise' of well-known men whose recollections are used as evidence, unframed through considerations of memory, narrative or historicising.[4] Scene myths – established and reiterated through the telling and retelling of certain stories about the northern soul past – have been reinscribed by scholars as the realities of the historic scene. Since 2019, however, Milestone, Street, and Gildart and Catterall have – through original and critically framed interviews and archival research – added diverse voices and divergent histories to our understanding of the northern soul scene past.[5] It is upon this latter work that we wish to build.

This chapter draws upon interviews, textual analysis, archival research and published scene memoirs which constitute a self-documented history of the scene.[6] Many of the older individuals (now in their sixties) who were interviewed for this chapter continue to attend events across the country, and all remembered a past which has been worked and reworked over the years as the speaker has reflected upon their experiences and, indeed, told these stories to others. As Ricœur argues, the stories that articulate this past order and organise not only time and self, but also self in relation to the others who equally lay claim to an authenticating past.[7] While this book focuses on youth cultures from the 1950s to the 1980s, we wish to consider the legacy of this authenticating past and the silencing of sexual experience. Drawing on interviews with the younger generation of the contemporary UK scene (undertaken 2015–18), we track the continued power and discursive role of dominant (and partial) histories and explore the ways in which young newcomers negotiate exclusionary notions of authentic scene participation.

The northern soul story: history, authenticity, remembering and forgetting

> In the space of just three years, the Highland Room had ceased to be the domain of the tattooed, vest-wearing, muscular Northern Soul dervishes dancing to pounding, aggressive beats. It was now the 'hip' place to be seen … Some of the male clientele looked decidedly unmacho.[8]

> Compare that with the average pop club, where the main aim of many blokes who go there is to swap saliva with a member of the opposite sex.[9]

The scene mythologies of northern soul as masculine, competitive and asexual emerge regularly in the retrospective narratives constructed by our participants and in the written histories of the 'original' generation (such as *Soul Survivors* and *Too Darn Soulful* quoted, respectively, at the start of this section). The 1970s British scene past is imagined as a coming together of musically enlightened individuals, bearing gifts of rare and underplayed records for discerning soul enthusiasts, welcoming all those who wished to dedicate themselves to the music and to the scene. However, the origin myths of where the records came from (rejects of the Motown industry 'discovered' by British record collectors and DJs), how the 'genre' of northern soul developed (through fast and competitive dancing), and how the scene was named (by *Blues & Soul* journalist Dave Godin),[10] all position northern soul as the product of heroic, male action.

The gendering of authenticity

The self-documenting histories of northern soul are intricately bound up in the mythologising of the scene, replicating and simplifying stories to demonstrate the insider knowledge of the author and to venerate the scene's development and continuation.[11] David Nowell's book remains one of the most well-read and well-considered. The passage from Nowell's (1999) book demonstrates the positioning of both the music and the dancing bodies of northern soul as innately masculine, discernible from the increasing presence of 'the beautiful people' of Bowie-era Britain: the male northern soulie is here written into mythology and becomes the key character in a totalising history of the scene. Tim Wall considered the 'heroic' nature of the acrobatic movements within the scene's dance style.[12] Here, the heroic cultivates a 'sense that important matters are at stake and that the success of one's actions are vital'[13]: the construction of the heroic separates the cultural 'inside' from 'out' and celebrates the unique nature of the scene and its members. In the origin myths of northern soul, the hero is a man and his traditionally masculine attributes made/make possible the development and continuation of the scene: the strength, power, physicality and speed of the dancer; the control, confidence and encyclopaedic knowledge of the DJ; the stabilising rules of hierarchy and respect, with age and experience equating to knowledge and legitimised influence.

Key scene practices involve activities that have been traditionally considered the musical activities of men, with record collection and DJing vital to the emergence and refining of northern soul's cultural form. Men dominated these activities in the 1970s, and many of the very same men continue to hold the influential roles of DJ, event organiser, record seller and (significantly) published scene historian. The increasingly mythologised story of northern soul is therefore narrated through a nostalgic male voice, in reference to the stories of other influential men as the writer establishes his insider credentials and networks.[14] These dominant histories and their very particular processes of creation have led to certain myths of self, the creation of pervasive northern soul masculinities, a silencing of sexuality and the loss of the female voice.

Narratives of authenticity evident within other music scenes also work to establish an idealised insider. Expectations of blues musicians as 'Black, male, born into poverty … and taught by a legend on a … homemade guitar', inform the idealised performers of the 'inside' and limit the perceived authenticity of those who fall on the discursive parameters (as noted by Johnson in her consideration of Black women blues guitarists).[15] Estranged from the production processes of the music, the performers of the northern soul scene are the dancers and DJs, both practices historically positioned as competitive, obsessive and masculine. The solo and spatially distanced nature of northern soul dancing does not sexualise or demote female dancers. However, the female dancer is removed from the collective imaginary of both insiders and outsiders by the retrospective construction of an archetypal *male* discursive body through the mythologised history of the scene: competitive, asexual, powerful, acrobatic, white and symbolically working class.[16] These expectations permeate discourses of authenticity, and while the 'original' participant of the 1970s is ageing, the image of the young male dancer continues to infuse the visual and material culture of the scene, be it through mediations or book and CD covers, flyers or photographic documentation.

While the acrobatic male dancer has become a dominant myth and pervasive image of the northern soul scene, the solely male competitive dancefloor noted by Barry Doyle in his 2005 article was not a reality in the 1970s.[17] Many members of the original scene, such as Simon quoted here, recall (during interviews) both men and women on and dominating the floor as 'dancers':

> There were as many girls at the clubs as there were lads. There were just as much. I think it was probably a 50/50 split, to be fair. Very well dressed, lovely ... The main thing is about the music and the dancing. And L.M [...] he won several dance competitions back in the day, and if you spoke to him today, he'd tell you that the best dancer he ever saw was a girl [...] The girls were just as good dancers as the blokes.[18]

Representing rare archival footage of a northern soul allnighter in the 1970s, *The Wigan Casino* film (directed by Tony Palmer for Granada TV series *This England* and broadcast in the UK in 1977) offers imagery that disrupts the myth of the dancefloor as a masculine space, panning across a gender-balanced dancefloor and spotlighting the skilful dancing of both women and men. Equally, the film also provides space for the voices of young men and women active on the scene through talking head sections. Yet the legacy of this material on the gendered roles of the scene has been partial, possibly due to both the comparatively stronger voice of the young male interviewee and the nature of subsequent scene engagement with the text itself. Although Palmer's inclusion of a female interviewee seemingly offers a strong, northern, working-class female voice (and one which has been documented for future generations), traditional and scene-specific gender roles persevere.

Through two brief sections, the young woman recalls her first time at the club, her struggles with disapproving parents and the monotony of her working week. Her male counterpart, on the other hand, takes the subtle role of the narrator as the film progresses, discussing local politics, the 'business' of northern soul (both record selling and event ticket revenue) and the complexities of youth identity; his voice threaded through much of the film, *he* becomes the scene expert. Whereas these dancefloor scenes have been heavily cannibalised by fans in the production of amateur montage videos posted on YouTube or Facebook, the focus has been primarily on the more acrobatic movements of primarily male dancers.[19] Generally, the acceptance of the film as a key scene text has been limited by the contemporary and ongoing scene backlash against the seemingly clumsy juxtaposition of contemporary and archival footage of an industrial, working-class north-western England (a conscious and political statement by Palmer),[20] and an association between this public exposure of an underground community to a mass audience and the decline of the scene in the late 1970s.[21]

Beyond the voice of the young woman in *The Wigan Casino* and the dancing bodies that have since been chopped up and edited, the many ways of engaging within the scene as a woman have remained experiential rather than a narrated part of the repeated and simplified dominant histories of the scene. As such, women have not become associated with certain practices or associated skills: the roles of women – both in the current scene and the remembered past – therefore lack the detail and direction afforded men.

Taking music seriously is a key distinction in the separation of the northern soul 'inside' from the mainstream 'out'. Unlike the supposedly fickle mainstream music fan, the northern soul insider – both historic and contemporary – attends events for the music alone, forgoing any potential distractions in order to more fully experience the music through a range of listening and appreciative practices. As part of this claim, a disinterest in members of the opposite sex is interwoven into the definitions and practices of the scene which has, in the following example (notably provided by a man), been retrospectively reworked through an almost emancipatory frame which once again reiterates a notion of freedom from the limitations of society beyond the walls of the northern soul all-nighter.

> [Michael] Back then, a single woman or a group of women could go and not be hassled, they were there for the music.'[22]

Echoing research into other music scenes, this establishing of scene boundaries not only associates mainstream (i.e. outsider, inauthentic) culture with sexuality,[23] but also with femininity.[24] Conversely, masculine behaviour is equated with 'authentic' musical engagement and practices and placed in opposition to the consumer-driven engagement of a feminised mainstream. As Maalsen and McLean note in their study, the positioning of women music participants as inauthentic by scholars – in the case of their work, categorising women record collectors as consumers – further perpetuates the gendering of 'authentic' music practices.[25] In her study of the UK drum 'n' bass scene, Joanna Hall identified hierarchies of value that privileged 'masculinity and the associations of intellectualism, complexity, seriousness and hardness'.[26] These qualities are ascribed to male and female club-goers but require the public performance of qualities culturally associated with masculinity to successfully demonstrate scene membership.

Similarly, northern soul is commonly positioned as musically separate from other scenes by its speed and the physicality of expected engagement, with all key practices (including dancing) viewed as the stage for male competition and the demonstration of knowledge and competency. Scene participants identify these embedded cultural values as the demonstration of 'authentic' and culturally valued engagement, building upon a foundation of shared discourses on gender and value, through which men (and their masculine, heteronormative actions) are valorised and the feminine is viewed as both subordinate and profane.

Asexuality and the northern soul scene

The profane 'outside' in scene definitions of northern soul (recounted) past and present also sets authentic engagement as separate from sexualised experience, acting to remove all public sexualised behaviour. It is commonly positioned (particularly by men – see Michael's quote in the previous section) that the asexual nature of the historic northern soul scene worked to provide increased freedom for women soulies to engage within scene practices, uninhibited by male harassment as a sexual object or chastised as a woman overstepping her cultural boundaries.[27] However, the remembered experiences of women on the 1970s northern soul scene suggest that a lack of female role models, a significant masculine culture and the dominance of men in these roles represented barriers to access. While the northern soul dancefloor in the 1970s was a more gender balanced space than dominant mythologies suggest, the roles of DJ and record collector were (and continue to be) heavily male dominated. As a quote from Brenda demonstrates, this all-male role was particularly daunting for young women soul fans in the 1970s and a lack of visible female role models in DJing has been a pervasive issue:

> Because I was quite shy and things like that then, I wish I'd got the courage and stuff what I've got now to have been out there, because I do enjoy my DJing. I wish I'd done it all those years ago … If I'd have known what a woman can do, if I could have said, 'right, can I do it?' I'd have done it then. And I think I might have carried on.[28]

In the stories told by women participants who were active on the 1970s scene, a more contested narrative also emerges in relation to sexuality. Being allowed out in the first place was a key concern for women who were often unmarried and living with parents when they first started going to all-nighters. This was less of an issue for young men, even within the same family, as Jayne notes:

> because me brother went to all-nighters, my dad's thought on it all was that they were all-night orgies, [laughs] don't ask me, but that's what he used to say, and he used to say, 'she's not going there with her brother I'm not having all that,' so I always were stopping at a friend's house. And I think because me dad were like that, I think that were a really good deterrent for me to think, no. I'm not gonna get involved with that kinda side of things, but, yeah it were definitely there.[29]

The reference to 'orgies' here emphasises the preoccupation of Jayne's father; his concern that Jayne may become involved in a form of sexuality which is positioned as deviant. And while this is a very vivid example, this paternalism is pervasive in the language used by men who discuss women on the scene in the 1970s. Despite the utopian and unifying narrative of the scene prevailing in retellings, the reality for women living in 1970s Britain meant that their gender could not be left at the door. This gendered experience of young women in the 1970s was documented at the time by Angela McRobbie and Jenny Garber in their 1970s contribution to (and critique of) the emerging 'subculture' approach of the Centre for Contemporary Cultural Studies (CCCS) at the University of Birmingham.[30] Women northern soulies recall navigating a complex terrain of authenticity whilst balancing a need (or want) to fulfil expectations to find a partner:

> [Brenda] I mean like, I don't know, if you go to a nightclub, kids stay in a little crowd don't you, whereas on the soul scene everybody talks to everybody, well, unless you've had some dingdongs with 'em, y'know, but it were like that then. There were a lot of jealousy around and things in them days because most of the girls were younger and wanting blokes and they were all after the same blokes, and you get that, that way. People having squabbles and stuff ... With being on the scene, it were very difficult to find a bloke. Or maybe it were just me! But then I met, well I knew my husband anyway, I knew him for years, but then I got with him and I'm still with him now, it's 40 years next year.[31]

Indeed, for the northern soul participants that we spoke to, meeting their current (or past partner) on the northern soul scene was a very common theme. For Brenda, and many others like her, sex and relationships were not something one did when the serious work of northern soul was done, but rather intertwined with their experiences on and off the dancefloor and a lasting legacy of their scene participation. It is in the subsequent acts of remembering and historicising the northern soul past that these aspects of youthful experience have been silenced, devalued and prohibited from the places of northern soul, both in memory and in current practice.

Queer experience and identity on the historic scene remain a peripheral part of the dominant northern soul story so far. This is perhaps unsurprising given that the scene's histories have been formalised through heteronormative and mythologising published narratives. Rather than having an explicit inclusion of queer voices and an engagement with gay/queer culture, what is common within the scene and among its participants is a mythologised and utopian notion that everyone was welcome. This is well articulated by Nigel:

> So yeah, it were hard times, and when you went into this place, and someone would just brush you, 'excuse me mate', 'sorry', thank you', and it was just like an oasis. When you went back outside again, don't get me wrong, you were back to square one again, back to seventies England.[32]

For many, northern soul events in the 1970s were likely to be quite different from this 'oasis', especially if we consider the youth of the participants, their drug use[33] and the homophobia of 1970s Britain (which was arguably fostered by the Conservative politics of Margaret Thatcher).[34] Several key characters within the dominant northern soul story were openly gay men, yet rather than contributing to a scene-wide adaptation of gay/queer culture, the sexuality of these figures was either quietly ignored or used nefariously within scene debates. For example, the active engagement of the Blackpool Mecca DJ Ian Levine with music emerging from the US disco scene and work as a record producer – two very divisive activities within a scene fast developing a particular canon of (and dedication to) 'rare soul' – was, for some critics, both intertwined with and denounced in reference to his sexuality. In his 'personal history' of the scene, Stuart Cosgrove notes that Levine 'came out as a gay man on what is frequently a tough scene, he met pockets of homophobic abuse, which may have receded with time but in the mid-seventies it was a stick to beat him with'.[35]

In terms of insight into the negotiation of gay (male) identity and northern soul (as a music and a scene), Gildart and Catterall highlight the value of the letters section of *Blues & Soul* in the mid-1970s.[36] While several of these letters advocate for a separation of sexuality and scene participation/the music, others offer claims to gay space on the 1970s northern soul scene. Dave Godin's editorial response reflects his work as a dedicated activist and radical – also clearly demonstrated through his equally strong support and advocacy for the Civil Rights Movement and issues concerning artist renumeration – and, while recognising the limits of a conservative 1970s British society, Godin encouraged the northern soul scene to support the Gay Liberation Front.[37] However, as succinctly argued by Street, fan responses to Godin's call to arms in *Blues & Soul* reveal that '[for] many soul fans, the music could be divorced from the socio-political contexts in which it was produced and experienced'.[38] Although Godin was an openly gay man strongly associated with the scene himself, it is important to note that his editorial engagement was that of a generational, socio-economic and (to a great extent) philosophical outsider.[39] It is also particularly significant for our discussion of silences that these letters (and the editorial response from Dave Godin) articulate the perspective of (self-identified) gay men. Less visible, even within detailed archival research such as that undertaken by Gildart and Catterall, is the voice of queer women or gender minorities.

Equally, many fan-penned and academic histories alike end with the closure of Wigan Casino in 1981, missing out the subsequent divergences of the scenes, its people and the music. Owing to the authenticating temporal boundaries of the northern soul past, little of this history has been documented. Grace, a now very well-known DJ who has been active on the rare soul and northern soul scenes since the 1970s, described her movement into the London gay scene in the 1980s and 1990s.[40] At a time when northern soul was moving into smaller, less-visible local venues, Grace found a home for her sounds in the sometime 'dangerous' and exciting gay clubs. Northern soul's overlap with disco and the sampling of soul records in house music offered Grace a logical new audience for her record collection. The movement of northern soul DJs and fans into overlapping club scenes – to queer clubs, acid jazz events and the emerging US house scene – have not yet been threaded into the dominant northern soul story and remain as personal tales told between individuals. As researchers such as Clifford-Napoleone highlight, the straightwashing of musical histories are products of authenticating (and sometimes moralistic) processes of reiterating certain stories and rendering invisible the messiness of diverse scenes, cities and genres.[41]

The silencing of sexual experience and queer identity has had a significant legacy on contemporary practices and subsequent historicising. As we will explore, this continued association between asexuality and authentic participation has meant that younger members of the scene have undertaken their explorations of sexuality either estranged from their northern soul identity or under the public radar. Equally, as one of our authors has noted in other work, the gender politics of the contemporary scene create significant barriers to the participation of younger women in particular.[42]

The legacy of sexual silences

[Nina, aged 19] When I went to normal nightclubs, I felt that everyone [was] there because they either just wanted to get really drunk or because they'd broken up with their boyfriend ... I don't think they're there because they love the music. Where [as] if you go to an all-nighter, and all you listen to is northern soul, like, the main reason that everybody is there [is that] the music makes them feel something.

[Des, in his 20s] It's in the middle of nowhere so you don't get any dickheads ... Like, nobody's going to walk down there in a pair of stilettos, you know what I mean?

In explaining their engagement, the younger members of the contemporary northern soul scene place their experiences in strict opposition to the perceived mainstream.[43] From these discussions, the mainstream was viewed as sexually promiscuous, feminine (the 'dickheads in stilettos'), focused on drinking and gaining sexual or physical proximity rather than 'serious' dancing and overly concerned with physical appearance. The scene 'inside' offered 'freedom' to dress for style rather than to be attractive, to escape the everyday realities of relationships, to dance until you sweat and, most importantly, to take the music and dancing seriously: as the primary focus of your activity, rather than merely a means to a drunken and sexual end. These mainstream activities are viewed as shallow and stereotypical, as restricting one's true and, indeed, meaningful identity.

Des's gendering of the scene outsiders is placed in opposition to an imagined and mythologised masculine archetypal scene participant, an archetype shared by other young people involved in this study and one which questions the nostalgic and sanitised dominant northern soul story as told by the original generation:

> [Des] But I, I still think there needs to be that element of it to be a bit seedy and like underground. It's got that stage now where it's like all handshakes and hooks and stuff. People forget that all those people pratting on about that now, yeah, you're all in your sixties, so when you were seventeen and stuff at Wigan, you'd have took that lad out into the car park and battered the shit out of him ... Do you know what I mean, like? I think that element of it's gone now ... I remember [my dad] saying ... Wigan ... all the massive Black guys outside in cars and stuff with like car boot open with a sawn-off shotgun next to a drugs cabinet asking if you wanted gear and shit.

For Des, these heroic, working-class masculine experiences, passed on to him through the tales of his father, are valorised as the 'true' history of the scene and, more widely, represents the central core of the northern soul past as constructed by younger members.[44] The stereotypical masculine actions of violence (notably between men), an emotive atmosphere of excitement and threat, and what Des considers to be the 'seedy underground' nature of venues and participation, constructs an idealised masculine past. The scene is therefore viewed as emerging out of a specifically masculine experience, no less heroic than the tales of transatlantic record searching. These hyper-masculine behaviours and situations are, however, allocated to the scene past (if rather begrudgingly by Des), adapting to fit the current expectations of member conduct in an ageing music scene.

As part of her interest in going to northern soul events, Nancy describes the scene as free from the sexualised experiences of mainstream clubbing. This lack of sexual predation offers her a safe environment within which she can fully dedicate her energies into developing her dancing skills or record knowledge.

> I love it because I was really fed up of drunken people in nightclubs trying to grope me, like, that is ... I mean, that's, you know, people must be there for that reason as well, but the main reason that everyone is there ... is for the music.
>
> [Rob, in his 20s] I think if you go ... [pauses] ... if you go out with somebody on the soul scene ... Um, I think, and you really get along, click, you've got something for life, in a way, 'cause ... you've both got a real shared interest

… Yeah, every teenager's after what you can get. Years back in the '90s and stuff, [women] used to take men in the toilets … Like strangers and just do what they want with them, they did … And it's 'cause they're out dancing and you're moving your body and it's very sexual and that, you know …

Both Nancy and Rob's insider relationships, and awareness of other relationships within the scene, were justified through the key desire to experience the music together, and to build a relationship around shared scene participation. The mythologised asexuality of the historic scene is also questioned by Rob based upon stories he has been told and his own experiences of being a teenage boy engaged in what he sees as 'sexual' practices, such as dancing. The mythologies of an asexual music scene experience are here reconfigured as a valuing of certain types of (heterosexual and heteronormative) relationships and the reasoning behind a lack of physical contact between couples at events.

[Nancy] But, I mean, like, with the dancing, you don't dance together, do you, so if someone come up to you, you'd be a bit like, 'look, mate, like, what are you doing, you're meant to be, you're meant to be giving me space to spin around!' [laughs]

[Rob] So I go off to my pals, the lads, and she goes off with her mates, but we're still together. We still might give each other a nod or something … [chuckles]… we party together but separate, in a way, so … [I]t's not like when you go in town and you're all cuddling on the dancefloor … It's a very selfish thing anyway, isn't it? You're partying, you're doing it for yourself … 'Cause you enjoy it.

Couples are hard to spot at events, rarely demonstrating physical affection and often spending much of their time with different groups of people. In explaining this distance, Nancy highlighted the individual nature of the northern soul dancing style, which afforded her freedom from the (sometimes unwanted) physical element of mainstream clubbing. Similarly, Rob explains his changing behaviour from the town centre club to the northern soul event through the same example of solo dancing, linking this to a desire to personally engage with the music, and dancing as a serious act of listening. In order to 'take northern soul seriously' and identify yourself as a scene insider, romantic relationships are placed temporarily on pause.

In addition to the centrality of asexuality to this authenticating discourse of 'taking it seriously', young couples are also a generational minority within an ageing music scene. The desire for a respectable and enjoyable night out for those now in their sixties and seventies has played a key role in positioning the scene as a friendly community, devoid of the sexual, intoxicant and violent excesses of the mainstream (and indeed, the historic scene itself).[45] As part of an ongoing positioning of self within the insider community of this ageing 'original' element, comparative invisibility of sexualised activity and drug use at public events has become necessary for those wishing to be viewed as an insider. When entered into through a shared passion for the scene, these participants viewed insider (monogamous) relationships as ideal, offering a solid foundation of shared interests and the ability to engage in the busy social calendar of the scene, with young soul fans keen to regularly attend all-night events across the country. However, the disruptive nature of sexual promiscuity within northern soul as a small, music-based community was placed in strict opposition to the potential benefits of the 'right' kind of relationship. Promiscuous behaviour is here vilified – the 'soap opera' of the assumed sexual promiscuity of the mainstream – as an unsettling force that intrudes on the ability of others to seriously engage in the scene.

> [Nina] That's the problem with, you get in relationships on the scene and it's like … If you start jumping from relationship to relationship, and then before you know it, nobody wants to talk to you … 'Cause we all know each other. It's too small. [T]here's no sisterhood in there, is there? There's no respect for yourself or others … Well, that's what frustrates me because it's like, it's a scene, like … Stop making it like a soap … Do you know what I mean, stop! … Just crack on with it, you're there!

The contemporary northern soul scene is not, therefore, a safe space within which young people can openly experiment with sex and sexuality – or drugs. Indeed, both explicit sexual and drug-related activities at northern soul events will earn the perpetrator subtle or explicit reminders that they have transgressed (and disrespected) the rules of the scene. While the continued illegality of recreational drugs in the UK necessitates subtle practices at venues, the intergenerational support evident at house events (for example) – with more experienced clubbers offering support and knowledge to newcomers in bathrooms and chill-out spaces to 'keep cool' or 'sip water' – is not a common practice at northern soul all-nighters. Equally, the stakes are much higher for those wishing to explore their sexuality as part of this small community, with young people wary of prompting harsh commentary similar to that articulated by Nina. This is, however, a generational expectation of the older participants for younger newcomers, with several interviewees from the original generation discussing the sexual opportunities of current northern soul events, further exposing the generational power dynamics of the contemporary scene.[46]

For Leon, although he hadn't experienced any discrimination based on being openly gay, he did position his northern soul lifestyle as problematic in relation to meeting other (openly) queer men:

> I don't think being gay is an issue on the scene at all. But I've always said I've fucked myself right up because I'm into soul music; where am I going to meet

a gay man? I know it sounds silly, but I think it's something that scares me 'cause if I was with someone they'd have to understand what I'm into, like. There's a lot of people on the soul scene who have been married to people who aren't into it and, you know, they're not with them anymore 'cause it just doesn't work.

Once again, while some experimentation in sexuality did take place between young soulies, it happened quietly and away from the public spaces of the scene. Social media platforms continue to occupy a liminal space in expressing sexual identity among the younger members of the scene, however this space is also limited. Facebook in particular represents a key tool for organising one's scene calendar and for connecting with friends made at events. It offers a clear demonstration of an individual's active participation on the scene and access to key individuals. As a platform, Facebook is therefore very scene-visible, and younger soulies noted processes of conscious self-curation to ensure that their virtual engagements fit within the discursive boundaries of the scene.[47] Instagram and TikTok do not offer the same scene functions, and as such offer more freedom for young soulies.

The continued association between scene authenticity and asexuality – and the pervasive gendering of northern soul practices and ideal soulies – has meant that young northern soulies cannot openly explore and express articulations of sexuality or gender identity in relation to their scene membership. Equally, they cannot use the in-person places of northern soul as a safe space for these explorations. Scene participants must therefore choose between their northern soul identity and their gendered, sexual identity once they step inside an all-nighter. In terms of power and dominance, the gender politics of the scene further sidelines a minority and comparatively disempowered group – women – and further reduces the claims of young newcomers to belong within the multigenerational scene. Furthermore, it is difficult for younger soulies of any gender identity to develop or demonstrate their identities as sexualised, empowered and desiring individuals in relation to their northern soul participation.

Conclusion

Through this chapter, we aimed to provide space for experiences which complicate the dominant narrative of asexuality, to explore the ways in which the historic northern soul scene has been remembered, and to ask: what is the legacy of the very particular inclusions, reworkings and silences that have now become an authenticating and restraining structure to contemporary scene participation? When we engage with the past and with memories through which that past is accessed and articulated, it is essential for scholars to ask: who creates the histories that are collectively shared and valued; whose experience is included and whose are silenced; when and why do these histories stop? And in terms of legacy, we must also ask and explore what these dominant and exclusionary narratives do to dissenting voices and to the experiences of those who follow and don't quite fit in.

As members of dance-focused music scenes ourselves, we do not wish to downplay the purposeful nature of events. We too behave differently on northern soul dancefloors than we would do in our local pubs. We too get frustrated when someone interrupts our flow as they cross the dancefloor to get a drink or attempt to speak to us in the middle of a song. And if you ask either of us why we attend northern soul nights, we will reply 'to dance'. Stop there and you will come away from that event persuaded that sex and relationships have no place on the northern soul dancefloor, dedicated as it is to the music. However, if you engage us a little more you will realise that dancing is just one of many interconnected practices that make up our participation; myriad ways of doing and saying northern soul that are key to our own claims to belong and to our embodied experience of a public scene event. Furthermore, as you talk to additional members of the contemporary scene, their practices and stories will begin to overlap and it will become clear that these actions and narratives are part of a wider, shared discourse which acts to validate the engagement of certain individuals and to restrict that of others. The stories that people tell during interviews and in snatched conversations at events, particularly about the past, should therefore be understood as purposeful constructions that do certain work in claims to belong. Equally, these stories narrate a very particular experience of the past, structured by the speaker's present and created for a particular audience. Ultimately, these stories potentially hold great power over our engagement in the present, particularly within exclusionary insider communities such as the northern soul scene. As storytellers, popular music scholars must also carefully consider what and whose histories they are telling and be mindful of the legacy of their own tales.

Notes

1 Sarah Raine, *Authenticity and Belonging in the Northern Soul Scene: The Role of History and Identity in a Multigenerational Music Culture* (Basingstoke: Palgrave Macmillan, 2020); Caitlin Shentall, 'Do All Roads Really Lead to Wigan?: A Reassessment of the History of the Northern Soul Scene in the "Crisis Decade" of the 1970s', Masters dissertation (University of Sheffield, 2018).
2 See Sarah Raine and Tim Wall, 'Myths on/of the Northern Soul Scene', in Sarah Raine, Tim Wall and Nicola Watchman Smith (eds), *The Northern Soul Scene* (Sheffield: Equinox Publishing, 2019), pp. 142–63.

3 See also Raine, *Authenticity and Belonging in the Northern Soul Scene*.
4 For example, Barry Doyle, 'More Than a Dance Hall, More a Way of Life: Northern Soul Masculinity and Working-class Culture in 1970s Britain', in Axel Schildt and Detlef Siegfried (eds), *Between Marx and Coca-Cola: Youth Cultures in Changing European Societies 1960–1980* (Oxford: Berghahn, 2005), pp. 313–28; Joanne Hollows and Katie Milestone, 'Welcome To Dreamsville: A History and Geography of Northern Soul', in Andrew Leyshon, David Matless and George Revill (eds), *The Place Of Music* (London: Guilford Press, 1998), pp. 83–103; Katie Milestone, 'Love Factory: The Sites, Practices and Media Relationships of Northern Soul', in *The Clubcultures Reader: Readings in Popular Cultural Studies* (Oxford: Blackwell, 1997), pp. 134–49; David Sanjeck, 'Groove Me: Dancing to the Discs Of Northern Soul', in Jill Terry and Neil A. Wynn (eds), *Transatlantic Roots Music: Folk, Blues and National Identities* (Jackson: University Press of Mississippi, 2012), pp. 227–45; Andrew Wilson, *Northern Soul: Drugs, Crime and Subcultural Identity* (Cullompton: Willan Publishing, 2007).
5 Keith Gildart and Stephen Catterall, *Keeping the Faith: A History of Northern Soul* (Manchester: Manchester University Press, 2020); Katie Milestone, 'Soul Boy, Soul Girl: Reflections on Gender and Northern Soul", in Raine, Wall and Watchman Smith (eds), *The Northern Soul Scene*, pp. 197–214; Joe Street, 'Dave Godin and the Politics of the British Soul Community', in Raine, Wall and Watchman Smith (eds), *The Northern Soul Scene*, pp. 120–41.
6 See also Raine and Wall, 'Myths on/of the Northern Soul Scene'; Raine, *Authenticity and Belonging in the Northern Soul Scene*.
7 Paul Ricœur, 'Life in Quest of Narrative', in David Wood (ed.), *On Paul Ricoeur: Narrative and interpretation* (London: Routledge, 1991), pp. 20–33.
8 David Nowell, *Too Darn Soulful: The History of Northern Soul* (London: Robson Books, 1999), p. 108.
9 Russ Winstanley and David Nowell, *Soul Survivors: The Wigan Casino Story* (London: Robson Books, 1998), p. 27.
10 Explored and nuanced further in Raine and Wall, 'Myths On/Of the Northern Soul Scene'; Raine, *Authenticity and Belonging in the Northern Soul Scene*.
11 Ibid.
12 Tim Wall, '"Out On The Floor": The Politics of Dancing on the Northern Soul Scene', *Popular Music*, 25:3 (2006), 431–55.
13 Douglas B. Holt and Craig J. Thompson, 'Man-of-Action Heroes: The Pursuit of Heroic Masculinity in Everyday Consumption', *Journal of Consumer Research*, 31:2 (2004), 439.
14 For further discussion see Raine, *Authenticity and Belonging in the Northern Soul Scene*; Tim Wall and Sarah Raine, 'Hidden in Plain Sight: Stories of Gender, Generation and Political Economy on the Northern Soul Scene", in Chris Anderton and Martin James (eds), *Media Narratives in Popular Music* (London: Bloomsbury, 2021), pp. 17–34.
15 Maria V. Johnson, 'Black Women Electric Guitarists and Authenticity in the Blues', in Elleen M. Hayes and Linda F. Williams (eds), *Black Women and Music: More than the Blues* (Champaign: University of Illinois Press, 2007),

p. 54. This idealised performer also forms a central thread in David Grazian, *Blue Chicago: The Search for Authenticity in Urban Blues Clubs* (Chicago: University of Chicago Press, 2003).
16 Wall and Raine, 'Hidden in Plain Sight'.
17 Doyle, 'More Than a Dance Hall, More a Way of Life'.
18 All interviews undertaken by Caitlin Shentall were conducted during 2016–17 in accordance with ethical requirements at the University of Sheffield. Updated consent was sought from all interviewees to include their comments in this book chapter, and their identities have been protected through pseudonyms. All interviewees from this project are now in their sixties and attended northern soul events in their late teens and early twenties.
19 See Raine and Wall, 'Myths On/Of the Northern Soul Scene'.
20 Tim Wall, 'Interviews with Tony Palmer, Elaine Constantine and Liam Quinn', in Raine, Wall and Watchman Smith (eds), *The Northern Soul Scene*, pp. 216–21.
21 Mentioned by our respondents and in Stuart Cosgrove, *Young Soul Rebels: A Personal History of Northern Soul* (Edinburgh: Polygon, 2016), p. 96.
22 Interview undertaken by Caitlin Shentall.
23 Sarah Thornton, *Club Cultures* (Cambridge: Blackwell, 1995); Rebekah Farrugia, 'Sisterdjs in The House: Electronic/Dance Music and Women-Centered Spaces on the Net', *Women's Studies in Communication*, 27:2 (2004), 236–62; Gretchen Larsen, '"It's a Man's Man's Man's World": Music Groupies and the Othering of Women in the World of Rock', *Organization*, 24:3 (2017), 397–417.
24 Also evident in Diane Railton, 'The Gendered Carnival of Pop', *Popular Music*, 20:3 (2000), 321–31; N. Coates, 'Teenyboppers, Groupies and Other Grotesques: Girls and Women and Rock Culture in the 1960s and early 1970s', *Journal of Popular Music Studies*, 31:3 (2007), 65–94; Marion Leonard, *Gender in the Music Industry: Rock, Discourse and Girl Power* (Aldershot: Ashgate, 2007); Sarah Baker, 'Teenybop and the Extraordinary Particularities of Mainstream Practice', in Sarah Baker, Andy Bennett and Jodie Taylor (eds), *Redefining Mainstream Popular Music* (London: Routledge, 2013), pp. 14–24.
25 Sophia Maalsen and Jessica McLean, 'Record Collections and Musical Archives: Gender, Record Collecting, and Whose Music Is Heard', *Material Culture*, 23:1 (2018), 39–57.
26 Joanna Hall, 'Rocking the Rhythm: Dancing Identified in Drum 'n' Bass Club Cultures', in Sherill Dodds and Susan Cook (eds), *Bodies of Sound: Studies Across Popular Music and Dance* (London: Routledge, 2013), pp. 103–16.
27 See, in relation to traditional Irish music, Helen O'Shea, '"Good Man, Mary!" Women Musicians and the Fraternity of Irish Traditional Music', *Journal of Gender Studies*, 17:1 (2008), 55–70.
28 Interview undertaken by Caitlin Shentall.
29 Ibid.
30 Angela McRobbie and Jenny Garber, 'Girls and Subcultures: An Exploration', in Stuart Hall and Tony Jefferson (eds), *Resistance Through Rituals* (London: Hutchinson, 1976), pp. 209–22.
31 Interview undertaken by Caitlin Shentall.

32 Ibid.
33 Wilson, *Northern Soul*; Andrew Wilson, 'Mixing the Medicine: The Unintended Consequence of Amphetamine Control on the Northern Soul Scene', *The Internet Journal of Criminology* (2008).
34 See, for example, Martin Durham, *Sex and Politics: The Family and Morality in the Thatcher Years* (London: Macmillan, 1991).
35 Cosgrove, *Young Soul Rebels*, p. 125.
36 Gildart and Catterall, *Keeping the Faith*, pp. 233–6.
37 Ibid., p. 234.
38 Street, 'Dave Godin and the Politics of the British Soul Community', p. 127.
39 See also Raine and Wall, 'Myths on/of the Northern Soul Scene'.
40 Interview with Raine, 2017.
41 Amber Clifford-Napoleone, *Queerness in Heavy Metal: Metal Bent* (New York: Routledge, 2015); Amber Clifford-Napoleone, *Queering Kansas City Jazz: Gender, Performance and the History of a Scene* (Lincoln: University of Nebraska Press, 2018).
42 Raine, *Authenticity and Belonging in the Northern Soul Scene*.
43 All interviews with the younger members of the northern soul scene were undertaken by Sarah Raine from 2015 until 2018 and in accordance with institutional ethical requirements. All names provided are pseudonyms and identifying aspects have been altered to protect individuals.
44 See Raine, *Authenticity and Belonging in the Northern Soul Scene*.
45 Sarah Raine, '"Back in the Day": Experiencing and Retelling the Past as a Claim to Belong in the contemporary Northern Soul Scene', in Sarah Baker, Lauren Istvandity and Zelmarie Cantillon (eds), *Remembering Popular Music's Past: Heritage-History-Memory* (London: Anthem Press, 2019), pp. 27–40; Raine, *Authenticity and Belonging in the Northern Soul Scene*.
46 One (male) interviewee described women at northern soul weekenders as 'Gangs of cougars on heat!'
47 For more, see Raine, *Authenticity and Belonging in the Northern Soul Scene*.

13

'Mummy ... what is a Sex Pistol?': SEX, sex and British punk in the 1970s

Matthew Worley

In June 1976, a magazine interview with Vivienne Westwood outlined her views on the clothes shop she ran with Malcolm McLaren. '[Our] message is simple. We want you to live out your wildest [...] fantasies to the hilt.' Their aim, she said, was to 'convert, educate and liberate'. 'We are really making a *political statement* with our shop by attempting to attack the system.'[1]

The shop, of course, was called SEX, located on the King's Road in London and soon-to-be forever associated with the gestation of British punk. Through it emerged the Sex Pistols, already beginning to court controversy in the music press at the time of Westwood's interview. In and around their wake came a 'new wave' of bands eager and able to reimagine popular music into the 1980s.[2] The clothes sold in SEX, meanwhile, would – in a matter of months – help redesign the cultural fabric. As the residual influence of early 1970s style began to give way to the bricolage of punk, so flares became straight and hair got cropped.[3] Black returned and new textures found an outlet; say goodbye to shades of brown and heavy denim.

'Punk', however, was not mentioned in the feature. Neither the word nor the associated musical style was fully formulated by the spring of 1976. In fact, the interview was conducted by Len Richmond for *Forum*, a top-shelf magazine that explored the sociological outreaches of all things sexual. Westwood and SEX were featured amid articles on women with younger lovers and a survey on oral sex. The focus was on the rubberwear items that lined the walls and the customers who frequented the shop. Only in the accompanying pictures, wherein Westwood bared her backside alongside Jordan (Pamela Rooke), Chrissie Hynde (later of The Pretenders), Danielle Lewis, Alan Jones and Sex Pistols' guitarist Steve Jones, was there glimpse of a nascent youth culture and the band that helped define it.

Quite evidently, sexual subversion was to the fore in the earliest moments of punk's becoming: 'the system' was to be attacked, in part, by unleashing (teenage) desire. As it was, the *Sturm und Drang* that consumed the Sex Pistols through 1976–77 all but buried this component of pre-punk provocation. The incendiary connotations of 'Anarchy in the UK' and 'God Save the Queen' lent punk and the Pistols a confrontational edge that appeared more seditious than sensual. It was the group's anti-social behaviour rather than their sexual predilections that prompted newspaper headlines from late 1976.[4] True, the stylistic innovations of what became punk are oft celebrated and recognised as integral to the shock effect generated in 1976–77. The subsequent career of Westwood as a doyenne of haute couture has been accompanied by countless exhibitions of punk clothing and design.[5] But watch a documentary – or flick through a magazine feature – on punk and stock images of derelict Britain rarely dwell on the relationship between disaffected youths and a T-shirt flashing a penis. In such a way, punk's use of sex to critique and assault the socio-moral complacencies of 1970s Britain diluted over time. 'We want to demystify sex', Westwood insisted in *Forum*, 'to free people of their sexual inhibitions. "Out of the bedroom and into the streets!", now that really would be revolutionary.'[6]

This chapter aims to locate the 'sex' in the Sex Pistols and explore how sexual subversion was key to punk's cultural intervention – at least in the beginning. To date, relatively few people have looked too hard in this direction. Paul Gorman's exhaustive biography of McLaren mined the history of SEX in ways deeper than any previous account of punk's formation, whereas James Anderson has applied a theoretical lens to 'punk and porn' more generally.[7] Both Jon Savage and John Scanlon have noted the influence of Wilhelm Reich on SEX's philosophy, while my own work has connected punk to the disembodied howls of the Marquis de Sade.[8] David Wilkinson, too, has critically dissected McLaren and Westwood's attitude to sex in the 1970s, noting in the process how Queer theorists have celebrated punk displays of sexual 'transgression'.[9] Typically, however, the transformation of fetishwear into fashionwear is observed rather than considered. Most brazenly, Toby Mott's 2016 *Showboat* project revelled in the salacious ephemera generated through punk, collating porn shoots and cataloguing the explicit material that decorated gig flyers and record sleeves through punk and American no wave, riot grrrl and queercore into the 2000s.[10]

The objective here is to recover and reassert the sexual dimension of punk's cultural assault. After all, when McLaren spoke to the short-lived music paper *Street Life* around the same time as Westwood's *Forum* interview, he envisaged SEX's ideal customer to be a teenage girl from the suburbs buying a rubber miniskirt at the weekend to wear to work on Monday.[11] And for a moment, as Jordan travelled to the King's Road from Seaford in a 'black rubber skirt and black silk stockings' that unsettled and maybe also excited her fellow commuters, his desire all but became a reality.[12]

SEX: craft must have clothes but truth loves to go naked

The backstory to SEX has been told many times.[13] McLaren – having worked his way through various London art schools – took up space in 430 King's Road in late 1971. With his friend Patrick Casey he named the shop Let it Rock, rubbing initially against the countercultural grain to reassemble the 1950s in the form of Teddy boy threads and early rock 'n' roll records. Casey soon drifted from the scene and Westwood got more involved, modifying clothing and reviving dead-stock ready for sale.[14] Inside the shop, a mocked-up front room was strewn with 1950s ephemera, including early 'cheesecake' porn magazines such as *Spick*, *Span* and *QT* – the latter quite possibly informing the name 'Kutie Jones and his Sex Pistols' that later featured on a T-shirt. Rocksploitation film posters – *Vive le Rock!* – and pictures of rock 'n' rollers covered the walls at the front-of-shop, where drape jackets and creepers were displayed next to rockabilly shirts and Slim Jim ties.

McLaren evidently sensed a cultural shift. Throughout 1972, he and Westwood helped service a rock 'n' roll revival that peaked with an all-day festival at Wembley Stadium in August and thereafter fed into films such as *That'll Be the Day* (1973), for which Let it Rock provided costumes. Extending the subcultural theme, rocker and biker-style leathers were added to the stock over 1973 as Let it Rock transformed into Too Fast To Live Too Young To Die. Therein, the spirit of *The Wild One* (1953) mixed with Kenneth Anger's *Scorpio Rising* (1963) in search of new expression. T-shirts and leather skirts were studded or decorated with evocative terms: 'Dominator', 'Venus', 'Perv'. Zips were fitted and clothes distressed; nudie pics were added to ties and shirts. By détourning the past to evoke the present, McLaren and Westwood began to innovate rather than excavate. In so doing, the sexual allure of youth subcultural style came more to the fore.

Such synergy found fruition with the opening of SEX in the early autumn of 1974. Inside, black leather and rubber accoutrements pointed towards darker, carnal sensibilities. Having travelled to New York in 1973, McLaren found himself awakened to the underground clubs frequented by the New York Dolls and the Warhol crowd, both of whom documented the city's sexual subterranea.[15] Not too long after his return, the shop was gradually transformed into a psychosexual playpen. Fetish garments and rubber clothing hung from gymnasium wall-bars alongside remnants of rock 'n' roll stock and a jukebox playing tunes predating the hippie 1960s. The *Forum* feature wrote of 'high-heeled boots, rubber panties, leather bras, leather wrist and ankle restraints [...] rubber mini-skirts (£12) [...] and six different styles of rubber masks and hoods (£20–£50)', one of which was inflatable to allow 'total pressure on the face'.[16] Quotes from pornographic novellas were applied to clothes and spray-painted on the wall next to surrealist and situationist slogans: 'Modernity killed every night'; 'Be reasonable, demand the impossible'. Breaking up the shop, latex curtains demarcated dressing rooms that complemented the racks of rubber mackintoshes and exotic shoes. A skin-coloured 'French-Letter Suit' was presented as an 'evening dress'.[17] Out front, black-curtained door panels were cast in the shadow of three large pink florescent letters spelling S-E-X. Graffitied underneath, Thomas Fuller's motto declared that 'craft must have clothes, but truth loves to go naked'.

As fetish and fashion began to coalesce, so the clothes and accoutrements stocked by SEX transformed style into revolt and revolt into style. On the one hand this meant transferring the private to the public: rubber bodices or stockings worn in the street; studded collars and cock-rings becoming jewellery. 'I dress like this all the time,' Jordan said in late 1975 whilst wearing only a black rubber bra and matching stockings, 'even for Sunday dinner.'[18] On the other, it inspired a range of designs intended to both incite and embolden. The idea, McLaren argued, was that 'wearing these clothes will affect your social life'.[19] By crossing over with rock 'n' roll and aligning their designs to more cerebral cultural rebellion, McLaren and Westwood directed their appeal towards young people looking for a 'movement that's hard and tough and in the open'.[20] No longer content to *imply* the correlation between youth culture and sex, McLaren and Westwood made the connection explicit.

They did this in various ways. First by the shop itself, which promised the possibility of sexual discovery whilst also making it feel tantalisingly forbidden behind the darkened exterior. Once through the door, new worlds – and experiences – might be discovered, be it on the clothes racks or by way of the jukebox and pictures from New York pinned to the walls. As the 1950s front room in Let it Rock suggested, 430 King's Road was as much an installation as a shop, a creative forum designed to stimulate and serve as a meeting place (to 'convert, educate and liberate'). Jordan described it as a 'social hub' and an 'information bureau', a space both enlightening and thrillingly intimidating.[21]

Second, SEX designs aestheticised fetishism and outré sexualities, extending their appeal from practitioners to fellow travellers alive to illicit adventure. Materials were fastidiously sourced, initially through PO box addresses found at the back of Sunday broadsheets via which McLaren would meet contacts who opened 'their doors and in the back rooms they were making rubber masks'.[22] A network was uncovered, with cottage industries across the UK providing clothes for fetishists. John Sutcliffe, whose *AtomAge* magazine documented the scene, supplied the more expensive rubberwear for SEX. Nearer to King's Road, the London Leatherman delivered bespoke leatherwear. Specialist shoemakers were sought to make the stilettos and boots suited to the fetishist. In the meantime, further visits to the USA by McLaren and others gathered materials for T-shirt designs and accessories.[23] In all cases, attention to detail was paramount.

Image-wise, fetishwear was complemented by customised clothing that bound sexuality to youth subculture. Distressed T-shirts served this best, often screen-printed by future Clash manager Bernard Rhodes and devised to communicate SEX's socio-cultural challenge. So, for example, three pornographic quotes were pulled from Alexander Trocchi, an erstwhile situationist and perennial junkie whose writing for Maurice Girodias' Olympia Press perfectly bridged the sensual and subversive. One – 'I groaned with pain as he eased the pressure in removing the thing which had split me […]' – came from *Helen and Desire* (1954); two more – 'softly she undulated her hips to smear her juices over his face […]' and 'she felt the seed stir at the pit of her belly in response to the strong tongue movements […]' – came from *School for Sin/School for Wives* (1955; 1967). A pair of breasts were also transposed to a T-shirt, the idea taken from a Rhode Island art school project McLaren found by chance on a trip to New Orleans.[24] Though ostensibly a simple design, the T-shirt's meaning and affect shifted depending on who was wearing it: male, female, younger, older.

Far more controversial were designs that provoked social prejudice as well as moral convention. So, for example, racial smears and fears were goaded by the naked image of Maurice Spencer, an African American footballer with his penis on full display. Latent homophobia was triggered by a Jim French illustration of two half-naked cowboys brought back from New York by McLaren in 1975. With their penises almost touching, one cowboy straightens the other's neckerchief as they bemoan the 'played 'aht' scene 'gettin' to[o] straight'. Extreme sexual acts – orgies and fisting – were later displayed through graphic illustration, though the 'smoking boy' shirt must now count among the most contentious of SEX's designs.[25] Taken from a magazine called *Boys Express* and envisaged to embody the idea of the Sex Pistols as 'sexy young assassins',[26] the shirt featured a naked pre-pubescent boy looking nonchalantly beyond the viewer with hand on hip and a cigarette.

Third, SEX's provocation was embodied by those who wore the clothes. In the shop, Jordan all but became the first Sex Pistol, bringing her own sense of style to bear on fetishwear worn to a rock 'n' roll soundtrack. Pictures from the time show her with a Ricci Burns beehive haircut, either modelling SEX's rubber lingerie or standing high-heeled in-and-outside the shop in a mix of mohair, leather, SEX shirts and see-through crinoline skirts. Her poise was always assertive and engaged, with bold make-up and a demeanour *Gallery International* magazine described as signalling 'sado sex for the seventies'.[27] Westwood, too, might be interviewed in a leather jerkin with zips and wrist-straps that could be bound to a dog collar. '[Not] the sight you expect to see in a noonday wine bar', one interviewer noted, 'and that, precisely, is [the] point'.[28] Indeed, public display brought reaction. Beyond Jordan causing awkward moments on her commute into London, Alan Jones was picked up by police in Piccadilly for wearing the semi-naked cowboys T-shirt. Jones, a regular customer and briefly an assistant at SEX, landed a charge of showing an obscene print in a public place recently made notorious as a rent boy hangout by Yorkshire TV's *Johnny Go Home* documentary.[29] SEX was duly raided the following day (29 July 1975), leading both to Jones and the shop receiving fines and effectively confirming to McLaren and Westwood that sex provided a ready means to unsettle the puritan core of English society.[30]

As for SEX's wider clientele, the odd Teddy boy and ageing rock star now rubbed shoulders with fetishists and a growing coterie of imaginative teenagers looking for clothes to negate the staid styles of the mid-1970s. The fetishists, among whom were reputedly TV personalities and establishment grandees, shopped for their private pleasure, ordering specialist items before reconvening in their suburban homes to play out fantasies both elaborate and rarefied.[31] The teenagers coalesced around the Sex Pistols to form the kernel of punk's expanding milieu. In fact, John Samson's film *Dressing for Pleasure* (1977) captured this unexpected relationship for posterity, as footage of the older 'rubber duck club' segues into the proto-punk SEX habitué.

The most well-known of the fledgling punks were the so-called 'Bromley Contingent', christened by the writer and activist Caroline Coon in an early feature for *Melody Maker*.[32] Among them was Siouxsie Sioux (Susan Ballion), whose penchant for Weimar chic took on dominatrix overtones when fused with SEX accoutrements. Her friends, a mix of genders and sexualities, adopted names that referred to Christopher Isherwood's tales of 1930s decadence (Bertie 'Berlin' Marshall) and Sacher-Masoch's erotic novel *Venus in Furs* (1870) via the Velvet Underground (Steve Severin). In the process, they – and the wider SEX milieu – cultivated bohemian sensibilities that intimated (and romanticised) deviant experience. Nowadays, a list of SEX's clientele reads as a Who's Who of punk and punk-related culture, be it the Pistols themselves or the likes of Chrissie Hynde, Peter Christopherson (Throbbing Gristle), Soo Catwoman, Steve Strange, Poly Styrene, Judy Nylon, Marco Pirroni, Adam Ant, Viv Albertine (The Slits), Boy George, Pauline Murray (Penetration) et al., many of whom came from the suburbs and further reaches of the UK, travelling to London before then proselytising the shop's possibilities on their return home.

SEX, then, opened the door to secret worlds. It promised transformation and transgression – but also demanded a commitment. A manifesto conceived by Rhodes and delivered with McLaren and Westwood set out the shop's stall on a 1974 T-shirt: 'You're gonna wake up one morning and <u>know</u> what side of the bed you've been lying on.' Here, sexual fetishists were listed next to radicals, rock 'n' rollers and revolutionaries. More importantly, SEX and its affiliates were set against socialites, sell-outs and the society of the spectacle. A weapon in the struggle, SEX's Sex Pistols were primed to shoot from the hip.

SEX and (pre-)punk Britain: saw you in a mag, kissing a man …

Paul Gorman has suggested, quite plausibly, that Nik Cohn's 1971 book *Today There Are No Gentleman* planted seeds for McLaren. Published just before Let it Rock opened, Cohn's book proposed that rock 'n' roll's sexual charge was aroused through shifts in youth cultural style.[33] For the Teddy boy, he wrote, 'their clothes said just three things: *I am different; I am tough; I fuck.*'[34] In effect, we can see the transition from Let it Rock to SEX – from Teddy boy revival to punk – as an attempt to work through Cohn's equation.

Of course, other influences also fed McLaren's fertile imagination. His art school training introduced him to radical ideas that reached through French situationists and conceptual art to the more extreme outposts of the counterculture. Obsessions, be they early rock 'n' roll or hidden histories found along London's byways and alleyways, led him toward sites of revolt and sounds of disorder. There he shared his manias with a rolling cast of acquaintances and collaborators, inciting actions that consistently repositioned the fixations of late twentieth-century culture. On visiting McLaren and Westwood's South London flat in 1977, the *Rolling Stone* writer Charles Young noted bookshelves containing 'Orwell, Dickens, de Sade and Wilhelm Reich's *The Mass Psychology of Fascism*', a potent mix that all but signposted punk's dystopian-psychosexual-delinquent impulse.[35]

Regarding SEX and sex, the early interviews undertaken by McLaren and Westwood in 1975–76 offer glimpses of ideas forming to help instigate cultural change. Not surprisingly, given SEX's focus on fetishism, these were often found in pornographic publications – though typically ones marketed as 'sex education' magazines (*Curious*) or journals of 'human relations' (*Forum*). Already, clothes sourced from 430 King's Road featured in *Club International* over 1973–75. These, more often than not, decorated fashion shoots and featurettes photographed by David Parkinson, with leather macs or stilettoed shoes providing the suitably seductive styling.[36] In 1975, *Curious* captured Jordan modelling clothes from the shop alongside more explicit shots of Karen Cook (aka Susan Shaw aka Mona Solomon) in a rubber mask and an array of SEX T-shirts.[37] *Parade*, in 1976, also featured a model wearing just the Trocchi 'groaned with pain ...' shirt, while the aforementioned *Forum* piece concentrated only on those in the shop on the day.[38] In each case, the images appeared incongruous next to more clichéd pornographic spreads. Interviews, however, allowed McLaren and Westwood to expound their ideas and present SEX as something more than a sleazy corner of Soho transported to Chelsea.

Key themes emerged. The alignment of youth subculture and sexual subculture was immediately apparent. 'I'm excited by cults', McLaren told *Curious* in 1975, 'that's why I opened Let it Rock. And now, the cults are the sex people. The leather people, rubber freaks, transvestites, shoe fetishists.'[39] 'I am primarily concerned', he continued later in the year, with 'young people, eighteen, nineteen years of age, who need to find expression in what they're doing,'[40] To this end, what the journalist David May described as a 'bizarre combination of sex and politics' was devised, fusing the sexually charged threat of the Teddy boy with the socially deviant practice of the fetishist.[41] Interestingly, however, the 'bulk of the customers' were recognised to include 'young working-class and middle-class girls', pre-empting Jordan's claim that the overt sexuality of SEX provided a challenge both to gender norms and social expectations. 'I'm completely opposed to the chic look', she told *Honey* magazine in 1976. 'I think it's unattractive. It takes any sexiness away from the body and to bring sexiness back is my aim [...] I think you need a really full body to wear this, so I never diet'.[42] It was young women, far more than men, who most overtly radicalised – and problematised – the dynamics of sexuality through punk: 'I looked powerful', Jordan said. 'I know I looked very intimidating.'[43]

Not coincidentally, the *politics* of sexual expression were highlighted in the interviews. That is: 'to bring onto the outside of the body some of the changes which the increasing sexual liberation of the last ten years have wrought inside the head'.[44] As this suggests, the clothes served as a commentary on the possibilities and limitations of 'sexual revolution', pushing the boundaries and testing the limits. '[We] began to see the pertinence of it', Westwood said. 'The fact is that if you really do want to find out how much freedom you have in this British society at the moment, the best way is just to make an overt sexual statement and you'll have all the hounds of hell on your back.'[45] Accordingly, SEX's designs confronted conformity by celebrating 'deviance': they demanded a reaction. But they also ventured into violent extremes, be it Valerie Solanas's SCUM (Society for Cutting Up Men) Manifesto or, even more disturbingly, the 'Cambridge Rapist' T-shirt that McLaren struggled to justify to *Gallery International*.

Solanas had shot Andy Warhol in 1968, responding to a perceived slight but also raging against 'degenerate' men whose 'ego consists of cock'. Men were even 'unfit for stud service', Solanas insisted, being little more than 'walking dildo[s]' for whom sex was akin to 'a good plumbing job'. The solution: to 'kill all men who are not in the Men's Auxiliary of SCUM [...] working diligently to eliminate themselves'.[46]

The Cambridge Rapist was the name given by the press to Peter Cook. Cook committed a series of rapes and sexual assaults over the course of 1974–75, from which the media picked up on his wearing a leather hood with the word 'rapist' etched across it. The possibility that Cook was a customer at SEX led to a visit by police. In response, McLaren designed a shirt depicting Cook's mask set next to a smaller insert repeating rumours of The Beatles' manager Brian Epstein's death in 1967 occurring as a result of sadomasochism. The shirt was titled 'It's Been a Hard Day's Night'. Accused of being exploitative, McLaren noted the T-shirt's commentary on the media's morally duplicitous fascination with sexual violence. But he also suggested Cook was as much a symptom as a perpetrator of sexual repression, a 'symbol of what is happening to everybody in this country'.[47]

Such dubious reasoning was in keeping with McLaren's moral detachment. For David Wilkinson, both McLaren and Westwood's desire to shock was ultimately contained within the same 'conservative orthodoxies' they sought to inflame. '[Rather] than consciously alternative or oppositional values, the designs deliberately inhabited dominant understandings of unsanctioned sexuality as perverse', Wilkinson argued.[48] Same-sex desire or interracial relationships were thereby rendered as 'deviant' alongside rape and a variety of fetishisms, suggesting provocation – not liberation – was always really the point. Indeed, the word 'punk' has, of course, an etymology that traces back to prostitution, evolving through time to accrue an array of (deviant) variations.[49] As a term used to identify a delinquent or a youth selling or passed around for sex, 1970s 'punk' inverted socio-sexual mores to turn the world upside down.

More resonant, perhaps, and crucial to later claims of punk's socio-political pertinence, was McLaren's suggestion that SEX captured a 1970s mood. 'There are always moods', he argued in 1975. '[But] it takes someone to articulate them. If it happens to be me, then it's me.'[50] Along with Westwood, he pondered the appeals of restriction and a growing fascination with sadomasochism that others, including the US writer Susan Sontag, recognised to be permeating the decade.[51] This, after all, was a period in which filmmakers, photographers, artists and writers were aestheticising and theorising about sexual fetishism, with 'Nazi-chic' and 'terrorist chic' being coined as terms to describe films such as *The Night Porter* (1974) or the *Vogue* fashion-shoots of Helmut Newton.[52] The bondage suit, modelled first by Johnny Rotten on the Sex Pistols' trip to Paris in September 1976, became the epitome of McLaren and Westwood's ruminations, at once alluding to fetishism but also signalling that the social restrictions they implied shaped sexual convention.[53]

The context, of course, was a period of economic and political instability combined with the ongoing advance of consumerism, liberalism and media spectacle. In Britain, industrial tensions and social antagonisms flared as faultlines in the post-war 'consensus' began to widen. A lexicon of 'crisis' and 'decline' determined at least one version of 1970s 'reality', resonating in a country scarred by the ongoing process of deindustrialisation.[54] The Second World War, not to mention the end of empire, cast shadows that masked deeper existential pains. Beneath the superficial optimism of the 'swinging sixties', moral conservatism seethed and feminist critiques pushed back against the liberatory claims made for the 'permissive society'. 'People all want to be guilty,' McLaren insisted, 'guilty of their own sexual desires.'[55] By so doing, he tapped into the same masochistic mode that Jon Savage applied in his 1976 fanzine *London's Outrage*. 'As for the kink gear,' Savage speculated, 'it fits a peculiarly English kind of decay; perversity thru repression given true expression.' To the right, Margaret Thatcher prepared to enact the necessary discipline, a 'Mother Sadist' to a supine nation.[56]

Informing such analysis was Wilhelm Reich, whose work Savage cut 'n' spliced to decorate his fanzine and whose ideas McLaren discussed with David May in *Gallery International*. 'If ideas like his [Reich's] became more significant,' McLaren said, 'then what I am doing [in SEX] would appear to be very ordinary.'[57] Reich, who married sexual repression to political oppression and fused Freud with Marx to analyse fascism, saw sexual gratification as the key to personal freedom. A sexual and moral revolution was needed to overcome the suppressive structures of bourgeois society, Reich insisted. McLaren concurred: 'if people were upfront about their sexual responses, I think the whole politics of this country would change'.[58] What was needed, he said, 'was a bit of sexual liberation' and, though he recognised the problems of promoting this through commodification and consumption, 'it is the best thing I can be doing at the moment and I try to do it in as political a way as possible'.[59]

Here, then, lay the attack on 'the system' that Westwood spoke of in *Forum*. McLaren, however, envisaged a more violent upheaval born of a brutal century that gave rise to the 'gruesome images' now '[pervading] the various SM magazines'. The array of sexual practices formulated through 'all these feelings ... the environment you live in ... the way you were brought up ... school' needed to be liberated. And 'if I take my fantasies to the extreme', he mused, then 'it is because the extremity is where it's at'.[60]

Punk and sex: two minutes and fifty seconds of squelching noises

As it happened, the Sex Pistols were not well enough endowed for sexual revolution. The band's members offered a mix of crude masculinity – summed up by Steve Jones's admitting 'I was all about a quick shag and see you later' (albeit on the back of an abusive childhood) – and Johnny Rotten's scrawny disaffection.[61] Where the former was always on the lookout for a furtive fumble, the latter exuded a sexlessness exacerbated by such quotes as 'love is two minutes and fifty seconds of squelching noises'.[62] His friend Sid Vicious claimed to find people 'very unsexy. I don't enjoy that side of life [...] I personally look upon myself as one of the most sexless monsters ever.'[63] True, there had been efforts early on to infuse the band with a sense of seditious sexuality. One formative Sex Pistols gig saw Jordan reveal all on stage in an attempt to disconcert the studied ennui of London's self-appointed glitterati at a party hosted by the artist and socialite Andrew Logan. Another showcase event was held in the Soho strip club El Paradiso. But if the apocryphal story of McLaren's suggesting the band write an S&M-themed song is true, then the fact Rotten turned 'Submission' into a 'submarine mission' heading 'down down' to 'watery love' suggests the band took such schtick with a pinch of salt.[64]

McLaren himself had an awkward relationship with sex. Brought up by his grandmother while his mother carried out numerous affairs, McLaren recognised he was 'fascinated with it [sex] from a fetishist point of view'.[65] '[I was] not scared of sex', he admitted in a 1995 interview, but found it 'a world that I didn't really know how to venture into in any major way'.[66] By all accounts, his and Westwood's relationship was tempestuous and sexually erratic: both were involved (awkwardly) with other partners and, like Rotten, their wearing SEX clothes desexualised fetishism rather than intensified it. The overt sexuality of SEX, Jon Savage noted, became an 'abstraction of sex'.[67]

Simultaneously, McLaren's threshold for boredom was low, meaning he was constantly searching for creative stimulation. His musical antenna had attuned to the New York Dolls, with whom he briefly collaborated in early 1975, feeding into the emergent punk scene in New York that spawned Richard Hell, Television and others. He was by this time already half-heartedly managing the fledgling Sex Pistols, to whom he gave greater attention from August 1975 when John Lydon joined to become Johnny Rotten. Akin to their fascination with fetishism, McLaren and Westwood began to incorporate other extremes into their designs, capturing again a *mood* of 1975–76. In a world beset by economic tumult and political instability, not to mention left-wing terrorist factions/brigades and, in Britain, the National Front's reinvigoration of the far right, so anarchist quotes and images of Marx festooned their shirts and accessories. Infamously, the swastika became part of punk's arsenal: clashing symbols signifying the political gestalt and evoking the 1930s' descent into chaos. As 1976 became 1977, therefore, SEX transformed into Seditionaries with a new range of outfits and a refitted shop showcasing motifs of destruction. 'Destroy' muslins and T-shirts were sold next to images of a bombed-out Dresden, for which signifiers of power and oppression – the swastika, a crucifix, the monarchy – were détourned or defaced. Concurrently, as the notoriety of the Sex Pistols increased, McLaren eased into his role as an anti-manager and Jamie Reid's artwork framed the band in ways that eclipsed the sexual politics of SEX. Generating controversy by demystifying the music industry and exposing the 'No Future' of 'England's dreaming' became paramount.

Despite such a shift, the dissemination of SEX's mission proved intriguing. Residual SEX ideas and stylings permeated media spaces and public places to subvert and reimagine in equal measure. In the pornographic press where SEX clothes first found exposure, the boldness of McLaren and Westwood's designs were soon codified to ensure such signifiers as spikey hair, horror make-up and safety pins became yet more fodder for the insatiable sex industry.[68]

Through SEX, too, those congregating as a proto-punk coterie were oft found on the sexual margins, drawn both by their own sexual proclivities and a unifying sense of outsiderdom. Louise's, a lesbian club on Soho's Poland Street, was a regular haunt, as was the gay hangout El Sombrero and Linda Ashby's home at the St James Hotel in London's Buckingham Gate SW1. Ashby worked from her flat as a maîtresse and bought 'equipment' from SEX, becoming in the process the landlady for Jordan and associated friends. Even The Roxy – the first renowned London punk club – was hosted in a dilapidated gay bar called Chaguaramas, a coming together repeated elsewhere in the UK as young punks sought sanctuary from a hostile 'straight' world.[69]

As to whether exposure to such spaces and places led to sexual liberation, the evidence is unclear. Though Westwood and Jordan spoke in admiring terms of SEX's rubber devotees, endeavouring to understand the feelings and sensations induced by the clothes they sold, neither admitted to experiencing sexual frisson through fetish.[70] For some, such as Dorothy 'Max' Prior as she navigated her proto-punk creativity with work as a stripper, there did seem to be some 'polymorphous perversity abounding' among her friends frequenting SEX and Louise's.[71] To be sure, Linda Ashby opened portals to hidden worlds and desires.[72] When Ashby 'was on the whipping sessions' in 1976, 15-year-old Debbie Wilson remembered 'camping it up down Park Lane with a gang of trannies. All my friends […] were on the game.'[73] Indeed, Berlin recalled hosting a bed-hopping 'baby bondage party' that culminated in cum-splattered purple sheets and whip-marks streaking the polystyrene ceiling of his parents' suburban home.[74] But while Berlin's own journey into an imagined world of Jean Genet, William Burroughs and Christopher Isherwood led to encounters both intense and terrifying, accounts from London's Roxy club suggest dalliances no more (or less) remarkable than nightlife shenanigans either side of punk.[75] Perhaps, as both Vivien Goldman and Viv Albertine suggested, 'punk love' affected the functional and unemotional, demystifying sex's allure as much as its taboo via 'Loud groans and yelps heard through a club toilet door clash[ing] with the thrash of a band onstage; a handjob fountains cum, ruins a vintage velvet frock on the backseat of [...] a late night 57 bus [...]; struggling with your bondage trousers for a three's up on a mattress [...] in a bare boards squat bedroom'; blowjobs born only of inquisitiveness and nothing else to do.[76] No doubt, different people had different experiences in different ways in different places. Goldman's and Albertine's evocations of handjobs and blowjobs point to a lop-sided gendering of punk's sexual 'liberation'. At the very least, however, punk enabled connections across sexual diversity and challenged sexual norms/expectations, albeit partially and with suitably teenage irreverence.[77]

Style-wise, subsequent McLaren/Westwood designs – such as the Joe Orton inspired gay-punk orgy T-shirt ('Prick Up Your Ears') – maintained the theme of sexual provocation. More immediately, the diffusion of punk stylings away from the King's Road briefly cultivated what the Sex Pistols' acolyte Nils Stevenson reputedly called a 'St Trinian's look': school blazers or shirts adorned and defaced, which young punk women offset with miniskirts, no skirts, stockings, tights and/or heels.[78] This, as Stevenson's comment reveals, triggered stereotypical ideas about the 'sexy schoolgirl' and lacked the panache of the original SEX crowd, who in turn were oft-dismissed as 'poseurs' and 'stuck up'.[79] More to the point, the DIY aesthetic that defined and evolved through punk soon widened beyond the initial impetus of SEX, with young male punks proving especially unresponsive or unwilling – maybe too embarrassed/naive/immature – to engage with and extend the sexual revolt instigated from King's Road. As a result, overt sexuality was diluted as punk's bricolage style drew from a broader range of symbols/signifiers and the culture culture unfolded across across a range of (often overlapping) scenes and musical forms. Ultimately, perhaps, the slow emergence of goth into the mid-1980s best traced the transmission of SEX's dark sexual aesthetic, fusing aspects of fetishwear with gothic tropes to formulate a distinct and long-lasting subculture. Or, not wholly coincidentally, we might look to the development of clubs and magazines such as Skin Two/*Skin Two* that reimagined fetishism and the aesthetics of sexuality within the context of 'lifestyle'.

Creatively, SEX's 'revolution' found responses both astute and crude. It was after visiting SEX in 1976 that Poly Styrene wrote 'Oh Bondage Up Yours' for her band X-Ray Spex, recording in her diary that reading Reich gave her 'a new sense of freedom [...] stimulated my brain cells. Am I over intellectual now [?] Saw some silly S&M imagery [...] and thought "Oh Bondage Up Yours!" "Oh Bondage No More!"'[80] For Styrene, punk signalled a way out of the sexual tropes that bound female expression. Her dismissal of S&M imagery also denoted an alternative reading of fetishism, recognising how the male gaze might embellish sex whilst maintaining the conventional lines of gender relations.

Soon to play only their second gig in support to X-Ray Spex, Adam and the Ants also found inspiration at 430 King's Road. Adam Ant (Stuart Goddard) was seduced by the deviant allure of SEX, obsessing about Jordan (who managed/collaborated with the Ants) and committing to use sex 'as my source material'. As well as 'pure fuck songs' ('Red Scab', 'Physical'), he explored the dynamics of fetishism across lyrics with titles such as 'Beat My Guest', 'Rubber People' and 'Bathroom Function'. Given Ant spent two years at Hornsey College of Art writing an unfinished dissertation on the artist Allen Jones, his interest in all things sexual came with an artistic twist. Visually, his band drew heavily from stylised readings of S&M, with gig posters and badges comprising text and imagery culled from John Willie's *The Adventures of Sweet Gwendoline* (1974) and similar publications. Increasingly, too, Ant's punk-infused fascination with fascism fed into songs referencing Weimar chic or the sexual charge oft-presumed to tremor beneath the Nazi veneer. 'I'm not personally into S/M', Ant insisted. 'It's the power, it's the imagery [...] which I find magnetic [and which] appeals to my imagination.'[81] As for the point and purpose, Ant echoed SEX's Reichian line prior to his pop-star breakthrough in 1980: 'I felt there were sexual repressions and taboos making people oppressed [...] but not being dealt with. I wanted to bring it out and push it to the limits.'[82]

Beyond SEX's immediate devotees, Manchester's Buzzcocks extended the Reichian motif through the New Hormones label set up with Richard Boon to release the *Spiral Scratch* EP in early 1977: catalogue number ORG-1. Their next single, 'Orgasm Addict' (1977), was fronted by a sexually explicit image provided by their friend Linder (Linda Mulvey). The song was a speedy, jittery homage to lustful teenage urges. The sleeve – a naked female torso with an iron for a head and smiles covering the nipples – was one of a series of photomontages created by Linder to explore how media images commodified and codified the female body. 'I collected images of women that mirrored every facet of social and sexual attitudes at the time', Linder recalled, 'lifting up the bonnet of the culture car and studying its engineering to understand it'. Far more critical than SEX's designs, Linder's work was informed by punk's approach to reveal the fragility of gender constructs, demystifying and exposing mediated depictions of sex and sexuality.[83]

Pornography was also used by Cosey Fanni Tutti (Christine Newby).[84] Cosey was part of the art collective COUM Transmissions that morphed into Throbbing Gristle in 1975–76, thereby helping forge what became industrial music. Developing parallel with punk, industrial music and culture shared an obsession with all things abject and taboo but went further with regard to probing mechanisms of socio-political control and the (often violent) outer limits of human behaviour. Throbbing Gristle's Peter Christopherson took some early photographs of the Sex Pistols, the rent boy and delinquent overtones of which have been noted.[85]

In October 1976, COUM's exhibition at London's Institute of Contemporary Arts (ICA) all but pre-empted the media furore that enveloped the Sex Pistols a few weeks later. Called 'Prostitution', the show featured Cosey's work as a pornographic model, her image culled from top-shelf magazines and repositioned within the walls of the (publicly funded) art establishment. Though COUM performances often included sex as part of their confronting social and cultural convention, Cosey's being a stripper and a model more pertinently challenged the interface between art, pornography and life itself. As this suggests, Cosey understood her work to be an investigation, a process of self-exploration. 'Sex is beautiful & ugly, tender & brutal both physically & mentally', she explained.[86] Her art served to decode pornography, revealing to her sexual archetypes and the power dynamics of a sex industry that transformed Cosey/Christine into 'Millie from Ross-on-Wye' or 'Nanette' the nurse from a sex-change clinic.[87] In the process, 'Prostitution' saw Cosey and COUM described as 'Sadistic […] the wreckers of civilisation' by the Tory MP Nicholas Fairbairn in the *Daily Mail*. To decorate the story, Siouxsie Sioux and others from SEX were pictured entering the ICA.

We could go on, referring to the ugly sex references of The Stranglers or, from the other extreme, Alternative TV's brilliant undermining of rock 'n' roll's potency via 'Love Lies Limp'. Fast forward to 1983 and Frankie Goes to Hollywood emerged from Liverpool's punk milieu with 'Relax', a number one single that found controversy in a style, lyric and video that rekindled the subterranean homosexual practices aestheticised in SEX. But as more and more bands formed and more and more records were released, so punk's sexual provocations became buried beneath a combination of speed, spit and social realism. The culture quickly evolved, diffusing and refracting to reflect new moods and varied sensibilities. Just as sex transformed into sedition, so punk's anger turned to alienation and other affectations. In the time it took to play a three-minute punk 7", the squelching noises all but stopped.

Leaving the twentieth century: Oh Bondage up yours!

With the demise of the Sex Pistols in January 1978 (and Westwood's turning towards haute couture), Malcolm McLaren proved himself not quite finished with sexual subversion. Just as his countercultural forebears propagated the emancipation of youthful desire,[88] so McLaren continued to do so whilst also exposing/exploiting the paedophilic tendencies that pulsed through the music industry. First, his plan for a film about the Sex Pistols (eventually realised as *The Great Rock 'n' Roll Swindle* in 1980) toyed with pornographic subplots before succumbing to multiple rewrites and reimagining. In the event, the film culminated with the porn star Mary Millington having sex with Steve Jones before the lewd folk song 'Friggin' in the Riggin'' [aka 'Good Ship Venus'] ushered people out of the cinemas – rather than out of the twentieth century as the situationists urged.[89]

Second, McLaren formed Bow Wow Wow in 1980, recruiting the 13-year-old Annabella Lwin as singer. Not surprisingly, Lwin's age caused controversy, especially when she appeared naked on a record sleeve enacting Édouard Manet's *Le Déjeuner Sur l'Herbe* (1862/3). There were other issues too: lyrics penned by McLaren that drew from pornographic filmscripts written whilst on sojourns to Paris in 1979; the plan to market the band's first cassette-only album on the front of a magazine that drew from paedophilic slang – *Chicken* – and proposed to feature images of kids posing alongside articles on 'pleasure tech'.[90] Generally, however, the music press were au fait with McLaren's schemes, framing Bow Wow Wow as such and never taking too seriously the talk of 'pornography for kids'.[91] More generally, this was a period in which 'naughty' schoolgirls and schoolgirl uniforms were a staple of the licit sexual landscape, be it openly via bawdy comedy or implicitly in the tabloids' fascination with topless teenage models. Throughout the 1970–80s, the lines of youthful *hetero*sexuality remained blurred enough to establish 'groupies' as a recognised part of rock 'n' roll culture and allow the likes of Jimmy Savile to abuse despite the 'rumours' John Lydon revealed at the time. Such rumours, he said, 'we all know about but are not allowed to talk about'.[92]

SEX and the Sex Pistols must therefore be located within the late twentieth century's broader grappling with the contested processes of liberalisation, commercialisation, commodification and media saturation. To be a 'Sex Pistol' was to be young, free and primed to destroy the socio-cultural strictures that bound and repressed. As this suggests, the transgression of perceived norms was part of the thrill, as was the discovery (and revelation) of all things hidden and forbidden. But it was the act and the agency – 'I wanna *be* Anarchy' – that mattered most, soon brokering initiatives and aesthetics beyond the confines of sex or sexuality. If SEX's revolution was sometimes messy and occasionally lost in a miasma of nihilism and abjection, then its 'political statement' remained liberatory: an invitation to live in *the now* and 'Fuck forever'.

Notes

My thanks to Russ Bestley, Natalie Thomlinson and Ian Trowell for their helpful and insightful comments.

1 Quoted in Len Richmond, 'Buy Sexual', *Forum*, June 1976, pp. 20–2. Emphasis in the original.
2 Jon Savage, *England's Dreaming: Sex Pistols and Punk Rock* (London: Faber & Faber, 1991); Simon Reynolds, *Rip it Up and Start Again: Postpunk, 1978–84* (London: Faber & Faber, 2005); Matthew Worley, *No Future: Punk, Politics and British Youth Culture, 1976–84* (Cambridge: Cambridge University Press, 2017).
3 Dick Hebdige, *Subculture: The Meaning of Style* (London: Methuen & Co., 1979).
4 Savage, *England's Dreaming*, pp. 244–75.
5 For example, MOMA, *Punk: Chaos to Couture* (New York: MOMA, 2013); Paul Stolper and Andrew Wilson, *No Future: SEX, Seditionaries and the Sex Pistols* (London: Horse Hospital, 2004).
6 Quoted in Richmond, 'Buy Sexual', p. 22.
7 Paul Gorman, *The Life and Times of Malcolm McLaren: The Biography* (London: Constable, 2020); James Anderson, 'Punk, Porn and Politics: The Aesthetics of Radical Sexualities' (University of Northumbria, PhD thesis, 2021).
8 Jon Savage, *London's Outrage*, 1 (1976); John Scanlon, *Sex Pistols: Poison in the Machine* (London: Reaktion Books, 2016), pp. 93–8; Matthew Worley, 'Whip in My Valise: British Punk and the Marquis de Sade, *Contemporary British History*, 36:2 (2022), 277–321.
9 David Wilkinson, 'Ever Fallen in Love (With Someone You Shouldn't Have?): Punk, Politics and Same-Sex Passion', *Keywords*, 13 (2015), 57–76; Lee Edelman, *No Future: Queer Theory and the Death Drive* (Durham: Duke University Press, 2004); Judith Jack Halberstam, *The Queer Art of Failure* (Durham: Duke University Press, 2011).
10 Toby Mott, *Showboat: Punk/Sex/Bodies* (London: Dashwood Books, 2016).
11 Rick Szymanski, 'Would You Buy a Rubber T-Shirt from This Man?', *Street Life*, 1–14 May 1976, p. 11.
12 Gordon Burn, 'Jordan Goes to Town', *Honey*, September 1976, pp. 12–14.
13 See, for just two examples: Savage, *England's Dreaming* and Gorman, *The Life and Times of Malcolm McLaren*.
14 Vivienne Westwood and Ian Kelly, *Vivienne Westwood* (London: Picador, 2014).
15 Gorman, *The Life and Times*, p. 195.

16 Richmond, 'Buy Sexual', pp. 21–2.
17 David May, 'Sado Sex for the Seventies', *Gallery International*, 1:4 (1976), 62.
18 Ibid., p. 62.
19 Szymanski, 'Would You Buy', p. 11.
20 Ibid., p. 11.
21 Jordan with Cathi Unsworth, *Defying Gravity: Jordan's Story* (London: Omnibus, 2019), pp. 93, 116.
22 Quoted in Gorman, *The Life and Times*, p. 216.
23 Ibid., pp. 216–17.
24 Ibid., p. 247. The American artist Robert Watts had previously prodcued a similar design in the 1960s.
25 PunkPistol, *SEX and Seditionaries* (London: First Edition, 2006).
26 Arena, *Punk and the Pistols* (directed by Paul Tickell, 1995).
27 May, 'Sado Sex for the Seventies', p. 60.
28 'Sex', *Curious*, 1:2 (1975), p. 18.
29 Michael Deakin and John Willis, *Johnny Go Home* (London: Futura, 1976).
30 Jane Mulvagh, *Vivienne Westwood: An Unfashionable Life* (London: Harper Collins, 2003), p. 67.
31 Jordan, *Defying Gravity*, pp. 95–6; May, 'Sado Sex', p. 62.
32 Caroline Coon, 'Parade of Punks', *Melody Maker*, 2 October 1976, p. 26.
33 Gorman, *The Life and Times*, pp. 121–2.
34 Nik Cohn, *Today There are No Gentlemen: The Changes in Englishmen's Clothes since the War* (London: Weidenfeld & Nicolson, 1971), p. 33.
35 Charles Young, 'Rock is Sick and Living in London: A Report of the Sex Pistols', *Rolling Stone*, 20 October 1977, p. 72.
36 See, for example, *Club International*, September 1974, December 1974 and June 1975.
37 'Sex', p. 18; Peter Stanfield, *Pin-Ups 1972: Third Generation Rock 'n' Roll* (London: Reaktion Books, 2022), p. 281.
38 *Parade*, September 1976.
39 'Sex', p. 18.
40 Quoted in David May, 'Sado Sex', p. 64.
41 Ibid., p. 62.
42 Burn, 'Jordan Goes to Town', p. 14.
43 Jordan, *Defying Gravity*, xv.
44 'Sex', p. 18.
45 Quoted in *Tacky/No Future*, 1 (1977), p. 11.
46 Valarie Solanas, *SCUM Manifesto* (London: Phoenix Press, 1991).
47 Quoted in May, 'Sado Sex', p. 64.
48 Wilkinson, 'Ever Fallen in Love', 63–4.
49 'Punk Etymology', in Johan Kugelberg and Jon Savage (eds), *Punk: An Aesthetic* (New York: Rizzoli, 2012), p. 348.
50 May, 'Sado Sex', p. 63.
51 Susan Sontag, 'Fascinating Fascism' [1974], in her *Under the Sign of Saturn* (London: Penguin, 2009); Michael Selzer, *Terrorist Chic* (New York: Hawthorn, 1979).

52　Worley, 'Whip in My Valise', 277–321.
53　May, 'Sado Sex', p. 64.
54　For alternative positions, see Lawrence Black, Hugh Pemberton and Pat Thane (eds), *Reassessing 1970s Britain* (Manchester: Manchester University Press, 2013).
55　McLaren quoted in May, 'Sado Sex', p. 64.
56　Jon Savage, *London's Outrage*, 1 (1976), 8.
57　Quoted in May, 'Sado Sex', p. 63.
58　Ibid., p. 64.
59　Ibid.
60　Ibid., p. 99.
61　Steve Jones, *Lonely Boy: Tales from a Sex Pistol* (London: Heinemann, 2016), p. 77.
62　Quoted in Young, 'Rock is Sick and Living in London', p. 74.
63　Quoted in Jonh Ingham, Jonh Ingham, 'Welcome to the (?) Rock Special', *Sounds*, 9 October 1976, p. 26.
64　John Lydon, *Rotten: No Irish, No Blacks, No Dogs* (London: Plexus, 1994), p. 231.
65　Quoted in Gorman, *The Life and Times*, p. 220.
66　Arena, *Punk and the Pistols* (directed by Paul Tickell, 1995).
67　Savage, *England's Dreaming*, p. 101.
68　See the shift from *Parade*, September 1976 to *Club International*, April 1977.
69　Wilkinson, 'Ever Fallen in Love', 67.
70　Richmond, 'Buy Sexual', pp. 21–2; May, 'Sado Sex', p. 63.
71　Dorothy Max Prior, 'Sex and the City', in Richard and Cabut (eds), *Punk is Dead: Modernity Killed Every Night* (London: Zero Books, 2017), pp. 107–16.
72　Simon Barker, *Punk is Dead* (Prague: Divus, 2011).
73　Quoted in Savage, *England's Dreaming*, p. 183.
74　Bertie Marshall, *Berlin Bromley* (London: SAF Publishing, 2006), pp. 43–5; Arena, *Punk and the Pistols* (directed by Paul Tickell, 1995).
75　Paul Marko, *The Roxy London WC2: A Punk History* (London: Punk 77 Books, 2007), pp. 124–5.
76　Quoted in Mott, *Showboat*, p. 178; Viv Albertine, *Clothes Music Boys* (London: Faber & Faber, 2014), pp. 113–15.
77　See the claims and recollections in Stephen Colegrave and Chris Sullivan, *Punk: A Life Apart* (London: Cassell, 2001).
78　Marko, *The Roxy*, pp. 114–15. See, for photographs, Derek Ridgers, *Punk London 1977* (London: Carpet Bombing, 2016).
79　*Sniffin' Glue*, 3 (1976), p. 7; *Gun Rubber*, 3 (1977).
80　'Diary of '77 Day 1', in Celeste Bell and Zoë Howe, *Dayglo: The Poly Styrene Story* (London: Omnibus, 2019), p. 49.
81　Quoted in *Ripped & Torn*, 8, 1977, pp. 5–6; 14, 1978, p. 11–13.
82　Simon Dwyer, 'Bury My Heart at Wounded Knee', *Sounds*, 15 November 1980, p. 18.
83　Linder, *Linderism* (London: Ridinghouse, 2015). See also her band Ludus.
84　Cosey Fanni Tutti, *Art Sex Music* (London: Faber & Faber, 2017).

85 John Kugelberg (ed.), *God Save Sex Pistols* (London: Rizzoli, 2016), pp. 23–5; Gorman, *The Life and Times*, p. 300.
86 Cosey Fanni Tutti, 'Sleevenotes' to *Time Will Tell* (CTI, 2000), written May 1988.
87 Maria Fusco and Richard Birkett (eds), *Cosey Complex* (London: Koenig Books, 2010).
88 See *OZ*, *International Times* and *Suck* for UK-based countercultural expressions of 'sexual liberation'.
89 *Internationale Situationniste*, 9 (1964).
90 Gorman, *The Life and Times*, pp. 452–505; Fred Vermorel, *Fashion + Perversity* (London: Bloomsbury, 1996), pp. 8–9; Craig Bromberg, *The Wicked Ways of Malcolm McLaren* (London: HarperCollins, 1989), pp. 234–40.
91 Michael Watts. 'The Rise and Fall of Malcolm McLaren', *Melody Maker*, 16 June 1979; Pete Silverton, 'Sun, Gold & Piracy', *Sounds*, 26 July 1980; Chris Salewicz, 'Malcolm McLaren', *The Face*, May 1981.
92 BBC Interview with John Lydon circa 1978 (YouTube, accessed 22 June 2021).

14

The 'style terrorism' of Siouxsie Sioux: femininity, early goth aesthetics and BDSM fashion

Claire Nally

On 20 September 1976, Siouxsie and the Banshees made their debut performance during the first night of the 100 Club Punk Festival in London. The Clash and the Sex Pistols were also on the bill, but as Siouxsie Sioux (born Susan Janet Ballion in 1957) recounts: 'The performance must have come across as quite shocking and bizarre, because there weren't any female performers around at the time.'[1] Later in the interview, Siouxsie also notes that: 'There were quite a few women in the audience – Viv Albertine, Palmolive and the rest of The Slits, Patti Palladin, even Chrissie Hynde.'[2] So Siouxsie's account captures women's contribution to punk and should not be underestimated.[3] However, whilst this picture seems like a Who's Who of women in 1970s punk, it still underscores the relative paucity of women on stage, something which continued in the traditional goth rock line-up of the Banshees through the 1980s.[4]

Theoretical analyses of the period, including Dick Hebdige's *Subculture: The Meaning of Style* (1979), have since been revised by several critics, including Angela McRobbie and Jenny Garber, who maintain 'Hebdige's usage of "style" structurally excludes women'.[5] McRobbie and Garber's analysis can also be used to highlight the double-bind of Siouxsie's sartorial practice: they note that 'punks appropriated the "illicit iconography of pornography", the male-defined discourse *par excellence* … it is the punk girls who wear the suspenders after all'.[6] Following this logic, in the analysis that follows, Siouxsie's spectacular visual iconography, and the way the popular music press identified her as a dominatrix, an 'ice queen' and a goth icon, reveals that women were emphatically carving a space for themselves in 1970s and 1980s subcultures, but that this was ultimately a partial victory in so far as it did little to destabilise gender. Rather, it performed a taboo sexuality and an aberrant femininity.

Indeed, Simon Reynolds and Joy Press cite how Siouxsie Sioux's influential style combined 'the dominatrix, the vampire and the Halloween witch into a singular form of style terrorism. She inspired a generation of British girls to adopt the gothic look (sepulchral clothes, pointy Cleopatra-style eye make-up, angular, jet-black hair, deathly-white make-up).[7] The problem is that each of these images present simultaneously the possibility of empowerment and traditional ideas about aberrant women. This is complex, because for some women, Siouxsie fostered an unconventional but nonetheless aspirational ideal.[8] Patricia Morrison (The Gun Club) notes that in 1980: 'No one was doing the Siouxsie thing in LA. There was me and this other girl and that was it! A lot of the spiky-haired punk thing didn't appeal to me, but Siouxsie had glamour, real dark glamour.'[9] Tracing these sartorial lineages through magazine and print culture, documentary footage and the Banshees' outputs through to their later successes in the 1980s, this chapter identifies how the broader issue of subcultural gendered performance is closely related to an aesthetic of perverse sexuality, which in turn developed into a complicated but crucial space for women in the subcultural music scene. As Worley notes in Chapter 13 of this volume, the representation of sex and sexuality (especially 'deviant' or alternative sexualities) through aggressive or outrageous dress was distinctly part of the 1970s punk ethos, which also reflects the punk origins of Siouxsie and the Banshees. Additionally, with the advent of what Brian McNair has called 'the pornographication of mainstream pop culture'[10], more and more hyper-sexual images appeared in advertising, art, on television chat shows and fashion: the exploration of fetish fashion through designers such as Vivienne Westwood or punk icons like Jordan being obvious examples.[11]

Swastikas, authority and femininity: The Bromley Contingent and early Banshees

In *The Punk Rock Movie* (1978), a fresh-faced backstage Siouxsie asks 'What shall I wear?', which in many ways frames this section of my argument.[12] Taking its cue from fashion theory, this chapter emphasises the importance of 'the sociocultural aspect of dress: that it is imbued with meaning understood by [the] wearer and viewer ... [D]ress [is] an assemblage of body modifications and/or supplements displayed by a person in communicating with other human beings.'[13] In this definition, 'dress' encompasses 'attachments' and 'modifications' to the body, such as clothes, but also jewellery and handheld objects. It is distinct from 'fashion', which implies 'mass acceptance', and is especially appropriate given Siouxsie's early participation in punk. It is also distinct from 'clothing', which implies 'personal or social values'. For example, if it covers then 'it surely must protect and be good. If it does not cover certain body parts, it may be immodest and bad, at least to some people.'[14] 'Dress' therefore navigates some of the key issues associated with Siouxsie's image – display of the body, subcultural identity, resistance and performativity.

Part of Siouxsie's early style revolt relates to her use of fetish and Nazi insignia, androgynous or outrageous hairstyles, and references to cult classics in cinema and literature (such as *A Clockwork Orange*, directed by Stanley Kubrick in 1971, from Anthony Burgess's 1962 novel of the same name). Unapologetic and intended to offend post-war society, this compendium of images links with the status of female performers in punk and accompanying ideas of authority. Siouxsie's later shift into a proto-goth image relates to the broader evolution of post-punk and underscores how far the gothic (as opposed to goth) provided Siouxsie and the Banshees with an aesthetic to articulate a coded dissatisfaction with their society. In that first performance of Siouxsie and the Banshees in 1976 at the 100 Club, we find all these contestations of mainstream society channelled through Siouxsie's early sartorial choices, which drew heavily on various intertextual signifiers such as BDSM subculture and bondage aesthetics, as well as film:

> On the day of the gig I sat at home and got my outfit together. Black vinyl drainpipes, bondage shoes, a black T-shirt with a few slashes in it and, for some reason, a pair of scissors around my neck. I needed something on top of it so I borrowed my sister's black pinstripe jacket out of her wardrobe. It was lucky she was out of the country or she would have killed me. I also had a swastika armband and I'd painted a black star over one eye, which was supposed to look a bit *Clockwork Orange*. My hair was slicked back and had red stripes in it. A few days earlier, the film *Cry of the Banshee* [1970] had been on the telly, so when the venue wanted to know what name we were going to use, I said 'Siouxsie and the Banshees'.[15]

There are several signifiers to unpick here, including the *Clockwork Orange* eye make-up, which Siouxsie also carefully donned in 1976, joining the Sex Pistols on Thames Television's *Today* programme to spark a media-driven moral panic. At the same time, there is a frisson of fear for the viewer of this spectacle. With BDSM paraphernalia and 'domestic' weaponry (scissors), there is a promise of violence, as well as a cut-up sensibility appropriate to punk. On the *Today* show, as well as the *Clockwork Orange* eye make-up, Siouxsie also sported peroxide blonde cropped hair and braces, articulating through punk a youthful dissatisfaction with contemporary society, which mirrored the subject matter of Kubrick's film: 'Ostensibly a science-fiction vision of a hypothetical, nightmare future, it seemed to many people uncomfortably close to a documentary about England, as bizarrely dressed, drugged youths ran amok through a post-industrial cityscape.'[16] For the young Siouxsie, this identification with Kubrick's cult classic posited her squarely against her parents' generation and advertised the dystopian future for 1970s youth of the 1970s: economic crises, social unrest, alienated consumerism and disaffection. It was also a contestation of gender normativity which would be a cornerstone of her dress code:

> Visually, Siouxsie is harsh, asexual. She wears shorts/skirts for freedom of movement. She is nicknamed 'Android' by the group. Her make-up, which eerily transforms her nervous, wistful, pale face into the hard-lined clown-tragedian, is the one concession to the audience.[17]

As with many other commentators on female-fronted bands, Paul Morley here focuses on Siouxsie's appearance (although whether she is quite as 'asexual' as he claims is another matter), but part of that spectacle is carefully curated to challenge the dominant discourse around sex, gender and authority. The swastika armband, which Siouxsie sported at various points in the 1970s, was very much a part of the combative, aggressive and intentionally offensive punk ethos: Jon Savage notes that at the same event, Sid Vicious (on the Banshees' drums) had swastikas felt-tipped on his T-shirt.[18] Certainly, part of Siouxsie's look was purely iconoclastic:

> It was always very much an anti-mums and anti-dads thing … We hated older people – not across the board but particularly in suburbia – always harping on about Hitler, 'We showed him', and that smug pride. It was a way of saying 'Well I think Hitler was very good, actually': a way of watching someone like that go completely red faced.[19]

Siouxsie's targets were the post-war generation, including the lower middle-class suburban ethos of places like Bromley. By contrast, John Lydon (aka Johnny Rotten) maintained: 'I thought Siouxsie and Sid were quite foolish … although I know the idea behind it was to debunk all this crap from the past, wipe clean history and have a fresh approach, it doesn't really work that way.'[20] Though ill-advised and indefensible, Siouxsie's use of a highly charged and deeply disturbing political signifier warrants closer attention. *Sounds* writer Jane Suck noted at the time that Siouxsie's aesthetic was 'more akin to Visconti's *The Damned* than the Third Reich', a film depicting the supposed decadence of pre-war Germany.[21] Indeed, at the 100 Club performance, Siouxsie sang an improvised rendition of 'Deutschland, Deutschland, Über Alles' (aka 'Das Lied der Deutschen'). This, whilst popularly associated with the Nazi regime, was adopted as the German national anthem in 1922 under the ill-fated Weimar republic.[22] It also provides an intersection with discourses of gender and sexuality. Siouxsie's milieu became known as the 'Bromley Contingent', whose regular haunts included rent boy/gay clubs, Louise's (a lesbian club) and the apartment of Linda Ashby (of whom Siouxsie says 'her work was never about sex. It was more about S&M').[23] By so doing, they tapped into the association of Weimar decadence with Nazism and sexual deviance. Thus, another Bromley Contingent member,

Bertie Marshall (aka Berlin), recalled Simon Barker and Steve Severin's 'Nuremberg Reunion Rally Party', where Siouxsie sported attire from SEX, including pink transparent stilettos, fishnets, a Chinese dress and swastikas painted on her cheekbones: 'It certainly wasn't pro-fascist, pro-Nazi. It was more "What's the worst thing you can do to your parents who'd fought and died in the War?" Really fuck them off.'[24]

This rejection of normative values extended to exhibitionist, public displays of sexuality. Berlin recalls one party as follows:

> Inevitably, the doorbell went and it was these typical nosy, opinionated, suburban middle-aged arseholes. Siouxsie, who was in fishnets, plastic apron, stilettos and nothing else, with cat-o'-nine-tails in her hand said, 'I'll go to the door, come with me'. There was this woman with grey hair and flyaway glasses mumbling something about calling the police. Then she looked Sioux up and down: 'You're just a little slut!' Sioux said, 'What did you say?' She repeated it: 'You're a slut!' Siouxsie pulled back her hand and smashed the woman round the face, making her glasses fly off.[25]

Berlin also remembers going to a bar called Cherries, where Siouxsie led him around on a dog lead.[26] She asked for a bowl of water for her dog and the pair were promptly removed from the premises.

Such public displays (we might almost think of them as performance art) seek to rethink conventional femininity. As a whip-wielding dominatrix, or a public debaser of men (it is no accident that the Banshees' bassist Steve Severin derived his name from the 1967 Velvet Underground song, itself drawing on Sacher-Masoch's 1870 novel *Venus in Furs*), Siouxsie and her early dress correlate with the use of Nazi symbology. Valerie Steele notes that 'some sadomasochists argue that SM makes explicit the power relationships that exist throughout society ... [utilizing] political themes and costumes to express sadomasochistic fantasies'.[27] Whilst borrowing from punk's shock tactics, Siouxsie's use of the swastika and S/M discourses also presents a fantasy of female power and control. The confrontation with the woman at the Nuremberg Party and the scene with Berlin at Cherries both render public what would ordinarily be a private and taboo sexual spectacle and, relatedly, Siouxsie's attire provided a commentary on, and corrective to, disempowered femininity.

Various music journalists and commentators have identified Siouxsie's dominatrix look. Savage comments on her 'dominatrix-style hauteur'; likewise, the cover of *Sounds* (3 December 1977) dubbed her the 'Ice Queen', a much-repeated appellation.[28] Whilst this persona would ultimately feed into the S/M influences informing goth as a subculture and a style choice, it also carefully manages a studied navigation of being a woman in the public sphere.[29] Siouxsie commented: 'I used to get really envious of the rest of the band and hate being the front person. There's so much more pressure when you're the focal point.'[30] As the centre of attention, she becomes a spectacle which needs self-protection and strength. Indeed, Siouxsie framed her dress choices in one interview as 'armour', and this is hardly surprising if we contextualise such dress alongside her experiences as a female performer in those early years.[31] In 1977, the Banshees' set at Rebecca's in Birmingham was punctuated by audience invocations to Siouxsie to 'show us your tits!'[32] Likewise, during a gig at the Rainbow Theatre in London (20 October 1977) Siouxsie was arrested and spent the night in prison: 'she was hauled out in the rain at 4.00 a.m. with no shoes on – they'd been seized as lethal weapons – she had to endure threats, dirty jokes and policemen sitting on her head'.[33] Her footwear, usually stiletto shoes or boots, become weapons and a means of defence. As Steele notes: 'To the extent that fetish fashion is popular with women, in large part this is because it adds the idea of *power* to femininity. Another word for *power* is *freedom*, since although power is oppressive when wielded by others, it is something that most people desire for themselves.'[34]

In 1976, Siouxsie and other members of the Bromley Contingent travelled to Paris to see the Sex Pistols perform at the Club Du Chalet Du Lac. Describing her attire for this gig, Siouxsie explains:

> It was the kitsch value of it all that appealed to me, the *Salon Kitty*, *Night Porter*, *Springtime for Hitler* thing. High camp, not death camp. I wore the outfit I'd worn for a Sex Pistols gig at the Screen on the Green – a black PVC bra and knickers, fishnet stockings, suspenders, a swastika, bondage stilettos from SEX and, of all things, a see-through plastic raincoat with white polka dots. Just in case it rained.[35]

There is something perverse and *unheimlich* about this image: the homely raincoat in case it rained, juxtaposed alongside bondage stilettos and Nazi symbols. The cornerstone of such attire, especially when showcased in the public sphere, is the idea (however illusory) of authority and agency: 'The bondage clothes were ostensibly restrictive ... but when you put them on they gave you a feeling of power.'[36] Whilst the correlation of BDSM subculture and punk is far from new, what is interesting is the way in which fetish was being used as a gendered site of resistance, rather than simply perverse pleasure.[37]

It is therefore noteworthy that despite the expectations of fans and Polydor, the first single, 'Hong Kong Garden', which reached number seven in the UK chart in 1978, did not feature an image of Siouxsie on the sleeve, but rather an image of a feminine figure hiding her face.[38] This decision suggests a navigation of the power dynamics from within the band (it highlights how Siouxsie and the Banshees are more than just the lead singer), but also identifies Siouxsie's visibility and the scopophilia attending her. It becomes a recognisable pattern in several early photos of the lead singer. The 1977 *Sounds* front cover shows Siouxsie with a T-shirt printed with a pair of naked breasts. In the same vein, the *NME* cover from 17 April 1982 pictures the singer simultaneously exposed and covered, as we cannot actually *see* anything other than her naked back. Thus, Siouxsie toys with the viewer in terms of their scopic desire. The same image also highlights the instability of the dominatrix's identity: no longer the sadist but rather a masochist, Siouxsie's image here references the character of Lucia Atherton (played by Charlotte Rampling) and her costume in *The Night Porter* (1974). Lucia suffered sadomasochistic abuse in a concentration camp but subsequently rekindles a relationship with Maximilian Theo Aldorfer, the former SS officer who abused (but also protected) her.

This shift in subject position is entirely in accord with the argument of 'Coldness and Cruelty', Deleuze's analysis of sadomasochism in Sade and Sacher-Masoch: 'the sadist enjoys being whipped as much as he enjoys whipping others ... there is a certain sadism in masochism'.[39] As such, we may conclude that Siouxsie's espousal of these differing, perverse identities underscores the contingency of her public selfhood, her (non-)normative sexuality and, in a curiously postmodern gesture, her denial of any real access to a coherent subjectivity. More broadly, by showcasing these S/M practices in the public domain, in common with *The Night Porter* itself, the image asks the viewer important questions about the nature of sexuality: 'whether sex can ever be divorced from the subjugation of one person by another (or whether, more subtly, it involves a collaboration for mutual surrender and the emergence of a felt sense of intimacy and consequent pleasure). The film also indirectly questions whether normative sexuality can be distinguished from traumatic compulsion.'[40] In many ways, the exposure of hierarchy, power, inequality and shame underneath a respectable veneer lies at the heart of both Liliana Cavani's film and Siouxsie's reproduction of it.

Siouxsie's rendition of *The Night Porter* eschews full-frontal nakedness but explores the nature of perverse sexuality and desire. By comparison, the now infamous erotic image of Budgie and Siouxsie in the shower for The Creatures' first shoot (taken in Newcastle upon Tyne, UK, August 1981 – one of these photos was later to feature on the cover for *A Bestiary of* from 1997) shows how strategic use of dress feeds into a broader discourse about the nature of women's sexuality.[41] In this shoot, Siouxsie wears a soggy vest and through it the viewer can see the contour of her nipples: we simultaneously can and cannot scrutinise the more intimate parts of her body. Whilst Siouxsie was not beyond exposing her breasts in the early years, this paradoxical revelation and coverage of the body is also familiar to *The Night Porter* shoot and S/M practice more generally: 'a dominatrix may sometimes show an expanse of naked thigh or bosom [but] it is more common for her to be almost completely covered by a second skin – from the mask that partially or completely covers her face down to her stiletto-heeled boots'.[42] This second skin, which may extend to the mask-like make-up (from *A Clockwork Orange* designs, to eyepatches and gothicised eyeliner and lipstick), all set up an erotic drama which permits and dismisses the audience, showcasing a dance of power, availability and spectacle. This is not to say that such an image is necessarily radical. As Deleuze suggests, the image and practice of the dominatrix is not without complexity, as ultimately – in the logic of S/M relations – the victim or submissive ultimately constructs the nature and practice of desire: 'the masochistic hero appears to be educated and fashioned by the authoritarian woman whereas basically it is he who forms her, dresses her for the part and prompts the harsh words she addresses to him. It is the victim who speaks through the mouth of his torturer.'[43] Hence the dominatrix is not as in control of her identity as much as we might like to think, and by this logic, the S/M image of Siouxsie is precarious. In many (but not all instances), this is a heterosexual fantasy imagined by the submissive rather than the dominatrix herself. Constructed through a plethora of media images, gigs, photographs and journalism, it is co-produced by Siouxsie, the band and record company curation, but also through audience reception and consumption. As a result, any claim to the 'style terrorism' of Siouxsie must be, at best, partial and qualified.

Sex and death: gothic Siouxsie and *Juju* (1981)

Writing in 1977 for *Sounds*, Jane Suck noted that whilst Siouxsie 'sounded like a cat being castrated', her appearance was positively 'orgasmic'.[44] Suck's correlation of sex and death ('when this lot play a gig … it's like throwing a party in a graveyard') provides a useful summary of some of the main themes in the evolution of post-punk and goth. It also sheds light – or casts shadow – on how Siouxsie's image contributed to a broader movement in gothicised popular culture, employing monstrosity, the Other and a darker, more romanticised ethos than punk presented. A recurrent theme of the band's output showcases that underneath polite society we find the return of the repressed: the brutal murderer, the fetishist, the pathological multiple personality.

The public revelation of this dark underworld ultimately feeds into the sartorial revolt of Siouxsie herself, complicating our understanding of (middle-class) femininity and especially domesticity, but it assists in identifying how Siouxsie's stage persona moved from a punk ethos to a more goth(ic) one. Commenting on the funereal palette of goth's colour scheme, Simon Reynolds notes that 'it represented the return of the repressed'.[45] The colour scheme worn by Siouxsie and the Banshees is entirely deliberate. Severin notes that by 1978 and *The Scream*, 'we all wore black. Siouxsie would wear an occasional flash of white or blue, but that was all. No other colours were allowed.'[46] Siouxsie's black dress choices (and black hair) are a part of a specifically gendered contestation of social mores. Indeed, black has signified at various historical junctures as a colour 'of opposition and resistance'.[47] Whilst it also denotes Victorian mourning and grief, it is fundamentally 'the colour of bourgeois society, but subverted, perverted, gone kinky. The modern "aesthetic of the ugly" loves the frisson black gives – and gives more powerfully since fascism eroticised the uniform, created a fetishized ideal, a whole philosophy of domination, cruelty and irrationalism.'[48] As an existentialist corruption of normative and middle-class values, black is the colour of contestation and challenge. This 'aesthetic of the ugly' seems more comprehensible when we position Siouxsie's style against normative expectations of femininity. The commonly lauded values of nurture, obedience, sexual modesty – all of which codify under expectations of women's behaviour in middle-class society – are inverted in Siouxsie's dress codes.

In style and in content (lyrical and visual), Siouxsie and the Banshees' iconography at this time registered a fascination with the underbelly of society. However, before exploring this aspect of the band in detail, a distinction between 'goth' and 'gothic' is important. Despite the various imitators of Siouxsie in the goth community, the band themselves were (in common with other goth icons) determined that they were never part of a goth scene, despite the use of that description since *Juju* was released in 1981.[49] Severin maintained that: 'goth was reacting much more to the way Siouxsie looked'.[50]

Despite Severin's caveat, the band seemed very much at home with gothic tropes: the allure of serial killers, dark sexuality, the supernatural, hidden secrets in the family home, all subjects which accord with a gothic sensibility and which coalesce on *Juju*. Severin notes that: 'We'd actually described *Join Hands* as "gothic" at the time of its release, but journalists hadn't picked up on it. Certainly, at that time, we were reading a lot of Edgar Allan Poe and writers like that. A song like "Premature Burial" from that album is definitely gothic in its proper sense.'[51] Even understanding goth as a subculture and gothic as a set of literary and cultural practices, what this distinction overlooks is how far 'gothic literary and cinematic tradition provides a ready-made lexicon of otherness and difference through which the disaffected [goths] are able to articulate their alienation'.[52] The 'literariness' and cinematic nature of the goth subculture is discernible from the band's formation, through the horror movie themes (including *Cry of the Banshee*) which influenced the band so extensively. These characteristics became especially foundational around the first album: 'We loved Hitchcock's psychological thrillers, and it was the spirit and emotion of his films that we were turning into music: making songs out of obsession and psychosis.'[53] Such influences are equally discernible in songs from *Juju* such as 'Voodoo Dolly', 'Night Shift', and 'Spellbound', as well as the kitschiness of a song like 'Halloween'.

The cultural zeitgeist of the late 1970s provided Siouxsie and the Banshees with inspiration for song lyrics and music videos, as well as a more gothicised image. The visibility of sex in the public domain in the late 1970s and early 1980s was codified in debates around disease and death following the discovery of HIV in the early 1980s, as well as Peter Sutcliffe's high-profile murders of at least thirteen women around Manchester and Yorkshire between 1975 and 1980. These circumstances meant that the dark underside of polite society – necrophilia, homosexuality, prostitution, murder and violence – were all subject to public scrutiny. The feminist response, including the Reclaim the Night protests which began in the UK in Leeds in 1977 as a partial rejoinder to the Yorkshire Ripper, was about recapturing women's rights to public spaces (the police at the time had advised women to stay indoors at night, rather than target the perpetrator himself). Siouxsie's evolving sartorial curation stands alongside these historical moments, as a questioning of traditional femininity, domesticity and middle-class values which would become a cornerstone of Banshee lyrics.

The psychopathy of a song like 'Night Shift', which was about the Yorkshire Ripper, was foreshadowed in the early song 'Carcass' (from *The Scream*). Capturing an early performance in *The Punk Rock Movie*, 'Carcass' shows Siouxsie prowling around the stage in black and white striped T-shirt, black trousers and cropped black hair: a form of dress suggestive of a proto-Tim Burton aesthetic but also of an aberrant femininity. Wiseman-Trowse notes that figures like Siouxsie were 'interrogating the very notion of feminization that suggests domesticity and hence middle-class experience. In some ways their project is more adventurous than their male counterparts, tapping in directly to Butler's notion of ambivalent performativity in the face of a discourse that shapes desire, gender and sex.'[54] So we can read through her onstage persona how Siouxsie performs some of the broader themes of the song. Reviews of *The Scream* emphasised Siouxsie's perverse femininity, noting the singer's 'cabaret/dominatrix uniform (new black boots and panties)' with vocals of 'icy intensity'.[55]

As a grotesque story of love and obsession, 'Carcass' tells an ambiguous story of a butcher: the lyrics suggest both that the carcass in question is a pig ('be a dead pork', 'don't whine, you swine'), but also they point towards a cannibalistic love affair. The butcher amputates his limbs in order to be forever 'limblessly in love' with the object of his affections. Given the romantic framing of the lyrics, the song functions metaphorically as a commentary on romance: the choice of porcine analogies suggestive of 'a long pig' are important here, whilst the song catalogues a monstrous drive to disembody the self and the other/lover. The lyrics subsequently shift to reflect on the monstrous feminine: 'Mother had her son for tea'.[56] This reference to the sow who eats her own farrow also functions on a metaphorical level, clearly bespeaking a broader anxiety about women and their bodies (they give birth and they destroy).

In describing the evolution of gothic and body horror in the 1980s to which this song can be linked, Clive Bloom notes that a cornerstone of the genre is how the 'body is split open and anatomised; our interiors have become the new architectural spaces of fear'.[57] So 'Carcass' showcases the vulnerability of the human body, the threat of the monstrous feminine and the need for its expulsion. Whilst 'Carcass' suggests the demise of mother/beloved and son/lover as both become carcasses, 'Night Shift' signifies 'one of the darkest cuts from the album *Juju*: a harrowing groove that explores street prostitution'.[58] The context of the Yorkshire Ripper case informing the content of the song, alongside the Reclaim the Night Movement, showcases the fightback from feminist communities, sex worker organisations and women who experienced gendered violence.[59] If, as Xavier Aldana Reyes claims, the role of gothic and body horror is to 'reveal anxieties regarding the vulnerability of the human flesh to attack, particularly from human beings', then a song like 'Night Shift' performs this anxiety in a highly gendered way.[60]

'Night Shift' opens with what seems to be the perspective of the necrophiliac murderer working 'in darkness'. The scene is constructed as a perverted love story:

> A bride by my side – I'm inside many brides
> Sometimes I wonder … what goes on in your mind
> Always silent and kind unlike the others
> Fuck the mothers kill the others
> Fuck the others kill the mothers.

In a repeat of 'Carcass', women become bride-mothers (or the monstrous Mother), providing a source of Oedipal anxiety, whilst the ideal woman is shown to be a corpse, or 'always silent and kind'. It becomes apparent that in common with gothic subgenres like body horror, the open and eviscerated body is a source of spectacular fascination and repulsion. Reyes notes that 'mutilation, degeneration and transformation (often hybridisation) are the main catalysts [for body horror]'.[61] Hence the speaker reflects on how the corpse is entirely pliable and without agency:

> The cold marble slab submits at my feet with a neat dissection …
> Looking so sweet to me – please come to me with your cold flesh –
>   my cold love
> Hissing not kissing …

Halberstam's discussion of female monstrosity in *Frankenstein* is especially applicable to this disturbing scene. They explain that dismemberment is 'a deconstruction of woman into her messiest and most slippery parts' and relates to 'the dehumanization of woman'.[62] Importantly, such a monstrous feminine body is 'the fleshy center that never speaks … but always haunts the articulate narrative'.[63] Thus the silence and deathly chill of the prone body in 'Night Shift' betokens a wider metaphor for women's silence and negation. The streetwalker's corpse is horrific but compelling, even though the dead body is also offensively ugly in its 'hissing' (a reference to the gases escaping the corpse on decomposition, which also challenges the victim's silence through inarticulate noise). The scene presents a refutation of romance, as much as it conveys an insight into the psychotic mind.

If the song ended with this perspective, it might in fact simply be gratuitous, sensationalist and exploitative. The lyrics seem to denote victim status or even blame, with these women uncomfortably 'submitting' to a *Liebestod* and, from the perspective of the killer (who is seductively 'always dressed in black'), getting what they deserve as sex workers. However, there are a number of competing voices in the song. The chorus repetition of 'Night Shift sisters' suggests a sorority of women (and therefore a speaker who is a survivor bearing witness to these crimes). At no point is this aspirational: the chorus emphasises the killer is a madman who blames women for his violence ('I'm out of my mind with you/ In heaven and hell with you'). The song ultimately refutes a coherent politicised or even feminist reading, but when situated alongside Siouxsie as vocalist and performer, it acquires further resonance. In *She-Bop*, Lucy O'Brien identifies Siouxsie as a final girl, a term borrowed from slasher films: 'A final girl is the heroine left at the end of the movie. When everyone around her has been killed off, she survives.'[64] By the end of the song, this speaker has yet to be killed. The live version of 'Night Shift', with Siouxsie's persona as gothic-dominatrix-chanteuse, provides a synecdoche for the uncomfortable and aberrant feminine identities that lurk underneath polite middle-class society. Whilst her streetwalker chic – of fishnets, PVC and leather, fur coats and thigh-high boots – glamorises and objectifies, it also *speaks*, through dress, of the complexity of women occupying public spaces making spectacles of themselves, constructing different versions of femininity and navigating vulnerability and desirability.[65]

Conclusion

In 1980, Siouxsie was a signatory to a campaign protesting a Private Member's Bill in parliament which would have restricted women's access to abortion. In an interview for *Record Mirror*, Siouxsie discussed some of the reasons behind her objections to the Bill:

> Socially, women have *changed* … Women want careers and that's difficult with children … I didn't want to think that it was any big deal being a girl, but I'm not exempt from discrimination either. I don't feel at all maternal, although it's rammed down girls' throats that they should feel that way [...] Some girls are given dolls that wet their nappies, or ironing boards and toys that they have to work with. And that's when they are at their most imaginative stage. Little boys are given spaceships, adventurous things. I didn't have many toys anyway, but I was given the old dolly [*sic*].[66]

In common with an early song like 'Suburban Relapse' (from *The Scream*, 1978), this identification of the comparatively limited options for women underscores Siouxsie's 'style revolt'. Similarly, the use of goth(ic) images from Weimar-era Germany, as well as disturbing symbols such as the swastika and the display of body horror, signify a protest against middle-class values of femininity and propriety rendered visible in Siouxsie's public persona and in the band's song lyrics. Sitting just below the surface of normative society are the nightmarish or frustrated mothers confined within the domestic sphere, the serial killer and his victims, and the fetishised dominatrix.

As a woman in punk and later an icon of the goth scene, Siouxsie and her visual spectacle, including her early dress choices as part of the Bromley Contingent became a hallmark of how she was described and consumed for scopic pleasure (and discomfort) in the music press at the time and on to the present day. Siouxsie's evolving visual iconography, from her mid-to-late 1970s stylings to her use of goth(ic) in the 1980s, also provided a cross-fertilisation for the band's lyrics and early music videos.[67] The idea of women's erotic pleasure became a cornerstone for Siouxsie and the Banshees at this time. 'Sin in My Heart' (*Juju*, 1981) is a clear example of this trajectory, and might be read alongside by a broader feminist culture emerging in the 1980s which petitioned for women's right to sexual pleasure:

> Oh sin in my heart
> When you grovel at my feet
> Oh sin in my heart.

This form of pleasure is inherently perverse ('when you grovel at my feet' is overt in its BDSM themes), but despite an implicit heteronormativity, it is also in part a potential challenge to more conventional ideas of passive female sexuality. Such a narrative continued on later releases by the band, most notably the orgasmic 'Melt' from *A Kiss in the Dreamhouse* (1982). Again, the romanticism of the lyrics is tempered by a playfully destructive and violent sexuality: 'You are beheaded/ Handcuffed in lace, blood and sperm' ('beheaded' of course is simultaneously literal and metaphorical). As a *Liebestod*, it is a compelling and complex account of the femme fatale. Written by Severin, it is in many ways a male fantasy, but ultimately it provides a voice to female desire, with a dominatrix speaker as active agent.

This chapter has explored how far these performances challenge broader societal conventions around femininity. The highly sexualised imagery of such visual performances can be emancipatory, ensuring some visibility for women in male-dominated music genres. However, these models of 'alternative femininities' are not without complexity, participating in stereotypes which also align women as objects of visual pleasure.

Notes

1 Mark Paytress, *Siouxsie & The Banshees: The Authorised Biography* (London: Sanctuary Publishing, 2003), p. 53.
2 Ibid., p. 55.
3 For women in punk, see Helen Reddington, *The Lost Women of Rock Music: Female Musicians of the Punk Era* (Aldershot: Ashgate, 2007); Lucy O'Brien, *She Bop II: The Definitive History of Women in Rock, Pop and Soul* (London: Continuum, 2005, revd edn); Lauraine Leblanc, *Pretty in Punk: Girls' Gender Resistance in a Boy's Subculture* (New Brunswick: Rutgers University Press, 1999); Vivien Goldman, *Revenge of the She-Punks: A Feminist Music History from Poly Styrene to Pussy Riot* (Austin: University of Texas Press, 2019).
4 Catherine Spooner, *Fashioning Gothic Bodies* (Manchester: Manchester University Press, 2004), p. 178.
5 Angela McRobbie and Jenny Garber, 'Girls and Subcultures', in Angela McRobbie, *Feminism and Youth Cultures From Jackie to Just Seventeen* (Basingstoke: Macmillan, 1991), p. 25. See also Christine Feldman-Barrett, 'Where the (Untypical) Girls Are: Inscribing Women's Experiences into Dick Hebdige's *Subculture: The Meaning of Style*', in The Subcultures Network (eds), *Hebdige and Subculture in the Twenty-First Century: Through the Subcultural Lens* (London: Palgrave Macmillan, 2021).
6 McRobbie and Garber, 'Girls and Subcultures', p. 26.
7 Simon Reynolds and Joy Press, *The Sex Revolts* (London: Serpent's Tail, 1995), p. 282.
8 Samantha Holland, *Alternative Femininities: Body, Ages and Identity* (London: Berg, 2004), p. 85. See also David Shumway and Heather Arnet, 'Playing Dress Up: David Bowie and the Roots of Goth', in Lauren M.E. Goodlad and Michael Bibby (eds), *Goth: Undead Subculture* (Durham: Duke University Press, 2007), p. 138.
9 Paytress, *Siouxsie*, p. 103.
10 Brian McNair, *Striptease Culture: Sex, Media and the Democratisation of Desire* (Abingdon: Routledge, 2002), p. 13.
11 See Frenchy Lunning's *Fetish Style* (London: Bloomsbury, 2013), pp. 47–8 for an account of the intersection of punk and fetish.

12 *The Punk Rock Movie*, dir. Don Letts (1978).
13 Joanne B. Eicher and Mary Ellen Roach-Higgins, 'Definition and Classification of Dress: Implications for Analysis of Gender Roles', in Joanne B. Eicher and Ruth Barnes (eds), *Dress and Gender: Making and Meaning* (Oxford: Berg, 1993), p. 15.
14 Mary Ellen Roach-Higgins and Joanne B. Eicher, 'Dress and Identity', in. Joanne B. Eicher, Mary Ellen Roach-Higgins and Kim K.P. Johnson (eds), *Dress and Identity* (New York: Fairchild Books, 1995), p. 7.
15 Paytress, *Siouxsie*, p. 52.
16 Jon Savage, *England's Dreaming: The Sex Pistols and Punk Rock* (London: Faber & Faber, revd edn, 2021), p. 77.
17 Paul Morley, 'Siouxsie and the Banshees: A World Domination By 1984 Special', *New Musical Express*, www.rocksbackpages.com/Library/Article/siouxsie-and-the-banshees-a-world-domination-by-1984-special (accessed 3 March 2021).
18 Savage, *England's Dreaming*, p. 219.
19 Ibid., p. 241.
20 Ibid., p. 242. For criticism at the time, see Julie Burchill, 'Siouxsie & The Banshees: *The Scream*', *NME*, 18 November 1978, p. 45. Reprinted in *NME Originals: Goth* (2005), p. 13.
21 Jane Suck, 'Siouxsie and the Banshees: Gimme Gimme Shock Treatment.' *Sounds*, http://rocksbackpages.com/Library/Article/siouxsie–the-banshees-gimme-gimme-shock-treatment (accessed 3 March 2021).
22 Relatedly, in her discussion of the later album *Peepshow* (1988), Samantha Bennett notes the influence of a 'Weimar aesthetic draw[n] from cabaret as well as photoplay', so this is a thematic trajectory the Banshees maintained throughout their career. Samantha Bennett, *Peepshow* (London: Bloomsbury, 2019), p. 25.
23 Paytress, *Siouxsie*, p. 40.
24 Ibid., p. 32.
25 Ibid., p. 37.
26 Ibid., p. 37.
27 Valerie Steele, *Fetish: Fashion, Sex & Power* (Oxford: Oxford University Press, 1996), p. 182. Here Steele also discusses the prevalence of Nazi uniforms in S/M scenarios.
28 Savage, *England's Dreaming*, p. 418.
29 Part of the issue with Bill Grundy on the *Today* show in 1976 was his seemingly lecherous suggestions. See Ibid, p. 259.
30 Paytress, *Siouxsie*, p. 123. On p. 187, Banshees' drummer (and former husband of Siouxsie) Budgie also commented: 'there was this compelling woman out front with the rest of them looking like ants behind her'.
31 Kris Needs, 'Siouxsie and The Banshees: the story of the band who saved punk from parody and invented goth', 2 March 2021, www.loudersound.com/features/siouxsie-and-the-banshees-the-story-of-the-band-who-band-who-saved-punk-from-parody-and-invented-goth (accessed 28 September 2021).
32 Paytress, *Siouxsie*, p. 60.

33 Vivien Goldman, 'Siouxsie and the Banshees', *Sounds*, 3 December 1977, p. 27, www.rocksbackpages.com/Library/Article/siouxsie-and-the-banshees (accessed 2 September 2021).
34 Steele, *Fetish*, p. 185.
35 Paytress, *Siouxsie*, p. 41.
36 Vivienne Westwood, quoted in Steele, *Fetish*, p. 37.
37 For a discussion of S&M clothing and punk, see ibid., pp. 37–8.
38 Paytress, *Siouxsie*, p. 68.
39 Gilles Deleuze, 'Coldness and Cruelty', in *Masochism* (New York: Zone Books, 1991), pp. 38–9.
40 Victor L. Schermer, 'Seuxality, Power, and Love in Cavani's *The Night Porter*: Psychological Trauma and Beyond', *Psychoanalytic Review* 94:6 (2007), 927–41, 927.
41 See Ray Stevenson's *Siouxsie and the Banshees Photo Book* (London: Symbiosis, 1983), p. 48.
42 Steele, *Fetish*, p. 169. See Savage, *England's Dreaming*, p. 195, for examples of Siouxsie's revealing dress in the Bromley Contingent years.
43 Deleuze, 'Coldness and Cruelty', p. 22. By comparison, see also Lunning, *Fetish Style*, p. 65, who argues the dominatrix is outside the norms of femininity.
44 Suck, 'Siouxsie and the Banshees: Gimme Gimme Shock Treatment'.
45 Simon Reynolds, *Rip It Up and Start Again: Postpunk 1978–1984* (London: Faber & Faber, 2005), p. 423.
46 Paytress, *Siouxsie*, p. 73.
47 Holland, *Alternative Femininities*, p. 76.
48 Elizabeth Wilson, *Adored in Dreams: Fashion and Modernity* (London: I.B. Tauris, 2010, revd edn), p. 189.
49 See Paytress, *Siouxsie*, pp. 106–7 for the band's ideas around goth and gothic.
50 Reynolds, *Post-Punk Interviews*, p. 157.
51 Paytress, *Siouxsie*, p. 107.
52 Shumway and Arnet, in *Goth: Undead Subculture*, p. 153.
53 Paytress, *Siouxsie*, p. 78.
54 Nathan Wiseman-Trowse, *Performing Class in British Popular Music* (Basingstoke: Palgrave, 2008), pp. 144–5.
55 Richard Riegel, 'Siouxsie & the Banshees: *The Scream* (Polydor)', *Creem*, September 1979, www.rocksbackpages.com/Library/Article/siouxsie–the-banshees-ithescreami-polydor (accessed 3 March 2021).
56 For the 'monstrous feminine', see Barbara Creed, *The Monstrous-Feminine: Film, Feminism, Psychoanalysis* (London: Routledge, 1993). Notably, 'Voodoo Dolly' invokes similar leitmotifs of destructive, non-normative femininity, romance and fear. On one level, this is a story of a haunted doll, common to many horror movies and tapping into an anxiety about the uncanny humanoid. But on another, the child-like doll is also a woman who consumes her lover: 'You're anaemic from her sucking/ And when you're dead she finds another.'
57 Clive Bloom, *Gothic Histories: The Taste for Terror 1764 to the Present* (London: Continuum, 2010), pp. 182–3.

58 Dave Simpson, 'Back in Black: The Goth Revival', *The Guardian*, 29 September 2006, www.rocksbackpages.com/Library/Article/back-in-black-the-goth-revival (accessed 3 March 2021).
59 In an uneasy double-bind, some feminists also complain that such protests present women as victims. See the discussion by Sarah Gamble, 'Postfeminism', in *The Routledge Companion to Feminism and Postfeminism* (Abingdon: Routledge 2001), pp. 43–54.
60 Xavier Aldana Reyes, *Body Gothic: Corporeal Transgression in Contemporary Literature and Film* (Cardiff: University of Wales Press, 2014), p. 18.
61 Xavier Aldana Reyes, 'Abjection and Body Horror', in Clive Bloom (ed.), *The Palgrave Handbook of Contemporary Gothic* (London: Palgrave 2020), p. 839.
62 J. Halberstam, *Skin Shows: Gothic Horror and the Technology of Monsters* (Durham: Duke University Press, 1995), p. 47.
63 Ibid., p. 49.
64 O'Brien, *She Bop II*, p. 132. See Sheila Whiteley (ed.), *Sexing the Groove: Popular Music and Gender* (Abingdon: Routledge 1997), p. 213, where Mary Celeste Kearney's article 'The Missing Links: Riot Grrrl – feminism – lesbian culture' queries whether 'Final Girl' is a useful term to apply to female performers: 'While the description is innovative in its implication that these female artists are survivors, O'Brien does not adequately address the different structures, relations, and roles (the "horrors") these musicians were and are fighting against. Moreover the use of "Final Girls" suggests that those horrors have been successfully eliminated.'
65 Ray Stevenson's *Juju Across America 1981 Part Two* (no place: Hanging Around Books, 2020) contains several examples of Siouxsie's dress, both on- and off-stage.
66 Rosalind Russell, 'Siouxsie & The Banshees: Siouxsie And The Bitter Pill', *Record Mirror* 1980, www.rocksbackpages.com/Library/Article/siouxsie–the-banshees-siouxsie-and-the-bitter-pill (accessed 3 March 2021).
67 See Reynolds and Press, *The Sex Revolts*, p. 233: 'Siouxsie Sioux ... shift[s] between a series of female archetypes in a strategy of investment and divestment.'

15

Coming of age Asian and Muslim in post-punk West Yorkshire

Nabeel Zuberi

This chapter reflects on sex in the wake of punk through a partly autobiographical account. As a 1962-born Pakistani who came to the UK with family in 1968 and was naturalised as a British citizen in 1973, my teenage years and young adulthood coincided with the punk/post-punk years of 1976–84, when I lived in the predominantly white small town of Ilkley where I also went to a comprehensive school. I spent more time at record shops, concerts and clubs as an unattending chemistry student at Leeds University (1981–83) and part-time A-level student at Bradford and Ilkley College (1983–84), still living at home in Ilkley while on the dole. I moved out of the family home in the autumn of 1984 to start an American Studies degree at Nottingham University and my parents moved south to Northwood, Middlesex. Post-punk discourses often have a strong attachment to education, and educational institutions, and experiences often feature in narratives about youth. Like many others of my generation in the Subcultures Network that work in educational institutions, punk and post-punk were formative.

This chapter considers punk and post-punk music culture as sex education, an archive of sounds, images and words that described and animated sex in diverse, startling and catchy ways. I situate these songs in the media and scholarship of punk and post-punk. I try to connect my experiences in school, the home and public culture to the racialised sexualisation and sexualised racialisation of British (South) Asians and British Muslims in media representations and discourses of film, television and literature then and now. My account negotiates the tropes and set-pieces of autobiographical and fictional narratives about British Asians of South Asian and Muslim descent, with the help of scholarship in literary, film, media and cultural studies that has critically examined such narratives for their normative sexualities and masculinities attached to nationalism, immigrant economic success and model minority discourses in white supremacist societies. The chapter grounds my narrative in articulations of the self in punk and post-punk writing and media. They contribute to memory, towards a reflexive nostalgia with as many echoes and hauntings as Martin Hannett's productions. This chapter adds another 'brown' perspective today shaped by the postcolonial 'political blackness' of the period to reflect on punk and post-punk and the racialisation of British music in relation to sex and sexualities.

Focusing on sex and race in post-punk might contribute to established threads in the study of youth culture: to the networked regionalism and northern geographies of punk and post-punk against London hegemony in the 'national music'; to approaches to music media, playback and recording technologies, listening and consumption that consider the (not-white) home and bedroom culture as much as the club; to the importance of friendships in the hospitable and hostile environments of schools and streets, pubs and clubs with their sexed, gendered and racial power relations; to how transcultural anti-racism might open up a space for punk and post-punk's other identities and sexualities to unsettle the white transgressions and liberations in punk and post-punk, including those related to sex.[1]

Method: safety-pin stuck inside of my heart[2]

Dick Hebdige has noted that 'perhaps punk's one true abiding legacy' is 'the war it waged on behalf of awkward syntax and the principle of dislocation against seamless flows, settled truths and closure'.[3] I approach this chapter in the spirit of punk and post-punk jaggedness, undecidability and their valuing of failure and the abject. I try to safety-pin together the sexual elements of music culture with the development of a racialised gendered and sexual self at school, at home and in public. The assemblage of academic and personal voices is indebted to the aesthetics of imperfection, do-it-yourself, montage and cut-up common to punk and post-punk music, performance, art, publishing, film and autobiographical narratives.[4] The relationship of the personal to the political in second-wave feminism and post-feminism is integral to rhetorical modes in punk and post-punk.[5] Recent years have amplified a sustained chord of punk and post-punk memoirs, mostly by musicians rather than fans or listeners.[6] Many of them are inspirations in their reappraisals and revisionist approaches to punk and post-punk. Their aesthetics of assemblage have influenced my approach as well as affect theories in cultural studies.[7]

My messthetic positionality is also attributable to bad memories and difficult, contradictory feelings in revisiting childhood and youth while working on this chapter. I've continued to listen to post-punk music over the years and my memories of living in the north are attached to the music. But this listening intensified with Jo Cox's murder in Batley in 2016, Brexit,

Windrush, Grenfell, and racist nationalisms in the political ascendancy. Even before being asked to contribute this chapter, my intensified listening of this music from the past increased to both cope with, but also colour, anxieties about the state of the nation and my family's safety and well-being during the Covid-19 pandemic. A diet of British news streams and current affairs podcasts brought stories of Yorkshire cricket racism that revived memories close to the bone, but shaped by a confusing tyranny and luxury of mediated distance from the UK. I haven't lived in England since 1988. I doubted another virtual return to Britishness and Englishness in my academic work. I suspected my desire to remember the less happy aspects of life in England was phantasmogorical. The uses of popular music and popular music studies seemed primarily therapeutic. Or could it be that was sinking into a breakdown of memory like the haze of an album by the Caretaker. Though my personal voice has appeared in previous academic writing, the opportunity to write about post-punk was a primary motivation rather than the focus on sex. This sex challenge made me nervous and ambivalent about writing about myself and my family members.

Sarah Attfield also warns that 'overvaluing the self' is one of the pitfalls of auto-ethnographies, and argues that in comparison to hip hop, punk writing has invited relatively more first-person accounts due to the distance of time and the whiteness of the music genre. Though I'm not white, I am a privileged member of a generation in the UK that had 'access to education and the kind of cultural capital required to develop an academic career' and for whom 'education was free'.[8] Attfield also cautions against claims to unmediated 'authenticity' in auto-ethnographic narratives, one reason that I am unable to abandon the reflexive and distancing strategies of academic writing. Attfield values auto-ethnographic writing for 'unofficial histories'. The 'performance' of faulty memories in writing may be empowering for authors and offer a pleasurable experience for readers. Gavin Butt writes of an approach to personal narrative that is 'a partial and open enactment of a subjectivity *in the process of being remembered, in the process of being written*' (italics in original).[9] I write in tension with the 'customary reification in discourse' of sex and sexuality, in particular the racialised sexualities of Asians and Muslims.[10]

Coming-of-age and 'coming out' narratives usually end in cultural assimiliation. As Sita Balani puts it, in the ideology of the Western neo-liberal subject, 'sexual orientation is seen to be a foundational characteristic of the self, the repression of which is dangerous, violent and uncivilized'.[11] Memoirs such as Sathnam Sanghera's *If You Don't Know Me By Now* (aka *The Boy with the Topknot*, 2008) and Sarfraz Manzoor's *Greetings from Bury Park* (2008), adapted for the 2019 film *Blinded by the Light*, and autobiographical novels about 'anxious Asian men' often follow a trajectory in which the protagonist achieves authentic selfhood and the good life as they come out of 'the closet' of dysfunctional families and communities, escaping from arranged marriages to sexualities based on love, often with white women. The heteronormative sexualities of these narratives have a *'submerged'* reliance on homosexuality, yet the texts betray little interest in the erotic'.[12] Pop cultural desires, including pop music in the case of Bruce Springsteen in Manzoor's text, substitute for religious or other cultural upbringing. These 'misery memoirs' have engendered subjects as 'safe' ethnic others and 'moderate Muslims' to counter the extremist masculinities of the War on Terror.

But similar narrative structures are present in the earlier (post-punk) works by Hanif Kureishi written in the early 1980s that tend to equate sexuality with freedom and transgression. In the film *Bend it Like Beckham* (2002) interracial romance stands for multicultural happiness.[13] The emasculated, passive and overly studious Asian male and hyper-masculine violent Muslim male are two abject figures.[14] These figures appear again in discourses about the 'failures of multiculturalism', and problems with Asian and Muslim masculinities in the M62 corridor region of northern England and towns within it, such as Oldham, Bradford and Dewsbury.[15] The view of dangerous masculine sexualities and 'sexual misery' racialised as primarily Muslim in the north of England's sex grooming gangs (bad Muslims) oscillate with representations of happy British Muslims.[16] The historicisation of these representations is responsive to contingency, context and contradictions, and to important shifts in discourses at moments like the Rushdie affair or 9/11.[17] One can argue that the British Asian was a more powerful identification in the public discourse than British Muslim in the late 1970s and early 1980s. However, genealogical approaches to sexualities remind us of the continuities and renaming of familiar essentialising discourses about South Asian and Muslim sexualities in British orientalism, colonialism and imperialism.[18]

In media studies, my narrative is embedded in what Dagmar Brunow terms 'pluri-medial networks' that produce meaning about post-punk. These include the audio, visual and audiovisual archives through which transcultural memories may question dominant representations of places and cultures, and be integral to the emergence of 'new memory communities' that rewrite nationalist and patriarchal histories.[19] Post-punk is an ever-changing formation in which the past is remediated in texts and experiences such as memoirs, films, videos, reissues, new music under the influence, revival tours, museum exhibits and academic research. A tea-towel carries a black and white image of The Cure's Robert Smith with the words 'Boys don't dry.' Peter Saville reworks the *Unknown Pleasures* (1979) album cover's radio waves into the near flat lines of a No Music on a Dead Planet T-shirt. Anton Corbijn's biopic of Ian Curtis, *Control* (2008), transforms Joy Division's 'Love Will Tear Us Apart' into a 'bizarre love triangle' as the recording accompanies

Deborah Curtis's (Samantha Morton's) frantic search for evidence of her husband's adulterous relationship just after Ian has asked her if she has ever thought about having sex with other people. The domestic hunt is intercut with the group in a reconstruction of the warehouse rehearsal in the original music video, and Deborah discovery of Annik Honoré's name and a phone number handwritten on Ian's copy of Siouxsie and the Banshees' *Join Hands* album as the song reaches it climax. The number is dialled, Deborah hears Annik's voice and hangs up in the dramatic moment that has brought Annik, Deborah and Siouxsie together, as the film cuts to the young men thrashing through to the end of the song, interrupted by manager Rob Gretton who tells them the good news of an impending US tour we know that they will never make. This is another moment of a biopic or documentary 'performing the archive'.[20] In this new iteration, 'Love Will Tear Us Apart' shares a closer affective affinity with the Scars' jagged and frenzied 'Adult/ery' with its imagining of 'a romantic liaison somewhere in the south of France'.[21]

Post-punk modes themselves heightened the engagement with the past: the gravestones and statues of Peter Saville's cover art for Joy Division's records, for example; goth subculture's Weimar and horror hauntings; the Second World War and fascinating fascism; industrialism and post-industrial decline. The darker aspects of Yorkshire in personal memory are mingled with an imagined north passed down in media representations, such as those of of the Peter Sutcliffe (the Yorkshire Ripper) and Jimmy Savile cases.[22] 'What a fucking place', says a detective in post-punk David Peace's 'fabulist docu-fiction' *Nineteen Eighty* (2018) as he approaches Leeds on 12 December 1980. The city is described as 'a collision of the worst of times, the worst of hells', a '[d]read spectre from a woken nightmare' and a 'a past trapped in a future, here and now'. The historical memory of post-punk is central to David Keenan's novel *This is Memorial Device*, with the author describing the book as 'a "memorial device" for the band Memorial Device. It's quite a heavy thing: it's a way of raising the dead, with a Shakespearean gravitas.'[23] Documentary filmmaking present the ghostly presences of post-punk artists such as Poly Styrene and Ari Up and tell stories of post-punk characters still alive to both trouble the present and repackage the past as more of the punk and post-punk generation come closer to death.[24] Social media platforms publish and share media content related to post-punk in a living, networked archive.

Before punk and post-punk

I spent several months as a toddler in Kingsbury, London, when my father had taken up a short medical fellowship in 1963, but the family migrated to Walsall in the Black Country in 1967 and 1968 as Pakistani refugees from the war in Aden. I was the product of (Enoch) Powellism and the 'Paki bashing' era.[25] The verbal abuse, threats and occasional violence at school from children and teenagers on our housing estate were a constant reminder of lower status than whites, despite good friends, academic accomplishments and selection for sports teams. The ambient racism had an impact on making sense of sexual feelings and imagining a sexual self. Playground jokes in primary and junior school deployed a confusing repertoire of ideas about Asian sexuality: Asians bred like rabbits in the loft where we'd hidden illegals. Boys parroted claims that Asian men were trying to 'take our women'. But the Asian male characters in the TV sitcoms we watched were mostly desexualised and sometimes featured white actors in brown face.[26] In news and current affairs programming, Asian women were usually shown on working-class doorsteps with inscrutable expressions gazing back at the camera as a white voice-over told us about something wrong with them or their community. The sober and serious Asians on the early morning Sunday TV ethnic magazine show *Nai Zindagi Naya Jeevan* were in stark contrast to the mute, passive or problematic Asians in most other mainstream media.[27]

My parents were Urdu-speaking Muhajirs (migrants) to Pakistan from Delhi and Meerut in Uttar Pradesh in India, moving just after Partition and independence in 1947. My father was a doctor who became an employment medical advisor in the civil service, my mother a 'housewife' with a BA in social sciences from the Open University in the early 1970s, where I first encountered the Black British scholar Stuart Hall in televised lessons. Their marriage had been arranged in 1960. My parents voted Labour and had a cosmopolitan set of friends and interests, were into arts and crafts, and organised mehfils and mushairahs at home with Hindustani classical and 'semi-classical' musicians and poets from India and Pakistan. Ghazal and qawaali singers on the stereo expressed the desires of their lovers' discourses. My father's records included western love songs and sexy songs by Cleo Laine, Shirley Bassey and Johnny Cash. My father talked to me after a best friend hit puberty before me and dropped me as a friend because I wasn't charged up enough yet to want to kiss any girl, not a particular girl. Baba explained that desires would arrive and be natural but would have to be controlled. He was physically intimate with his children and comfortable in his body around us. At home in front of the children my father often initiated exuberant hugs and kisses with my mother, kisses on the cheeks not the lips. My mother was witty and flirtatious with words. They both loved Urdu poetry and Quranic recitation. My father laughed with us at the sexual comedies of *Carry On* films and 1970s television with their music-hall archetypes and pantomime sexualities. The open bookshelves included English literary and pulp novels, poetry and psychology best-sellers that included sex. There was no gender segregation in our home or social life, but going out with girls or boys for the short or long term was unlikely to happen. In Urdu my parents would disparage young people's public displays of affection. An upcoming school disco involved arguments, negotiations and often tears on all sides. My sister had a harder time than me or my two brothers but my parents gave us permission and freedom, as well as prohibition. As the firstborn child, I didn't have a desire to have sex until an arranged marriage to a Muslim from a family of similar religious and ethnic background, possibly related from the extended family, but only after I had a job and was settled, and before my three younger siblings. These attitudes to sexuality were expressed in terms of family ethos and morality rather than explicitly religious language. The homosexuality in the extended family was on open secret. Such fragmented moments in this generalised condensation of everyday life are typical of the moments of teen narratives and comedies such *Goodness, Gracious Me* and *The Kumars at No. 42*.

But whiteness inevitably gets a walk-on part. When I was 10 or 11, one of my best friends told me that 'girls would fancy you if you were white'. It was meant as a compliment. I took it at face value. Whiteness was unattainable and desirable. You show me yours and I'll show you mine with a girlfriend in a back garden tent when I was about seven and pre-pubescent friendships with girls in my class and tingles dancing with them to Showaddywaddy failed to develop into anything beyond crushes. There was no skin. At the Manor Farm Comprehensive School I attended in Rushall in Walsall I was often called a 'poof' or 'poofter', I thought at the time because I was a swot.

A promotion for my father brought him to an office in Bradford then Leeds so we moved to the more affluent and Tory town of Ilkley in June 1976, primarily for the 'good schools' after the experience of racist educational policies and bussing in Walsall.[28] I attended a state secondary school, a co-ed comprehensive that clung to the word 'grammar'. In school and in the town centre, white locals would often mistake Zuberi siblings for the Doshi siblings and vice versa since we seemed like the only two Asian families that had children with National Health specs. There was one 'West Indian' boy in a school of a thousand pupils. My life at school was almost exclusively homosocial. The girls were academic competitors. I had a handful of regular white friends, all boys, who were opinionated and argumentative about football, music and books and for left-wing politics. They would later introduce me to drugs and alcohol, pubs and clubs. The natural beauty of Ilkley and a much bigger house with individual bedrooms and a large garden transformed play inside and outside the house. I now had a room of my own to devour the weekly music papers *Sounds* and *NME*, play records, tape songs from John Peel's show and I would re-tune the radio after midnight to Dave Fanning on RTE 2 from Dublin.

The photo of school-uniformed lads messing about on the cover of *Resistance Through Rituals*, Stuart Hall and Paul Jefferson's edited volume of papers on 'youth cultures in post-war Britain', doesn't take me to the friends circle of my teenage years, but to the boys and their older mates who hung around outside the school gates at the end of most days, impressing their girlfriends by shouting 'Paki cunt', 'dirty Paki' or 'nignog' at me to sniggers and open laughter.[29] That ritual primed me for punk, with its anger and anti-nationalism finding a willing convert from pre-pubescent Beatlemania. I went quickly from arguing with my friend Mike that the Sex Pistols were tuneless shock merchants with disgusting spitting fans to punk making perfect sense when I danced to 'Pretty Vacant' at a school disco in 1977.[30] Like T. Rex boogie crossed with the anthemic choruses of Slade, Wizzard and Gary Glitter, the word 'vacant' reminded me of toilet doors and Johnny Rotten's 'we don't care' was attuned to my own anti-nationalist negations. Mike was soon recommending *Sounds* rather than *Melody Maker* or the *NME* as a place to learn more.

Punk and post-punk

As with any post-, post-punk discourse is preoccupied with the relative weight of the new to the old, the difference between before and after, continuities and discontinuities. These conceptions affect how we might consider the sexual content of post-punk. Stressing novelty has been a logic of the music industries since its early days.[31] 'Post-punk' emerged as a term in the British music press in 1978 and most studies position it as roughly 1978–85, arguably book-ended by the break-up of the Sex Pistols and the dissemination of post-punk's edgier musicalities into more commercially oriented music, including new wave, new pop, synthpop, indie and industrial music, among others. Simon Reynolds defines post-punk by its desire to fulfil 'punk's uncompleted musical revolution' through the exploration of 'new sonic possibilities'.[32] Matthew Worley writes that post-punk is an extension of some of punk's most important aesthetic strategies and techniques, with 'an emphasis on originality and innovation: a "new musick" or a "new pop" that evaded preconceived ideas and genres to perpetuate punk's tendency to confront, demystify and reassemble'.[33] There is an elastic relationship between the 'two genres' or cultural formations, such as in the approach of the academic journal *Punk and Post-Punk* with no definitive break, even though Garry Bushell earlier criticised post-punk for its middle-class distanciation from punk's working-class elements.[34] Mimi Haddon notes, 'the boundaries between the different categories of punk, new wave, and post-punk were more fluid and porous at the time than they are seen today by both writers and fans'.[35]

The logic of novelty in the music industries aligns in some respects with the ideologies and discourses of the music press and the desire for the new in writing by music critics and academics. Andy Bennett notes that the dominant historiography of 1970s music has tended to stress discontinuities rather than continuities in musical styles, and been 'rockist', downplaying more commercial or pop genres such as bubblegum, glam and soul.[36] Simon Reynolds and Mark Fisher privilege the futuristic aspects of popular modernism, radical contingency, the avant-garde, experimentalism, art rock and electronic music. Even as they are deeply interested in uses of the past in their writings on retromania and hauntology, innovation and change are valued more. Pushing back against this tendency, Gavin Butt points out that many post-punk artists were involved in the 'reworking of an earlier historical moment' of funk and 1960s psychedelia, as well as reggae, dub and folk music.[37]

The music was omnivorous and expressed sex through many of the sonic, instrumental and lyrical conventions of established genres that had their own racialised histories of race and sex. The Cramps drew on burlesque and rock 'n' roll tropes in talk about sex in songs like 'Can Your Pussy Do the Dog?' and 'What's Inside a Girl?' At the Futurama festival at Queens Hall, Leeds in 1980, the animated bony topless body of Lux Interior dived into the crowd while Poison Ivy chewed gum in bustier and fishnet stockings in the pose of a bad girl from 1950s rocksploitation flicks. Bauhaus's Pete Murphy intoned a frenzied sexual encounter with 'Dark Entries' when I saw them at the Fan Club in Leeds with their *Caligari* pastiche film and dry ice. On *Top of the Pops*, Squeeze's hit 'Up the Junction' was a kitchen-sink movie in song about a romance with an unplanned pregnancy and broken relationship. Alternative TV's 'Love Lies Limp' used dub (reggae) to wind down the libido and describe the 'bother' and anxiety of sex. Jazz-funk underpins Ian Dury's 'Wake Up and Make Love With Me', in which his voice describes roaming over a body, touching parts, with the ellipsis of 'what happens next is private, it's also very rude' leading to an instrumental break punctuated by Chas Jankel's piano.[38].

Post-punk sexed

Punk and post-punk culture offered a sex education, part of what Kodwo Eshun, in conversation with Green (Gartside) of Scritti Politti at a 2010 conference at Goldsmiths, University of London, describes as 'an alternative curriculum in which music functions as a portal that leads you into different kinds of culture'.[39] Eshun adds that the 'discontent' of late 1970s post-punk was focused on 'education' alongside music and youth. Education is one of the major themes in post-punk scholarship. According to Gavin Butt, for students from different backgrounds in art schools in Leeds, 'the band became a particularly potent "world-making" machine at this time'.[40] Punk often appears in debates about radical democratic pedagogy, DIY and auto-didacticism.[41] The scalpel, typewriter, camera, photocopier and lists of records, films, television and books in zines and the major music press were among the tools that could reorganise the world, and cultivate knowledge and experience in the arts to shape identity formation and radical democratic politics. For many in the Subcultures Network, the post-punk ethos encouraged interest in studying further and sometimes teaching jobs, careers in educational institutions, and pedagogies for critique and social justice.

Post-punk often made direct allusions to sex education. The Sheffield band They Must Be Russians reproduced a sex education lesson from what might be a relatively progressive social studies curriculum of the 1970s in 'Don't Try to Cure Yourself' (1980), produced by Richard Kirke (*sic*) and Stephen Mallinder of Cabaret Voltaire at Western Works.[42] The spoken-word lead vocal mimics a lesson on venereal diseases in which a series of pictures of gonorrhea and syphillis elicit a noise of vocal horror with a synthesiser squeal to simulate the spread of microbes and crab lice in 'the moist recesses of the human body'. A backing vocalist emphasises certain phrases in this lesson, 'yeah, yeah, pubic hair'. The cover of the 7-inch record includes microscope images of the offending organisms. Lizzy Mercier Descloux's 'Herpes Simplex' (1979) was another frank lesson, with Descloux 'yelping about the STI in fractured hysterics'.[43] As a fifth former, my friends and I distributed a 1979 National Union of School Students (NUSS) pamphlet that called for the greater availability of contraception products. The pamphlet included a photo of Jilted John (Graham Fellows) in school uniform from the photo session for his novelty hit of the same name. 'Jilted John' (1978) produced by Martin Zero (Martin Hannett) was post-punk in its parody of punk gestures. The album *True Love Stories* (1978), also produced by Hannett, was an homage to the teenage magazines aimed mostly at girls that boys like myself had scoffed at but also read over the shoulders of girls on the school bus, particularly the drawn or photographic comic strips with their speech bubbles of awkward encounters and the lists of what boys and girls hated and liked about each other.[44] The song 'I Was a Pre-pubescent' remains comical in its autobiographical tale of a working-class boy who describes the golden age before all the erupting changes of body and voice and the shock of 'words I didn't know' such as 'pubescence, adolescence … fornication, copulation, menstruation, contraception, masturbation'. The *pièce de résistance* is the squeeky comically forlorn male backing vocal of 'pre-pubescent, now he's not' that closes out the song.

'Why Theory?' the Gang of Four sang on the Rock Against Racism album, posing the question 'we've all got opinions, where do they come from?' as an entré into critical thinking about ideology. The group introduced us to anti-foundational theories of sex in 'Natural's Not In It' (1979). The yelps of 'fornication makes you happy' and 'repackaged sex keeps your interest' were earworms like the slogans of politicians or advertising in dystopian science fiction.[45] But in the song 'Damaged Goods' the group also included phrases about sweaty sex and 'heated couplings in the night' over a propulsive beat that made sex between imperfect bodies sound like an exciting clash. The choppy and discordant guitars of funk and Jamaican reggae and dub were a turning away from the 'cock rock' that guitarists and singers like Eric Clapton had appropriated from African American blues forebears then developed into musical virtuosity to boost their white masculinities.[46] The Au Pairs' 'Come Again' also used the instrumental techniques of African American funk to animate its public revelation of the labour required to achieve sexual pleasure. Over this beat, Lesley Woods repeats 'Is your finger aching? I can feel you hesitating' in rising impatience. According to Budgie, drummer on the sessions for the Slits' *Cut* album, Pennie Smith's famous cover photo of Ari Up, Viv Albertine and Tessa Politt topless and covered in mud in an English country garden was the band's rebuke to Trojan Records and other record companies that featured pictures of unclothed, sexualised Black women for the British reggae-buying public.[47]

Poly Styrene's voice rattled the cage of gender with its 'bondage' metaphor from the experience of slavery as well as a critical engagement with sex fashion. Punk and post-punk validated queer and transgressive sex, fetishism and sado-masochism. The sounds and poses also echoed many of the established ways in which sex was present in 'mainstream' popular culture. The Undertones' desire to 'hold her tight and get teenage kicks right through the night' could have been on a 1960s album. Blondie's urge to see a lover 'in the flesh' made more explicit the sexual ellipses of 1960s girl group songs with harmonies that echoed that sound. The period's 'sex beat' (to borrow from The Gun Club song) inevitably drew on genealogies of sex in a range of well-established music genres and cultures that informed punk and post-punk, offering a breadth of sexual encounters, desires and fantasies in music, image and performance. The music remains a rich archive of sex talk, sexual feelings, sexual experiences, sexed subjectivities with an edgy new frankness and ease in articulating sex. Punk and post-punk developed in the wake of the sexual revolution of the 1960s, second-wave feminism and gay and lesbian liberation in the 1970s. As Jon Savage has articulated in writing and compilations, punk was an influence in the emergence of queer identities and activism in the 1980s and 1990s. The post- in post-punk were enmeshed with the posts in post-feminism and post-modernism and their approaches to sex and sexualities.

One of the ur-texts then and now of punk and post-punk sex is Buzzcocks' briefly banned-on-the-BBC single 'Orgasm Addict' (1977) which kicked off their stunning series of singles on United Artists that bridged punk and post-punk.[48] Inspired by William Burroughs and cut-up in Pete Shelley's recollections, it is part acknowledgement and part critique of relentless desire, a polymorphously perverse series of sexual encounters and masturbatory scenarios with all kinds of people from 'schoolkids', 'winos and heads of state' to 'international women with no body hair'. Shelley's orgasmic oh-oh-ohs were mimicked by punk comrades to laughter. The record cover features Linder Sterling's striking photomontage that implicates and returns the male gaze on the naked woman's body with the domestic iron as a face and grinning smiles replacing nipples. The cover art may be the Mona Lisa of punk graphics as much as Jamie Reid's image of Queen Elizabeth II. Linder used her archive of women's magazines and pornography, 'slow-moving lumpen targets' for her 'surgeon's scalpel to liberate the images from the page' and reposition them with 'the sticky permanence of the adhesive' to comment on 'the mechanics of desire as democratic, the same techniques used to sell an eyeshadow as for a Mercedes Benz'.[49] Sterling and Jon Savage's *The Secret Republic* (1978) fanzine released on Buzzcocks' New Hormones label featured a montage of a heterosexual couple with television sets for heads and TV remotes and aerials replacing genitalia in an act of mutual masturbation.[50] Linder's spoken-word segment in the single 'Breaking the Rules' sounds like a lecture on 'the various combinations of romance, love and marriage' with sex intruding with 'too many rules' as she recites other utopian sexual formations to try out: 'female plus female/male loving male/female plus female plus female/male plus male plus male plus male'.[51]

Punk and post-punk approaches to pornography both critiqued its imagery and disseminated pornographic images more widely, contributing to what Dick Hebdige terms the 'pornetration' of popular culture brought about by the Internet.[52] Responses to pornography were often carnivalesque. John Cooper Clarke celebrated 'the monstrous feminine' in his post-punk poetry and music. The 'credo' of women bikers or 'sexational psycle sluts' captured 'the collective libido like lariats'. I would see the 'lean leonine leatherette lovelies of the Leeds intersection' at gigs at the University, the Fan Club or Warehouse.[53] The comical 'Readers Wives' celebrates the women photographed with 'cold flesh the colour of potatoes/In an Instamatic living room of sin' at the expense of the boring husband 'happily married to his wrist'.[54] Soft Cell put a thoroughfare of one of central London's sex zones Soho on the cover of their debut album *Non-Stop Erotic Cabaret* (1981) and Marc Almond dwelt on the heavy breathing and groping hands of people watching 'seedy films' and the 'sex dwarf luring disco dollies to a life of vice'.

The urban spaces of sex work and sometimes sex workers appeared in the West Yorkshire media more often during the late 1970s, due to Peter Sutcliffe's serial murders and attacks on women, often in the 'red light' areas of West Yorkshire and Lancashire cities. Watching a July 1977 episode of *Calendar*, Yorkshire TV's evening news and current affairs magazine programme, in which journalist Marilyn Webb interviews incompetent Assistant Chief Constable George Oldfield, one is struck by the disparaging discourse of 'women of the streets', 'ladies of the night', 'girls who like the high life' and Oldfield's certainty that 'prostitutes' rather than any women are the Yorkshire Ripper's targets.[55] Webb interviews sex workers in a Chapeltown pub who have a clearer idea of the killer's motives as someone who hates women. I notice the South Asian men at the bar that may be friends or customers. Joan Smith's account of the Ripper case in *Misogynies* recounts the police's disparaging attitudes to the 'morality' of working-class white women that had relationships with Black men.[56] Lucy O'Brien has recalled the intensity of shows by Siouxsie and the Banshees and Au Pairs at the University of Leeds in early 1981 soon after the arrest of Peter Sutcliffe in January.[57] Siouxsie and the Banshees recorded 'Night Shift' about the motivations of the murderer and the fears of sex workers. I saw the Au Pairs in July of the same year at the Carnival Against Racism in Potternewton Park, Chapeltown, where they performed 'Kerb Krawler', a song that counters the gaze of the cruising driver 'hiding behind his window screen, searching you out with his headless beams'.[58]

Punk and post-punk culture outside the home were predominantly white spaces even if they played dub on the PA. I was aware of Aki Nawaz from Bradford when I saw the Southern Death Cult at the Warehouse in Leeds, and Amrik Rai in Sheffield who wrote for the *NME*, and I hoped that Leyla Sanai, also in the *NME*, was an Asian or Muslim writer and not just an orientalist pseudonym. At Leeds University, Leeds Polytechnic or the Fan Club, I would exchange a look of recognition with the rare fellow Asian. The level of comfort in music venues was contingent on gauging safety and danger in the huddle of a closely packed crowd. The sensual moment of being pressed into someone's patchouli-impregnated leather jacket could be interrupted by someone else taking umbrage for a spilled drink or losing their footing, and fights would occasionally break out.

Leeds was a dangerous place with the National Front active in the city and on the football terraces of Elland Road. At around 11 p.m., when the pubs let out their punters, Asian taxi and bus drivers were often the objects of abuse. I negotiated that landscape and its spaces mostly with white male friends as a layer of protection. I rarely entered a pub on my own unless I knew for certain they were already there. My punkish friends who were natives of Yorkshire would often parody the Tetley Bittermen machismo on display at local hostelries and the rugby and cricket clubs.[59] Bouncers at dance clubs would bar entry, looking you up and down and shaking their heads. Though it is set earlier in the 1970s, the scene in the film *East is East* (1999) in which two Pakistani brothers manage to enter a Salford club by pretending they are Italian is a reminder of racist door policies.

Once I started Leeds University in 1981, still commuting from Ilkley to spend days wandering around Leeds record shops and spending my grant on records, I found the Warehouse, and became a weekend regular for about two years with a small group of my school friends, including two young women. I was naive and barely aware of the sex acts in the toilets joked about on the Warehouse 1981–88 Facebook page. When I messengered Leeds music producer and Warehouse regular Choque Hosein as a first approach for an interview, the reply was simply 'Cock'. I wasn't sure if that was an automatic message, an insult or a crystallisation of sex at the Warehouse. 'Pulling' seemed less important than posing. The soundtrack of DJs such as Ian Dewhirst invited dancing by oneself in a crowd to an eclectic mix of sounds of US boogie, early hip hop, post-punk and industrial dance music from England and Europe; playlists like the ones Tim Lawrence has documented from contemporaneous clubs and DJs in New York City.[60] The Warehouse seems relatively glamorous in my memories compared with the more accurate realism of documentary *A Night at the Xclusiv Club in Batley* in 1984.[61] Friends with big hair listen to a soundtrack of post-punk and goth staples with the odd Glenn Miller tune thrown in too. They discuss their spectacular, angular hairstyles and homemade clothes, sway on the dancefloor to The Human League's 'Sound of the Crowd' and in pointy boots step towards new mutations of themselves to the reverberating twang of The Cramps' 'Human Fly'.

The sexual education that punk and post-punk gave me didn't lead to any sexual relationships or intimacies during those years. Punk's repercussions dispersed a multivalent and ironic attitude to sex and tempered the collective phwoah of tabloid culture. I yearned for romance more than sex, but had some resolve and hope that once I moved away from home, both were possible. Post-punk contributed to the deferral of sexual pleasures. The sensual experience of the dancefloor and the erotics of writing celebrated and articulated by music journalists Paul Morley and Ian Penman, drawing from French poststructuralists and Nietszche, sublimated sex in the pleasures of language and the semiotics of images and clothes. The commodity fetishism around 12-inch and 7-inch records was another sublimation. The political and sexual education largely shaped by punk and post-punk and early Thatcherism while I was at Leeds University meant a reorientation of education towards the arts. A couple of years later I was reading Marcuse's *Eros and Civilisation* in an American Studies programme at Nottingham University. Post-punk was a gateway into a wider world of sounds and experiences in music and dance, beyond only white musicians, white critics and white fans to what I believe is a more fundamental infrastructure of Caribbean sound systems and African American music in the UK. Punk and post-punk should continue to be analysed and revised as multi-ethnic and transcultural to question a predominantly white British popular music history and heritage of the late 1970s and early 1980s. These music cultures gave me and many others a sex education. Punk and post-punk's frank and critical approach to normative sexualities also gifted the techniques to not tell the full story of a sex life as a way to question how British Asians and Muslims have been sexualised.

Notes

Thank you to Isabella Skinner for research assistance as a University of Auckland Faculty of Arts Summer Research Scholar, Lucy Robinson for an invaluable review, and Matthew Worley for gentle editorial guidance and patience.

1 Jayna Brown, '"Brown Girl in the Ring": Poly Styrene, Annabella Lwin, and the Politics of Anger', *Journal of Popular Music Studies*, 23:4 (2011), 455–78; Richard T. Rodriguez, *A Kiss Across the Ocean: Transatlantic Intimacies of British Post-Punk and US Latinadad* (Durham: Duke University Press, 2022).
2 Patrik Fitzgerald, *Safety-Pin Stuck in my Heart* (Small Wonder Records, 1978).
3 Dick Hebdige, 'Afterword After Shock: From Punk to Pornetration to "Let's Be Facebook Frendz!!"', in The Subcultures Network (eds), *Subcultures, Popular Music and Social Change* (Newcastle upon Tyne: Cambridge Scholars Publishing, 2014), p. 267.
4 Stacy Thompson, 'Punk Cinema', in Nicholas Rombes (ed.), *New Punk Cinema* (Edinburgh University Press, 2005), pp. 2–38.
5 David Wilkinson, *Post-Punk, Politics and Pleasure in Britain* (Basingstoke: Palgrave Macmillan, 2016).
6 See for example, Viv Albertine, *Clothes, Clothes, Clothes. Music, Music, Music. Boys, Boys, Boys* (London: Faber & Faber, 2015); Tracey Thorn, *Bedsit Disco Queen: How I Grew Up and Tried to Be a Pop Star* (London: Virago, 2013); Lavinia Greenlaw, *The Importance of Music to Girls* (London: Faber & Faber, 2017); Cosey Fanni Tutti, *Art Sex Music* (London: Faber & Faber, 2017).
7 Jasbir Puar, *Terrorist Assemblages: Homonationalism in Queer Times* (Durham: Duke University Press, 2007).

8 Sarah Attfield, 'Punk Rock and the Value of Auto-ethnographic Writing about Music', *Portal: Journal of Multidisciplinary International Studies*, 8:1 (2011), 6.
9 Gavin Butt, 'Happenings in History, or, the Epistemology of the Memoir', *Oxford Art Journal*, 24:2 (2001), 120.
10 Ibid., 124.
11 Sita Balani, 'Anxious Asian Men: "Coming Out" into Neo-Liberal Masculinity', *Journal of Postcolonial Writing*, 55:3 (2019), 383.
12 Ibid., 385.
13 Ruvani Ranasinha, 'Racialized Masculinities and Postcolonial Critique in Contemporary British Asian Male-authored Texts', *Journal of Postcolonial Writing*, 45:3 (2009), 297–307.
14 Virinder Kalra, 'Between Emasculation and Hypermasculinity: Theorizing British South Asian Masculinities', *South Asian Popular Culture*, 7:2 (2009), 113–25.
15 Shamim Miah, Pete Sanderson and Paul Thomas, *'Race', Space and Multiculturalism in Northern England: The (M62) Corridor of Uncertainty* (Cham: Palgrave Macmillan/Springer Nature Switzerland AG, 2020), p. 3.
16 Claire Chambers, Richard Phillips, Nahfesa Ali, Peter Hopkins and Raksha Pande, '"Sexual Misery" or "Happy British Muslims"?: Contemporary Depictions of Muslim Sexuality', *Ethnicities*, 19:1 (2019), 66–94.
17 Peter Cherry, *Muslim Masculinities in Literature and Film: Transcultural Identity and Migration in Britain* (London: I.B. Tauris, 2022).
18 Indrani Chaterjee, 'When "Sexuality" Floated Free of Histories in South Asia', *The Journal of Asian Studies*, 71:4 (2012), 945–62.
19 Dagmar Brunow, *Remediating Transcultural Memory: Documentary Filmmaking as Archival Intervention* (Berlin/Boston: De Gruyter, 2015), pp. 6–9.
20 Maurizio Corbella, 'Unpacking Performance in the Biopic', in Julia Merrill (ed.), *Popular Music Today: Proceedings of IASPM 2017* (Cham: Springer International Publishing, 2017), pp. 67–74.
21 Scars, *Adult/ery / Horrorshow* (Fast Product, 1979).
22 Ewa Mazierska (ed.), *Heading North: The North of England in Film and Television* (Cham: Palgrave Macmillan/Springer International Publishing, 2017).
23 Josh Kimblin, 'An Interview with David Keenan', *New Writing North*, 12 October 2017, https://newwritingnorth.com/journal/article/interview-david-keenan/.
24 Darren Ambrose (ed.), *K-Punk: The Collected and Unpublished Writings of Mark Fisher (2004–2016)* (London: Repeater Books, 2018); *Here to Be Heard: The Story of the Slits* (William E. Badgley, Head Gear Films, Metrol Technology, Molasses Manifesto, 2018); *Poly Styrene: I Am a Cliché* (Celeste Bell and Paul Sng, Generation Indigo Films, Polydoc Films, Tyke Films, 2021).
25 Paul Gilroy, *There Ain't No Black in the Union Jack* (London: Routledge, 1987); Claudette / The Corporation – Skinheads A Bash Them / Walkin Through Jerusalem (1970, 4 Prongs Push-out Centre, vinyl) – Discogs.
26 *It Ain't Half Racist, Mum* (Maggie Steed and Stuart Hall, BBC Television episode, 1 March 1979).
27 Sarita Malik, *Representing Black Britain: Black and Asian Images on Television* (London: Sage, 2001).

28 Anandi Ramamurthy, *Black Star: Britain's Asian Youth Movements* (London: Pluto Press, 2013), p. 17.
29 Stuart Hall and Tony Jefferson (eds), *Resistance through Rituals: Youth Subcultures in Post-war Britain* (Birmingham/London: Centre for Contemporary Cultural Studies, 1976 / Routledge, 1991).
30 Sex Pistols, 'Pretty Vacant' (Virgin, 1977).
31 Elodie A. Roy, 'Total Trash: Recorded Music and the Logic of Waste', *Popular Music*, 39:1 (2020), 88–107.
32 Simon Reynolds, *Rip It Up and Start Again: Postpunk 1978–1984* (London: Faber & Faber, 2009).
33 Matthew Worley, *No Future: Punk, Politics and Youth Culture, 1976–1984* (Cambridge University Presss, 2017, p. 9.
34 Philip Kiszely and Alex Ogg, 'Editorial', *Punk and Post-Punk*, 1:1 (2012), 3–4.
35 Mimi Haddon, *What is Post-Punk? Genre and Identity in Avant-Garde Popular Music 1977–82* (Ann Arbor, University of Michigan Press, 2020), p. 17.
36 Andy Bennett, 'The Forgotten Decade: Rethinking the Popular Music of the 1970s', *Popular Music History*, 2:1 (2007), 5–24.
37 Gavin Butt, Kodwo Eshun and Mark Fisher (eds), *Post-Punk Then and Now* (London: Repeater Books, 2016), p. 15.
38 Ian Dury, *New Boots and Panties* (Stiff Records, 1977).
39 Quoted in Butt, Eshun and Fisher (eds), *Post-Punk Then and Now*, p. 305.
40 Ibid., p. 102. See also Gavin Butt, *No Machos or Pop Stars: When the Leeds Art Experiment Went Punk* (Durham: Duke University Press, 2022).
41 Wilkinson, *Post-Punk, Politics and Pleasure*, pp. 115–54; Gareth Dylan Smith, Mike Dines and Tom Parkinson (eds), *Punk Pedagogies: Music, Culture and Learning* (London: Routledge, 2017).
42 They Must Be Russians, 'Don't Try to Cure Yourself (Fresh Records, 1979).
43 Laura Snapes, 'Lizzy Mercier Descloux, Press Color', *Pitchfork*, 10 August 2015, https://pitchfork.com/reviews/albums/20767-press-color/.
44 Jilted John, *True Love Stories* (EMI, 1979); Angela McRobbie, *Feminism and Youth Culture: From* Jackie *to* Just 17 (London: Macmillan, 1991).
45 Gang of Four, *Entertainment* (EMI, 1979).
46 Lucy O'Brien, 'Can I Have a Taste of your Ice Cream?', *Punk & Post-Punk*, 1:1 (2012), 29.
47 Lol and Budgie, *Curious Creatures* Episode 10: Cut: The Slits (2021), https://curiouscreaturespodcast.com/?p=2608.
48 The Buzzcocks, 'Orgasm Addict' (United Artists, 1977).
49 Linder Sterling, Through the Looking Glass, and What Linder Found There', in Johan Kugelberg and Jon Savage (eds), *Punk: An Aesthetic* (New York: Rizzoli, 2012), p. 287.
50 Linder Sterling and Jon Savage, *The Secret Public* (Manchester: New Hormones, 1978).
51 Ludus, 'Breaking the Rules' (Sordide Sentimental, 1983).
52 Hebdige, 'Afterword After Shock', p. 278.
53 John Cooper Clarke, *Innocents E.P.* (Rabid Records, 1977).
54 John Cooper Clarke, *Disguise in Love* (CBS, 1978).

55 *Calendar*, News Special, 19 July 1977. https://youtu.be/u3U7nyy3w8I.
56 Joan Smith, 'There's Only One Yorkshire Ripper,', in *Misogynies* (London: The Westbourne Press, 1989/2013 edn), pp. 193–239.
57 O'Brien, 'Can I Have a Taste ...', 33.
58 Au Pairs, 'You' (021 Records, 1979).
59 Seething Wells, 'Godzilla vs. The Tetley Bittermen' from Seething Wells and Attila the Stockbroker, *Rough, Raw and Ranting* (Radical Wallpaper Records, 1982).
60 Tim Lawrence, *Love and Death on the New York Dance Floor 1980–1983* (Durham: Duke University Press, 2016).
61 The Height of Goth: 1984: A Night at the Xclusiv Nightclub: Batley, West Yorkshire, UK. https://youtu.be/A9sMZ_5NjM8.

16

'I'm your man': heartthrobs and banter in *Smash Hits*

Hannah Charnock

The pop band Wham! of the 1980s were never afraid of toying with their masculinity. After their brazen defence of life on the dole in their first single 'Wham! Rap' and the playboy attitude of 'Young Guns', the band's third single put forward a fun-seeking, rebellious and emotionally aloof vision of male sexuality.[1] The song 'Bad Boys' described a lifestyle full not only of fights but of 'Easy girls and late nights, cigarettes and love bites'.[2] Reviewing the single in *Smash Hits*, future Pet Shop Boy Neil Tennant asserted that the song would be 'a hit in the gay clubs (and everywhere else for that matter)'.[3] In the same issue, the magazine ran a feature on the band under the headline 'Bad Boys Stick Together'. While the imagery depicted the Wham! boys in unzipped leather jackets with greased-back hair, the text of the article offered another less 'cool' image of masculine sexuality. As Andrew Ridgeley and George Michael recounted their years-long friendship, the band revealed the embarrassing state of their teenage love lives. Ridgeley recalled how, having got 'absolutely blind drunk' at a house party in their mid-teens, Michael fell over, got his new trousers dirty and 'was off, bawling his head off for an hour about how no-one fancied him'.[4]

Bringing together scholarship on the history of teenage magazines and the music press with work on pop/rock sexuality, this chapter uses a case study of *Smash Hits*' coverage of Wham! to interrogate sexualised magazine discourse in the late twentieth century. In doing so, the chapter demonstrates the extent to which cultures of youthful gender and sexuality changed across the second half of the twentieth century. The research shows that sex was a constant theme in much of how the magazine presented Wham! This was manifest in both the visual imagery and textual copy of the magazine, and represented both the band's self-presentation (as in their music, self-chosen marketing and interviews) as well as the magazine's editorial commentary. Two tropes of heterosexuality stand out in the coverage. The first was the tradition of the 'male pop star as heartthrob', although, as we will see, the pop star pin-up was increasingly sexualised with a particular emphasis placed on male stars' bodies as well as their romantic credentials and nice faces. At the same time, *Smash Hits* presented Wham! in a more 'laddish' mode which was underpinned by various forms of sexual banter. Both of these tropes had precedents in the sexual cultures of earlier periods but took on new forms at this time, not least because in *Smash Hits* they coexisted.

In part, we could explain the coexistence of these two tropes which had historically been highly gendered (heartthrobs for girls, banter for boys) by the fact that *Smash Hits* was a publication seeking to appeal to both young men and women. Magazines such as *Smash Hits* and *The Face* were part of a new wave of teen-facing popular culture that sought not to appeal to boys or girls exclusively, but to appeal to young people of both genders.[5] In the 1970s and early 1980s, at the same time that the Gay and Women's Liberation Movements had been making social and political challenges to the accepted gender order, subcultures such as punk, glam rock and the New Romantics had used make-up, fashion and music to push against hegemonic ideals of gender. The popularity of pop acts such as Elton John, T-Rex and David Bowie among both young men and young women was a powerful indication of the potential for mass-appeal popular culture that transcended gender binaries. In its emphasis on ungendered 'fans' and its coverage of an extremely wide variety of music acts (from Cliff Richard to The Specials, Bucks Fizz to The Cure), *Smash Hits* can be seen as meeting that demand.

The real significance of *Smash Hits*' discourse, however, lay in how it went beyond bringing together differently gendered registers of sex talk to blur the two together. It is certainly true that different sections of the magazine tended to discuss sex in different modes, but reading the magazine as a whole (and even when reading single features) readers would have encountered various different forms of sex talk. Within *Smash Hits* at least, all readers were included in and expected to understand sexual banter, while also appreciating (or at least not minding) the pin-up presentation of pop stars (both male and female). In this way, the chapter highlights how youthful sexual cultures of the 1980s were distinctly different to what had come before but were by no means settled. Sex was a commodity used to market bands to young audiences of both genders by playing on erotic forms of sexuality as well as sex's potential for satire, hubris and laughs.

Wham!

The band Wham! was formed by Andrew Ridgeley and George Michael in 1981. Ridgeley and Michael met at Bushey Meads Comprehensive school in 1975 and, bonding over their shared love of pop music, became best friends.[6] In their late teens, they recorded a demo of their first song 'Wham! Rap', and parts of 'Club Tropicana' and 'Careless Whisper', using a Fostex porta-studio that a friend of a friend had loaned them for £20. They were signed by the new record label Innervision in 1982. Having made reference to being on the dole in 'Wham! Rap', the music press jumped on Wham! as an exciting new socially-conscious and 'authentic' pop act.[7] *NME* and *Melody Maker* quickly became disillusioned, however, when it became apparent that Michael and Ridgeley's intent was to make catchy pop songs rather than offer biting social commentary.[8] Although Ridgeley had co-writing credits on a handful of Wham!'s biggest singles (including Michael's solo hit 'Careless Whisper'), it was Michael who took the lead on the musical direction of the group and provided the lead vocals on all of their songs. Contemporary commentators (both professional and amateur) were often dismissive of Ridgeley's role in the band, regularly portraying him as dead weight. The band's manager Simon Napier-Bell recognised the appeal of Ridgeley and Michael's duality, however, noting that: 'Their image is what Hollywood has sold films on for the past 50 years [...] Think of Butch Cassidy and the Sundance Kid.'[9] As one reporter wrote: 'The strength of Wham! lies in the way they supply different needs and balance each other out.'[10]

Wham!'s funk-and-soul-inspired pop took them to the height of pop superstardom. Between 1981 and 1986 when the group disbanded, Wham! had five number one singles and two chart-topping albums in the United Kingdom and their second album, *Make It Big* (1984), got to number one in the United Kingdom, the USA, Australia, Canada, Japan, the Netherlands, Norway and Switzerland. Wham! toured around the world and were only the second Western pop act to perform in China. Throughout the band's existence, Wham! generated much copy for *Smash Hits*. Having first been mentioned in the magazine in October 1982, the boys starred on the cover of *Smash Hits* in August 1983.[11] Between then and the band's break-up in 1986, Wham!, Ridgeley or Michael featured on the cover another seven times. Wham! were the subject of fourteen long-form articles (including a feature on their China tour that ran over two issues) and were centrefold or back-cover poster stars on a number of other occasions. *Smash Hits* readers voted the band's debut album, *Fantastic*, their favourite album of 1983 and Wham! made the top five in the *Smash Hits* Readers' Poll 'Best Group' category in 1983, 1984, 1985 and 1986.[12]

Only teenagers themselves as they entered the music industry, Wham! explicitly positioned themselves as a band for young people. As Ridgeley explained in an early interview: 'The trouble over the past few years is that kids are trying to relate to bands with images that are much more adult than they want to be.'[13] Reflecting in 2020 on why Wham! disbanded in

1986, Ridgeley suggested that this was because the boys were 'unable to outlive our youth': 'Continuing to distil the very essence of teenage emotion once we grew up was a pop alchemy beyond even George's prodigious songwriting talents.'[14] Youth was at the core of what Wham! was and what it meant.

Over the following decades, George Michael went on to achieve success and acclaim as a solo artist. Throughout his career, both with Wham! and after, Michael's sexuality was a point of interest for the press. In an interview with *Gay Times* in 2007, Michael described his sexuality as 'a real slow development' and that he 'really didn't self-identify as gay' at an early age. By the time Wham! was having success he 'really wanted to come out' but 'as the band became really, really successful, I lost my nerve [...] what else are you going to do at [19]?'[15] While Michael and Ridgeley 'played about with' their homoerotic dynamic, especially in the early years of Wham!, their public presentation was fairly consistently coded as heterosexual. Michael's later solo work obliquely addressed his relationships with men but Wham!'s music played on imagery of male–female relationships. When Michael was arrested in Los Angeles in 1998 for 'lewd behaviour', his subsequent coming out as gay came as a surprise to many fans even as music industry insiders insisted that Michael's sexuality had been an 'open secret' within the scene for years.[16]

In its analysis of coverage of Wham! in *Smash Hits*, this chapter does not seek to 'decode' the band's marketing and self-presentation to uncover hints of Michael's 'real' sexuality. Rather, the chapter is interested in the archetypes and discourses of sexuality articulated and depicted in *Smash Hits* during this period and the selection of Wham! as its case study reflects the band's direct positioning as an act directed at teenage fans. For the analysis undertaken here, the reality of Michael and Ridgeley's sexuality is less relevant than the cultures of sex talk that surrounded them, true or otherwise.

Smash Hits

Founded in 1978 by former *NME* editor Nick Logan, *Smash Hits* changed the landscape of music journalism and became an integral part of the British pop music scene in the final decades of the twentieth century. In the 1970s, music journalism, particularly that at *NME*, had become increasingly intellectualised. The 'Inkies' (cheaply produced weekly music magazines such as *NME*, *Melody Maker* and *Sounds*, whose ink stained readers' fingers) treated music as 'a serious affair',[17] publishing 'sprawling essays where musical textures and musicians were decoded, deciphered and deconstructed'.[18]

Smash Hits broke this mould not only in terms of the physical format of the magazine – it was printed in glossy full-colour – but in its ethos. Former members of the editorial team from *Smash Hits*' early years have recalled a desire to create an 'incredible, fantasy parallel universe' in which pop music was treated with loving irreverence.[19] Former *Smash Hits* writer Dave Rimmer summarised the lessons learned from his time at the magazine as: 'the value of mischief, the beauty of concision, the importance of having fun with your work and how to use that in giving personality to a publication, the necessity of never underestimating your audience'.[20] The defining characteristic of *Smash Hits* was its sense of humour and its unceasing desire to undermine the pomposity and self-importance that characterised much of the music industry.[21] As former editor David Hepworth explained: 'We thought pop stars were terrific, but absurd, so we developed a way of dealing with this supposedly glamorous world in a mundane style.'[22] This formula proved hugely popular. In the mid-1980s, the fortnightly magazine sold in excess of half-a-million copies per issue.

In many ways, *Smash Hits* functioned as a hybrid of the traditional music press and magazines aimed at teenage girls. Britain had a long history of periodicals marketed at girls and young women. Publications such as the *Girl's Own Paper* in the nineteenth and earlier twentieth century were joined by swathes of girls' comics in the first half of the twentieth century. While early publications focused on schoolgirl adventures, from the late 1940s a number of new publications such as *Girls' World* and *Miss Modern* were launched aimed directly at teenage girls. In both their fictional stories and their features, these publications often centred on romance and domestic femininity.[23] With the rise of rock 'n' roll in the 1950s, another wave of magazines emerged to capitalise on girls' interest in stars such as Cliff Richard and Donny Osmond offering readers interviews, backstage news and posters of their favourite acts. The quintessential girl's magazine of the post-war period, *Jackie*, combined both the romance paper tradition with the new fascination with the stars of popular music, creating a vision of girlhood in which pop music fandom was incorporated into everyday femininity.[24] With its combination of music reviews, lyric sheets, pull-out full-colour posters, behind-the-scenes gossip, letters pages and irreverent interviews, *Smash Hits* occupied a new space in the publishing landscape, offering music journalism to a younger and less explicitly masculine audience.

Yet, Neil Kirkham has questioned the assumption that *Smash Hits* had, and attempted to appeal to, an exclusively female audience. Although ascertaining the exact nature of the magazine's readership is difficult, *Smash Hits*' content suggests that it had (or at least it perceived itself to have) a mixed audience. Covering a wide range of acts across multiple genres of music (including disco, reggae, electronica and pop), *Smash Hits* was designed to engage readers beyond the rock fans catered to by the Inkies.[25] Letters to the magazine in the mid-1980s indicate a diverse readership and advertisements printed in the magazine sold a range of gendered and generic products from make-up, fashion and the magazine *Dirt Bike Rider* to blank cassette tapes and the latest music releases. As we shall see, the magazine's coverage of pop stars and pop music certainly deployed heartthrob discourses long-associated with girls' pop star fandom and teen magazines, but *Smash Hits* also tapped in to more masculine sexual discourse through its use of sexualised 'banter'.

Heartthrobs

Throughout history, British women have been 'desiring subjects' and male pop stars have long been the object of young women's romantic and sexual fantasies. The most famous manifestation of this came in the 1960s with the onset of Beatlemania but across the 1960s and 1970s pop acts such as Cliff Richard, Donny Osmond, David Cassidy, Mark Bolan and the Bay City Rollers similarly captivated young female audiences.[26] Without dismissing fans' enjoyment and appreciation of the music itself, many fans' adulation and adoration of their favourite pop stars went beyond musical taste. These stars elicited intense feelings in fans that were at once affectionate, desiring, possessive, lustful and loving. As Carol Dyhouse has noted, 'performers with the capacity to drive girls wild [were] a potential gold mine' for pop stars and their management.[27] Young fans bought every record their favourite stars released and every magazine that featured their idols. They learned all the lyrics to every song, sent off for posters and signed pictures, rushed home after school or work to ensure they caught bands' appearances on *Top of the Pops*, subscribed to fan clubs, travelled across the country to attend concerts, and even staked out the hotels in which they believed their favourite stars were staying. Pop star marketing was designed to encourage and sustain this feeling and teenage magazines played a key role in this. In her 1968 study *Magazines Teenagers Read*, Connie Alderson found that: 'More than 50 per cent of the material printed in teenage magazines [was] devoted to pictures of and features about the current pop stars.'[28]

In fact, there is a case to be made that by the 1980s, the arrival of new glossy magazines such as *Smash Hits* and, later, *Just Seventeen*, as well as the emergence of MTV and the rise of the music video, actually intensified pop music's investment in the pop star pin-up. While many aspects of music culture in the 1970s had pushed back against the shiny, romantic and explicitly commercial aspects of popular culture, the New Pop of the 1980s, building on glam rock and the New Romantic 'movement', was far more willing to embrace a commercial (if still eccentric and DIY) aesthetic.[29] Acts such as Adam Ant, Duran Duran, Spandau Ballet and Culture Club embraced their status as objects of desire, using this for commercial gain. They entered into a mutually beneficial heartthrob economy with *Smash Hits*. As Neil Kirkham has explained: 'In the early 1980s, pin-ups such as John Taylor of Duran Duran would cement their reputation as "most fanciable male" by appearing in provocative and objectifying shoots for the magazine.'[30] The coverage of Wham! in *Smash Hits* certainly played into the heartthrob trope with Michael and Ridgeley capitalising on their good looks.

While Wham! remained heartthrobs across the time the band was active, they played with different versions of pin-up masculinity, subtly shifting their look and presentation between contexts and over time. In the band's early days, at the time they were promoting the singles 'Wham! Rap', 'Bad Boys' and 'Young Guns', two slightly different constructions of the band were played out. The singles and their marketing deployed stereotypes of a roguish masculinity. A photograph of Michael and Ridgeley, posed on their sides, each reclining on one arm, back-to-back, wearing leather jackets left open to reveal bare chests, was used in the full-page advert to promote the 'Bad Boys' single in an April 1983 issue of *Smash Hits*.[31] With their slicked-back hair and eyes looking directly to camera, a colour-version of this photo was also used in a *Smash Hits* feature article on the band the following fortnight.[32] When *Smash Hits* printed the lyrics to 'Wham! Rap' in February 1983, the photo used to accompany these had tapped into the same tropes. The black and white photograph showed Michael standing slightly in front of Ridgeley, wearing an unzipped, sleeveless leather jacket with his arms crossed over his chest. Looking directly at camera, neither man was smiling.[33] This imagery stood in contrast to the song lyrics themselves which, while speaking to life on the dole, ultimately insisted that young people should 'make the most of everyday, don't let hard times stand in your way'.[34] This material deployed trappings of 'rocker' culture but, through the open jackets and bare arms and chests, offered this rebelliousness up to the young female gaze. It was a form of male sexuality premised on a mainstream edginess rather than actual rebellion.

At the same time, however, other *Smash Hits* features saw Wham! presented in a much more 'ordinary' way. Their first *Smash Hits* centrefold saw the boys featured alongside Wham! dancers Pepsi and Shirley, striking very awkward poses while dressed in seemingly 'high-street' jumpers and jeans, standing in front of a winter scene painted backdrop. Minus the winter scene, a similar set-up was used when Wham! first featured in one of *Smash Hits*' giant colour posters. The very act of being chosen as poster stars indicates a conviction that Wham! were pop star pin-up material. The selection of these images for the posters perhaps reflects a belief that teenage and/or female audiences were interested in 'approachable' masculinities that did not appear too distant from their own lives.

Between these two characterisations we can see Wham! pushing at the edges of respectable young masculinity while never pushing too far. As David Rimmer claimed about the New Pop of the 1980s, the appeal of these 'pretty [...] rather than butch and aggressively masculine' stars was that they were 'safe and unthreatening while at the same time being deviant enough to annoy your average parent'.[35] Wham! cultivated an appealing yet 'safe' sexuality. The band themselves acknowledged that their 'clean' characters, at least in their official presentation, was crucial to their success both at home and abroad: when Wham! became only the second Western pop act to perform in China, Michael asserted that this was because 'we're at the total opposite end of the scale to what China sees as the decadent rock acts of The West. You know – sex, drugs, scandal'.[36]

Wham!'s heartthrob presentation did change over time, moving from this initial bad boy/boy-next-door contrast, through the short-shorts-wearing, summer-love-interest persona of 'Club Tropicana' and the 'Fantastic' tour era, to a more mature and explicitly masculine heterosexuality as the singles 'I'm Your Man' and 'Everything She Wants' were released. A particular turning point came in the summer of 1984 as George Michael released his first solo single, 'Careless Whisper'. *Smash Hits* reporter Neil Tennant was sent to Miami to cover the filming of Michael's music video. This video portrayed Michael in a new light with 'George being in close physical contact with two models' for large portions of the shoot. The opening of Tennant's article reads like a romance novel:

> Here, in one of America's favourite holiday cities, George Michael lounges, clad only in a white bathrobe, on a bed shimmering with red satin sheets. Sunlight streams through the blinds, streaking the walls of the room. Standing at the dressing-table is a fair-haired young girl, also in a white bathrobe. George stares at her and smiles warmly. She walks over to the bed. They fall into each other's arms and kiss.

Asked about this 'sexy' and 'glamorous' new direction, Michael and Ridgeley reflected on their differing characterisations:

> One of the differences between Wham!-sexy and 'Careless Whispers'-*sexy* is
>   that 'Careless Whispers'-*sexy* is –
> 'Adult!' interjects Andrew.
> 'Straight-faced', continues George.

The article played with this duality. While two of the article's inset photographs depicted the Wham! boys looking sultry and model-like, the full-page photo alongside the article depicted the two of them pulling faux-macho poses on the beach with silly grins on their faces.[37] Wham!'s manager, Simon Napier-Bell, once remarked that part of the band's appeal lay in their buddy-boy homoeroticism.[38] In the article Wham! talked about sex and in the photos they may have had their shirts off but the fact of their pairing together and their cheeky back-and-forth defused any threatening potential of their sexuality.

Wham!'s increasing embrace of explicit heartthrob sexuality was heightened towards the end of 1985. In this period, *Smash Hits* ran two cover articles in which Ridgely and Michael were featured individually. The first of these appeared in October 1985. Entitled, 'Wham!: Randy Andy in Naked Five-in-a-Bed Tug-of-Love Porno Sex-Change Wife-Swap Spy Riddle', the article focused heavily on the bad reputation Andrew Ridgeley had acquired in the tabloid press. Images of some salacious tabloid headlines were inset into the piece, potentially revealing a side of Ridgeley of which younger fans were unaware, relating to drunkenness, brawling and promiscuity. However, the featured imagery used on the cover of the magazine and to illustrate the piece doubled down on Ridgeley's heartthrob status. The cover featured Ridgeley reclining on a chair, appearing to be dressed only in a white robe. With his hand running through his hair, he gazes directly at the reader. Another full-page photo sees him in a camel-hair coat with the collar covering his face so only his eyes are visible as he looks down the camera lens. In the final image he is wearing smart black trousers with an unbuttoned white shirt. Standing against a wall with his hands behind his back, he looks off into the distance. In contrast to the bright colours, Fila sportswear and cheeky grins often associated with mid-era Wham!, the colour palette of the whole feature is neutral and muted. This is Ridgeley in the mode of glamorous and aspirational heartthrob.[39]

Five issues later, Michael was the cover star with a close-up of his face gracing the front of *Smash Hits*.[40] Michael's hair, eyes, facial hair and outfit made a palette of brown tones, a departure from Wham!'s colourful styling. The cover's strapline was direct about the band's shift in direction: '"I'm Your Man" is more us … It's more about sex'. In the article itself, Michael explained that whereas previous Wham! records had been about sex in the 'soap opera … kiss and cuddle' sense, new tracks were rooted in the sex lives of twenty-somethings. Michael also pushed back on the public impression that he offered kids 'some clean harmless fun': '[The press] could easily have chased me round and found me in as many compromising positions'. Once again he drew out distinctions between his Wham! and solo artist personas: 'Well, the idea was for the ballads and the more romantic things to be for the George Michael solo LP and the more overtly sexual stuff could go on the Wham! LP. But now I think I should put something really filthy on my solo LP.'[41] Michael understood his pop-star sexuality to be dynamic, and he was conscious of his ability to take this in different directions. Within this interview, Michael was toying with various heterosexual characterisations acknowledging both his romantic lead persona as well as more explicitly 'stud'-like traits.

In these ways, then, *Smash Hits*' coverage of Wham! indicates the evolution of youthful sexual culture in Britain across the post-war period. While magazine heterosexuality had revolved around romance for decades, by the 1980s magazine discourse was embracing a more openly sexual culture in which sex was not taboo and where the sexual desires of readers were openly catered for. Magazines did not entirely abandon older models of romantic pop star masculinity but, especially through their visual copy and emphasis on male bodies, leaned into notions of sexual fantasy.

'What a lad, eh!'[42]

Late twentieth-century British culture was not only more explicitly sexual but was also increasingly casual in its expressions of sexuality. In the case of Wham! and their coverage in *Smash Hits*, discussions of sex variously characterised the boys as 'cheeky', cool or relatable. In all cases, it was taken for granted that modern youth culture did not entirely reify sexual activity as something that exclusively revolved around romantic love, intimacy and/or privacy.[43]

At the same time that visual coverage of the band played into a heartthrob mode of heterosexuality, *Smash Hits* also bought into a characterisation of Wham! as typical 'cheeky' lads. In several articles, Andrew Ridgeley was quoted making slang references to male genitalia. Commenting on his fractious relationship with the tabloid press, Ridgeley quipped: 'I know what angle they'd take: "Andrew Talks Frankly About the Size Of His Willy"!'[44] In a later article, George Michael stated: 'Andrew does have a lot to do with the filthy content of the Wham! stuff. When I'm writing he walks in and goes "oh don't put that – put cock"!'[45] With the arrival of *Just Seventeen* in 1983 it was increasingly common for teen magazines to address matters of sex and sexuality but they usually did so in an earnest and educational mode. Pop stars' off-the-cuff remarks about penises featuring in print marked a significant departure from teen press pasts.

Wham!'s sexual banter came to the fore during their first major tour as silly sexuality became a central part of their act. During the 'Club Fantastic' show, the boys would come out in sports gear and play badminton on stage. Infamously, they put shuttlecocks down their shorts. This set piece was widely reported in the music press, whose tour reviews were scathing of the band and highly dismissive of the group's fans. One reporter wrote:

'They touch the shuttlecocks (hey! symbolic, huh?) and lob them into the audience. George places his last shuttlecock down his shorts, then launches it at us. Good old George, eh? What a frigging *jerk*.'[46] The following year, Wham! reflected on this part of their act and the response it elicited:

> [George:] 'It was one of the highlights of the show [...] But the number of people who got offended was amazing! You should have seen the reactions of the crowd when we did those parts: all the girls screamed and all the blokes laughed which is what we wanted. [...]'
>
> 'You're in a position where everything you do gets screamed at, so you just parody that,' adds Andrew. 'The wiggle of the hips, the wink, everything.'

For Wham! making visual innuendos on stage was a harmless form of performative banter. Crucially, as Michael explained, this was a sexual presentation that appealed to fans of both genders: 'The girls love it – right? – and all the blokes who like you think it's a laugh.' In the context of live performance Wham! embraced their status as objects of desire, amplifying this in a form of playful, rather than necessarily erotic, sexuality.[47]

Having established this reputation, *Smash Hits*' future coverage of the band leaned into this. References to George Michael's 'pelvic thrusting' and 'hip wiggling' became something of a running joke in the magazine's discussions of Wham! In a feature on Wham! concerts in December 1985, a *Smash Hits* writer described the show as 'pure pantomime' and captions of the accompanying photographs were tongue-in-cheek. Seemingly quoting the man himself, a photograph of Michael on stage was captioned: 'Singing "Careless Whisper" and showing off *those* trousers: "I was determined to do the shuttlecocks again because everybody found it so offensive. But I couldn't get them down these ski-pants – or if I did I wouldn't be able to get them out again."'[48]

In the spring of 1985, as news came out about Wham's upcoming tour to China, much was made of the band's image. While, as we've already seen, the band's clean and apparently wholesome image underpinned the visit, *Smash Hits* made much of how this would involve adjusting the group's on-stage act. 'Mutterings' (the magazine's celebrity gossip column) noted that while the group's lyrics had been deemed inoffensive, 'The Chinese won't however have the pleasure of seeing Our George's "sexy thrusts and bottom wiggles" – he discovered on their recent Japanese dates that such thrilling behaviour gets barely a cheer out east'.[49] The sentiment was echoed two issues later: 'George and Andrew have just returned from China where, despite the lack of sexy hip wiggles [...] they apparently went down a storm.'[50] *Smash Hits* presented Wham!'s dance moves as an integral part of their act and, while it gently mocked the high-energy sexuality of the group, the magazine acknowledged it as a central part of the group's appeal to many UK-based fans.

In addition to highlighting the sexualised nature of their performances, *Smash Hits* featured coverage of the boys' 'actual' sex lives. In certain places this came from the band themselves. Behind the scenes with the band on tour in 1984, *Smash Hits* journalist Chris Heath was part of a conversation with George Michael and his sister about women's magazines: '"There's always a couple in them who look like they've just had the most perfect sex. It's so unrealistic. The earth's never moved for me. But", he adds, "I'm open to offers!"'[51] The following year Heath wrote a feature on 'George Michael: The Story So Far'. The article described Michael's life history from his early years to the present. A number of paragraphs were dedicated to Michael's relationships with girls. In describing how he lost his virginity at 12, Michael and the magazine leant into the now-clichéd 'bad deflowering by an older woman' trope: '"She was a right old dog." How charmingly put. "I was so young and so absolutely inexperienced … it was so embarrassingly bad that I went to school and didn't tell anyone.''[52] These slightly tragic accounts of youthful sexuality may well have worked to humanise superstar George Michael, showcasing his 'everyman' origins as a normal, sexually curious but awkward teenager. This register of self-deprecating sex talk could function to humanise the band in eyes of the young women who desired them and young men who aspired to be them.

Of course, the need to ground Michael and Ridgeley's sexuality was necessary because of the heightened nature of their public sexual personas and their extremely atypical lifestyles. In part, this could be attributed to the simple facts of global superstardom but it also lay in the very specific ways that Ridgeley and Michael were portrayed in the press, including *Smash Hits*. *Smash Hits* had to walk a fine line in its treatment of pop stars. In relation to Wham!, the magazine could be scathing of the 'old twaddle' of the tabloid press and directly framed its feature on Ridgeley in 1985 as an opportunity for him 'to dispel a few Fleet Street "shock horror" stories'.[53] At the same time, however, *Smash Hits*' coverage of the band often leaned into a characterisation of Wham! that played upon old tropes of masculine rock star sexuality. In this way the New Pop stars of the 1980s and their coverage in *Smash Hits* represented an evolution of the musical sexuality described by Simon Frith and Angela McRobbie in 1978. While Frith and McRobbie identified two seemingly opposite forms of rock star sexuality – 'teenypop' (in which artists played upon an emotional and explicitly romantic notion of young female sexuality) and 'cock rock' (which was more aggressively sexual) – in the 1980s, the lines between these genres of male rock sexuality blurred. To update McRobbie and Frith's term, coverage of Wham! represented a new form of 'cock pop'.[54]

Once in the public eye, the boys of Wham! quickly gained reputations as womanisers. In *Smash Hits* this characterisation tended to be expressed in the 'incidental' sections of the magazine, in contrast to feature articles. For example, in 1983, Wham! guest edited the singles review section. Reviewing the Frank Barber Orchestra's single 'Disco Band', Michael wrote: 'If I were the sexist pig I've been accused of being, I'd probably say that the only decent thing about this record are the tasty birds on the cover. But I'm not, so I won't.'[55] This hyper-sexual image would have been clear in the minds of readers who, earlier in the issue, would have seen a photograph of Michael snogging a woman at a showbiz party. A more uncomfortable form of macho male sexuality was expressed in a George Michael quote cited in the 'Mutterings' section of the magazine in 1985. Talking about his video for 'Careless Whisper', Michael reflected: 'Because of its sensual nature, we had to select girls who wouldn't be embarrassed in bedroom scenes. So when we were interviewing the models who applied, I wore only swimming trunks … to see how they reacted'. To their credit, the magazine annotated this quote, 'Mutterings say: yeuch!' and a Kipper Williams cartoon punctured the bravado of this episode.[56]

As time went on, it was Andrew Ridgeley's sexual exploits that became the focus of *Smash Hits*' banter surrounding the band. In early 1985, for example, the 'Mutterings' page repeated claims of one of Ridgeley's ex-girlfriends that she used to 'tease him and wear all the kinky clothes he loves'.[57] Feature articles on the band often turned to Michael to discuss the band's music but primarily discussed Ridgeley in terms of his social life. While Michael addressed the band's legal battles with their record label in the May 1984 feature, it was Ridgeley's partying that was worthy of note. Celebrating the party culture of Fort Lauderdale, Ridgeley described a scene in which 'lots of girls and all the guys are on the make' and asserted that he '[took his] pleasure seeking very seriously'.[58] *Smash Hits* repeatedly characterised Ridgeley as 'a bit of a lad'.[59] Just prior to the China tour, Ridgeley made headlines in relation to drunken exploits at a rugby club in Bristol. *Smash Hits*' reporting of this incident was hardly complementary: 'A "drunken" Andrew Ridgeley apparently removed girls' bras at a student party in Bristol t'other week then "staggered about twanging girls' suspenders and fondled a man in drag mistaking him for a girl." What a lad, eh!'[60] A few months later, the magazine feigned innocence, suggesting that it was 'the papers' that wrote 'such horrible things about Ridgeley'.[61] In this way, *Smash Hits* played both sides. At the same time that it embraced and encouraged stars to discuss their sexual exploits as a way to juice up their gossip columns, it presented these stories with the textual equivalent of an eye-roll. Pop stars' banter was the subject of the magazine's banter. The magazine moved between 'insider' and 'outsider' status, riding the wave of pop stars' cool sexuality when it suited them, cashing in on 'sex as scandal' tropes when it was beneficial, but also offering critique when stars' sexual conduct was deemed to have gone too far or become unappealing.

Smash Hits was a marketing tool for bands, and pop acts benefited greatly from good coverage in its pages. Yet, *Smash Hits*' own credibility relied upon maintaining good relationships with and access to pop groups with large fan followings. As such, the magazine was very much in the groups' hands. For all that *Smash Hits* prided itself on, and has been remembered for, its satire and self-aware humour, it often played into bands' own self-image. Feature articles largely let bands speak for themselves and it was only in the more peripheral sections of the magazine (in cartoons, gossip columns and generalist news sections) that it took jabs at the stars. Here, however, the magazine was not afraid to draw attention to the artifice of Wham's sex talk. In 1984, 'Mutterings' took aim at Wham!'s apparent willingness to characterise their sexuality differently to appeal to difference audiences:

> George Michael of Wham! in the *News of the World*: 'And I go to clubs to pull girls. The whole thing revolves around sex. [...]' A few days later George Michael in *Just Seventeen*: 'It's funny. Here we are with all these women available to us, but you find you just don't want to take advantage of it.'[62]

The following year, when the magazine quoted Andrew Ridgeley stating 'All we appear to have talked about for the last two years is our sex lives. Actually, we made it all up', there was a hint of derision. But having been complicit in this sex talk by publishing it, *Smash Hits* could not really critique the band.[63] Although *Smash Hits* often played along for its own benefit, contemporaneous coverage of the band recognised elements of performance and role-playing as underpinning bands' navigation of the pop scene at this time.

Conclusion

Smash Hits' coverage of Wham! does not reveal any 'truth' about the reality of pop star sexuality in this period, but it is a useful demonstration of the extent to which youthful sexual cultures had changed in the four decades after the Second World War. The overlapping celebrations and satirising of myriad forms of heterosexuality showcases the messiness of sexual culture at this time. Most importantly, while the two core sexual tropes *Smash Hits* was toying with – that of the heartthrob and that of bawdy banter – had long precedents in the sexual cultures of previous periods, by the 1980s these had both evolved and coexisted in mainstream discourse. In *Smash Hits*, heartthrobs were not just romantic idols based in fantasies of love but were objects of physical sexual desire. The magazine embraced a female gaze in which men were aesthetic objects to be looked at and their bodies fantasised about. This represented a significant shift from the coverage of pop stars in *Jackie* and *Valentine* in the 1960s. At the same time, sexual humour and innuendo had moved beyond the music hall and the locker room and become an everyday feature of youth culture.

These two visions of heterosexuality were deeply gendered – it appears to have been assumed that heartthrobs were for girls while banter was for the 'lads' – yet single pop acts and *Smash Hits*' coverage of them often moved seamlessly between the two, sometimes oscillating several times in a single article. In part, we can attribute this to the mixed audience of *Smash Hits* which meant that the magazine was always seeking to speak to both young men and women, trying to exclude neither entirely. Yet I believe that this is also an indication of how late twentieth-century discourse of gender blurred the boundaries of masculine and feminine sexuality. By the 1980s, it was assumed that girls would 'get the joke', finding sex talk amusing rather than shocking or taboo. At the same time, while it was not necessarily expected that young men would stick posters of Wham! on their bedroom walls, *Smash Hits* felt that such imagery could be aspirational for men, or at least that it would not deter men from reading the magazine. *Smash Hits* in the 1980s did not contain 'explicit' sexual content and its humour worked to defuse much of the erotic potential of its coverage of bands like Wham! However, its coverage was highly sexualised and, perhaps even more so than its sister publication *Just Seventeen*, it is evidence of just how much young people's sexual culture had transformed by the late twentieth century. For *Smash Hits* and the bands featured within it, sex was not a problem but a selling point.

Notes

1 Wham!, 'Wham! Rap (Enjoy What You Do)' (Innervision, 1982); Wham!, 'Young Guns (Go For It)' (Innervision, 1982).
2 Wham!, 'Bad Boys' (Innervision, 1983).
3 *Smash Hits*, 116 (12–25 May 1983).
4 Dave Rimmer, 'Bad Boys Stick Together', *Smash Hits*, 116 (12–25 May 1983).
5 Examples of this popular culture include films by the American director John Hughes, the novels of Aidan Chambers, British youth programming such as *Grange Hill* and later *Brookside*, and male bands of the 'New Pop' such as Duran Duran and Spandau Ballet.
6 Andrew Ridgeley, *Wham! George and Me* (London: Penguin Books, 2020).
7 Adrian Thrills, 'Wham!', *NME*, 19 June 1982; Lynn Hanna, 'Wham! Young Brats Go For It', *NME*, 27 November 1982.

8. Ian Birch, 'Wham! Make It Bigger', *Smash Hits*, 152 (27 September–10 October 1984).
9. Simon Napier-Bell quoted in Mike Bygrave, 'A Meaningful Relationship', *The Mail on Sunday Magazine*, 30 September 1984.
10. Ian Birch, 'The Sundance Kids', *Smash Hits*, 123 (18–31 August 1983).
11. *Smash Hits*, 102 (28 October–10 November 1982); *Smash Hits*, 123 (18–31 August 1983).
12. They also made the top 5 in the 'Worst Band' category in 1985 and 1986 as well!
13. Thrills, 'Wham!'.
14. Ridgeley, *Wham! George and Me*, p. 17.
15. George Michael, quoted in Steve Pafford and Richard Smith, 'George Talks: His Frankest Interview Ever', *Gay Times* (July 2007).
16. 'George's Closet Encounter with the Law', *Vox* (1 June 1998); Fiona Russell Powell, 'George Michael: My High Times with Gay George', *Punch* (March 1998).
17. Jason Toynbee, 'Policing Bohemia, Pinning up Grunge: The Music Press and Generic Change in British Pop and Rock', *Popular Music*, 12:3 (1993), 291.
18. Eamonn Forde, 'From Polyglotism to Branding: On the Decline of Personality Journalism in the British Music Press', *Journalism*, 2:1 (2001), 25.
19. Mark Ellen quoted in Forde, 'From Polyglotism to Branding', 27.
20. Dave Rimmer, *Like Punk Never Happened: Culture Club and the New Pop* (London: Faber & Faber, 2011), p. xi.
21. Diane Railton, 'The Gendered Carnival of Pop', *Popular Music*, 20:3 (2001), 329.
22. David Hepworth quoted in David Simpson, 'How we Made Smash Hits Magazine', *The Guardian* (6 August 2018), www.theguardian.com/culture/2018/aug/06/how-we-made-smash-hits-magazine (accessed 5 October 2021).
23. Penny Tinkler, *Constructing Girlhood: Popular Magazines for Girls Growing Up in England 1920–50* (London: Taylor & Francis, 1995).
24. Joan Ormrod, 'Reading Production and Culture: UK Teen Girl Comics from 1955 to 1960', *Girlhood Studies*, 11, no. 3 (2018), 18–33.
25. Stephen Hill, 'Lost in the Seventies: *Smash Hits* and the Televisual Aesthetics of British Pop', in Laurel Forster and Sue Harper (eds), *British Culture and Society in the 1970s: The Lost Decade* (Newcastle: Cambridge Scholars Publishing, 2010), pp. 175–85.
26. Barbara Ehrenreich, Elizabeth Hess and Gloria Jacobs, 'Beatlemania: Girls Just Want to Have Fun', in Lisa A. Lewis (ed.), *The Adoring Audience: Fan Culture and Popular Music* (London: Taylor & Francis, 1992); Sheryl Garratt, 'All of Me Love All of You', in John Aizlewood (ed.), *Love is the Drug: Living as a Pop Fan* (London: Penguin, 1994).
27. Carol Dyhouse, *Heartthrobs: A History of Women and Desire* (Oxford: Oxford University Press, 2017), p. 61.
28. Connie Alderson, *Magazines Teenagers Read* (London: Pergamon Press, 1968), p. 42.

29 Rimmer, *Like Punk Never Happened*.
30 Kirkham, 'Polluting Young Minds'.
31 *Smash Hits*, 116 (28 April–11 May 1983).
32 Rimmer, 'Bad Boys Stick Together'.
33 *Smash Hits*, 109 (3 February–16 February 1983).
34 Wham!, 'Wham! Rap' (Innervision, 1982).
35 Rimmer, *Like Punk Never Happened*, p. 10.
36 Peter Martin, 'Wham! in China (Part One)', *Smash Hits*, 168 (8–21 May 1985).
37 Neil Tennant, 'The Beach Boys', *Smash Hits*, 143 (24 May–6 June 1984).
38 Napier-Bell quoted in Mike Bygrave, 'A Meaningful Relationship'.
39 Peter Martin, 'Wham!: Randy Andy in Naked Five-in-a-Bed Tug-of-Love Porno Sex-Change Wife-Swap Spy Riddle', *Smash Hits*, 177 (11 September–24 September 1985).
40 *Smash Hits*, 182 (20 November–3 December 1985).
41 Peter Martin, '"I'm Your Man" is More us … it's More about Sex', *Smash Hits*, 182 (20 November–3 December 1985).
42 *Smash Hits*, 166 (11–24 April 1985).
43 On the increasing social status of sexual experience among teenagers see: Hannah Charnock, 'Teenage Girls, Female Friendship and the Making of the Sexual Revolution in England, *c*.1950–80', *Historical Journal*, 63:4 (2020), 1032–53.
44 Martin, 'Wham!: Randy Andy'.
45 Martin, 'I'm Your Man'.
46 David Quantick, 'Wham!: Hammersmith Odeon, London', *New Musical Express*, 5 November 1983. For a more scathing account see Helen Fitzgerald, 'Wham! Lyceum, London', *Melody Maker*, 26 November 1983.
47 Tennant, 'Beach Boys'.
48 Chris Heath, 'Will George Michael ever Appear on Stage again?', *Smash Hits*, 159 (3–16 January 1985).
49 *Smash Hits*, 165 (28 March–10 April 1985).
50 *Smash Hits*, 167 (24 April–7 May 1985).
51 Heath, 'Will George Michael'.
52 Chris Heath, 'George Michael: The Story So Far', *Smash Hits*, 192 (9–22 April 1986).
53 *Smash Hits*, 184 (18–31 December 1985); Martin, 'Wham! Randy Andy'.
54 Frith and McRobbie, 'Rock and Sexuality'.
55 *Smash Hits*, 119 (23 June–6 July 1983).
56 *Smash Hits*, 150 (30 August–12 September 1984).
57 *Smash Hits*, 161 (17–30 January 1985).
58 Tennant, 'Beach Boys'.
59 *Smash Hits*, 173 (17–30 July 1985); 177 (11–24 September 1985).
60 *Smash Hits*, 166 (11–24 April 1985).
61 Martin, 'Wham! Randy Andy'.
62 *Smash Hits*, 135 (2–15 February 1984).
63 *Smash Hits*, 156 (22 November–5 December 1984).

Index

100 Club (club), 258, 260, 261

Abrams, Lyn, 78
Ackroyd, Peter, 172
A Clockwork Orange (book), 259
A Clockwork Orange (film), 259, 265
Actor Network Theory (ANT), 114, 125, 127
Adam and the Ants, 251
Adorno, Theodore, 201
A Hard Day's Night (film), 124
A Kiss in the Dreamhouse (Siouxsie and the Banshees), 270
Albertine, Viv, 243, 250, 258, 260
Alderson, Connie, 298
Alderson, David, 187
Alternative TV, 252, 283
Anderson, Perry, 190
Anger, Kenneth, 175, 240
Ani, Marimba, 210
A Night at the Xclusiv Club in Batley (film), 288
Ant, Adam (Stuart Goddard), 243, 251, 299
Antonioni, Michelangelo, 170–81 *passim*, 186
Arena Three, 135, 146
Ashby, Linda, 249, 261
Asher, Jane, 186, 197
Aston, Mathew, 26
AtomAge, 241
Attfield, Sarah, 277
Attwell, Winifred, 23

August, Andrew, 69
Au Pairs, 285, 287

Baby Doll (film), 50
Bailey, David, 173
Bailey, Peter, 8
Bamboo Bar, 67
Barbarella (film), 172
Barker, Simon, 262
Barnes, Richard, 116, 123
Bart, Lionel, 123
Bassey, Shirley, 23, 158, 280
Bauhaus, 283
Bay City Rollers, 298
BBC, 19–21, 23, 24, 83, 124, 134, 159, 206, 286
'Beat' writers, 62, 69–70
Beatles, The, 2, 16, 29–30, 34, 39, 51, 52, 69, 123–4, 175, 186, 246, 282
Beausoleil, Bobby, 175
Beck, Jeff, 180
Bend it Like Beckham (film), 278
Bengry, Justin, 45, 49
Bennett, Andy, 283
Berry, Chuck, 28, 46, 63, 65
Bingham, Adrian, 41, 45, 49, 52, 68
Birkin, Jane, 170, 177
Blackman, Shane, 119
Blondie, 285
Blowup (film), 170–81 *passim*, 186
Blues & Soul, 220–2, 228
Bolan, Marc (Mark Feld), 116, 298
Boon, Richard, 251

Boone, Pat, 26, 30
Bowie, David, 156, 160, 162, 294
Bow Wow Wow, 253
Boyfriend, 77
Boy George (George O'Dowd), 160, 243
Boys Express, 242
Brake, Michael, 113
Bragg, Rick, 49
Bronski Beat, 160
Brooke, Stephen, 94
Brookside, 134
Brown, Callum, 7
Brown, Mary, 97
Browne, Ken, 116, 117
Brunow, Dagmar, 278
Bryne, Richard, 95
Bucks Fizz, 294
Burgess, Anthony, 259
Burnette, Johnny, 30
Burroughs, William, 7, 250, 286
Burton, Peter, 121
Bushell, Garry, 282
Buster, Prince, 211
Butler, Judith, 59
Butt, Gavin, 277, 283, 284
Buzzcocks, 251, 286
Byrds, The, 172

Cabaret Voltaire, 284
Cambridge Rapist (Peter Cook), 245–6
Campaign for Homosexual Equality (CHE), 136, 152, 154, 156–7, 163
Can, 185
Carter, Fan, 78
Casey, Patrick, 240
Cash, Johnny, 32, 46, 280
Cassidy, David, 298
Catwoman, Soo (Sue Lucas), 243
Cavani, Liliana, 264
Centre for Contemporary Cultural Studies (CCCS), 113, 114, 119–20, 125, 127, 191, 227
Chaguaramas (club), 249
Chaplin, Charlie (reggae DJ), 213
Charnock, Hannah, 85, 94
Christopherson, Peter, 243, 252
Civil Rights Movement, 228
Clapton, Eric, 180, 285

Clark, Petula, 28
Clash, The, 242, 258
Clause 28, 9, 164
Club International, 244
Cochran, Eddie, 65, 68
Cohen, Stanley, 118–20
Cohn, Nik, 3, 58–72 *passim*, 123, 244
Cole, Nat King, 22, 30, 31
Communist Party of Great Britain (CPGB), 25
Connell, R. W., 59
consumerism, 16–36 *passim*
contraception, 5, 75, 80–7, 89, 101, 115, 196, 284
Control (film), 278–9
Cook, Karen, 244
Cook, Matt, 153
Cooke, Sam, 28
Coon, Caroline, 243
Cooper Clarke, John, 286
COUM Transmissions, 252
Cramps, The, 283, 288
Creatures, The, 264
Cry of the Banshee (film), 260, 266
Crystals, The, 27
Culture Club, 160
Cure, The, 278, 294
Curious, 244–5
Curtis, Ian, 278
Cut (The Slits), 285

Daily Express, 41, 96–8
Daily Mail, 41, 47–8, 50, 51
Daily Mirror, 40, 43, 48, 50, 96–8, 106
Damned, The (film), 261
Day, Doris, 22
Dear, Michael, 172
Debord, Guy, 174
Deep End (film), 185–201
Deleuze, Gilles, 264–5
Delfont, Bernard, 23
Dene, Terry, 45–46, 66–67
Descloux, Lizzy Mercier, 284
Dewhirst, Ian, 288
Diamond The Girls' Best Friend Sound System, 213
Doncaster, Patrick, 41
Dors, Diana, 45, 193, 198–9

Douglas, Craig, 28
Doyle, Barry, 223
Dressing for Pleasure (film), 243
drugs, 3, 52, 75, 121, 125, 136, 144, 179, 228, 230, 232, 260, 281, 300
Drummond, Paul, 180
Duffy, Maureen, 137, 141, 144
Duran Duran, 159, 299
Dyhouse, Carol, 298
Dylan, Bob, 70, 179

Eager, Vince, 40
East is East (film), 288
Echo, General, 214–17
Elizabeth, Hannah, 79
El Paradiso (club), 248
El Sombrero (club), 249
Epstein, Brian, 23, 26, 30, 64, 123–4, 246
Everly Brothers, 31

Fabulous, 77
Fairburn, Nicholas, 252
Faith, Adam, 27, 41
Faithful, Marianne, 52
Fantastic (Wham!), 295
Farren, Mick, 62, 63
Fisher, Mark, 190, 199, 283
Forum, 238, 239, 240, 244–5, 247
Foucault, Michel, 6, 59
Four Tops, The, 157
Fraser, Roy, 81, 86
Freed, Alan, 46
Freeman, Elizabeth, 135
French, Jim, 242
Freud, Sigmund, 70, 79, 247
Frith, Simon, 70, 304
Fryer, Peter, 82
Fury, Billy, 27
Futurama festival, 283

Gallery International, 242, 245, 247
Gang of Four, 285
Garber, Jane, 227, 258
Gartside, Green, 283
Gateways, The (club), 135, 140–2, 144, 145
Gay Liberation Front (GLF), 147, 156–7, 162, 228

Gay News, 155, 157, 162
Gay Times, 296
Gaynor, Gloria, 157, 160
Gay's The Word (shop), 154
Gay Youth, 159
Geffen, Sasha, 30
Geldof, Bob, 160
Genet, Jean, 250
Ghettotone Sound System, 208
Giddens, Anthony, 17
Gildart, Keith, 70, 153, 159, 221, 228
Gilroy, Paul, 208, 216
Girl, 132, 134
Girl's Own Paper, 297
Girls' World, 297
Girodias, Maurice, 242
Glitter, Gary (Paul Gadd), 9, 282
Godin, Dave, 220–2, 228
Goldman, Vivien, 250
Good, Jack, 42
Gorer, Geoffrey, 100
Gorman, Paul, 239, 244
Granny Takes A Trip (shop), 122
Great Rock 'n' Roll Swindle, The (film), 253
Greer, Germaine, 188
Grimes, Carol, 156
Gub Club, The, 259, 285

Haddon, Mimi, 282
Halberstam, Jack, 199, 269
Haley, Bill, 25, 38, 40, 43, 65
Haley, William, 20
Hall, Lesley, 17, 79
Hall, Stuart, 118, 280, 282
Hancock, Herbie, 170, 178–9
Hannett, Martin, 276, 284
Harper's & Queen, 60
Heath, Chris, 304
Hebdige, Dick, 67, 114, 118–19, 126, 258, 276, 286
Hemmings, David, 170–81 *passim*
Hepworth, David, 297
Hesmondhalgh, David, 59
High Numbers, The, 123
Holly, Buddy, 30, 40, 46, 65
Honey, 75–90 *passim*, 245
Honoré, Annik, 279
Horn, Matthew, 20
Hosein, Charlie, 288

Human League, The, 288
Hunt, Leon, 10
Hynde, Chrissie, 238, 243, 258

International Times, 7, 62, 156
Institute of Contemporary Arts (ICA), 252
Invocation of My Demon Brother (film), 175
Isherwood, Christopher, 243, 250

Jackie, 29, 77, 81, 297, 307
Jackson, Louise, 43, 99
Jah Shaka Sound System, 208
Jagger, Mick, 1, 9, 10, 52
Jamieson, Frederic, 189
Jefferson, Tony, 118, 282
Jerry, Brigadier, 215–16
Jilted John, 284
John, Elton, 160, 294
Johnny Go Home, 243
Join Hands (Siouxsie and the Banshees), 266, 279
Jones, Alan, 238, 243
Jones, Allen, 251
Jones, Steve, 138, 248, 253
Jordan (Pamela Rooke), 238–44, 245, 248, 249, 251, 259
Joy Division, 278–9
JuJu (Siouxsie and the Banshees), 266, 267, 268, 270
Just Seventeen, 298, 307

Katz, David, 209
Kennan, David, 279
Kennedy, John, 66
Killing of Sister George, The (film), 142
King, Jonathan, 9
Kirkham, Nick, 297, 299
Korner, Alexis, 67, 68
Kubrick, Stanley, 259
Kureishi, Hanif, 278
Kynaston, David, 44

La Dolce Vita (film), 114
Lady Saw, 212
Laine, Cleo, 23, 280
Lamar, Angie, 212–13
Lambert, Kit, 123

Langhamer, Claire, 5, 17, 25, 27, 96
Lawrence, D. H., 6
Lawrence, Tim, 288
Le Duce (shop), 121
Led Zeppelin, 180
Lee, Bunny 'Striker', 209
Leech, Kenneth, 117
Let it Rock (shop), 240, 241, 244, 245
Levine, Ian, 228
Lewis, Danielle, 238
Lewis, Jerry Lee, 1, 9, 32, 38–53 *passim*, 63
Lewis, Myra, 47–51
Linder (Linder Mulvey/Linder Sterling)), 251–2, 286
Logan, Andrew, 248
Logan, Nick, 296
London Leatherman, 241
London's Outrage, 247
Louise's (club), 249
Lovegrove, Elizabeth, 78
Lovin' Spoonful, The, 179
Lukács, György, 194
Lwin, Annabella, 253

MacInnes, Colin, 117
Make it Big (Wham!), 295
Male West One (shop), 123
Man About Town, 122
Man Who Sold the World, The (David Bowie), 162
Marcuse, Herbert, 194, 200, 289
marriage, 5, 7, 8, 27, 40, 46–8, 50–1, 80–5, 89, 90, 100, 134, 280
Marriott, Steve, 117
Marshall, Bertie (Berlin), 243, 249–50, 262
Martino, Al, 22
Marx, Karl, 247, 248
May, David, 245, 247
Mazierska, Ewa, 188–9, 197–8
McCartney, Paul, 186
McLaren, Malcolm, 238–54 *passim*
McNair, Brian, 259
McRobbie, Angela, 3, 103, 227, 258, 304
Meek, Joe, 26, 123
Meier, Leslie, 59

Melly, George, 41, 123, 173
Melody Maker, 19, 41, 42, 43, 162, 243, 282, 295, 296
Michael, George, 160, 293–307 *passim*
Mirabelle, 78
Miles, Barry, 121
Miles, Sarah, 17
Millington, Mary, 253
Mills, Helena, 94, 100
Minorities Research Group, 135, 143, 146
Miss Modern, 297
Mitchell, Gillian, 66
Mods and Rockers (film), 117
Moorcock, Michael, 186
moral panic, 5
Morley, Paul, 261, 288
Morrison, Patricia, 259
Mort, Frank, 44, 58
Mott, Toby, 239
Murray, Pauline, 243

Nai Zindagi Naya Jeevan, 280
Napier-Bell, Simon, 294, 301
National Front, 248, 287
National Union of School Students, 284
Nawaz, Aki, 287
New Hormones, 251
New Musical Express (*NME*), 17, 42, 264, 281, 287, 288, 295, 296
New Penny, The (club), 136
News of the World, 29, 44, 52, 306
Newton, Helmut, 246
New York Dolls, 240, 248
Night Porter, The (film), 246, 264
Non-Stop Erotic Cabaret (Soft Cell)
Notting Hill riots (1958), 43–4
Nowell, David, 222
Numan, Gary, 160
Nuttall, Jeff, 4, 188, 191

O'Brien, Lucy, 269, 287
Oh Boy!, 42
Olympia Press, 242
Orbison, Roy, 30, 32, 144
Orton, Joe, 250
Osmond, Donny, 297
OZ, 7

Page, Jimmy, 170, 180
Page, Larry, 48
Palladin, Patti, 258
Palmer, Tony, 224
Parade, 244
Parkinson, David, 244
Parnes, Larry, 23, 26, 40, 41, 122, 123, 124
Peace, David, 279
Penman, Ian, 288
Performance (film), 171
Perkins, Carl, 46
Pet Shop Boys, 293
Petticoat, 75–90 *passim*
Pirroni, Marco, 243
Plummer, Ken, 153, 158
Polari, 224
popular individualism, 6
pornography, 6, 29, 238, 240, 244, 249, 251–2
Powers, Ann, 2
Presley, Elvis, 26, 30, 32, 34, 42, 46, 65, 68
Pres, Joy, 258
Price, Antony, 26
Priestley, J. B., 24
Prior, Dorothy (Max), 249
Prostitution (exhibition), 252
Punk Rock Movie, The (film), 259

QT, 240
Quant, Mary, 125

Radio Caroline, 60
Radio Luxembourg, 62
Radio One, 159
Rai, Amrik, 287
Railway Tavern, 155–6
Rampling, Charlotte, 264
Rawlins, Terry, 121
Ray, Johnny, 22, 23, 31, 32, 43, 64
Ready, Steady, Go!, 114
Reclaim the Night, 267, 268
Record Mirror, 157, 270
Reel, Penny, 116
Regency Club, 139
Reich, Wilhelm, 244, 247, 251
Reid, Jamie, 249, 286
Reith, John, 20
Reyes, Xavier Aldana, 268

Reynolds, Simon, 258, 282, 283
Rhodes, Bernard, 242, 243
Richard, Cliff, 42, 45, 51, 297, 298
Richard, Little, 2, 26, 30, 34, 61, 64, 65
Richards, Keith, 69
Richmond, Len, 238
Ricky Tick (club), 179–80
Ridgeley, Andrew, 293–307 *passim*
Rimmer, Dave, 297, 300
Robinson, Emily, 6
Robinson, Lucy, 153
Robinson, Tom, 156, 159
Rock Against Racism (RAR), 285
Rock Around the Clock (film), 25, 38
Rocking and Swing (General Echo), 215
Rodriguez, Antonia, 158
Rolling Stone, 244
Rolling Stones, 1, 9, 10, 52, 67, 69, 70
Romeo, Max, 206–9, 212, 217
Ronettes, The, 27
Rotten, Johnny (John Lydon), 246, 248, 253, 261, 282
Ross, Diana, 158
Roxy, The (club), 249, 250
Roza, Lita, 23

Sacher-Masoch, Leopold von, 243, 282
Samson, John, 243
Samuel, Raph, 187
Sanai, Leyla, 287
Sappho, 146
Savage, Edna, 66
Savage, Jon, 159, 239, 247, 248, 261, 262, 285, 286
Savile, Jimmy, 9, 29, 63, 253, 279
Saville, Peter, 278, 279
Saxon Sound System, 208
Scanes, Richard, 157, 160
Scanlon, John, 239
Schofield, Camilla, 6
Schofield, Michael, 8, 82
Scorpio Rising (film), 240
Scream, The (Siouxsie and the Banshees), 266, 267, 270
Scritti Politti, 283
Secret Public, The, 286
Seditionaries, 249

Severin, Steve (Steve Bailey), 243, 262, 266, 270
SEX (shop), 238–54 *passim*, 262
Sex Discrimination Act (1975), 162
Sexual Offences Act (1967), 113, 145, 152
Sex Pistols, 238–54 *passim*, 258, 282
Shapiro, Helen, 27, 144
Shelley, Pete, 286
Shirelles, The, 27
Showbiz Club, 161
Sioux, Siouxsie (Susan Ballion), 243, 252, 258–71 *passim*
Siouxsie and the Banshees, 258–71 *passim*, 279, 287
Skin Two (club), 250
Skin Two, 250
Skolimowski, Jerzy, 185–201
Slade, 282
Slits, The, 243, 259, 285
Slaughter, Audrey, 77–8
Small Faces, 117
Smash Hits, 157, 159, 164, 293–307 *passim*
Smith, Mandy, 9
Smith, Pennie, 285
Smith, Robert, 278
Soft Cell, 286–7
Solanas, Valerie, 245
Somerville, Jimmy, 160
songs
    '2-4-6-8 Motorway' (Tom Robinson Band), 156
    'Adultery' (Scars), 279
    'All I Have To Do Is Dream' (Everly Brothers), 32
    'Anarchy in the UK' (Sex Pistols), 239
    'Bad Boys' (Wham!), 299
    'Bathroom Function' (Adam and the Ants), 252
    'Beat My Guest' (Adam and the Ants), 251
    'Be Bop A Lula' (Gene Vincent), 25
    'Big Five' (Prince Buster), 211
    'Blind Date' (Lezlee Lyrix), 214
    'Blue Suede Shoes' (Elvis Presley), 25
    'Born Too Late' (The Poni Tails), 28
    'Boys Don't Cry' (The Cure), 278

'But I Might Die Tonight' (Cat Stevens), 186, 191
'Can Your Pussy Do the Dog?' (The Cramps), 283
'Carcass' (Siouxsie and the Banshees), 267–8
'Careless Whisper' (Wham!), 295, 300, 305
'Club Tropicana' (Wham!), 295
'Come Again' (Au Pairs), 285
'Damaged Goods' (Gang of Four), 285
'Dark Entries' (Bauhaus), 283
'Did You Ever Have to Make Up Your Mind' (Lovin' Spoonful), 179
'Don't Try to Cure Yourself' (They Must Be Russians), 284
'Everything She Wants' (Wham!), 300
'Friggin' in the Riggin'' (Sex Pistols), 253
'Glad To Be Gay' (Tom Robinson Band), 159
'Glory be to God' (Lady Saw), 212
'Go Away Little Girl' (Mark Winter), 28
'God Save the Queen' (Sex Pistols), 239
'Good Golly Miss Molly' (Little Richard), 26
'Groove is in the Heart' (Dee-Lite), 178
'Halloween' (Siouxsie and the Banshees), 267
'Happy Birthday Sweet Sixteen' (Neil Sedaka), 28
'Herpes Simplex' (Lizzy Mercier Descloux), 284
'Heart of Teenage Girl' (Craig Douglas), 28
'Hong Kong Garden' (Siouxsie and the Banshees), 263
'Human Fly' (The Cramps), 288
'I'm Just a Baby' (Louise Cordet)
'I'm Your Man' (Wham!), 300
'I Was a Pre-pubescent' (Jilted john), 284
'I Will Survive' (Gloria Gaynor), 160

'Kerb Crawler' (Au Pairs), 287
'La Bamba' (Antonia Rodriguez), 158
'Last Night Was made for Love' (Billy Fury), 27
'Let's Spend the Night Together' (Rolling Stones), 1
'Love Lies Limp' (Alternative TV), 252, 283
'Love to Love You, Baby' (Diana Ross), 158
'Love Will Tear Us Apart' (Joy Division), 278–9
'Melt' (Siouxsie and the Banshees), 270
'Mother Sky' (Can), 186, 195
'Move it' (Cliff Richard), 42
'Natural's Not In It' (Gang of Four), 285
'Night Shift' (Siouxsie and the Banshees), 267–9, 287
'No One Gets the Prize' (Diana Ross), 158
'Oh Bondage, Up Yours!' (X-Ray Spex), 251, 285
'Only the Lonely' (Roy Orbison), 32, 144
'Only Sixteen' (Craig Douglas), 28
'Orgasm Addict' (Buzzcocks), 251, 286
'Physical' (Adam and the Ants), 251
'Poor Me' (Adam Faith), 27
'Premature Burial' (Siouxsie and the Banshees), 266
'Pretty Vacant' (Sex Pistols), 282
'Pretty Woman' (Roy Orbison), 32
'Readers' Wives' (John Cooper Clarke), 286
'Red Scab' (Adam and the Ants), 251
'Relax' (Frankie Goes to Hollywood), 252
'Rock Around the Clock' (Bill Haley), 25
'Rubber People' (Adam and the Ants), 251
'She Was Hot' (Rolling Stones), 10
'Sin in My Heart' (Siouxsie and the Banshees), 270

'Smalltown Boy' (Bronski Beat), 160
'Sound of the Crowd' (The Human League), 288
'Spellbound' (Siouxsie and the Banshees), 277
'Stray Cat Blues' (Rolling Stones), 9
'Stroll On' (The Yardbirds), 170, 179
'Submission' (Sex Pistols), 248
'Suburban Relapse', (Siouxsie and the Banshees), 270
'Suffragette City' (David Bowie), 156
'Sweet Little Sixteen' (Chuck Berry), 28
'Teenage Kicks' (The Undertones), 285
'The Girl's in Love With You' (Dusty Springfield, 132, 144
'The Twist' (Chubby Checker), 68
'This is My Life' (Shirley Bassey), 158
'Train Kept A Rollin'' (The Yardbirds), 180
'Tutti Frutti' (Little Richard), 2, 61
'Up the Junction' (Squeeze), 283
'Voodoo Dolly' (Siouxsie and the Banshees), 267
'Wet Dream' (Max Romeo), 206–10
'Wham Rap' (Wham!), 293, 295, 299
'What's Inside a Girl?' (The Cramps), 283
'When Will I See You Again' (Three Degrees), 159
'Whole Lot of Shakin' Going On' (Jerry Lee Lewis), 1, 25, 63
'Why Theory' (Gang of Four), 285
'Wreck a Buddy' (Soul Sisters), 211
'Wreck a Pum Pum' (Prince Buster), 211–12
'You Never Can Tell' (Jerry Lee Lewis), 63
'Young Guns' (Wham!), 293, 299
'You're Sixteen' (Johnny Burnette), 28
Sontag, Susan, 245
Soul Sisters, 211–12
Sounds, 262, 265, 281, 296
sound systems, 208

Southern Death Cult, 287
Span, 240
Spandau Ballet, 299
Specials, The, 294
Spector, Phil, 69
Spencer, Maurice, 242
Spick, 240
Spiral Scratch (Buzzcocks), 251
Springfield, Dusty, 27, 121, 132, 135, 138, 140, 144–5
Springsteen, Bruce, 278
Squid, 156
Steele, Tommy, 40, 41, 43, 65–7, 69
Stephen, John, 115, 117, 121, 122
Stevens, Cat, 185, 193
Stevenson, Nils, 250
Strange, Steve (Steve Harrington), 243
Stratton, Jon, 16
Street Life, 239
Street-Porter, Janet, 180
Styrene, Poly (Marianne Elliott-Said), 243, 251, 279, 285
Suck, Jane, 261, 265
Sun, The, 6
Sunday Times, 126
Sutcliffe, John, 241
Sutcliffe, Peter (Yorkshire Ripper), 267–8, 279, 287
Sutcliffe-Braithwaite, Florence, 6

Tasker, Yvonne, 194
Taylor, John, 299
Tebbutt, Melanie, 78
Tennant, Neil, 300
Thatcher, Margaret, 4, 9, 228, 247
That'll Be the Day (film), 240
They Must Be Russians, 284
Thomlinson, Natalie, 6
Three Degrees, 159
Throbbing Gristle, 252
Time, 172
Tinkler, Penny, 78, 104
Too Fast To Live Too Young To Die (shop), 240
Top of the Pops, 19, 21, 159, 283, 298
Town, 116
Townshend, Pete, 116, 123
T. Rex, 282, 294
Trocchi, Alexander, 242, 245

Trojan Records, 285
True Love Stories (Jilted John), 284
Tutti, Cosey Fanni (Christine Newby), 251

Uncle Dog, 156
Undertones, The, 285
Unknown Pleasures (Joy Division), 278

Valentine, 307
Variety Club, 140, 142
Velvet Underground, 180, 243, 262
Venus in Furs, 243, 282
Vicious, Sid (John Ritchie), 248, 261
Vince Man's Shop, 121–2
Vincent, Gene, 31, 62
Vogue, 246

Walkowitz, Judith, 17, 23
Wall, Tim, 222
Ward, Christopher, 75
Warhol, Andy, 240, 245
Waterhouse, Keith, 97
Weeks, Jeffrey, 29, 85, 154
Weight, Richard, 115

West Side Story (film), 117
Westwood, Vivienne, 238–54 *passim*, 259
Wham!, 293–307 *passim*
Whiteley, Sheila, 3
Whitehouse, Mary, 9
Who, The, 115, 116, 123, 180
Wigan Casino, The (film), 224
Wilde, Marty, 40
Wild One, The (film), 240
Wilkinson, David, 59, 239, 246
Williams, Raymond, 62, 190, 198
Williams, William, 105–6
Willie, John, 251
Wilson, Debbie, 249
Wilson, Harold, 179
Woodhead, Colin, 122
Wyman, Bill, 9

X-Ray Spex, 251

Yardbirds, The, 170, 179, 180
Youth News, 163

Zabriskie Point (film), 171, 175, 181

Milton Keynes UK
Ingram Content Group UK Ltd.
UKHW011342140324
439519UK00007B/121